Nigeria
a country study

Federal Research Division
Library of Congress
Edited by
Helen Chapin Metz
Research Completed
June 1991

DT
515
.22
.N53
1992

On the cover: Bronze head of an *oni*, or king, of Ife, spiritual head of the Yoruba people

Fifth Edition, First Printing, 1992.

Library of Congress Cataloging-in-Publication Data

Nigeria: a country study / Federal Research Division, Library of
   Congress ; edited by Helen Chapin Metz. — 5th ed.
      p.   cm. — (Area handbook series, ISSN 1057-5294) (DA
   pam ; 550-157)
      "Research completed December 1990."
      Includes bibliography (pp. 341-361) and index.
      ISBN 0-8444-0738-0
      1. Nigeria.   I. Metz, Helen Chapin, 1928-   . II. Library of
   Congress. Federal Research Division.   III. Series.
   DT515.22.N53   1992   92-9026
   966.9—dc20   CIP

Headquarters, Department of the Army
DA Pam 550-157

Foreword

This volume is one in a continuing series of books prepared by the Federal Research Division of the Library of Congress under the Country Studies—Area Handbook Program sponsored by the Department of the Army. The last page of this book lists the other published studies.

Most books in the series deal with a particular foreign country, describing and analyzing its political, economic, social, and national security systems and institutions, and examining the interrelationships of those systems and the ways they are shaped by cultural factors. Each study is written by a multidisciplinary team of social scientists. The authors seek to provide a basic understanding of the observed society, striving for a dynamic rather than a static portrayal. Particular attention is devoted to the people who make up the society, their origins, dominant beliefs and values, their common interests and the issues on which they are divided, the nature and extent of their involvement with national institutions, and their attitudes toward each other and toward their social system and political order.

The books represent the analysis of the authors and should not be construed as an expression of an official United States government position, policy, or decision. The authors have sought to adhere to accepted standards of scholarly objectivity. Corrections, additions, and suggestions for changes from readers will be welcomed for use in future editions.

Louis R. Mortimer
Chief
Federal Research Division
Library of Congress
Washington, D.C. 20540

Acknowledgments

The authors wish to acknowledge the contributions of the following individuals who wrote the 1982 edition of *Nigeria: A Country Study:* Robert Rinehart, Irving Kaplan, Donald P. Whitaker, Jean R. Tartter, and Frederick Ehrenreich. Their work provided the basis of the present volume, as well as substantial portions of the text.

John N. Paden, Robinson Professor of International Studies at George Mason University, made an extremely useful critique of the entire manuscript, helping the authors and the editor to focus their efforts more sharply. Revisions to Chapter 4 were made by Richard Joseph and Amy Poteete.

The authors are grateful to individuals in various government agencies and private institutions who gave their time, research materials, and expertise to the production of this book. These individuals include Ralph K. Benesch, who oversees the Country Studies—Area Handbook program for the Department of the Army. Special thanks are owed to the Embassy of Nigeria, which provided numerous photographs as well as a mounted map of Nigeria with a superimposed head that served as the basis for the cover art of this volume. Graphics support was supplied by Greenhorne and O'Mara; Harriet R. Blood, who prepared the topography and drainage map; Carlyn Dawn Anderson, who designed the illustrations on the title pages of the chapters; and Wayne Horne, who designed the cover.

The authors also wish to thank members of the Federal Research Division who contributed directly to the preparation of the manuscript. These people include Sandra W. Meditz, who reviewed all drafts and graphic material and served as liaison with the sponsoring agency; Tim L. Merrill, who assisted in preparing maps; David P. Cabitto, who provided invaluable graphic assistance and supervised graphics productions; and Marilyn Majeska, who managed editing and production. Also involved in preparing the text were editorial assistants Barbara Edgerton and Izella Watson.

Individual chapters were edited by Barbara Harrison and Vincent Ercolano. Catherine Schwartzstein performed the final prepublication review, and Joan C. Cook compiled the index. Linda Peterson of the Library of Congress Composing Unit prepared the camera-ready copy, under the supervision of Peggy Pixley.

Contents

Chapter 4. Government and Politics 203
Eghosa Osaghae

Chapter 5. National Security 253
Joseph P. Smaldone

Appendix. Tables 323
Bibliography 341
Glossary 363

List of Figures

Preface

Like its predecessor, this study is an attempt to treat in a concise and objective manner the dominant historical, social, political, economic, and military aspects of contemporary Nigerian society. Sources of information included scholarly journals and monographs, official reports of government and international organizations, newspapers, and numerous periodicals. Chapter bibliographies appear at the end of the book; brief comments on some of the more valuable sources suggested as possible further reading appear at the end of each chapter. Measurements are given in the metric system; a conversion table is provided to assist those readers who are unfamiliar with metric measurements (see table 1, Appendix). A glossary is also included.

Place-names generally have been spelled in accordance with those established by the United States Board on Geographic Names and the Permanent Committee on Geographic Names for British Official Use, known as the BGN/PCGN system. The spelling of other proper names conforms to the current usage in the country (where the official language is English) or to the most authoritative available sources.

Nigeria created nine more states on August 27, 1991, bringing the total number of states to thirty. The map on the frontispiece reflects the 1991 status, whereas the map at the end of chapter 1 reflects the status of Nigeria from 1987 to August 1991.

The body of the text reflects information available as of December 1990. Certain other portions of the text, however, have been updated. The Introduction discusses significant events that have occurred since the completion of research; the Country Profile includes updated information as available; and the Bibliography lists recently published sources thought to be particularly helpful to the reader.

Country Profile

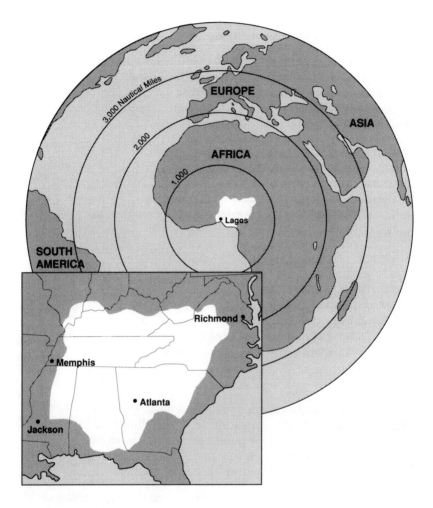

Country

Formal Name: Federal Republic of Nigeria.

Short Form: Nigeria.

Term for Nationals: Nigerian(s).

Capital: Lagos (projected to complete gradual move to Abuja in Federal Capital Territory in late 1991).

Date of Independence: October 1, 1960.

Geography

Size: 923,768 square kilometers.

Boundaries: Southern limits set by Gulf of Guinea (bights of Benin and Biafra); inland frontiers shared with Cameroon (east), Chad (northeast), Niger (north), and Benin (west). No demarcation reached regarding Nigeria-Chad-Niger-Cameroon boundary in Lake Chad, leading to disputes.

Topography: Five major geographic divisions: low coastal zone along Gulf of Guinea; succeeded northward by hills and low plateaus; Niger-Benue river valley; broad stepped plateau stretching to northern border with highest elevations over 1,200 meters; mountainous zone along eastern border, which includes country's highest point (2,042 meters).

Climate: Tropical with variations governed by interaction of moist southwest monsoon and dry northeast winds. Mean maximum temperatures of 30–32°C (south), 33–35°C (north). High humidity in south February-November, June-September in north; low humidity during dry season. Annual rainfall decreases northward; about 2,000 millimeters in coastal zone (Niger Delta averages over 3,550 millimeters); 500 to 750 millimeters in north.

Society

Population: Population and growth estimates varied widely. World Bank estimated 1990 population at 119 million; however, 1991 preliminary census figures published in 1992 gave population total of 88.5 million. Growth rate in 1990 estimated about 3.3 percent; 28 percent of population urban in 1985.

Ethnic Groups: 250 to 400 or more recognized groups, many divided into subgroups of considerable social and political importance. Most important ethnolinguistic categories: Hausa and Fulani in north, Yoruba in southwest, and Igbo in southeast, all internally subdivided. Next major groups: Kanuri, Ibibio, Tiv, and Ijaw.

Languages: Number of languages estimated at 350 to 400, many with dialects. Most important: Hausa, Yoruba, and Igbo. Hausa major language in north. English official language used in government, large-scale business, mass media, and education beyond primary school. Several other languages also recognized for primary education. Classical Arabic of religious significance in north.

Religion: In last officially accepted census (1963), about 47 percent of population self-identified as Muslims (chiefly adherents of Sunni Islam), nearly 35 percent as Christians, and more than 18 percent as other (almost entirely adherents of indigenous religions). Majority of north Muslim; south mainly non-Muslim, primarily Christian; middle belt mixed faiths. Mission-related Christian churches (Anglican, Roman Catholic, Methodist, and others), African independent churches, and Aladura Church present.

Education: Universal primary education (six-year program) responsibility of state and local governments. Great increase in enrollments (about 12 million in government primary schools, additional millions in Muslim and Christian private schools in 1985). Responsibility for secondary education shared by federal and state governments; also some private schools; 3.7 million in government secondary schools in 1985. In 1990 between 150,000 and 200,000 in thirty-five colleges, universities, and higher technical schools.

Health: Major prevalent diseases included cerebrospinal meningitis, yellow fever, Lassa fever, acquired immune deficiency syndrome (AIDS), malaria, guinea worm, schistosomiasis, onchocerciasis, and malnutrition among young children. Medical establishments owned by federal, state, and local governments and private groups. Shortage of medical facilities and physicians in rural areas. Primary Health Care Plan launched in late 1980s, including expanded immunization campaign.

Economy

Gross National Product (GNP): US$30.0 billion, 1989; US$230 per capita, 1990.

Agriculture, Forestry, and Fishing: Agriculture represented 39.1 percent of gross domestic product (GDP) in 1988. In 1990, 34 million hectares, or 42 percent of arable land under cultivation; 18 million hectares of pastureland; 20 million hectares of forests. 1991 drought forced substantial increase in food imports. Cash crops: cocoa, palm oil, rubber, cotton, peanuts. Major food crops: cassava, yams, taro, sweet potatoes, sorghum, millet, corn, rice. Livestock: cattle, goats, sheep, horses, camels, pigs, poultry, representing 2.0 percent of GDP. Forests used extensively, and government engaged in afforestation projects. Fisheries catch did not meet domestic needs; modernization projects underway.

Industry: Constituted 10.0 percent of GDP in 1988. Primary processing industries: palm oil, peanuts, rubber, petroleum, wood, hides and skins. Manufacturing industries: food products, textiles, cement, building materials, footwear, chemical products, ceramics, small appliances.

Mining, Petroleum, and Energy: Main items mined: coal, tin, columbite for domestic use. Nigeria world's sixth largest oil exporter; domestic consumption 250,000 barrels per day; 11 percent of extracted oil refined domestically. Natural gas constituted more than 20 percent of commercial energy sources in 1990. Emphasis on expanding hydroelectric power (14 percent of energy consumed in 1980s) and oil- and gas-generated electricity.

Exports: Petroleum, cocoa.

Imports: Machinery, transportation equipment, chemicals, manufactured goods, food, live animals.

Major Trading Partners: United States, Britain, other European Economic Community countries, Japan, Canada. Nigeria had negative trade balance.

Currency: Naira (N); 1 naira = 100 kobo; average exchange rate in 1990: N8.04 per US$1.00.

Transportation and Communications

Roads: In 1990, 108,000 kilometers of roads, of which 30,000 kilometers paved, 25,000 kilometers gravel; rest unimproved earth. Most state capitals and large towns accessible by paved road.

Railroads: In 1990, 3,500 kilometers of narrow-gauge (1.067-meter) track. Nigerian Railway Corporation declared bankruptcy in 1988 and system in serious operational difficulties.

Civil Aviation: Three airports handled international flights: Murtala Muhammad International at Lagos, Aminu Kano International at Kano, and Port Harcourt. Twenty-nine other airports with paved runways. Nigeria Airways parastatal with domestic and international flights.

Ports: Three major complexes: Lagos (including Apapa and Tin Can Island), which handled majority of cargo, Delta (including Warri and Sapele on Niger River), and Rivers (including Port Harcourt); Calabar (on Cross River), major eastern port. Crude oil exported through Bonny, near Port Harcourt, and Burutu, near Warri.

Communications: Telecommunications being expanded in 1990; domestic satellite stem linked all major urban areas; good international telecommunications system. Also 65 AM radio stations and various television stations.

Government and Politics

Government: Federal republic under strong presidential administration. Became parliamentary democracy at independence; under military rule 1966 to 1979, 1983– . Constitution of 1979 amended February 1984. New constitution promulgated 1989 and scheduled to take effect January 1993; provides for three independent branches of government: executive, legislative, judicial. National Assembly dissolved in 1983, had not been reinstated as of mid-1991. Transition to civilian rule scheduled to be completed January 1993.

Administrative Divisions: Thirty states divided into local councils; Federal Capital Territory of Abuja projected to become operational as national capital in 1991 as federal departments transfer from Lagos.

Judicial System: Legal system based on English common law modified by Nigerian rulings, constitution of 1979, legislative enactments, and decrees of military government in effect. Draft constitution of 1989 to take effect at start of Third Republic. Customary and Muslim sharia law recognized in personal status matters. Federal system included Supreme Court, federal courts of appeal, and federal high courts. Supreme Court had original jurisdiction in constitutional disputes.

Politics: In 1989 two political parties established by government: National Republican Convention, slightly right of center, and Social Democratic Party, slightly left of center. Presidential elections scheduled for December 1992.

Foreign Relations: Nonaligned; active member of United Nations, Organization of African Unity, Commonwealth of Nations, and Economic Community of West African States. Main principles of foreign policy: noninterference in internal affairs and inviolability of national borders in Africa.

National Security

Armed Forces: In 1990 armed forces totaled at least 94,500; components were army, 80,000; navy, 5,000; and air force, 9,500; no organized reserves; service entirely voluntary.

Major Tactical Units: Army had two mechanized infantry divisions, one armored division, and one airborne division; air force tactical command had three interceptor/strike squadrons, one maritime reconnaissance squadron, and five transport squadrons. Equipment inventory over 260 aircraft. Navy equipped with modern fleet of frigates, corvettes, transports, and patrol craft; defended territorial waters and was developing amphibious warfare capability.

Major Military Suppliers: Diversified military procurement sources included Italy, Germany, Britain, United States, and Eastern Europe. Small but important domestic defense industry.

Military Costs: Between 1977 and 1987, military spending decreased 80 percent to less than 1 percent of GNP; in 1990 defense budget N2.19 billion, or about US$277 million.

Security Forces: Size of national police (Nigeria Police Force) variously estimated at between 20,000 and 152,000, organized into seven area commands under Nigeria Police Council that included president, chief of staff, minister of internal affairs, and police inspector general. Also Port Security Police (total about 12,000) and Quick Intervention Force (number not known) in each state. Security services reorganized in 1986 into State Security Service for domestic intelligence, National Intelligence Agency for foreign intelligence and counterintelligence, and Defence Intelligence Agency for military intelligence.

Introduction

THE MOST POPULOUS COUNTRY IN AFRICA and the largest in area of the West African states, Nigeria was an early twentieth century colony that became an independent nation in 1960. A country of great diversity because of the many ethnic, linguistic, and religious groups that live within its borders, Nigeria is also a country with a long past. The history of the peoples that constitute the present state dates back more than 2,000 years. The earliest archaeological finds were of the Nok, who inhabited the central Jos Plateau between the Niger and Benue rivers between 300 B.C. and 200 A.D. A number of states or kingdoms with which contemporary ethnic groups can be identified existed before 1500. Of these, the three dominant regional groups were the Hausa in the northern kingdoms of the savanna, the Yoruba in the southwest, and the Igbo in the southeast.

The European slave trade that occurred in Africa as early as the late fifteenth century and that crested between the 1650s and the 1850s had a significant impact on Nigeria. Britain declared the slave trade illegal in 1807 and sent its navy to West African waters to enforce the ban. Britain's action led ultimately to British intervention in Nigeria, which had become a major area for the slave trade. Meanwhile, whereas European missionaries were bringing Christianity to the peoples of southern Nigeria, Islam had been introduced along the caravan routes of northern Nigeria. The jihad, or holy war, waged within what became the Sokoto Caliphate between 1804 and 1808, was instrumental in spreading the Muslim faith not only in the north but also into adjacent regions, such as the area that came to be known as the middle belt, running from the Niger River valley in the west to the Cameroon Highlands in the east.

Initially, the slave trade had been the area's primary attraction for the European powers, but other products, including palm oil and cocoa, also played a role. To safeguard trade from the instability resulting from the ongoing Yoruba wars that began in the 1830s, Britain established a colony in Lagos as early as 1861. The Royal Niger Company was chartered for trading purposes in 1886, shortly after the Berlin Conference of 1885 had sought to resolve overlapping European colonial activities on the African continent. Until 1900 British control of the area was limited to the coastal region and Lokoja, at the confluence of the Niger and Benue rivers. In that year, Britain named Frederick Lugard high commissioner of the Protectorate of Northern Nigeria. His tenure, which lasted until 1918, stressed indirect British control using local rulers. When Northern Nigeria and Southern Nigeria were united in 1914, Lugard continued as Britain's chief representative. Hugh Clifford, who succeeded him as governor from 1919 to 1925, sought to bring Western economic development, to build on educational progress made in the south, and to introduce new governmental structures such as the 1922 constitution and the Legislative Council.

British rule and economic and educational development produced a rising nationalism that was reflected particularly in the organized labor movement and the creation of various political parties during World War II. Following the war, Nigeria developed under two colonial constitutions, those of 1946 and 1951. They expanded the Legislative Council and introduced the federal principle, combining regional autonomy with federal union and stipulating that civil service personnel and personnel in other public spheres should reflect the various parts of the country. In 1952-53 a census indicated that 54 percent of the population resided in the northern part of the country. Because population was the basis for allocating revenues as well as political representation, census findings always aroused considerable controversy as to their accuracy. The 1962 census was voided, and the 1963 census has become the accepted basis for planning purposes. The 1973 census, which claimed that 64 percent of the population lived in the north, was subsequently disallowed. (The November 1991 census was conducted by restricting movement of the population for two days in 250,000 enumeration areas. In mid-March 1992 the government announced that the overall population was only 88.5 million, considerably less than anticipated.)

Nigeria gained its independence on October 1, 1960, and the First Republic is generally held to have begun then, although the nation actually became a republic on October 1, 1963. The political scene, unfortunately, was clouded by the trial of two leading politicians, who were charged with conspiracy; and widespread political abuses and corruption caused the electorate to become disillusioned. The 1964-65 elections saw very low voter participation, followed by increasing violence that led to the death of as many as 2,000 persons. After an abortive coup attempt in January 1966, the army took over under Major General Johnson Aguiyi Ironsi, an Igbo, and a Federal Military Government was formed. Ironsi's tenure was short-lived because northern officers staged a countercoup in July, in which Ironsi was killed and Lieutenant Colonel Yakubu Gowon, a Christian from the middle belt area, took control. Tension increased between the infantry, who were mainly of northern origin, and the Igbo soldiers in the south. The conflict led to the bloody civil war of 1967-70 (also known as the Biafran War) that took the lives of about 2 million persons.

Gowon, who intended that his be an interim rule preparing for return to civilian government, concentrated on economic development. In the late 1960s, the discovery of petroleum in commercial quantities caused oil to replace cocoa, peanuts, and palm products as Nigeria's major foreign exchange earner; and in 1971 Nigeria became a member of the Organization of the Petroleum Exporting Countries (OPEC). The economy suffered, however, from the 1972-74 drought and rising unemployment as farm workers flocked into the cities.

Discontent increased, and in 1975 military forces deposed Gowon in a bloodless coup. They brought in Brigadier Murtala Muhammad, soon to became general, who began demobilizing the military, cutting the civil service, and creating new states (the number of states eventually came to nineteen) in order to weaken regional ethnic ties. Dissatisfaction within the military over these measures led to Murtala Muhammad's assassination in 1976. He was succeeded by his next in command, Lieutenant General Olusegun Obasanjo, who concentrated on preparing the country for civilian rule in accordance with the draft of the constitution, which was promulgated in 1979, and the elections held under it.

The resulting Second Republic lasted from 1979 to 1983 under civilian president Shehu Shagari. The weak political coalition government, the end of the oil boom, the strain of recession, and fraud in the 1983 elections caused the army to step in again at the end of December 1983 under Major General Muhammadu Buhari, who sought to end widespread corruption. The army removed Buhari in August 1985, substituting Major General Ibrahim Babangida and calling the new governing military body the Armed Forces Ruling Council. Babangida also attempted to prepare Nigeria for civilian government, initially through economic measures. He declared a National Economic Emergency in 1986 and undertook Nigeria's own version of a rigorous structural adjustment program (SAP), as a result of which it received aid from the World Bank (see Glossary).

Economic measures designed to raise the overall standard of living of Nigerians had to take into account the pluralistic nature of the society. The country contained between 250 and 400 ethnic groups (depending on the way they were defined), speaking about 400 languages. Of these, the Hausa were the dominant group in the northern area, followed by the Kanuri; the Nupe and Tiv predominated in the middle belt; and the southern area was fragmented: the major groups being the Yoruba concentrated in the southwest and the Igbo in the southeast. Whereas 80 percent of Nigeria's population in 1990 lived in farming villages, the country experienced perhaps the fastest growing urbanization in the world in the 1970s and had the largest total urban population of any state in sub-Saharan Africa. The search for employment drew males to the cities, leaving most rural areas with a population composed largely of women, children, and the elderly.

Religion also has been pluralist. The far northern areas of Nigeria have commonly been considered Muslim, but the middle belt has a mixture of Muslim and Christian adherents. In the south, traditionally considered Christian and featuring Protestant and Africanized churches, such as the Aladura movement among the Yoruba and Roman Catholicism among the Igbo, there was also a sizeable Muslim population in 1992. In addition, traditional religion, characterized by worship of primordial spirits, dead ancestors, and spirits of places, is practiced, especially in rural areas.

Education, too, has followed a varied pattern. By 1992, Nigeria had a nationwide indigenous system in which English had come to be the language of instruction beyond primary school; traditional Quranic schools, both in the rural and urban areas of the north; and private and parochial schools in the cities, which provided a European-style education (such schools were taken over by the government in the mid-1970s but allowed to resume private operation in 1990).

Health facilities were uneven in quality as of 1992. Babangida launched a Primary Health Care plan in 1987 designed to expand immunization and improve inadequate rural health facilities and the geographic maldistribution of medical facilities. Significant health progress had been made nationally, however, since World War II. One of the most challenging health problems of the early 1990s was the increasing prevalence of acquired immune deficiency syndrome (AIDS). In the spring of 1992, the minister of health announced that about 400,000 Nigerians (nearly 0.5 percent of the population) were carriers of the virus that caused AIDS.

The relatively high percentage of secondary school and university graduates in Nigeria represented both an asset and a liability to the economy. Although an educated work force was useful in promoting technology and the professions, in the recession of the late 1980s, Nigeria had an unemployment rate for secondary school graduates of 35 to 40 percent, a potential source of unrest. Efforts to decrease unemployment were hampered by the dependence of the economy on petroleum. In 1988 oil produced 87 percent of the country's export income and 77 percent of total federal revenues.

This situation made the economy very vulnerable to world oil price fluctuations. For example, the fall in oil prices and output in the latter 1980s caused a drastic decline in Nigeria's gross national product (GNP—see Glossary). GNP went from US$830 per capita in 1983 to US$250 per capita in 1989. As a result, in 1989, for the first time, Nigeria was listed by the World Bank as a low-income country. The fall in the price of oil caused Nigeria not only to incur a trade deficit but also to begin foreign borrowing, resulting in 1989 in the largest public debt of any sub-Saharan state.

In addition to petroleum, Nigeria's major exports in the early 1990s continued to be primary products such as cocoa and, to a lesser degree, peanuts, cotton, and palm oil products. (In 1990 a law was passed banning the export of cocoa beans as of January 1991 in order to promote domestic processing. This law caused concern because despite various projects for establishing processing plants, Nigeria was unable to process all the cocoa beans produced.) The United States replaced Britain in the late 1980s as Nigeria's best customer, but Britain remained Nigeria's largest single source of imports.

Babangida's introduction of the SAP in 1986 represented an effort to increase domestic production and to institute financial and import restrictions that would strengthen the economy. Measures taken under the SAP entailed control of the value of the naira (see Glossary) by creating the second-tier foreign exchange market, strict control of the money supply and credits, a budget deficit limited to 4 percent of gross domestic product (GDP—see Glossary), privatization of major state-owned companies together with a new industrial policy, easing of trade restrictions, and debt rescheduling. The SAP was still in place in early 1992; the floating of the naira against international currencies in March 1992 was a bold step but was expected to result in further inflation.

Babangida's SAP was not Nigeria's first attempt at economic planning. Early government planning efforts, beginning in the late 1940s, had limited results; therefore, in 1990 Nigeria adopted a three-year rolling plan system that could readily be modified when changed circumstances required. The major goals were to reduce inflation, which had averaged 20 percent or more annually between 1973 and 1984; to maintain the infrastructure—Nigeria had one of the best-developed transportation systems in Africa but maintenance had been poor; to achieve agricultural self-sufficiency, and to reduce the SAP burden. As with most other developing countries, the share that agriculture contributed to GDP declined. It went from 65.7 percent in fiscal year (see Glossary) 1959 to 39.2

percent in 1988. Moreover, Nigeria's hope of achieving food self-sufficiency was at least temporarily dashed when in early 1991 drought forced Nigeria to increase substantially its food imports. Manufacturing's share in GDP gradually rose from 4.4 percent in fiscal year 1959 to 10.0 percent in 1988. The growth in manufacturing resulted in part from the Nigerian Enterprises Promotion decrees of 1972, 1977, and 1981 that facilitated indigenous majority ownership. These decrees were relaxed in 1985, however, to encourage foreign investment and thus stimulate the economy.

The major goals of economic development were integrating agriculture and industry more closely, including privatization or commercialization of a number of parastatals and government-owned enterprises; improving the infrastructure with particular reference to increasing electric power generation, enlarging and modernizing communications systems, and performing needed maintenance on existing transportation systems; reducing dependence on oil; and creating an effective national planning body. By the end of 1991, privatization measures had taken effect in such areas as agriculture, banking, railroads, and telecommunications. Nigeria, however, for the most part lacked the capital necessary for large-scale development and depended upon foreign loans to implement its programs. For example, it received a 1990 European Economic Community grant for rural development and telecommunications of 3.54 billion naira (for value of the naira—see Glossary) under the Fourth Lomé Convention (see Glossary) and a 1991 British loan of £223.3 million to expand the electric power system. As a result of such borrowing, at the end of 1991 Nigeria owed an estimated US$34 billion in external debt; 44 percent was owed to members of the Paris Club and 20 percent to foreign commercial banks. Throughout 1990 and 1991, Nigeria engaged in extensive debt rescheduling with Paris Club countries such as Britain, Italy, Japan, and Sweden.

Among other major development projects that Nigeria was pursuing was the large Ajaokuta steelworks, begun with Soviet funding and subsequently funded by the World Bank, due for completion at the end of 1992. On a smaller scale was a European currency unit (ECU) 48 million loan from the European Investment Bank under the Third Lomé Convention for the development of palm oil refining facilities. In addition, despite its efforts to diversify its economy, Nigeria was expanding its oil production. The expansion came, most notably, through the discovery of an offshore field near Akwa Ibom, which was scheduled to increase oil production by one-third by 1994. Expansion also resulted from the renovation of oil refineries at Warri and Kaduna; the development of petrochemical plants; an oil condensate project at Oso on the Niger Delta coast; and the planned construction, beginning in 1992, of facilities to enable the export of liquefied natural gas from Bonny.

Despite this economic progress, the implementation of the SAP led to decreased spending on social programs in the late 1980s. The decrease caused some domestic dissatisfaction, which was reflected in strikes and student demonstrations. Since achieving independence in 1960, Nigeria has faced a number of incidents reflecting domestic discontent; in many instances the incidents were initiated by the army or its leaders. Such dissension, of which the most serious outbreak was the Biafran civil war, has led to twenty-two years of military rule; democratic government under the First Republic and the Second Republic was limited to ten years. Sources of military dissatisfaction have arisen not only from the personal ambitions of various military leaders but also from general dismay at the corruption, bribery, favoritism, and inefficiency prevalent in the government. Many Nigerians initially saw the army as the most effective body to control the country, but with the understanding that military rule was an interim measure and that plans must go forward for the transition to democratic government. In support of this view, a number of organized interest groups, such as professional associations, trade unions, student associations, women's organizations, and the media have exerted pressures in favor of democratic processes.

The 1989 constitution that Nigeria adopted as the basis for its transition to democratic government was modeled on the United States federal system. It provided for a president; two legislative houses, one based on population and the other on states; and an independent judiciary. A timetable was established for a series of elections at the local government area, state, and national levels. At first, officeholders in any previous government were barred from holding office in an attempt to eliminate corruption and undue political influence; in mid-December 1991 the ban was lifted, making only Babangida ineligible.

In 1989 Babangida also rejected the applications of all political entities to be recognized as political parties and instead in October 1989 created two parties: the Republican National Convention, "a little to the right of center," and the Social Democratic Party, "a little to the left of center." This action, which generated considerable controversy, was designed to create parties that would cross ethnic, religious, regional, and socioeconomic lines. Results of the various elections held in 1991 appeared to indicate that previously cohesive blocs were indeed being eroded. On August 27, 1991, the number of states was increased from twenty-one to thirty (see fig. 1). Irregularities in the gubernatorial primaries in October 1991 in nine states caused the election results to be canceled in November and new elections to be rescheduled for early December, with the final state gubernatorial and state assembly elections occurring in mid-December. Although by Nigerian standards the elections went relatively smoothly, there was some criticism of the system of open balloting by which voters stood behind a photograph of their chosen candidate and were counted.

Among the difficulties involved in encouraging the democratic process have been ethnic and religious tensions arising among the multitudinous groups in the country. Outbreaks of violence caused by religious tensions resulting in losses of life have occurred in the past and recurred in the 1980s and 1990s. Most recently, in 1991 and 1992 they took place in Bauchi, Benue, Kaduna, Kano, Taraba, and other states. Desire for ethnic self-assertion and for the power and financial wherewithal resulting from statehood have largely constituted the basis for the creation of new states. Nigeria has moved from three regions at independence to four regions in 1963, twelve states in 1967, nineteen states in 1976, twenty-one states in 1987, and thirty states in August 1991. Government leaders including Babangida have endeavored, however, to diversify ethnic representation in a state so as to prevent the dominance of a single group. The move of the federal capital from Lagos to Abuja in December 1991 resulted not only from the tremendous overcrowding and pressure on transportation and other infrastructure facilities in Lagos but also from the desire to locate the capital in a central area that lacked association with a particular ethnic group. Some issues continued to be controversial, such as the impact the move to Abuja would have on Lagos. Moreover, the relationship of states to the federal government, with particular reference to the division of revenues among them, had as of early 1992 not been resolved to general satisfaction, nor had the highly controversial matter of the establishment of Muslim sharia courts of appeal in southern states.

Despite these domestic difficulties, Nigeria has continued to play a prominent role not only in West Africa but also in the world community. Nigeria was a prime organizer of the Economic Community of West African States (ECOWAS) and of the ECOWAS Cease-fire Monitoring Group (ECOMOG) that stemmed from it. ECOMOG provided a peacekeeping force for Liberia to which Nigeria contributed 900 personnel in August 1990 as well as leadership. To reduce the financial burden on Nigeria of participation in African peacekeeping forces, Babangida, at the 27th annual meeting of the Organization of African Unity (OAU), held in Abuja in June 1991, again raised the matter of a volunteer pan-African defense force, suggesting that such a force be organized on a regional basis.

In 1991–92 Babangida served as president of the OAU, thereby enhancing his mediator role. During this period, he met with the prime ministers of Chad and Niger and the president of Cameroon concerning border problems between Nigeria and these countries. A meeting of the four states in July 1990 had failed to resolve the Lake Chad boundary question, and in the summer of 1991 Cameroon had occupied nine Nigerian border villages or islands. Because it had a higher standard of living than its neighbors, Nigeria was also facing an influx of workers from surrounding countries. In November 1991, in an attempt to deal with the problem, Nigeria announced that it planned to create a frontier force to control illegal immigration. Nigeria's major role in the African continent was particularly highlighted by the visit of South African president Frederick W. de Klerk to Nigeria in early April 1992. The visit laid a foundation for possible future recognition of a transitional South African government by the OAU and other African states.

Nigeria has sought to play a responsible role in OPEC as well as in various United Nations bodies. Nigeria's position toward the Arab-Israeli dispute has been influenced by its domestic religious divisions. Babangida reinstated Nigeria's diplomatic relations with Israel in August 1991, and shortly thereafter invited Palestine Liberation Organization head Yasir Arafat to visit, greeting him with a twenty-one-gun salute reserved for heads of state. The same month Babangida suspended Nigeria's membership in the Organization of the Islamic Conference. He had initiated membership in 1986 without any prior consultation, a move that had created a furore among Nigerian Christians. Because of its position as a former British colony, its membership in the British Commonwealth of Nations, and its position as a world oil producer, Nigeria's national interests have led it to align itself primarily with the West, including the European Economic Community.

Nigeria's role as an African regional leader, peacekeeper, and mediator has emerged at the same time that the country's army was being drastically reduced from approximately 250,000 personnel during the civil war to about 80,000 in 1991. Additional cuts were projected in order to bring the force to approximately 60,000. This process, together with a large-scale restructuring of the armed forces beginning in 1990 and still underway in early 1992, occurred in preparation for the transition to civilian government under the Third Republic.

The size of the armed forces reflected not only Nigeria's expanse but also the domestic instability the country had experienced since achieving independence in 1960. In the period between 1966 and 1985, Nigeria underwent no less than six coups d'état, in addition to several attempted coups. (A serious recent failed coup was that led by Major Gideon Ockar, a middle belt Christian, in April 1991. He advocated the "excising" from Nigeria of the five northern Muslim states—the coup attempt occurred prior to the creation of Nigeria's nine additional states—on the grounds that the true Nigeria was the Christian southern part of the country.)

Economic and social conditions worsened in the 1980s, increasing the discontent resulting from ethnic, sectional, and religious cleavages. To these forces for instability were added such factors as the potential for foreign subversion, caused in part by the large number of illegal workers from other African states; the fluctuation of oil prices and particularly the impact of decreasing oil income on the economy; the pressures of the rising foreign debt; and the growing Islamism, or Islamic activism (sometimes seen as fundamentalism), as well as increasing Christian fundamentalism.

Public disenchantment with the military in the 1980s and 1990s caused increasing demands for democracy, the elimination of military tribunals, and an end to Decree Number 2, passed during the Buhari regime. In 1992 this decree still permitted the jailing of individuals for up to six weeks without charge and set limits on freedom of speech and the press. Pressure groups, such as labor unions, academic, and student groups, and especially the media, agitated for reforms and a greater role in government decision making, particularly in the economic field. Such activity led the government to jail various individuals on a number of occasions. Another public concern was the rising crime rate, especially in urban areas, and the marked increase in drug-related crime and international narcotics trafficking. Numerous jail sentences resulted, leading to overcrowding and causing periodic amnesties to empty penal facilities.

Despite Nigeria's recent history of military domination of politics, in April 1992 Babangida appeared committed to turning over power to a new civilian government in January 1993. Part of Babangida's transition process entailed the demilitarization of the government. Demilitarization was accomplished in part in September 1990 by retiring from military service all cabinet ministers except for Babangida and the minister of defense. The officers continued to serve in a civilian capacity. The post of chief of the General Staff was likewise eliminated; the incumbent, Vice Admiral Augustus Aikhomu, who had also been retired from the military, was named vice president. In addition, numerous state military governors were retired and replaced by lower-ranking officers; in each state, a civilian deputy governor served under the military governor in order to become familiar with the duties entailed. In December 1991, the newly elected civilian governors took office.

Serious questions remained, however, as to whether or not Babangida's goals for the professionalization of the armed forces and the reeducation of the military concerning their subordinate role in a forthcoming civilian government were attainable. Concurrently, Babangida stressed educating the citizenry about their responsibilities for active, knowledgeable participation in government. The question was also raised as to whether or not democracy could be achieved by a military government that established rules for the transition but that simultaneously imposed strict limits on the democratic process and sought to silence critics both of the domestic political scene and of the government's economic policies, particularly the SAP. The House of Representatives elections and the Senate elections (which will return two senators from each state and one from Abuja to the newly structured sixty-one-member Senate) scheduled for November 1992 and the presidential elections scheduled for December 1992 would be the final test in the transition to the Third Republic slated to occur in January 1993.

April 15, 1992   Helen Chapin Metz

Chapter 1. Historical Setting

Nok terra-cotta head dating from the first millennium B.C.

LIKE SO MANY OTHER MODERN AFRICAN states, Nigeria is the creation of European imperialism. Its very name—after the great Niger River, the country's dominating physical feature—was suggested in the 1890s by British journalist Flora Shaw, who later became the wife of colonial governor Frederick Lugard. The modern history of Nigeria—as a political state encompassing 250 to 400 ethnic groups of widely varied cultures and modes of political organization—dates from the completion of the British conquest in 1903 and the amalgamation of northern and southern Nigeria into the Colony and Protectorate of Nigeria in 1914. The history of the Nigerian people extends backward in time for some three millennia. Archaeological evidence, oral traditions, and written documentation establish the existence of dynamic societies and well-developed political systems whose history had an important influence on colonial rule and has continued to shape independent Nigeria. Nigerian history is fragmented in the sense that it evolved from a variety of traditions, but many of the most outstanding features of modern society reflect the strong influence of the three regionally dominant ethnic groups—the Hausa in the north, the Yoruba in the west, and the Igbo in the east.

There are several dominant themes in Nigerian history that are essential in understanding contemporary Nigerian politics and society. First, the spread of Islam, predominantly in the north but later in southwestern Nigeria as well, began a millennium ago. The creation of the Sokoto Caliphate in the jihad (holy war) of 1804–8 brought most of the northern region and adjacent parts of Niger and Cameroon under a single Islamic government. The great extension of Islam within the area of present-day Nigeria dates from the nineteenth century and the consolidation of the caliphate. This history helps account for the dichotomy between north and south and for the divisions within the north that have been so strong during the colonial and postcolonial eras.

Second, the slave trade, both across the Sahara Desert and the Atlantic Ocean, had a profound influence on virtually all parts of Nigeria. The transatlantic trade in particular accounted for the forced migration of perhaps 3.5 million people between the 1650s and the 1860s, while a steady stream of slaves flowed north across the Sahara for a millennium, ending at the beginning of the twentieth century. Within Nigeria, slavery was widespread, with social implications that are still evident today. The Sokoto Caliphate, for

3

example, had more slaves than any other modern country, except the United States in 1860. Slaves were also numerous among the Igbo, the Yoruba, and many other ethnic groups. Indeed, many ethnic distinctions, especially in the middle belt—the area between the north and south—were reinforced because of slave raiding and defensive measures that were adopted for protection against enslavement. Conversion to Islam and the spread of Christianity were intricately associated with issues relating to slavery and with efforts to promote political and cultural autonomy.

Third, the colonial era was relatively brief, lasting only six decades or so, depending upon the part of Nigeria, but it unleashed such rapid change that the full impact was still felt in the contemporary period. On the one hand, the expansion of agricultural products as the principal export earner and the corresponding development of infrastructure resulted in severely distorted economic growth that has subsequently collapsed. On the other hand, social dislocation associated with the decline of slavery and the internal movement of population between regions and to the cities necessitated the reassessment of ethnic loyalties, which in turn have been reflected in politics and religion.

In the three decades since the independence of Nigeria in 1960, a period half as long as the colonial era, Nigeria has experienced a number of successful and attempted military coups d'état and a brutal civil war, let corrupt civilian governments siphon off the profits from the oil boom of the 1970s, and faced economic collapse in the 1980s. As the most populous country in Africa, and one of the ten most populous countries in the world, Nigeria has a history that is important in its own right but that also bears scrutiny if for no other reason than to understand how and why this nation became as it is today.

Early History

All evidence suggests the early settlement of Nigeria millennia before the spread of agriculture 3,000 years ago, and one day it probably will be possible to reconstruct the high points of this early history. Although archaeological research has made great strides in identifying some major developments, comparatively little archaeological work has been undertaken. Consequently, it is possible only to outline some of the early history of Nigeria.

The earliest known example of a fossil skeleton with negroid features, perhaps 10,000 years old, was found at Iwo Elero in western Nigeria and attests to the antiquity of habitation in the region. Stone tools, indicating human settlement, date back another 2,000 years. Microlithic and ceramic industries were developed by pastoralists in the savanna from at least the fourth millennium B.C. and were continued by grain farmers in the stable agricultural communities that subsequently evolved there. To the south, hunting and gathering gradually gave way to subsistence farming on the fringe of the forest in the first millennium B.C. The cultivation of staple foods, such as yams, later was introduced into forest clearings. The stone ax heads, imported in great quantities from the north and used in opening the forest for agricultural development, were venerated by the Yoruba descendants of Neolithic pioneers as ''thunderbolts'' hurled to earth by the gods.

The primitive iron-smelting furnaces at Taruga dating from the fourth century B.C. provide the oldest evidence of metalworking in West Africa, while excavations for the Kainji Dam revealed the presence of ironworking there by the second century B.C. The transition from Neolithic times to the Iron Age apparently was achieved without intermediate bronze production. Some scholars speculate that knowledge of the smelting process may have been transmitted from the Mediterranean by Berbers who ventured south. Others suggest that the technology moved westward across the Sudan (see Glossary) from the Nile Valley, although the arrival of the Iron Age in the Niger River valley and the forest region appears to have predated the introduction of metallurgy in the upper savanna by more than 800 years. The usefulness of iron tools was demonstrated in the south for bush cutting and in the north for well digging and the construction of irrigation works, contributing in both regions to the expansion of agriculture.

The earliest culture in Nigeria to be identified by its distinctive artifacts is that of the Nok people. These skilled artisans and ironworkers were associated with Taruga and flourished between the fourth century B.C. and the second century A.D. in a large area above the confluence of the Niger and Benue rivers on the Jos Plateau. The Nok achieved a level of material development not repeated in the region for nearly 1,000 years. Their terra-cotta sculpture, abstractly stylized and geometric in conception, is admired both for its artistic expression and for the high technical standards of its production.

Information is lacking from the ''silent millennium'' (first millennium A.D.) that followed the Nok ascendancy, apart from evidence of iron smelting on Dala Hill in Kano from about 600 to 700 A.D. It is assumed, however, that trade linking the Niger region with North Africa played a key role in the continuing development of the area. Certainly by the beginning of the second millennium A.D., there was an active trade along a north-south axis from North Africa through the Sahara to the forest, with the savanna people acting as intermediaries in exchanges that involved slaves, ivory, salt, glass beads, coral, cloth, weapons, brass rods, and other goods.

Early States Before 1500

Long before 1500, much of present-day Nigeria was divided into states, which can be identified with the modern ethnic groups that trace their history to the origins of these states. These early states included the Yoruba kingdoms, the Edo kingdom of Benin, the Hausa cities, and Nupe. In addition, numerous small states to the west and south of Lake Chad were absorbed or displaced in the course of the expansion of Kanem, which was centered to the northeast of Lake Chad. Borno, initially the western province of Kanem, became independent in the late fourteenth century. Other states probably existed as well, but oral traditions and the absence of archaeological data do not permit an accurate dating of their antiquity.

Yoruba Kingdoms and Benin

As far as historical memory extends, the Yoruba have been the dominant group on the west bank of the Niger. Of mixed origin, they were the product of the assimilation of periodic waves of migrants who evolved a common language and culture. The Yoruba were organized in patrilineal descent groups that occupied village communities and subsisted on agriculture, but from about the eleventh century A.D., adjacent village compounds, called *ile*, began to coalesce into a number of territorial city-states in which loyalties to the clan became subordinate to allegiance to a dynastic chieftain. This transition produced an urbanized political and social environment that was accompanied by a high level of artistic achievement, particularly in terra-cotta and ivory sculpture and in the sophisticated metal casting produced at Ife. The brass and bronze used by Yoruba artisans was a significant item of trade, made from copper, tin, and zinc imported either from North Africa or from mines in the Sahara and northern Nigeria.

The Yoruba placated a pantheon headed by an impersonal deity, Olorun, and included lesser deities, some of them formerly mortal, who performed a variety of cosmic and practical tasks. One of them, Oduduwa, was regarded as the creator of the earth and the ancestor of the Yoruba kings. According to a creation myth, Oduduwa founded the city of Ife and dispatched his sons to establish other cities, where they reigned as priest-kings and presided over cult rituals. Formal traditions of this sort have been interpreted as poetic illustrations of the historical process by which Ife's ruling dynasty extended its authority over Yorubaland. The stories were attempts to legitimize the Yoruba monarchies—after they had supplanted clan loyalties—by claiming divine origin.

Ife was the center of as many as 400 religious cults whose traditions were manipulated to political advantage by the *oni* (king) in the days of the kingdom's greatness. Ife also lay at the center of a trading network with the north. The *oni* supported his court with tolls levied on trade, tribute exacted from dependencies, and tithes due him as a religious leader. One of Ife's greatest legacies to modern Nigeria is its beautiful sculpture associated with this tradition.

The *oni* was chosen on a rotating basis from one of several branches of the ruling dynasty, which was composed of a clan with several thousand members. Once elected, he went into seclusion in the palace compound and was not seen again by his people. Below the *oni* in the state hierarchy were palace officials, town chiefs, and the rulers of outlying dependencies. The palace officials were spokesmen for the *oni* and the rulers of dependencies who had their own subordinate officials. All offices, even that of the *oni*, were elective and depended on broad support within the community. Each official was chosen from among the eligible clan members who had hereditary right to the office. Members of the royal dynasty often were assigned to govern dependencies, while the sons of palace officials assumed lesser roles as functionaries, bodyguards to the *oni*, and judges.

During the fifteenth century, Oyo and Benin surpassed Ife as political and economic powers, although Ife preserved its status as a religious center even after its decline. Respect for the priestly functions of the *oni* of Ife and recognition of the common tradition of origin were crucial factors in the evolution of Yoruba ethnicity. The *oni* of Ife was recognized as the senior political official not only among the Yoruba but also at Benin, and he invested Benin's rulers with the symbols of temporal power.

The Ife model of government was adapted at Oyo, where a member of its ruling dynasty consolidated several smaller city-states under his control. A council of state, the Oyo Mesi, eventually assumed responsibility for naming the *alafin* (king) from candidates proposed from the ruling dynasty and acted as a check on his authority. Oyo developed as a constitutional monarchy; actual government was in the hands of the *basorun* (prime minister), who presided over the Oyo Mesi. The city was situated 170 kilometers north of Ife and about 100 kilometers north of present-day Oyo. Unlike the forest-bound Yoruba kingdoms, Oyo was in the savanna and drew its military strength from its cavalry forces, which established hegemony over the adjacent Nupe and the Borgu kingdoms and thereby developed trade routes farther to the north (see fig. 2).

7

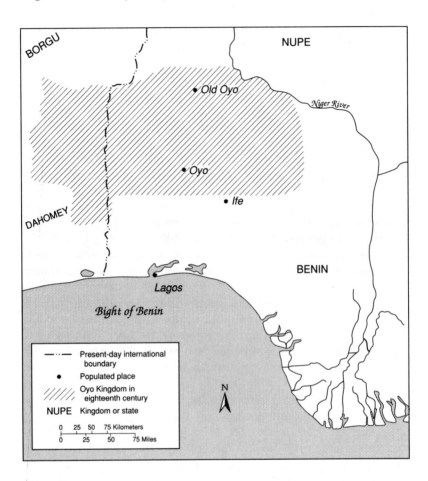

Figure 2. Yorubaland, Eleventh to Nineteenth Centuries

Benin was already a well-established agricultural community in the Edo-speaking area, east of Ife, when it became a dependency of Ife at the beginning of the fourteenth century. By the fifteenth century, it took an independent course and became a major trading power in its own right, blocking Ife's access to the coastal ports as Oyo had cut off the mother city from the savanna. Political power and religious authority resided in the *oba* (king), who according to tradition was descended from the Ife dynasty. The *oba* was advised by a council of six hereditary chiefs, who also nominated his successor. Benin, which may have housed 100,000 inhabitants at its height, spread over twenty-five square kilometers that were enclosed by three concentric rings of earthworks. Responsibility for administering the urban complex lay with sixty trade guilds, each with its own quarter, whose membership cut across clan affiliations and owed its loyalty directly to the *oba*. At his wooden, steepled palace, the *oba* presided over a large court richly adorned with brass, bronze, and ivory objects. Like Ife and the other Yoruba states, Benin, too, is famous for its sculpture.

Unlike the Yoruba kingdoms, however, Benin developed a centralized regime to oversee the administration of its expanding territories. By the late fifteenth century, Benin was in contact with Portugal (see European Slave Trade in West Africa, this ch.). At its apogee in the sixteenth and seventeenth centuries, Benin even encompassed parts of southeastern Yorubaland and the small Igbo area on the western bank of the Niger. Dependencies were governed by members of the royal family, who were assigned several towns or villages scattered throughout the realm rather than a block of territory that could be used as a base for revolt against the *oba*.

As is evident from this brief survey, Yoruba and Benin history were interconnected. In fact, areas to the west of Nigeria, in the modern Republic of Benin, were also closely associated with this history, both in the period before 1500 and afterward.

The Igbo: A Stateless Society?

Most scholars have argued that Igbo society was "stateless" and that the Igbo region did not evolve centralized political institutions before the colonial period. According to this theory, the relatively egalitarian Igbo lived in small, self-contained groups of villages organized according to a lineage system that did not allow social stratification. An individual's fitness to govern was determined by his wisdom and his wisdom by his age and experience. Subsistence farming was the dominant economic activity, and yams were the staple crop. Land, obtained through inheritance, was the measure of wealth. Handicrafts and commerce were well developed, and a relatively dense population characterized the region.

Despite the absence of chiefs, some Igbo relied on an order of priests, chosen from outsiders on the northern fringe of Igboland, to ensure impartiality in settling disputes between communities. Igbo gods, like those of the Yoruba, were numerous, but their relationship to one another and to human beings was essentially egalitarian, thereby reflecting Igbo society as a whole. A number of oracles and local cults attracted devotees, while the central deity, the earth mother and fertility figure, Ala, was venerated at shrines throughout Igboland.

9

The weakness of this theory of statelessness rests on the paucity of historical evidence of precolonial Igbo society. There are huge lacunae between the archaeological finds of Igbo Ukwu, which reveal a rich material culture in the heart of the Igbo region in the eighth century A.D., and the oral traditions of the twentieth century. In particular, the importance of the Nri Kingdom, which appears to have flourished before the seventeenth century, often is overlooked. The Nri Kingdom was relatively small in geographical extent, but it is remembered as the cradle of Igbo culture. Finally, Benin exercised considerable influence on the western Igbo, who adopted many of the political structures familiar to the Yoruba-Benin region.

The Northern Kingdoms of the Savanna

Trade was the key to the emergence of organized communities in the savanna portions of Nigeria. Prehistoric inhabitants, adjusting to the encroaching desert, were widely scattered by the third millennium B.C., when the desiccation of the Sahara began. Trans-Saharan trade routes linked the western Sudan with the Mediterranean from the time of Carthage and with the upper Nile from a much earlier date, also establishing an avenue of communication and cultural influence that remained open until the end of the nineteenth century. By these same routes, Islam made its way south into West Africa after the ninth century A.D.

By then a string of dynastic states, including the earliest Hausa states, stretched across the western and central Sudan. The most powerful of these states were Ghana, Gao, and Kanem, which were not located within the boundaries of present-day Nigeria but which nonetheless had an indirect influence on the history of the Nigerian savanna. Ghana declined in the eleventh century but was succeeded by Mali, which consolidated much of the western Sudan under its imperial rule in the thirteenth century. Songhai emerged as an empire out of the small state of Gao in the fifteenth century. For a century, Songhai paid homage to Mali, but by the last decade of the fifteenth century it attained its independence and brought much of the Malian domains under its imperial sway. Although these western empires had little political influence on the savanna states of Nigeria before 1500, they had a strong cultural and economic impact that became more pronounced in the sixteenth century, especially because these states became associated with the spread of Islam and trade. In the sixteenth century, moreover, much of northern Nigeria paid homage to Songhai in the west or to Borno, a rival empire in the east (see fig. 3).

Borno's history is closely associated with Kanem, which had achieved imperial status in the Lake Chad basin by the thirteenth century. Kanem expanded westward to include the area that became Borno. Its dynasty, the Sayfawa, was descended from pastoralists who had settled in the Lake Chad region in the seventh century. The *mai* (king) of Kanem ruled in conjunction with a council of peers as a constitutional monarch. In the eleventh century, the *mai* and his court accepted Islam, as the western empires also had done. Islam was used to reinforce the political and social structures of the state, although many established customs were maintained. Women, for example, continued to exercise considerable political influence.

The *mai* employed his mounted bodyguard, composed of *abid* (slave-soldiers), and an inchoate army of nobles to extend Kanem's authority into Borno, on the western shore of Lake Chad. By tradition the territory was conferred on the heir to the throne to govern during his apprenticeship. In the fourteenth century, however, dynastic conflict forced the then-ruling group and its followers to relocate in Borno, where as a result the Kanuri emerged as an ethnic group in the late fourteenth and fifteenth centuries. The civil war that disrupted Kanem in the second half of the fourteenth century resulted in the independence of Borno.

Borno's prosperity depended on its stake in the trans-Sudanic slave trade and the desert trade in salt and livestock. The need to protect its commercial interests compelled Borno to intervene in Kanem, which continued to be a theater of war throughout the fifteenth and into the sixteenth centuries. Despite its relative political weakness in this period, Borno's court and mosques under the patronage of a line of scholarly kings earned fame as centers of Islamic culture and learning.

By the eleventh century, some of the Hausa states—such as those at Kano, Katsina, and Gobir—had developed into walled towns that engaged in trade and serviced caravans as well as manufactured cloth and leather goods. Millet, sorghum, sugarcane, and cotton were produced in the surrounding countryside, which also provided grazing land for cattle. Until the fifteenth century, the small Hausa states were on the periphery of the major empires of the era.

According to tradition, the Hausa rulers descended from a "founding hero" named Bayinjida, supposedly of Middle Eastern origin, who became *sarki* (king) of Daura after subduing a snake and marrying the queen of Daura. Their children founded the other Hausa towns, which traditionally are referred to as the Hausa *bakwai* (Hausa seven). Wedged in among the stronger Sudanic kingdoms,

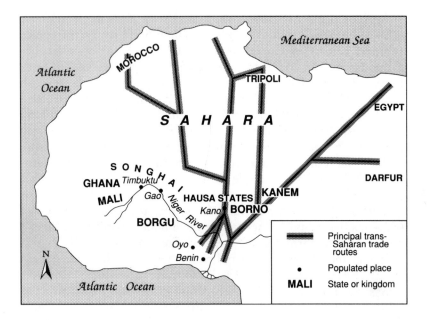

Figure 3. Principal Trans-Saharan Trade Routes, Ninth to Seventeenth Centuries

each of the Hausa states acquired special military, economic, or religious functions. No one state dominated the others, but at various times different states assumed a leading role. They were under constant pressure from Songhai to the west and Kanem-Borno to the east, to which they paid tribute. Armed conflict usually was motivated by economic concerns, as coalitions of Hausa states mounted wars against the Jukun and Nupe in the middle belt to collect slaves, or against one another for control of important trade routes.

Commerce was in the hands of commoners. Within the cities, trades were organized through guilds, each of which was self-regulating and collected taxes from its members to be transmitted to the *sarki* as a pledge of loyalty. In return, the king guaranteed the security of the guild's trade. The surrounding countryside produced grain for local consumption and cotton and hides for processing.

Islam was introduced to Hausaland along the caravan routes. The famous Kano Chronicle records the conversion of Kano's ruling dynasty by clerics from Mali, demonstrating that the imperial influence of Mali extended far to the east. Acceptance of Islam was gradual and was often nominal in the countryside, where folk

religion continued to exert a strong influence. Non-Islamic practices also were retained in the court ceremonies of the Hausa kings.
Nonetheless, Kano and Katsina, with their famous mosques and
schools, came to participate fully in the cultural and intellectual
life of the Islamic world.

Fulbe pastoralists, known in Nigeria as Fulani, began to enter
the Hausa country in the thirteenth century, and by the fifteenth
century they were tending cattle, sheep, and goats in Borno as well.
The Fulani came from the Senegal River valley, where their ancestors had developed a method of livestock management and
specialization based on transhumance. The movement of cattle
along north-south corridors in pursuit of grazing and water followed the climatic pattern of the rainy and dry seasons. Gradually,
the pastoralists moved eastward, first into the centers of the Mali
and Songhai empires and eventually into Hausaland and Borno.
Some Fulbe converted to Islam in the Senegal region as early as
the eleventh century, and one group of Muslim Fulani settled in
the cities and mingled freely with the Hausa, from whom they became racially indistinguishable. There, they constituted a devoutly
religious, educated elite who made themselves indispensable to the
Hausa kings as government advisers, Islamic judges, and teachers.
Other Fulani, the lighter-skinned pastoral nomads, remained aloof
from the Hausa and in some measure from Islam as well, herding
cattle outside the cities and seeking pastures for their herds.

The Savanna States, 1500–1800

The sixteenth century marked a high point in the political history of northern Nigeria. During this period, the Songhai Empire
reached its greatest limits, stretching from the Senegal and Gambia rivers in the far west and incorporating part of Hausaland in
the east. At the same time, the Sayfawa Dynasty of Borno asserted itself, conquering Kanem and extending its control westward
to Hausa cities that were not under Songhai imperial rule. For
almost a century, much of northern Nigeria was part of one or the
other of these empires, and after the 1590s Borno dominated the
region for 200 years.

Songhai's sway over western Hausaland included the subordi-
nation of Kebbi, whose *kanta* (king) controlled the territory along
the Sokoto River. Katsina and Gobir also paid tribute to Songhai,
while Songhai merchants dominated the trade of the Hausa towns.
It was at this time that the overland trade in kola nuts from the
Akan forests of modern Ghana was initiated. Largely because of
Songhai's influence, there was a remarkable blossoming of Islamic learning and culture.

The influence of Songhai collapsed abruptly in 1591, when an army from Morocco crossed the Sahara and conquered the capital city of Gao and the commercial center of Timbuktu. Morocco was not able to control the whole empire, and the various provinces, including the Hausa states, became independent. The collapse undermined Songhai's commercial and religious hegemony over the Hausa states and abruptly altered the course of history in the region.

Borno reached its apogee under *mai* Idris Aloma (ca. 1569–1600), during whose reign Kanem was reconquered. As a result of his campaigns, several Hausa cities, including Kano and Katsina, became tributaries. The destruction of Songhai left Borno uncontested as an imperial force, and during the seventeenth and eighteenth centuries Borno continued to dominate the political history of northern Nigeria. Now Borno became the center of Islamic learning and trade. Its capital at Birni Gazargamu, on the Komadugu Yobe River that flows eastward into Lake Chad, was well situated in the midst of a prosperous agricultural district. Textile production was a mainstay of its economy. Borno also controlled extensive salt deposits, which supplied its most important export to the west and south. These reserves were located at Bilma and Fachi in the Sahara, in the districts of Mangari and Muniyo adjacent to Birni Gazargamu, and on the northeastern shores of Lake Chad.

Despite Borno's hegemony, the Hausa states wrestled for ascendancy among themselves for much of the seventeenth and eighteenth centuries. Gobir, Katsina, Zamfara, Kano, Kebbi, and Zaria formed various alliances, but only Zamfara ceased to exist as an autonomous state, falling to Gobir in the eighteenth century. Borno collected tribute from Kano and Katsina, and its merchants dominated the trade routes that passed through Hausaland. Gradually, however, Borno's position began to weaken. Its inability to check the political rivalries of the competing Hausa cities was one example of this decline. Another factor was the military threat of the Tuareg, whose warriors, centered at Agades in the center of present-day Nigeria, penetrated the northern districts of Borno. They even diverted the salt trade of Bilma and Fachi from Birni Gazargamu. Tuareg military superiority depended upon camels, which also were used to transport salt and dates to the savanna.

The major cause of Borno's decline was a severe drought and famine that struck the whole Sahel (see Glossary) and savanna from Senegal to Ethiopia in the middle of the eighteenth century. There had been periodic droughts before; two serious droughts, one of seven years' duration, hit Borno in the seventeenth century. But the great drought of the 1740s and 1750s probably caused the most severe famine that the Sahel has known over the past several hundred years, including that of the 1970s. As a consequence of the mid-eighteenth century drought, Borno lost control of much of its northern territories to the Tuareg, whose mobility allowed them the flexibility to deal with famine conditions through war and plunder. Borno regained some of its former might in the succeeding decades, but another drought occurred in the 1790s, again weakening the state.

The ecological and political instability of the eighteenth century provided the background for the momentous events of the first decade of the nineteenth century, when the jihad of Usman dan Fodio revolutionized the whole of northern Nigeria. The military rivalries of the Hausa states and the political weakness of Borno put a severe strain on the economic resources of the region, just at a time when drought and famine undermined the prosperity of farmers and herders. Many Fulani moved into Hausaland and Borno at this time to escape areas where drought conditions were even worse, and their arrival increased tensions because they had no loyalty to the political authorities, who saw them as a source of increased taxation. By the end of the eighteenth century, some Muslim clerics began to articulate the grievances of the common people. Political efforts to eliminate or control these clerics only heightened the tensions. The stage was set for jihad (see Usman dan Fodio and the Sokoto Caliphate, this ch.).

European Slave Trade in West Africa

A desire for glory and profit from trade, missionary zeal, and considerations of global strategy brought Portuguese navigators to the West African coast in the late fifteenth century. Locked in a seemingly interminable crusading war with Muslim Morocco, the Portuguese conceived of a plan whereby maritime expansion might bypass the Islamic world and open new markets that would result in commercial gain. They hoped to tap the fabled Saharan gold trade, establish a sea route around Africa to India, and link up with the mysterious Christian kingdom of Prester John. The Portuguese achieved all these goals. They obtained access to the gold trade by trading along the Gulf of Guinea, establishing a base at Elmina ("the mine") on the Gold Coast (Ghana), and they made their way into the Indian Ocean, militarily securing a monopoly of the spice trade. Even the Christian kingdom turned out to be real—it was Ethiopia; Portuguese adventures there, however, turned sour very quickly. Portugal's lasting legacy for Nigeria, in the end, was its initiation of the transatlantic slave trade.

By 1471 Portuguese ships had reconnoitered the West African coast south as far as the Niger Delta, although they did not know that it was the delta, and in 1481 emissaries from the king of Portugal visited the court of the *oba* of Benin. For a time, Portugal and Benin maintained close relations. Portuguese soldiers aided Benin in its wars; Portuguese even came to be spoken at the *oba*'s court. Gwatto, the port of Benin, became the depot to handle the peppers, ivory, and increasing numbers of slaves offered by the *oba* in exchange for coral beads; textile imports from India; European-manufactured articles, including tools and weapons; and *manillas* (brass and bronze bracelets that were used as currency and also were melted down for objets d'art). Portugal also may have been the first European power to import cowrie shells, which were the currency of the far interior.

Benin profited from its close ties with the Portuguese and exploited the firearms bought from them to tighten its hold on the lower Niger area. Two factors checked the spread of Portuguese influence and the continued expansion of Benin, however. First, Portugal stopped buying pepper because of the availability of other spices in the Indian Ocean region. Second, Benin placed an embargo on the export of slaves, thereby isolating itself from the growth of what was to become the major export from the Nigerian coast for 300 years. Benin continued to capture slaves and to employ them in its domestic economy, but the Edo state remained unique among Nigerian polities in refusing to participate in the transatlantic trade. In the long run, Benin remained relatively isolated from the major changes along the Nigerian coast.

The Portuguese initially bought slaves for resale on the Gold Coast, where slaves were traded for gold. For this reason, the southwestern coast of Nigeria and neighboring parts of the present-day Republic of Benin (not to be confused with the kingdom of Benin) became known as the "slave coast." When the African coast began to supply slaves to the Americas in the last third of the sixteenth century, the Portuguese continued to look to the Bight of Benin as one of its sources of supply. By then they were concentrating activities on the Angolan coast, which supplied roughly 40 percent of all slaves shipped to the Americas throughout the duration of the transatlantic trade, but they always maintained a presence on the Nigerian coast.

The Portuguese monopoly on West African trade was broken at the end of the sixteenth century, when Portugal's influence was challenged by the rising naval power of the Netherlands. The Dutch took over Portuguese trading stations on the coast that were the source of slaves for the Americas. French and English competition later undermined the Dutch position. Although slave ports from Lagos to Calabar would see the flags of many other European

maritime countries (including Denmark, Sweden, and Branden-
burg) and the North American colonies, Britain became the
dominant slaving power in the eighteenth century. Its ships handled two-fifths of the transatlantic traffic during the century. The
Portuguese and French were responsible for another two-fifths.

Nigeria kept its important position in the slave trade throughout the great expansion of the transatlantic trade after the middle
of the seventeenth century. Slightly more slaves came from the
Nigerian coast than from Angola in the eighteenth century, whereas
in the nineteenth century perhaps 30 percent of all slaves sent across
the Atlantic came from Nigeria. Over the period of the whole trade,
more than 3.5 million slaves were shipped from Nigeria to the
Americas. Most of these slaves were Igbo and Yoruba, with significant concentrations of Hausa, Ibibio, and other ethnic groups. In
the eighteenth century, two polities—Oyo and the Aro confederacy—
were responsible for most of the slaves exported from Nigeria. The
Aro confederacy continued to export slaves through the 1830s, but
most slaves in the nineteenth century were a product of the Yoruba
civil wars that followed the collapse of Oyo in the 1820s.

The expansion of Oyo after the middle of the sixteenth century
was closely associated with the growth of slave exports across the
Atlantic. Oyo's cavalry pushed southward along a natural break
in the forests (known as the Benin Gap, that is, the opening in the
forest where the savanna stretched to the Bight of Benin), and thereby gained access to the coastal ports.

Oyo experienced a series of power struggles and constitutional
crises in the eighteenth century that directly related to its success
as a major slave exporter. The powerful Oyo Mesi, the council
of warlords that checked the king, forced a number of kings to com-
mit suicide. In 1754 the head of the Oyo Mesi, *basorun* Gaha, seized
power, retaining a series of kings as puppets. The rule of this military oligarchy was overcome in 1789, when King Abiodun successfully staged a countercoup and forced the suicide of Gaha.
Abiodun and his successors maintained the supremacy of the
monarchy until the second decade of the nineteenth century,
primarily because of the reliance of the king on a cavalry force that
was independent of the Oyo Mesi. This force was recruited largely from Muslim slaves, especially Hausa, from farther north.

The other major slave-exporting state was a loose confederation
under the leadership of the Aro, an Igbo clan of mixed Igbo and
Ibibio origins, whose home was on the escarpment between the
central Igbo districts and the Cross River. Beginning in the late
seventeenth century, the Aro built a complex network of alliances
and treaties with many of the Igbo clans. They served as arbiters

in villages throughout Igboland, and their famous oracle at Arochukwu, located in a thickly wooded gorge, was widely regarded as a court of appeal for many kinds of disputes. By custom the Aro were sacrosanct and were allowed to travel anywhere with their goods without fear of attack. Alliances with certain Igbo clans who acted as mercenaries for the Aro guaranteed their safety. As oracle priests, they also received slaves in payment of fines or dedicated to the gods by their masters as scapegoats for their own transgressions. These slaves thereby became the property of the Aro priests, who were at liberty to sell them.

Besides their religious influence, the Aro established their ascendancy through a combination of commercial acumen and diplomatic skill. Their commercial empire was based on a set of twenty-four-day fairs and periodic markets that dotted the interior. Resident Aro dominated these markets and collected slaves for export. They had a virtual monopoly of the slave trade after the collapse of Oyo in the 1820s. Villages suspected of violating treaties with the Aro were subject to devastating raids that not only produced slaves for export but also maintained Aro influence. The Aro had treaties with the coastal ports—especially Calabar, Bonny, and Elem Kalabari—from which slaves were exported. The people of Calabar were Efik, a subsection of Ibibio, whereas Bonny and Elem Kalabari were Ijaw towns.

The Ijaw, who occupied the tidal area in proximity to the Igbo, had wrested a frugal living from the sale of dried fish and sea salt to the inland communities for centuries before the rise of the slave trade. Traditionally, they had lived in federated groups of villages with the head of the ranking village presiding over general assemblies attended by all the males. During the heyday of the slave trade in the eighteenth century, the major Ijaw villages grew into cities of 5,000 to 10,000 inhabitants ruled by local strongmen allied with the Aro. Their economies were based on the facilities they offered to slave traders. They were entrepreneurial communities, receiving slaves from the Aro for resale to European agents. Personal wealth rather than status within a lineage group was the basis for political power and social status. Government typically was conducted by councils composed of leading merchants and headed by an *amanyanabo* (chief executive), an office that in time became hereditary.

By the end of the eighteenth century, the area that was to become Nigeria was far from a unified country. Furthermore, the orientation of the north and the south was entirely different. The savanna states of Hausaland and Borno had experienced a difficult century of political insecurity and ecological disaster but otherwise continued in a centuries-long tradition of slow political and economic change that was similar to other parts of the savanna. The southern areas near the coast, by contrast, had been swept up in the transatlantic slave trade. Political and economic change had been rapid and dramatic. By 1800 Oyo governed much of southwestern Nigeria and neighboring parts of the modern Republic of Benin, whereas the Aro had consolidated southeastern Nigeria into a confederation that dominated that region. The Oyo and the Aro confederations were major trading partners of the slave traders from Europe and North America.

The Nineteenth Century: Revolution and Radical Adjustment

In the first decade of the nineteenth century, two unrelated developments that were to have a major influence on virtually all of the area that is now Nigeria ushered in a period of radical change. First, between 1804 and 1808, the Islamic holy war of Usman dan Fodio established the Sokoto Caliphate, which not only expanded to become the largest empire in Africa since the fall of Songhai but also had a profound influence on much of Muslim Africa to the west and to the east (see fig. 4). Second, in 1807 Britain declared the transatlantic slave trade to be illegal, an action that occurred at a time when Britain was responsible for shipping more slaves to the Americas than any other country. Although the transatlantic slave trade did not end until the 1860s, it was gradually replaced by other commodities, especially palm oil; the shift in trade had serious economic and political consequences in the interior, which led to increasing British intervention in the affairs of Yorubaland and the Niger Delta. The rise of the Sokoto Caliphate and the economic and political adjustment in the south strongly shaped the course of the colonial conquest at the end of the nineteenth century.

Usman dan Fodio and the Sokoto Caliphate

By the late eighteenth century, many Muslim scholars and teachers had become disenchanted with the insecurity that characterized the Hausa states and Borno. Some clerics (*mallams*) continued to reside at the courts of the Hausa states and Borno, but others, who joined the Qadiriyah brotherhood, began to think about a revolution that would overthrow existing authorities. Prominent among these radical *mallams* was Usman dan Fodio, who, with his brother and son, attracted a following among the clerical class. Many of his supporters were Fulani, and because of his ethnicity he was able to appeal to all Fulani, particularly the clan leaders and wealthy cattle owners whose clients and dependents provided

19

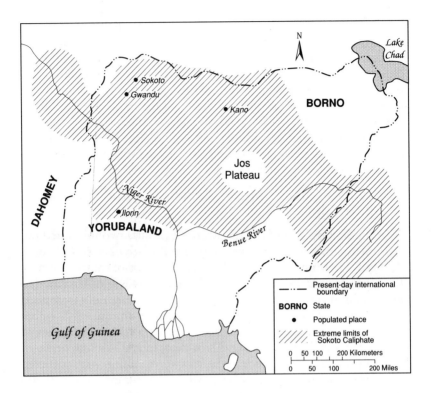

Figure 4. The Sokoto Caliphate, Mid-Nineteenth Century

most of the troops in the jihad that began in Gobir in 1804. Not all *mallams* were Fulani, however. The cleric whose actions actually started the jihad, Abd as Salam, was Hausa; Jibril, one of Usman dan Fodio's teachers and the first cleric to issue a call for jihad two decades earlier, was Tuareg. Nonetheless, by the time the Hausa states were overthrown in 1808, the prominent leaders were all Fulani.

Simultaneous uprisings confirmed the existence of a vast underground of Muslim revolutionaries throughout the Hausa states and Borno. By 1808 the Hausa states had been conquered, although the ruling dynasties retreated to the frontiers and built walled cities that remained independent. The more important of these independent cities included Abuja, where the ousted Zaria Dynasty fled; Argungu in the north, the new home of the Kebbi rulers; and Maradi in present-day Niger, the retreat of the Katsina Dynasty. Although the Borno *mai* was overthrown and Birni Gazargamu destroyed, Borno did not succumb. The reason, primarily, was that another cleric, Al Kanemi, fashioned a strong resistance that eventually forced those Fulani in Borno to retreat west and south. In the end, Al Kanemi overthrew the centuries-old Sayfawa Dynasty of Borno and established his own lineage as the new ruling house.

The new state that arose during Usman dan Fodio's jihad came to be known as the Sokoto Caliphate, named after his capital at Sokoto, founded in 1809. The caliphate was a loose confederation of emirates that recognized the suzerainty of the commander of the faithful, the sultan. When Usman dan Fodio died in 1817, he was succeeded by his son, Muhammad Bello. A dispute between Bello and his uncle, Abdullahi, resulted in a nominal division of the caliphate into eastern and western divisions, although the supreme authority of Bello as caliph was upheld. The division was institutionalized through the creation of a twin capital at Gwandu, which was responsible for the western emirates as far as modern Burkina Faso—formerly Upper Volta—and initially as far west as Massina in modern Mali. As events turned out, the eastern emirates were more numerous and larger than the western ones, which reinforced the primacy of the caliph at Sokoto.

By the middle of the nineteenth century, there were thirty emirates and the capital district of Sokoto, which itself was a large and populous territory although not technically an emirate. All the important Hausa emirates, including Kano, the wealthiest and most populous, were directly under Sokoto. Adamawa, which was established by Fulani forced to evacuate Borno, was geographically the biggest, stretching far to the south and east of its capital at Yola into modern Cameroon. Ilorin, which became part of the caliphate in the 1830s, was initially the headquarters of the Oyo cavalry that had provided the backbone of the king's power. An attempted coup d'état by the general of the cavalry in 1817 backfired when the cavalry itself revolted and pledged its allegiance to the Sokoto Caliphate. The cavalry was largely composed of Muslim slaves from farther north, and they saw in the jihad a justification for rebellion. In the 1820s, Oyo had been torn asunder, and the defeated king and the warlords of the Oyo Mesi retreated south to form new cities, including Ibadan, where they carried on their resistance to the caliphate and fought among themselves as well.

Usman dan Fodio's jihad created the largest empire in Africa since the fall of Songhai in 1591. By the middle of the nineteenth century, when the Sokoto Caliphate was at its greatest extent, it stretched 1,500 kilometers from Dori in modern Burkina Faso to southern Adamawa in Cameroon and included Nupe lands, Ilorin in northern Yorubaland, and much of the Benue River valley. In addition, Usman dan Fodio's jihad provided the inspiration for a series of related holy wars in other parts of the savanna and Sahel far beyond Nigeria's borders that led to the foundation of Islamic states in Senegal, Mali, Ivory Coast, Chad, Central African Republic, and Sudan. An analogy has been drawn between Usman dan Fodio's jihad and the French Revolution in terms of its widespread impact. Just as the French Revolution affected the course of European history in the nineteenth century, the Sokoto jihad affected the course of history throughout the savanna from Senegal to the Red Sea.

The Yoruba Wars

Oyo, the great exporter of slaves in the eighteenth century, collapsed in a civil war after 1817, and by the middle of the 1830s the whole of Yorubaland was swept up in these civil wars. New centers of power—Ibadan, Abeokuta, Owo, and Warri—contested control of the trade routes and sought access to fresh supplies of slaves, which were important to repopulate the turbulent countryside. At this time, the British withdrew from the slave trade and began to blockade the coast (see Abolition of the Slave Trade, this ch.). The blockade required some adjustments in the slave trade along the lagoons that stretched outward from Lagos, whereas the domestic market for slaves to be used as farm laborers and as porters to carry commodities to market easily absorbed the many captives that were a product of these wars.

War and slave raiding were complementary exercises among the Yoruba, who needed capital to buy the firearms with which they fought in a vicious cycle of war and enslavement. Military leaders were well aware of the connection between guns and enslavement.

Some of the emerging Yoruba states started as war camps during the period of chaos in which Oyo broke up and the Muslim revolutionaries who were allied to the caliphate conquered northern Yorubaland. Ibadan, which became the largest city in black Africa during the nineteenth century, owed its growth to the role it played in the Oyo civil wars. Ibadan's *omuogun* (war boys) raided far afield for slaves and held off the advance of the Fulani. They also took advantage of Benin's isolation to seize the roads leading to the flourishing slave port at Lagos. The threat that Ibadan would dominate Yorubaland alarmed its rivals and inspired a military alliance led by the Egba city of Abeokuta. Dahomey, to the west, further contributed to the insecurity by raiding deep into Yorubaland, the direction of raids depending upon its current alliances.

Abolition of the Slave Trade

In 1807 the Houses of Parliament in London enacted legislation prohibiting British subjects from participating in the slave trade. Indirectly, this legislation was one of the reasons for the collapse of Oyo. Britain withdrew from the slave trade while it was the major transporter of slaves to the Americas. Furthermore, the French had been knocked out of the trade during the French Revolution beginning in 1789 and by the Napoleonic wars of the first fifteen years of the nineteenth century. Between them, the French and the British had purchased a majority of the slaves sold from the ports of Oyo. The commercial uncertainty that followed the disappearance of the major purchasers of slaves unsettled the economy of Oyo. Ironically, the political troubles in Oyo came to a head after 1817, when the transatlantic market for slaves once again boomed. Rather than supplying slaves from other areas, however, Oyo itself became the source of slaves.

British legislation forbade ships under British registry to engage in the slave trade, but the restriction was applied generally to all flags and was intended to shut down all traffic in slaves coming out of West African ports. Other countries more or less hesitantly followed the British lead. The United States, for example, also prohibited the slave trade in 1807 (Denmark actually was the first country to declare the trade illegal in 1792). Attitudes changed slowly, however, and not all countries cooperated in controlling the activity of their merchant ships. American ships, for instance, were notorious for evading the prohibition and going unpunished under United States law. It should be noted, moreover, that the abolition movement concentrated on the transatlantic trade for more than five decades before eventually turning to a full-fledged attack on slave trading within Africa itself.

The Royal Navy maintained a prevention squadron to blockade the coast, and a permanent station was established at the Spanish colony of Fernando Po, off the Nigerian coast, and given responsibility for patrolling the West African coast. For several decades, as many as one-sixth of all British warships were assigned to this mission, and a squadron was maintained at Fernando Po from 1827 until 1844. Slaves rescued at sea were usually taken to Sierra Leone, where they were released. British naval crews were permitted to divide prize money from the sale of captured slave ships. Apprehended slave runners were tried by naval courts and were liable to capital punishment if found guilty.

Still, a lively slave trade to the Americas continued into the 1860s. The demands of Cuba and Brazil were met by a flood of captives taken in wars among the Yoruba and shipped from Lagos, and the Aro continued to supply the delta ports with slave exports through the 1830s. Despite the British blockade, almost 1 million slaves were exported from Nigeria in the nineteenth century. The risk involved in running the British blockade obviously made profits all the greater on delivery.

The campaign to eradicate the slave trade and substitute for it trade in other commodities increasingly resulted in British intervention in the internal affairs of the Nigerian region during the nineteenth century and ultimately led to the decision to assume jurisdiction over the coastal area. Suppression of the slave trade and issues related to slavery remained at the forefront of British dealings with local states and societies for the rest of the nineteenth century and even into the twentieth century.

Lagos, where the British concentrated activities after 1851, had been founded as a colony of Benin in about 1700. A long dynastic struggle, which became entwined with the struggle against the slave trade, resulted in the overthrow of the reigning *oba* and the renunciation of a treaty with Britain to curtail the slave trade. Britain was determined to halt the traffic in slaves fed by the Yoruba wars and responded to this frustration by annexing the port of Lagos in 1861. Thereafter, Britain gradually extended its control along the coast. British intervention became more insistent in the 1870s and 1880s as a result of pressure from missionaries and liberated slaves returning from Sierra Leone. There was also the necessity of protecting commerce disrupted by the fighting. The method of dealing with these problems was to dictate treaties that inevitably led to further annexations.

Commodity Trade

The development of "legitimate" trade was the final phase of private and official British efforts to find a positive alternative to the traffic in slaves. Earlier aspects of such constructive interest had included the founding of the colony at Sierra Leone in 1787 as a refuge for liberated slaves, the missionary movement designed to bring Christianity to the region, and programs of exploration sponsored by learned societies and scientific groups, such as the London-based African Association.

The principal commodities of legitimate trade were palm oil and palm kernels, which were used in Europe to make soap and as lubricants for machinery before petroleum products were developed for that purpose. Although this trade grew to significant proportions—palm oil exports alone were worth £21 million a year by 1840—it was concentrated near the coast, where palm trees grew in abundance. Gradually, however, the trade forced major economic and social changes in the interior, although it failed to undermine slavery and the slave trade. Quite the contrary, the incidence of slavery in local societies actually increased.

Initially most palm oil (and later kernels) came from Igboland, where palm trees formed a canopy over the densely inhabited areas of the Ngwa, Nri, Awka, and other Igbo peoples. Palm oil was used locally for cooking, the kernels were a source for food, trees were tapped for palm wine, and the fronds were used for building material. It was a relatively simple adjustment for many Igbo families to transport the oil to rivers and streams that led to the Niger Delta for sale to European merchants. The rapid expansion in exports, especially after 1830, occurred precisely at the time slave exports collapsed. Instead, slaves were redirected into the domestic economy, especially to grow the staple food crop, yams, in northern Igboland for marketing throughout the palm-tree belt. As before, Aro merchants dominated trade, including the sale of slaves within Igboland as well as palm products to the coast. They maintained their central role in the confederation that governed the region.

The Niger Delta and Calabar, which once had been known for the export of slaves, now became famous for the export of palm oil, so much so that the delta streams were given the name the "oil rivers." The basic economic units in each town were "houses," family-operated entities that were also the focus of loyalty for those employed in them. A "house" included the extended family of the trader, both his retainers and slaves. As its head, the master trader taxed other traders who were members of his "house" and was obligated to maintain a war vessel, which was a large dugout canoe that could hold several tons of cargo and dozens of crew, for the defense of the harbor. Whenever a trader could afford to keep a war canoe, he was expected to form his own "house." Economic competition among these "houses" was so fierce that trade often erupted into armed battle between the large canoes.

Because of the hazards of climate and disease for Europeans and the absence of any authority responsive to their interests on the mainland, European merchants ordinarily moored their ships outside harbors or in the delta and used the ships as trading stations and warehouses. In time, however, they built depots onshore and eventually moved up the Niger River to stations established in the interior, like that at Onitsha, where they could bargain with local suppliers and purchase products likely to turn a profit. Some European traders switched to legitimate business only when the commerce in slaves became too hazardous. Disreputable as many of the traders had been, they often suffered from the precariousness of their position and were at the mercy of what they considered to be unpredictable coastal rulers. Accordingly, as the volume of trade increased, the British government responded to repeated requests of merchants to appoint a consul to cover the region. Consequently in 1849, John Beecroft was accredited as consul for the bights of Benin and Biafra, a jurisdiction stretching from Dahomey to Cameroon. Beecroft was the British representative to Fernando Po, where the British navy's prevention squadron was stationed.

Exploration of the Niger Basin had a commercial as well as scientific motivation, but curiosity about the course and destination of the river also played a part. The delta masked the mouth of the great river, and for centuries Nigerians chose not to tell Europeans the secrets of the interior, initially probably because no one thought to ask but by the nineteenth century because of the commercial implications. In 1794 the African Association commissioned Mungo Park, an intrepid Scottish physician and naturalist, to search for the headwaters of the Niger and follow the river downstream. Park reached the upper Niger the next year by traveling inland from the Gambia River. Although he reported on the eastward flow of the Niger, he was forced to turn back when his equipment was lost to Muslim slave traders. In 1805 he set out on a second expedition, sponsored by the British government, to follow the Niger to the sea. His mission failed, but Park and his party covered more than 1,500 kilometers, passing through the western portions of the Sokoto Caliphate, before being drowned in rapids near Bussa.

On a subsequent expedition to the Sokoto Caliphate, Hugh Clapperton learned where the Niger River flowed to the sea, but Clapperton also died before he could substantiate his information. It was his servant, Richard Lander, and Lander's brother, John, who actually demonstrated that the Niger flowed into the delta. The Lander brothers were seized by slave traders in the interior and sold down the river to a waiting European ship.

Initial attempts to open trade with the interior by way of the Niger could not overcome climate and disease, which took the lives of a third of a British riverine expedition in 1842. Use of quinine to combat malaria on similar expeditions in the 1850s enabled a Liverpool merchant, Macgregor Laird, to open the river. Laird's efforts were stimulated by the detailed reports of a pioneer German explorer, Heinrich Barth, who traveled through much of Borno and the Sokoto Caliphate and recorded information about the region's geography, economy, and inhabitants.

Royal Niger Company

The legitimate trade in commodities attracted a number of rough-hewn British merchants to the Niger River, as well as some men who formerly had been engaged in the slave trade but who had changed their line of wares. The large companies that subsequently opened depots in the delta cities and in Lagos were as ruthlessly competitive as the delta towns themselves and frequently used force to compel potential suppliers to agree to contracts and to meet their demands. The most important of these trading companies, whose activities had far-reaching consequences for Nigeria, was the United Africa Company, founded by George Goldie in 1879. In 1886 Goldie's consortium was chartered by the British government as the Royal Niger Company and granted broad concessionary powers in "all the territory of the basin of the Niger." Needless to say, these concessions emanated from Britain, not from any authority in Nigeria.

The terms of the charter specified that trade should be free in the region—a principle systematically violated as the company strengthened its monopoly to forestall French and German trade interests. The company also was supposed to respect local customs "except so far as may be necessary in the interests of humanity." The qualifying clause was aimed at slavery and other activities categorized as "barbarous practices" by British authorities, and it foreshadowed the qualifications applied to noninterference as a guide to official policy when Britain assumed formal colonial responsibility in Nigeria.

Meanwhile, the Royal Niger Company established its headquarters far inland at Lokoja, from where it pretended to assume responsibility for the administration of areas along the Niger and Benue rivers where it maintained depots. The company interfered in the territory along the Niger and the Benue, sometimes becoming embroiled in serious conflicts when its British-led native constabulary intercepted slave raids or attempted to protect trade routes. The company negotiated treaties with Sokoto, Gwandu, and Nupe that were interpreted as guaranteeing exclusive access to trade in return for the payment of annual tribute. Officials of the Sokoto Caliphate considered these treaties quite differently; from their perspective, the British were granted only extraterritorial rights that did not prevent similar arrangements with the Germans and the French and certainly did not surrender sovereignty.

Under Goldie's direction, the Royal Niger Company was instrumental in depriving France and Germany of access to the region. Consequently, he may well deserve the epithet "father of Nigeria," which imperialists accorded him. He definitely laid the basis for British claims.

Influence of the Christian Missions

Christianity was introduced at Benin in the fifteenth century by Portuguese Roman Catholic priests who accompanied traders and officials to the West African coast. Several churches were built to serve the Portuguese community and a small number of African converts. When direct Portuguese contacts in the region were withdrawn, however, the influence of the Catholic missionaries waned and by the eighteenth century had disappeared.

Although churchmen in Britain had been influential in the drive to abolish the slave trade, significant missionary activity was renewed only in the 1840s and was confined for some time to the area between Lagos and Ibadan. The first missions there were opened by the Church of England's Church Missionary Society (CMS). They were followed by other Protestant denominations from Britain, Canada, and the United States and in the 1860s by Roman Catholic religious orders. Protestant missionaries tended to divide the country into spheres of activity to avoid competition with each other, and Catholic missions similarly avoided duplication of effort among the several religious orders working there. Catholic missionaries were particularly active among the Igbo, the CMS among the Yoruba.

The CMS initially promoted Africans to responsible positions in the mission field, an outstanding example being the appointment of Samuel Adjai Crowther as the first Anglican bishop of the Niger. Crowther, a liberated Yoruba slave, had been educated in Sierra Leone and in Britain, where he was ordained before returning to his homeland with the first group of missionaries sent there by the CMS. This was part of a conscious "native church" policy pursued by the Anglicans and others to create indigenous ecclesiastical institutions that eventually would be independent of European tutelage. The effort failed, however, in part because church authorities came to think that religious discipline had grown too lax during Crowther's episcopate but especially because of the rise of prejudice. Crowther was succeeded as bishop by a British cleric. Nevertheless, the acceptance of Christianity by large numbers of Nigerians depended finally on the various denominations coming to terms with local conditions and involved the participation of an increasingly high proportion of African clergy in the missions.

In large measure, European missionaries were convinced of the value of colonial rule, thereby reinforcing colonial policy. In reaction some African Christian communities formed their own independent churches.

Colonial Nigeria

Prodded by the instability created by the Yoruba wars and by the activities of other European powers, Britain moved cautiously but inexorably toward colonial domination of the lower Niger Basin. In the decades that followed Britain's abolition of the slave trade, British diplomacy wove a fabric of treaties with kings and chieftains whose cooperation was sought in suppressing the traffic. British interests also dictated occasional armed intervention by the Royal Navy and by the Royal Niger Company Constabulary to staunch the flow of slaves to the coast, to protect legitimate commerce, and to maintain peace. Moreover, the missionaries cried out for protection and assistance in stamping out slavery and other "barbarous practices" associated with indigenous religions. Finally, the posting of consular officials by the Foreign Office to service the increasing amount of trade in the ports of the bights of Benin and Biafra helped project British influence inland.

For many years, official hesitation about adding tropical dependencies to the British Empire outweighed these factors. The prevailing sentiment, even after Lagos became a colony in 1861, was expressed in a parliamentary report in 1865 urging withdrawal from West Africa. Colonies were regarded as expensive liabilities, especially where trading concessions could be exercised without resorting to annexation. Attitudes changed, however, as rival European powers, especially France and Germany, scurried to develop overseas markets and annexed territory (see fig. 5).

Inevitably, imperial ambitions clashed when the intentions of the various European countries became obvious. In 1885 at the Berlin Conference, the European powers attempted to resolve their conflicts of interest by allotting areas of exploitation. The conferees also enunciated the principle, known as the dual mandate, that the best interests of Europe and Africa would be served by maintaining free access to the continent for trade and by providing Africa with the benefits of Europe's civilizing mission. Britain's claims to a sphere of influence in the Niger Basin were acknowledged formally, but it was stipulated here as elsewhere that only effective occupation would secure full international recognition. In the end, pressure in the region from France and Germany hastened the establishment of effective British occupation.

Extension of British Control

British expansion accelerated in the last decades of the nineteenth century. The early history of Lagos Colony was one of repeated attempts to end the Yoruba wars. In the face of threats to the divided

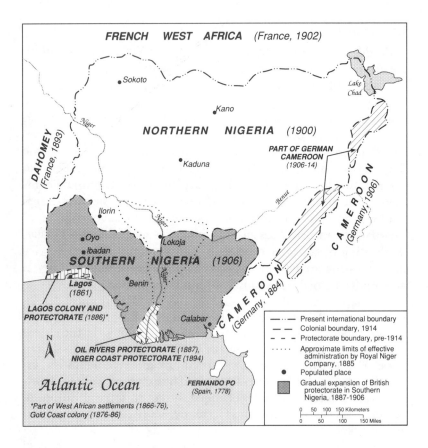

Figure 5. British Presence in the Niger Region, 1861–1914

Yoruba states from Dahomey and the Sokoto Caliphate, as represented by the emirate of Ilorin, the British governor—assisted by the CMS—succeeded in imposing peace settlements on the interior.

Colonial Lagos was a busy, cosmopolitan port, reflecting Victorian and distinctively Brazilian architecture and the varied backgrounds of a black elite, composed of English-speakers from Sierra Leone and of emancipated slaves repatriated from Brazil and Cuba. Its residents were employed in official capacities and were active in business. Africans also were represented on the Lagos Legislative Council, a largely appointed assembly.

After the Berlin Conference, Britain announced formation of the Oil Rivers Protectorate, which included the Niger Delta and extended eastward to Calabar, where the British consulate general was relocated from Fernando Po. The essential purpose of the protectorate was to control trade coming down the Niger. Vice consuls were assigned to ports that already had concluded treaties of cooperation with the Foreign Office. Local rulers continued to administer their territories, but consular authorities assumed jurisdiction for the equity courts established earlier by the foreign mercantile communities. A constabulary force was raised and used to pacify the coastal area. In 1894 the territory was redesignated the Niger Coast Protectorate and was expanded to include the region from Calabar to Lagos Colony and Protectorate, including the hinterland, and northward up the Niger River as far as Lokoja, the headquarters of the Royal Niger Company. As a protectorate, it did not have the status of a colony but remained under the jurisdiction of the Foreign Office.

Continued expansion of the protectorate was accomplished largely by diplomatic means, although military force was employed to bring Ijebu, Oyo, and Benin into compliance with dictated treaty obligations. The conquest of Benin in 1897 completed the British occupation of southwestern Nigeria. The incident that sparked the expedition was the massacre of a British consul and his party, who were on their way to investigate reports of ritual human sacrifice in the city of Benin. In reprisal a marine detachment promptly stormed the city and destroyed the *oba*'s palace. The reigning *oba* was sent into exile, and Benin was administered indirectly under the protectorate through a council of chiefs.

Although treaties were signed with rulers as far north as Sokoto by 1885, actual British control was confined to the coastal area and the immediate vicinity of Lokoja until 1900. The Royal Niger Company had access to the territory from Lokoja extending along the Niger and Benue rivers above their confluence, but there was no effective control, even after punitive expeditions against Bida and Ilorin in 1897. The clear intent was to occupy the Sokoto Caliphate, but for that purpose the Royal Niger Company was not deemed to be a sufficient instrument of imperialism. Consequently, on December 31, 1899, Britain terminated the charter of the company, providing compensation and retention of valuable mineral rights.

Lugard and Indirect Rule

Frederick Lugard, who assumed the position of high commissioner of the Protectorate of Northern Nigeria in 1900, often has been regarded as the model British colonial administrator. Trained as an army officer, he had served in India, Egypt, and East Africa, where he expelled Arab slave traders from Nyasaland and established the British presence in Uganda. Joining the Royal Niger Company in 1894, Lugard was sent to Borgu to counter inroads made by the French, and in 1897 he was made responsible for raising the Royal West African Frontier Force (RWAFF) from local levies to serve under British officers.

During his six-year tenure as high commissioner, Lugard was occupied with transforming the commercial sphere of influence inherited from the Royal Niger Company into a viable territorial unit under effective British political control. His objective was to conquer the entire region and to obtain recognition of the British protectorate by its indigenous rulers, especially the Fulani emirs of the Sokoto Caliphate. Lugard's campaign systematically subdued local resistance, using armed force when diplomatic measures failed. Borno capitulated without a fight, but in 1903 Lugard's RWAFF mounted assaults on Kano and Sokoto. From Lugard's point of view, clear-cut military victories were necessary because their surrenders weakened resistance elsewhere.

Lugard's success in northern Nigeria has been attributed to his policy of indirect rule, which called for governing the protectorate through the rulers who had been defeated. If the emirs accepted British authority, abandoned the slave trade, and cooperated with British officials in modernizing their administrations, the colonial power was willing to confirm them in office. The emirs retained their caliphate titles but were responsible to British district officers, who had final authority. The British high commissioner could depose emirs and other officials if necessary. Lugard reduced sharply the number of titled fief holders in the emirates, weakening the rulers' patronage. Under indirect rule, caliphate officials were transformed into salaried district heads and became, in effect, agents of the British authorities, responsible for peacekeeping and tax collection. The old chain of command merely was capped with a new overlord, the British high commissioner.

The protectorate required only a limited number of colonial officers scattered throughout the territory as overseers. Depending on local conditions, they exercised discretion in advising the emirs and local officials, but all orders from the high commissioner were transmitted through the emir. Although the high commissioner possessed unlimited executive and legislative powers in the protectorate, most of the activities of government were undertaken by the emirs and their local administrations, subject to British approval. A dual system of law functioned—the sharia (Islamic law) court continued to deal with matters affecting the personal status of Muslims, including land disputes, divorce, debt, and slave emancipation. As a consequence of indirect rule, Hausa-Fulani domination was confirmed—and in some instances imposed—on diverse ethnic groups, some of them non-Muslim, in the so-called middle belt.

The accomplishments of Lugard and his successors in economic development were limited by the revenues available to the colonial government. One of Lugard's initial acts was to separate the general treasury of each emirate from the emir's privy purse. From taxes collected by local officials, first one-quarter and later one-half was taken to support services of the colonial regime, which were meager because of the protectorate's lack of public resources. In the south, missionaries made up for the lack of government expenditure on services; in the north, Lugard and his successors limited the activities of missionaries in order to maintain Muslim domination. Consequently, educational and medical services in the north lagged behind those in the south. Progress was made in economic development, however, as railroad lines were constructed to transport tin from Jos Plateau and northern-grown peanuts and cotton to ports on the coast.

Efforts to apply indirect rule to the south, which was formally a protectorate from 1906, in emulation of Lugard's successful policy in the north set off a search for legitimate indigenous authorities through whom the policy could be implemented. The task proved relatively easy in Yorubaland, where the governments and boundaries of traditional kingdoms were retained or, in some instances, revived. In the southeast, where Aro hegemony had been crushed, the search for acceptable local administrators met with frustration. As a result, the tasks of government initially were left in the hands of colonial officials, who antagonized many Igbo. The Igbo therefore stressed traditional egalitarian principles as a justification for their early opposition to colonial rule; in Yorubaland and in the north, the devolution of administrative duties to the indigenous ruling elites contained much of the early opposition. Resistance to colonial rule was mitigated to the extent that local authorities and courts were able to manage affairs.

The British prohibited the enslavement of free persons and suppressed slave trading. All children in the north who were born to persons in bondage on or after April 1, 1900, were declared free. The relations between existing slaves and their owners, however, were allowed to continue indefinitely, on the assumption that wholesale liberation would cause more harm than good by disrupting the agricultural economy. As a consequence, at least several hundred thousand slaves deserted their masters in the early years of colonial rule. In 1906 a radical, allegedly Mahdist, Muslim uprising that received the support of many fugitive slaves was brutally crushed. In the south, slaves legally could be forced to return to their owners until 1914. In the north, vagrancy laws and the enforcement of proprietary rights to land were used to try to check the flight of slaves. Slaves in the northern emirates could secure their freedom upon application to an Islamic court, but comparatively few used this option. Throughout the colonial period in the Muslim north, many slaves and their descendants continued to work for their masters or former masters and often received periodic payments leading to emancipation.

Unification of Nigeria

After having been assigned for six years as governor of Hong Kong, Lugard returned to Nigeria in 1912 to set in motion the merger of the northern and southern protectorates. The task of unification was achieved two years later on the eve of World War I. The principle of indirect rule administered by traditional rulers was applied throughout Nigeria, and colonial officers were instructed to interfere as little as possible with the existing order. In 1916 Lugard formed the Nigerian Council, a consultative body that brought together six traditional leaders—including the sultan of Sokoto, the emir of Kano, and the king of Oyo—to represent all parts of the colony. The council was promoted as a device for allowing the expression of opinions that could instruct the governor. In practice Lugard used the annual sessions to inform the traditional leaders of British policy, leaving them with no functions at the council's meetings except to listen and to assent.

Unification meant only the loose affiliation of three distinct regional administrations into which Nigeria was subdivided—northern, western, and eastern regions (see fig. 6). Each was under a lieutenant governor and provided independent government services. The governor was, in effect, the coordinator for virtually autonomous entities that had overlapping economic interests but little in common politically or socially. In the Northern Region, the colonial government took careful account of Islam and avoided any appearance of a challenge to traditional values that might incite resistance to British rule. This system, in which the structure of authority focused on the emir to whom obedience was a mark of religious devotion, did not welcome change. As the emirs settled more and more into their role as reliable agents of indirect rule, colonial authorities were content to maintain the status quo, particularly in religious matters. Christian missionaries were barred, and the limited government efforts in education were harmonized with Islamic institutions.

In the south, by contrast, traditional leaders were employed as vehicles of indirect rule in Yorubaland, but Christianity and Western education undermined their sacerdotal functions. In some instances, however, a double allegiance—to the idea of sacred monarchy for its symbolic value and to modern concepts of law and administration—was maintained. Out of reverence for traditional kingship, for instance, the *oni* of Ife, whose office was closely identified with Yoruba religion, was accepted as the sponsor of a Yoruba political movement. In the Eastern Region, appointed officials, who were given "warrants" and hence called warrant chiefs, were vehemently resisted because they had no claims on tradition.

In practice, however, British administrative procedures under indirect rule entailed constant interaction between colonial authorities and local rulers—the system was modified to fit the needs of each region. In the north, for instance, legislation took the form of a decree cosigned by the governor and the emir, whereas in the south, the governor sought the approval of the Legislative Council. Hausa was recognized as an official language in the north, and knowledge of it was expected of colonial officers serving there, whereas only English had official status in the south. Regional administrations also varied widely in the quality of local personnel and in the scope of the operations they were willing to undertake. British staffs in each region continued to operate according to procedures developed before unification. Economic links among the regions increased, but indirect rule tended to discourage political interchange. There was virtually no pressure for fuller unity until the end of World War II.

Public works, such as harbor dredging and road and railroad construction, opened Nigeria to economic development. British soap and cosmetics manufacturers tried to obtain land concessions for growing oil palms, but these were refused. Instead, the companies had to be content with a monopoly of the export trade in these products. Other commercial crops such as cocoa and rubber also were encouraged, and tin was mined on the Jos Plateau. The only significant interruption in economic development arose from natural disaster—the great drought of 1913–14. Recovery came quickly, however, and improvements in port facilities and the transportation infrastructure during World War I furthered economic development. Nigerian recruits participated in the war effort as laborers and soldiers. The Nigeria Regiment of the RWAFF, integrating troops from the north and south, saw action against German colonial forces in Cameroon and in German East Africa. During the war, the colonial government earmarked a large portion of the Nigerian budget as a contribution to imperial defense. To raise additional revenues, Lugard took steps to institute a uniform tax structure patterned on the traditional system that he had adopted in the north during his tenure there. Taxes became a source

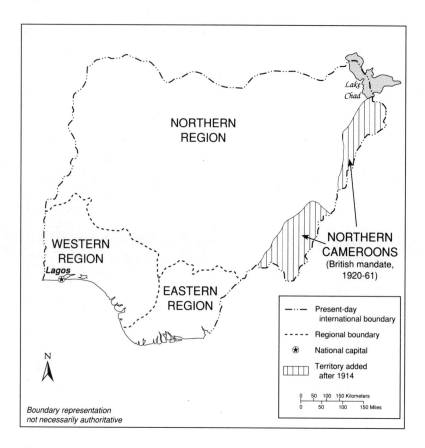

Figure 6. Unification of Nigeria, 1914

of discontent in the south, however, and contributed to disturbances protesting British policy. In 1920 portions of former German Cameroon were mandated to Britain by the League of Nations and were administered as part of Nigeria.

Until he stepped down as governor general in 1918, Lugard was primarily concerned with consolidating British sovereignty and with assuring local administration through traditional leaders. He was contemptuous of the educated and Westernized African elite, and he even recommended transferring the capital from Lagos, the cosmopolitan city where the influence of these people was most pronounced, to Kaduna in the north. Although the capital was not moved, Lugard's bias in favor of the Muslim north was clear at the time. Nevertheless, Lugard was able to bequeath to his successor a prosperous colony when his term as governor general expired.

Further Development of Colonial Policy

Lugard's immediate successor, Hugh Clifford (1919–25), was an aristocratic professional administrator with liberal instincts who had won recognition for his enlightened governorship of the Gold Coast. The approaches of the two governors to colonial development were diametrically opposed. In contrast to Lugard, Clifford argued that it was the primary responsibility of colonial government to introduce as quickly as practical the benefits of Western experience. He was aware that the Muslim north would present problems, but he evinced great hopes for progress along the lines that he laid down in the south, where he anticipated "general emancipation" leading to a more representative form of government. Clifford emphasized economic development, encouraging enterprises by immigrant southerners in the north while restricting European participation to capital-intensive activity.

Uneasy with the amount of latitude allowed traditional leaders under indirect rule, Clifford opposed further extension of the judicial authority held by the northern emirs, stating bluntly that he did "not consider that their past traditions and their present backward cultural conditions afford to any such experiment a reasonable chance of success." He did not apply this rationale in the south, however, where he saw the possibility of building an elite educated in schools modeled on a European method. These schools would teach "the basic principles that would and should regulate character and conduct." In line with this attitude, he rejected Lugard's proposal for moving the capital from Lagos, the stronghold of the elite in whom he placed so much confidence for the future.

Clifford also believed that indirect rule encouraged centripetal tendencies, and he argued that the division into two separate colonies was advisable unless a stronger central government could bind Nigeria into more than just an administrative convenience for the three regions. Whereas Lugard had applied lessons learned in the north to the administration of the south, Clifford was prepared to extend to the north practices that had been successful in the south. The Colonial Office, where Lugard was still held in high regard, accepted that changes might be due in the south, but it forbade fundamental alteration of procedures in the north. A.J. Harding, director of Nigerian affairs at the Colonial Office, defined the official position of the British government in its continued support of indirect rule when he commented that "direct government by impartial and honest men of alien race . . . never yet satisfied a nation long and . . . under such a form of government, as wealth and education increase, so do political discontent and sedition.''

Clifford's recommendations, as modified by the Colonial Office, were embodied in the 1922 constitution (known as the Clifford Constitution). Whereas administration in the north was left untouched, a new legislative council was established in common for the two southern regions, replacing the Lagos Legislative Council and the moribund Nigerian Council. For the first time, direct elections took place outside Lagos, although only four of the council's forty-six members were elected. Moreover, the introduction of the legislative principle encouraged the emergence of political parties and ultimately the growth of nationalism in Nigeria. By 1931 strong sentiments had emerged in the north in reaction to Clifford's reforms.

Emergence of Nigerian Nationalism

British colonialism created Nigeria, joining diverse peoples and regions in an artificial political entity. It was not unusual that the nationalism that became a political factor in Nigeria during the interwar period derived both from an older political particularism and broad pan-Africanism rather than from any sense of a common Nigerian nationality. Its goal initially was not self-determination, but rather increased participation in the governmental process on a regional level. Inconsistencies in British policy reinforced cleavages based on regional animosities by attempting simultaneously to preserve the indigenous cultures of each area and to introduce modern technology and Western political and social concepts. In the north, appeals to Islamic legitimacy upheld the rule of the emirs, so that nationalist sentiments there were decidedly anti-Western. Modern nationalists in the south, whose thinking was shaped by European ideas, opposed indirect rule, which had entrenched what was considered to be an anachronistic ruling class in power and shut out the Westernized elite.

The ideological inspiration for southern nationalists came from a variety of sources, including prominent United States-based activists such as Marcus Garvey and W.E.B. Du Bois. Nigerian students abroad joined those from other colonies in pan-African groups, such as the West African Students Union, founded in London in 1925. Early nationalists tended to ignore Nigeria as the focus of patriotism; rather, the common denominator was based on a newly assertive ethnic consciousness, particularly Yoruba and Igbo. Despite their acceptance of European and North American influences, the nationalists were critical of colonialism for its failure to appreciate the antiquity of indigenous cultures. They wanted self-government, charging that only colonial rule prevented the unshackling of progressive forces in Africa.

Political opposition to colonial rule often assumed religious dimensions. Independent Christian churches had emerged at the end of the nineteenth century because many European missionaries were racist and blocked the advancement of a Nigerian clergy. European interpretations of Christian orthodoxy also refused to allow the incorporation of local customs and practices, even though the various mission denominations themselves interpreted Christianity very differently. It was acceptable for the established missions to differ, but most Europeans were surprised and shocked that Nigerians would develop new denominations independent of European control. Christianity long had experienced "protestant" schisms; the emergence of independent Christian churches in Nigeria was another phase of this history. The pulpits of the independent congregations provided one of the few available avenues for the free expression of attitudes critical of colonial rule.

In the 1920s, there were several types of associations that were ostensibly nonpolitical. One group consisted of professional and business associations, such as the Nigerian Union of Teachers, which provided trained leadership for political groups; the Nigerian Law Association, which brought together lawyers, many of whom had been educated in Britain; and the Nigerian Produce Traders' Association, led by Obafemi Awolowo.

Ethnic and kinship organizations that often took the form of a tribal union also emerged in the 1920s. These organizations were primarily urban phenomena that arose after large numbers of rural migrants moved to the cities. Alienated by the anonymity of the urban environment and drawn together by ties to their ethnic homelands—as well as by the need for mutual aid—the new city dwellers formed local clubs that later expanded into federations covering whole regions. By the mid-1940s, the major ethnic groups had formed such associations as the Igbo Federal Union and the Egbe Omo Oduduwa (Society of the Descendants of Oduduwa), a Yoruba cultural movement, in which Awolowo played a leading role.

A third type of organization that was more pointedly political was the youth or student group, which became the vehicle of intellectuals and professionals. They were the most politically conscious segment of the population and stood in the vanguard of the nationalist movement. Newspapers, some of which were published before World War I, provided coverage of nationalist views.

The opportunity afforded by the 1922 constitution to elect a handful of representatives to the Legislative Council gave politically

39

conscious Nigerians something concrete to work on. The principal figure in the political activity that ensued was Herbert Macauley, often referred to as the father of Nigerian nationalism. He aroused political awareness through his newspaper, the Lagos *Daily News,* while leading the Nigerian National Democratic Party (NNDP), which dominated elections in Lagos from its founding in 1922 until the ascendancy of the National Youth Movement (NYM) in 1938. His political platform called for economic and educational development, Africanization of the civil service, and self-government for Lagos. Significantly, however, Macauley's NNDP remained almost entirely a Lagos party, popular only in the area with experience in elective politics.

The NYM first used nationalist rhetoric to agitate for improvements in education. The movement brought to public notice a long list of future leaders, including H.O. Davies and Nnamdi Azikiwe. Although Azikiwe later came to be recognized as the leading spokesman for national unity, his orientation on return from university training in the United States was pan-African rather than nationalist, emphasizing the common African struggle against European colonialism. He betrayed much less consciousness of purely Nigerian goals than Davies, a student of Harold Laski at the London School of Economics, whose political orientation was considered left-wing.

By 1938 the NYM was agitating for dominion status within the British Commonwealth of Nations, so that Nigeria would have the same status as Canada and Australia. In elections that year, the NYM ended the domination of the NNDP in the Legislative Council and moved to establish a genuinely national network of affiliates. This promising start was stopped short three years later by internal divisions in which ethnic loyalties emerged triumphant. The departure of Azikiwe and other Igbo members of the NYM left the organization in Yoruba hands; during World War II, it was reorganized into a predominantly Yoruba political party, the Action Group, by Awolowo. Yoruba-Igbo rivalry had become a major factor in Nigerian politics (see Ethnic Relations, ch. 2).

During World War II, three battalions of the Nigeria Regiment fought in the Ethiopian campaign. Nigerian units also contributed to two divisions serving with British forces in Palestine, Morocco, Sicily, and Burma, where they won many honors. Wartime experiences provided a new frame of reference for many soldiers, who interacted across ethnic boundaries in ways that were unusual in Nigeria. The war also made the British reappraise Nigeria's political future. The war years,. moreover, witnessed a polarization between the older, more parochial leaders inclined toward gradualism and the younger intellectuals, who thought in more immediate terms.

The rapid growth of organized labor in the 1940s also brought new political forces into play. During the war, union membership increased sixfold to 30,000. The proliferation of labor organizations, however, fragmented the movement, and potential leaders lacked the experience and skill to draw workers together.

In the postwar period, party lines were sharply drawn on the basis of ethnicity and regionalism. After the demise of the NYM, the nationalist movement splintered into the Hausa- and Fulani-backed Northern People's Congress (NPC), the Yoruba-supported Action Group, and the Igbo-dominated National Council of Nigeria and the Cameroons (NCNC, later the National Council of Nigerian Citizens). These parties negotiated with the British government over constitutional changes, but cooperation among them was the result of expediency rather than an emerging sense of national identity. Because of the essentially regional political alignments of the parties, the British government decided to impose a political solution for Nigeria based on a federally structured constitution.

The first political party in Nigeria to have nationwide appeal was the NCNC, founded in 1944 when Azikiwe encouraged activists in the National Youth Movement to call a conference in Lagos of all major Nigerian organizations to "weld the heterogeneous masses of Nigeria into one solid bloc." The aged Macauley was elected president of the new group, and Azikiwe became its secretary general. The party platform renewed the National Youth Movement's appeal for Nigerian self-government within the Commonwealth under a democratic constitution.

At its inception, party membership was based on affiliated organizations that included labor unions, social groups, political clubs, professional associations, and more than 100 ethnic organizations. These bodies afforded unusual opportunities for political education in existing constituencies, but the NYM, which was fading out, was absent from the list of NCNC affiliates. Leadership of the NCNC rested firmly with Azikiwe, in large part because of his commanding personality but also because of the string of newspapers he operated and through which he argued the nationalist cause. In the late 1940s, the NCNC captured a majority of the votes in the predominantly Yoruba Western Region, but increasingly it came to rely on Igbo support, supplemented by alliances with minority parties in the Northern Region. The NCNC backed the creation of new regions, where minorities would be ensured a larger voice, as a step toward the formation of a strong unitary national government.

The Action Group arose in 1951 as a response to Igbo control of the NCNC and as a vehicle for Yoruba regionalism that resisted the concept of unitary government. The party was structured democratically and benefited from political spadework done by the NCNC in the Western Region in the late 1940s. As a movement designed essentially to exploit the federal arrangement to attain regional power, however, the Action Group became the NCNC's competitor for votes in the south at the national level and at the local level in the Western Region.

The Action Group was largely the creation of Awolowo, general secretary of Egbe Omo Oduduwa and leader of the Nigerian Produce Traders' Association. The Action Group was thus the heir of a generation of flourishing cultural consciousness among the Yoruba and also had valuable connections with commercial interests that were representative of the comparative economic advancement of the Western Region. Awolowo had little difficulty in appealing to broad segments of the Yoruba population, but he strove to prevent the Action Group from being stigmatized as a "tribal" group. Despite his somewhat successful efforts to enlist non-Yoruba support, the regionalist sentiment that had stimulated the party initially could hardly be concealed.

Another obstacle to the development of the Action Group was the animosity between segments of the Yoruba community—for example, many people in Ibadan opposed Awolowo on personal grounds because of his identification with the Ijebu Yoruba. Despite these difficulties, the Action Group rapidly built an effective organization. Its program reflected greater planning and was more ideologically oriented than that of the NCNC. Although he did not have Azikiwe's compelling personality, Awolowo was a formidable debater as well as a vigorous and tenacious political campaigner. He used for the first time in Nigeria modern, sometimes flamboyant, electioneering techniques. Among his leading lieutenants were Samuel Akintola of Ibadan and the *oni* of Ife.

The Action Group was a consistent supporter of minority-group demands for autonomous states within a federal structure, and it even supported the severance of a midwest state from the Western Region. This move assumed that comparable alterations would be made elsewhere, an attitude that won the party minority voting support in the other regions. It also backed Yoruba irredentism in the Fulani-ruled emirate of Ilorin in the Northern Region and separatist movements among non-Igbo in the Eastern Region.

The Northern People's Congress (NPC) was organized in the late 1940s by a small group of Western-educated northern Muslims who obtained the assent of the emirs to form a political party capable of counterbalancing the activities of the southern-based parties. It represented a substantial element of reformism in the Muslim north. The most powerful figure in the party was Ahmadu Bello, the *sardauna* (war leader) of Sokoto, a controversial figure who aspired to become the sultan of Sokoto, still the most important political and religious position in the north. Often described by opponents as a "feudal" conservative, Bello had a consuming interest in the protection of northern social and political institutions from southern influence. He also insisted on maintaining the territorial integrity of the Northern Region, including those areas with non-Muslim populations. He was prepared to introduce educational and economic changes to strengthen the north. Although his own ambitions were limited to the Northern Region, Bello backed the NPC's successful efforts to mobilize the north's large voting strength so as to win control of the national government.

The NPC platform emphasized the integrity of the north, its traditions, religion, and social order. Support for broad Nigerian concerns occupied a clear second place. A lack of interest in extending the NPC beyond the Northern Region corresponded to this strictly regional orientation. Its activist membership was drawn from local government and emirate officials who had access to means of communication and to repressive traditional authority that could keep the opposition in line.

The small contingent of northerners who had been educated abroad—a group that included Abubakar Tafawa Balewa and Aminu Kano—was allied with British-backed efforts to introduce gradual change to the emirates. The support given by the emirs to limited modernization was motivated largely by fear of the unsettling presence of southerners in the north and by the equally unsettling example of improving conditions in the south. Those northern leaders who were committed to modernization were firmly connected to the traditional power structure. Most internal problems within the north—peasant disaffection or rivalry among Muslim factions—were concealed, and open opposition to the domination of the Muslim aristocracy was not tolerated. Critics, including representatives of the middle belt who plainly resented Muslim domination, were relegated to small, peripheral parties or to inconsequential separatist movements.

In 1950 Aminu Kano, who had been instrumental in founding the NPC, broke away to form one such party, the Northern Elements Progressive Union (NEPU), in protest against the NPC's limited objectives and what he regarded as a vain hope that traditional rulers would accept modernization. NEPU formed a parliamentary alliance with the NCNC.

The NPC continued to represent the interests of the traditional order in the preindependence deliberations. After the defection of Kano, the only significant disagreement within the NPC related to the awareness of moderates, such as Balewa, that only by overcoming political and economic backwardness could the NPC protect the foundations of traditional northern authority against the influence of the more advanced south.

In all three regions, minority parties represented the special interests of ethnic groups, especially as they were affected by the majority. The size of their legislative delegations, when successful in electing anyone to the regional assemblies, was never large enough to be effective, but they served as a means of public expression for minority concerns. They received attention from major parties before elections, at which time either a dominant party from another region or the opposition party in their region sought their alliance.

The political parties jockeyed for positions of power in anticipation of the independence of Nigeria. Three constitutions were enacted from 1946 to 1954 that were subjects of considerable political controversy in themselves but inevitably moved the country toward greater internal autonomy, with an increasing role for the political parties. The trend was toward the establishment of a parliamentary system of government, with regional assemblies and a federal House of Representatives.

In 1946 a new constitution was approved by the British Parliament and promulgated in Nigeria. Although it reserved effective power in the hands of the governor and his appointed executive council, the so-called Richards Constitution (after Governor Arthur Richards, who was responsible for its formulation) provided for an expanded Legislative Council empowered to deliberate on matters affecting the whole country. Separate legislative bodies, the houses of assembly, were established in each of the three regions to consider local questions and to advise the lieutenant governors. The introduction of the federal principle, with deliberative authority devolved on the regions, signaled recognition of the country's diversity. Although realistic in its assessment of the situation in Nigeria, the Richards Constitution undoubtedly intensified regionalism as an alternative to political unification.

The pace of constitutional change accelerated after the promulgation of the Richards Constitution, which was suspended in 1950. The call for greater autonomy resulted in an interparliamentary conference at Ibadan in 1950, when the terms of a new constitution were drafted. The so-called Macpherson Constitution, after the incumbent governor, went into effect the following year.

The most important innovations in the new charter reinforced the dual course of constitutional evolution, allowing for both regional autonomy and federal union. By extending the elective principle and by providing for a central government with a Council of Ministers, the Macpherson Constitution gave renewed impetus to party activity and to political participation at the national level. But by providing for comparable regional governments exercising broad legislative powers, which could not be overridden by the newly established 185-seat federal House of Representatives, the Macpherson Constitution also gave a significant boost to regionalism. Subsequent revisions contained in a new constitution, the Lyttleton Constitution, enacted in 1954, firmly established the federal principle and paved the way for independence.

In 1957 the Western and the Eastern regions became formally self-governing under the parliamentary system. Similar status was acquired by the Northern Region two years later. There were numerous differences of detail among the regional systems, but all adhered to parliamentary forms and were equally autonomous in relation to the federal government at Lagos. The federal government retained specified powers, including responsibility for banking, currency, external affairs, defense, shipping and navigation, and communications, but real political power was centered in the regions. Significantly, the regional governments controlled public expenditures derived from revenues raised within each region.

Ethnic cleavages intensified in the 1950s. Political activists in the southern areas spoke of self-government in terms of educational opportunities and economic development. Because of the spread of mission schools and wealth derived from export crops, the southern parties were committed to policies that would benefit the south of the country. In the north, the emirs intended to maintain firm control on economic and political change. Any activity in the north that might include participation by the federal government (and consequently by southern civil servants) was regarded as a challenge to the primacy of the emirates. Broadening political participation and expanding educational opportunities and other social services also were viewed as threats to the status quo. Already there was an extensive immigrant population of southerners, especially Igbo, in the north; they dominated clerical positions and were active in many trades.

The cleavage between the Yoruba and the Igbo was accentuated by their competition for control of the political machinery. The receding British presence enabled local officials and politicians to gain access to patronage over government jobs, funds for local development, market permits, trade licenses, government contracts, and even scholarships for higher education. In an economy with many qualified applicants for every post, great resentment was generated by any favoritism authorities showed to members of their own ethnic group.

In the immediate post-World War II period, Nigeria benefited from a favorable trade balance. The principal exports were agricultural commodities—peanuts and cotton from the Northern Region, palm products from the Eastern Region, and cocoa from the Western Region. Marketing boards, again regionally based, were established to handle these exports and to react to price fluctuations on the world market. During the 1950s, the marketing boards accumulated considerable surpluses. Initially, imports lagged behind exports, although by the mid-1950s imports began to catch up with exports, and the surpluses decreased. Expansion in the nonagricultural sectors required large imports of machinery, transport equipment and, eventually, intermediate materials for industry. In time there also were increased administrative costs to be met. Although per capita income in the country as a whole remained low by international standards, rising incomes among salaried personnel and burgeoning urbanization expanded consumer demand for imported goods.

In the meantime, public sector spending increased even more dramatically than export earnings. It was supported not only by the income from huge agricultural surpluses but also by a new range of direct and indirect taxes imposed during the 1950s. The transfer of responsibility for budgetary management from the central to the regional governments in 1954 accelerated the pace of public spending on services and on development projects. Total revenues of central and regional governments nearly doubled in relation to the gross domestic product (GDP—see Glossary) during the decade.

The most dramatic event, having a long-term effect on Nigeria's economic development, was the discovery and exploitation of petroleum deposits. The search for oil, begun in 1908 and abandoned a few years later, was revived in 1937 by Shell and British Petroleum. Exploration was intensified in 1946, but the first commercial discovery did not occur until 1956, at Olobiri in the Niger Delta. In 1958 exportation of Nigerian oil was initiated at facilities constructed at Port Harcourt. Oil income was still marginal, but the prospects for continued economic expansion appeared bright and further accentuated political rivalries on the eve of independence.

The election of the House of Representatives after the adoption of the 1954 constitution gave the NPC a total of seventy-nine seats, all from the Northern Region. Among the other major parties, the NCNC took fifty-six seats, winning a majority in both the Eastern and the Western regions, while the Action Group captured only twenty-seven seats. The NPC was called on to form a government, but the NCNC received six of the ten ministerial posts. Three of these posts were assigned to representatives from each region, and one was reserved for a delegate from the Northern Cameroons.

As a further step toward independence, the governor's Executive Council was merged with the Council of Ministers in 1957 to form the all-Nigerian Federal Executive Council. NPC federal parliamentary leader Balewa was appointed prime minister. Balewa formed a coalition government that included the Action Group as well as the NCNC to prepare the country for the final British withdrawal. His government guided the country for the next three years, operating with almost complete autonomy in internal affairs.

The preparation of a new federal constitution for an independent Nigeria was carried out at conferences held at Lancaster House in London in 1957 and 1958 and presided over by the British colonial secretary. Nigerian delegates were selected to represent each region and to reflect various shades of opinion. The delegation was led by Balewa of the NPC and included party leaders Awolowo of the Action Group, Azikiwe of the NCNC, and Bello of the NPC; they were also the premiers of the Western, Eastern, and Northern regions, respectively. Independence was achieved on October 1, 1960.

Elections were held for a new and greatly enlarged House of Representatives in December 1959; 174 of the 312 seats were allocated to the Northern Region on the basis of its larger population. The NPC, entering candidates only in the Northern Region, confined campaigning largely to local issues but opposed the addition of new regions. The NCNC backed creation of a midwest state and proposed federal control of education and health services. The Action Group, which staged a lively campaign, favored stronger government and the establishment of three new states, while advocating creation of a West Africa Federation that would unite Nigeria with Ghana and Sierra Leone. The NPC captured 142 seats in the new legislature. Balewa was called on to head a NPC-NCNC coalition government, and Awolowo became official leader of the opposition.

Independent Nigeria

By an act of the British Parliament, Nigeria became an independent country within the Commonwealth on October 1, 1960. Azikiwe was installed as governor general of the federation and Balewa continued to serve as head of a democratically elected parliamentary, but now completely sovereign, government. The governor general represented the British monarch as head of state and was appointed by the crown on the advice of the Nigerian prime minister in consultation with the regional premiers. The governor general, in turn, was responsible for appointing the prime minister and for choosing a candidate from among contending leaders when there was no parliamentary majority. Otherwise, the governor general's office was essentially ceremonial.

The government was responsible to a parliament composed of the popularly elected 312-member House of Representatives and the 44-member Senate, chosen by the regional legislatures.

In general, the regional constitutions followed the federal model, both structurally and functionally. The most striking departure was in the Northern Region, where special provisions brought the regional constitution into consonance with Islamic law and custom. The similarity between the federal and regional constitutions was deceptive, however, and the conduct of public affairs reflected wide differences among the regions.

In February 1961, a plebiscite was conducted to determine the disposition of the Southern Cameroons and Northern Cameroons, which were administered by Britain as United Nations Trust Territories. By an overwhelming majority, voters in the Southern Cameroons opted to join formerly French-administered Cameroon over integration with Nigeria as a separate federated region. In the Northern Cameroons, however, the largely Muslim electorate chose to merge with Nigeria's Northern Region.

Politics in the Crisis Years

During the first three years after independence, the federal government was an NPC-NCNC coalition, despite the conflicting natures of the two partners. The former was regionalist, Muslim, and aristocratic; the latter was nationalist, Christian, and populist. Moreover, the NCNC supported opponents of the NPC in regional elections in the Northern Region. Although a more natural ideological alignment of the Action Group and the NCNC was called for by some Action Group leaders, it held no attraction for the NCNC as long as the NPC was assured of a parliamentary majority.

Domination of the Northern Region by the NPC and NCNC control of the Eastern Region were assured. Action Group control of the Western Region, however, was weakened and then collapsed because of divisions within the party that reflected cleavages within

*Abubakar Tafawa Balewa,
first prime minister
(1960–66), speaking at
Organization of African Unity
meeting in Addis Ababa
Courtesy Embassy of Nigeria,
Washington*

Yoruba society. This loss of stability in one region gradually under-mined the political structure of the whole country.

The leadership of the Action Group, which formed the official opposition in the federal parliament, split in 1962 as a result of a rift between Awolowo and Akintola, prime minister of the Western Region. Awolowo favored the adoption of democratic socialism as party policy, following the lead of Kwame Nkrumah's regime in Ghana. The radical ideology that Awolowo expressed was at variance with his earlier positions, however, and was seen as a bid to make the Action Group an interregional party that drew support across the country from educated younger voters, whose expectations were frustrated by unemployment and the rising cost of living. Akintola, in reaction, attempted to retain the support of conservative party elements who were disturbed by Awolowo's rhetoric. He called for better relations with the NPC and an all-party federal coalition that would remove the Action Group from opposition and give its leaders greater access to power.

Awolowo's radical majority staged the expulsion of Akintola from the party. The governor of the Western Region demanded Akintola's resignation as prime minister (although he had not lost a vote of confidence in the regional legislature) and named a successor recommended by the Action Group to head the government. Akintola immediately organized a new party, the United People's Party, which pursued a policy of collaboration with the NPC–NCNC government in the federal parliament.

Akintola's resignation in May 1962 sparked bloody rioting in the Western Region and brought effective government to an end as rival legislators, following the example in the streets, introduced violence to the floor of the regional legislature. The federal government declared a state of emergency, dissolved the legislature, and named a federal administrator for the Western Region. One of his first acts was to place many Action Group leaders under house arrest.

Investigations by the federal administrator led to accusations of criminal misuse of public funds against Awolowo and other Action Group leaders. A special commission found that Awolowo had funneled several million pounds from public development corporations to the Action Group through a private investment corporation when he was prime minister of the Western Region in the 1950s. The regional government seized the corporation's assets and pressed legal claims against the Action Group.

In the course of the financial investigation, police uncovered evidence linking Awolowo with a conspiracy to overthrow the government. With a number of other Action Group leaders, he was arrested and put on trial for treason. Authorities charged that 200 activists had received military training in Ghana and had smuggled arms into Nigeria in preparation for a coup d'état. Awolowo was found guilty, along with seventeen others, and was sentenced to ten years in prison. Anthony Enahoro, Awolowo's chief lieutenant who had been abroad at the time of the coup, was extradited from Britain and also was convicted of treason and imprisoned.

In the meantime, the state of emergency was lifted and Balewa, determining that Akintola had been improperly dismissed, obtained his reinstatement as prime minister of the Western Region at the head of a coalition between the NCNC and the United People's Party. The Action Group successfully contested the legality of this action in the courts, but a retroactive amendment to the Western Region's constitution that validated Akintola's reappointment was quickly enacted. As Balewa told parliament, the legalities of the case "had been overtaken by events."

Later in 1963, Nigeria became a republic within the Commonwealth. The change in status called for no practical alteration of the constitutional system. The president, elected to a five-year term by a joint session of the parliament, replaced the crown as the symbol of national sovereignty and the British monarchy as head of state. Azikiwe, who had been governor general, became the republic's first president.

New State Movements

After independence the attitudes of the major parties toward the formation of new states that could accommodate minority aspirations varied widely. The NCNC espoused self-determination for ethnic minorities but only in accordance with its advocacy of a unitary state. The Action Group also supported such movements, including the restoration of the northern Yoruba area (Ilorin) to the Western Region, but as part of a multistate, federal Nigeria. The NPC steadfastly opposed separatism in the Northern Region and attempted with some success to win over disaffected minorities in the middle belt.

Proposals were introduced for the creation of three states as a means of restructuring the regions along ethnic lines. The most extensive revision sought the separation of the middle belt from the Northern Region, a move the United Middle Belt Congress promoted. Serious riots in Tivland in 1960 and 1964 were related to this agitation. Another plan was put forward by the Edo and western Igbo to create the Midwestern Region by separating the whole tract adjacent to the Niger River from the Yoruba-dominated Western Region. At the same time, Ijaw and Efik-Ibibio ethnic groups proposed that the coast between the Niger Delta and Calabar become a new region in order to end Igbo dominance in that area. At this time, however, only the Midwestern Region achieved formal approval, despite opposition of the Action Group. The creation of the region was confirmed by plebiscite in 1963.

The creation of the Midwestern Region reopened the question of the internal restructuring of Nigeria. One motive for a more drastic restructuring was the desire to break up the Northern Region. That region, having more than half the country's population, controlled a majority of the seats in the House of Representatives. There was also the fear that the Igbo-dominated NCNC would gain control of the Midwestern legislature and thereby become even more powerful. A new political coalition, the Midwest Democratic Front (MDF), was formed by leaders of the Action Group and the United People's Party to contest the Midwestern Region election with the NCNC. During the campaign, the conservative United People's Party accepted support from the NPC, a fact that NCNC candidates stressed in their call to keep northern influence out of the region. Many Action Group workers withdrew support from the MDF in protest, and some allied themselves with the NCNC. In the 1964 elections, the NCNC won by a landslide.

The Census Controversy

Because seats in the House of Representatives were apportioned on the basis of population, the constitutionally mandated decennial census had important political implications (see Population, ch. 2; The First Republic, ch. 4). The Northern Region's political strength, marshaled by the NPC, had arisen in large measure from the results of the 1952-53 census, which had identified 54 percent of the country's population in that area. A national campaign early in 1962 addressed the significance of the forthcoming census. Politicians stressed the connection between the census and parliamentary representation on the one hand, and the amount of financial support for regional development on the other. The 1962 census was taken by head count, but there was evidence that many enumerators obtained their figures from heads of families, and many persons managed to be counted more than once.

Southern hopes for a favorable reapportionment of legislative seats were buoyed by preliminary results, which gave the south a clear majority. A supplementary count was immediately taken in the Northern Region that turned up an additional 9 million persons reportedly missed in the first count. Charges of falsification were voiced on all sides and led to an agreement among federal and regional governments to nullify the count and to conduct a new census.

The second nationwide census reported a population of 60.5 million, which census officials considered impossibly high. A scaled-down figure of 55.6 million, including 29.8 million in the Northern Region, finally was submitted and adopted by the federal government, leaving legislative apportionment virtually unchanged.

Demographers generally rejected the results of the 1963 census as inflated, arguing that the actual figure was as much as 10 million lower. Controversy over the census remained a lively political issue. NCNC leaders publicly charged the Northern Region's government with fraud, a claim that was denied by Balewa and by Bello, the regional prime minister.

Popular Disillusionment and Political Realignment

The conspiracy trials that led to the conviction of two of the country's most dynamic politicians, Awolowo and Enahoro, severely weakened public confidence in the political and judicial systems. Abuses were widespread, including intimidation of opponents by threats of criminal investigation, manipulation of the constitution and the courts, diversion of public funds to party and private use, rigging of elections, and corruption of public officials whose political patrons expected them to put party interests ahead of their legal responsibilities. Popular disillusion also intensified because politicians failed to produce benefits commensurate with expectations of constituents.

The volatile political scene leading up to elections in 1964 was ominous. The Action Group virtually disappeared from the federal parliament as a result of the Awolowo affair, thereby fundamentally altering political alignments at the national level. By early 1964, therefore, the federal parliament no longer had a recognized opposition. Akintola's party, which was renamed the Nigerian National Democratic Party in an effort to attract more support, now dominated the Western Region. The federal government nominally consisted of a consensus of the ruling parties of all four regions, but it was a fragile alliance at best and had emerged as a result of heavy-handed tactics. The NCNC had strengthened its position by gaining firm control of the Midwestern Region, so that it dominated two of the four regions. Akintola managed to undermine the NCNC in the Western Region, even though nationally he was pledged to an alliance with the NCNC. For its part, the NCNC denounced Akintola's party as a "tool of the NPC" and allied itself with remnants of the Action Group.

Political realignment was deceptive, however, because the basic divisions within the country remained unaltered. The NPC was reasonably secure in the Northern Region, despite the presence of minor parties, but it could not govern Nigeria alone, and alliances with any of the southern parties were ideologically incompatible and very tenuous. The NPC continued its dominance because of the inability of the other parties to find common ground among themselves and with northern progressives. Awolowo's pointed remarks in 1963 that democracy could be secured only if the Action Group and the NCNC could reach an accommodation that would remove the deadweight of the NPC from power fueled NPC concerns. The detention of Awolowo prevented that alliance from maturing, but it did not result in greater political stability. Indeed the alliance between the NPC and NCNC, which had dominated federal politics and destroyed the Action Group, now fell apart.

The 1964-65 Elections

The federal parliamentary election campaign in December 1964—the first since independence—was contested by two political alliances incorporating all the major parties. The Nigerian National Alliance (NNA) was composed of the NPC, Akintola's Western-based Nigerian National Democratic Party, and opposition parties representing ethnic minorities in the Midwestern and Eastern regions. It was opposed by the United Progressive Grand Alliance (UPGA), which joined the NCNC and the remnants of the Action Group with two minority-based northern allies, the Northern Elements Progressive Union and the United Middle Belt Congress.

Not surprisingly, the NNA adopted a platform that reflected the views of the northern political elite and, hence, was an attempt by the NPC to gain firmer control of federal politics through an alliance with the Western Region. Its appeal to voters outside the north was based essentially on the advantages to be gained from associating with the party in power. The NNA preyed on Yoruba fears of Igbo domination of the federal government. The UPGA was employed in an attempt by the NCNC to use the two regional governments that it controlled as a springboard to domination of the federal government. Strategically it offered a reformist program, combining a planned economy that endorsed increased public spending while also encouraging private enterprise. The UPGA proposed to divide the country into states that reflected ethnicity. Its proposals were intended to undermine the existing regional basis of political power by creating a sufficient number of states in each region so that none of the major ethnic groups—Hausa, Yoruba, or Igbo—could dominate a region. The UPGA presented itself as an alternative to northern and, more specifically, to Hausa-Fulani domination of the federal government. Convinced that it would win if the election were held in an atmosphere free from interference by ruling parties in the Northern Region and the Western Region, the UPGA spent most of its efforts denouncing what it regarded as NNA intentions to rig the election in those regions.

The election was postponed for several weeks because of discrepancies between the number of names on voting rolls and on census returns. Even then the UPGA was not satisfied and called on its supporters to boycott the election. The boycott was effective in the Eastern Region, where polling places did not open in fifty-one constituencies that had more than one candidate running for office. In other constituencies in the region, UPGA candidates ran unopposed. Nationwide, only 4 million voters cast ballots, out of 15 million who were eligible. The NNA elected 198 candidates, of whom 162 represented the NPC, from the 261 constituencies returning results. After an embarrassing delay, President Azikiwe agreed to ask Balewa to form a government with the NNA majority. The boycott had failed to stop the election, and in March 1965 supplementary elections were held in those areas in the Eastern Region and in Lagos where the boycott had been honored. UPGA candidates were elected in all these constituencies, bringing the

Third session of the Enugu Provincial Assembly in the early 1960s
Courtesy Embassy of Nigeria, Washington

NCNC-dominated coalition a total of 108 seats in the House of Representatives. The UPGA became the official opposition.

After this decisive defeat, the UPGA prepared for the November 1965 legislative election in the Western Region in an attempt to gain control of the three southern regions and the Federal Territory of Lagos, the region surrounding the capital. If successful, the NPC-dominated NNA still would have controlled the House of Representatives, but it would have given the predominantly southern UPGA a majority in the Senate, whose members were chosen by the regional legislatures.

Once more NCNC strategy failed. Amid widespread charges of voting irregularities, Akintola's NNDP, supported by its NPC ally, scored an impressive victory in November. There were extensive protests, including considerable grumbling among senior army officials, at the apparent perversion of the democratic process. In the six months after the election, an estimated 2,000 people died in violence that erupted in the Western Region. In the face of the disorders, the beleaguered Balewa delegated extraordinary powers to the regional governments to deal with the situation. By this time, Azikiwe and the prime minister were scarcely on speaking terms, and there were suggestions that Nigeria's armed forces should restore order.

In January 1966, army officers attempted to seize power. In a well-coordinated action, the conspirators, most of whom were Igbo, assassinated Balewa in Lagos, Akintola in Ibadan, and Bello in Kaduna, as well as senior officers of northern origin. In a public proclamation, the coup leaders pledged to establish a strong and efficient government committed to a progressive program and eventually to new elections. They vowed to stamp out corruption and to suppress violence. Despite the bloody and calculated character of the coup, these sentiments appealed directly to younger, educated Nigerians in all parts of the country.

The army's commander in chief, Major General Johnson Aguiyi Ironsi, quickly intervened to restore discipline within the army. In the absence of Azikiwe, who was undergoing treatment in a London hospital, Balewa's shaken cabinet resigned, leaving the reins of authority to the armed forces. Ironsi, also an Igbo, suspended the constitution, dissolved all legislative bodies, banned political parties, and as an interim measure formed a Federal Military Government (FMG) to prepare the country for a return to civilian rule at an unspecified date. He appointed military governors in each region and assigned officers to ministerial positions, instructing them to implement sweeping institutional reforms.

Ironsi and his advisers favored a unitary form of government, which they thought would eliminate the intransigent regionalism that had been the stumbling block to political and economic progress. A decree issued in March abolished the federation and unified the federal and regional civil services. Civilian experts, largely Igbo, set to work on a new constitution that would provide for a centralized unitary government such as the NCNC had favored since the 1950s.

Although the decree contained a number of concessions to regional interests, including protection of northerners from southern competition in the civil service, Ironsi's action showed dangerous disregard for the nuances of regional politics and badly misjudged the intensity of ethnic sensitivities in the aftermath of the bloody coup. The failure of the military government to prosecute Igbo officers responsible for murdering northern leaders stirred animosities further. Igbo civil servants and merchants residing in the north made the situation even worse through their triumphant support for the coup. Furthermore, Ironsi was vulnerable to accusations of favoritism toward the Igbo. The coup was perceived not so much as an effort to impose a unitary government as a plot by the Igbo to dominate Nigeria. Likewise, many Muslims saw the military decrees as Christian-inspired attempts to undermine emirate government.

Troops of northern origin, who made up the bulk of the infantry, became increasingly restive. Fighting broke out between them and Igbo soldiers in garrisons in the south. In June mobs in the northern cities, abetted by local officials, carried out a pogrom against resident Igbo, massacring several hundred people and destroying Igbo-owned property. Some northern leaders spoke seriously of secession. Many northerners feared that Ironsi intended to deprive them of power and to consolidate further an Igbo-dominated centralized state.

In July northern officers and army units staged a countercoup, during which Ironsi and a number of other Igbo officers were killed. The Muslim officers named thirty-one-year-old Lieutenant Colonel (later Major General) Yakubu ''Jack'' Gowon, a Christian from a small ethnic group (the Anga) in the middle belt, as a compromise candidate to head the FMG. A young and relatively obscure officer serving as army chief of staff, Gowon had not been involved in the coup, but he enjoyed wide support among northern troops who subsequently insisted that he be given a position in the ruling body. His first act was to repeal the Ironsi decree and to restore federalism, a step followed by the release of Awolowo and Enahoro from prison.

Civil War

Throughout the remainder of 1966 and into 1967, the FMG sought to convene a constituent assembly for revision of the constitution that might enable an early return to civilian rule. Nonetheless, the tempo of violence increased. In September attacks on Igbo in the north were renewed with unprecedented ferocity, stirred up by Muslim traditionalists with the connivance, Eastern Region leaders believed, of northern political leaders. The army was sharply divided along regional lines. Reports circulated that troops from the Northern Region had participated in the mayhem. The estimated number of deaths ranged as high as 30,000, although the figure was probably closer to 8,000 to 10,000. More than 1 million Igbo returned to the Eastern Region. In retaliation, some northerners were massacred in Port Harcourt and other eastern cities, and a counterexodus of non-Igbo was under way.

The Eastern Region's military governor, Lieutenant Colonel Chukwuemeka Odumegwu Ojukwu, was under pressure from Igbo officers to assert greater independence from the FMG. Indeed, the eastern military government refused to recognize Gowon's legitimacy on the ground that he was not the most senior officer in the chain of command. Some of Ojukwu's colleagues questioned whether the country could be reunited amicably after the outrages committed against the Igbo in the Northern Region. Ironically, many responsible easterners who had advocated a unitary state now called for looser ties with the other regions.

The military commanders and governors, including Ojukwu, met in Lagos to consider solutions to the regional strife. But they failed to reach a settlement, despite concessions offered by the northerners, because it proved impossible to guarantee the security of Igbo outside the Eastern Region. The military conferees reached a consensus only in the contempt they expressed for civilian politicians. Fearing for his safety, Ojukwu refused invitations to attend subsequent meetings in Lagos.

In January 1967, the military leaders and senior police officials met at Aburi, Ghana, at the invitation of the Ghanaian military government. By now the Eastern Region was threatening secession. In a last-minute effort to hold Nigeria together, the military reached an accord that provided for a loose confederation of regions. The federal civil service vigorously opposed the Aburi Agreement, however. Awolowo, regrouping his supporters, demanded the removal of all northern troops garrisoned in the Western Region and warned that if the Eastern Region left the federation, the Western Region would follow. The FMG agreed to the troop withdrawal.

In May Gowon issued a decree implementing the Aburi Agreement. Even the Northern Region leaders, who had been the first to threaten secession, now favored the formation of a multistate federation. Meanwhile, the military governor of the Midwestern Region announced that his region must be considered neutral in the event of civil war.

The Ojukwu government rejected the plan for reconciliation and made known its intention to retain all revenues collected in the Eastern Region in reparation for the cost of resettling Igbo refugees. The eastern leaders had reached the point of rupture in their relations with Lagos and the rest of Nigeria. Despite offers made by the FMG that met many of Ojukwu's demands, the Eastern Region Consultative Assembly voted May 26 to secede from Nigeria. In Lagos, Gowon proclaimed a state of emergency and unveiled plans for abolition of the regions and for redivision of the country into twelve states. This provision broke up the Northern Region, undermining the possibility of continued northern domination and offering a major concession to the Eastern Region. It was also a strategic move, which won over eastern minorities and deprived the rebellious Igbo heartland of its control over the oil fields and access to the sea. Gowon also appointed prominent civilians, including

Awolowo, as commissioners in the federal and new state governments, thus broadening his political support.

On May 30, Ojukwu answered the federal decree with the proclamation of the independent Republic of Biafra, named after the Bight
of Biafra. He cited as the principal cause for this action the Nigerian
government's inability to protect the lives of easterners and suggested its culpability in genocide, depicting secession as a measure taken reluctantly after all efforts to safeguard the Igbo people
in other regions had failed.

Initially, the FMG launched "police measures" to restore the
authority of Lagos in the Eastern Region. Army units attempted
to advance into secessionist territory in July, but rebel troops easily stopped them. The Biafrans retaliated with a surprise thrust into
the Midwestern Region, where they seized strategic points.
However, effective control of the delta region remained under federal control despite several rebel attempts to take the non-Igbo area.
The federal government began to mobilize large numbers of recruits
to supplement its 10,000-member army.

By the end of 1967, federal forces had regained the Midwestern
Region and secured the delta region, which was reorganized as the
Rivers State and the Southeastern State, cutting off Biafra from
direct access to the sea. But a proposed invasion of the rebel-held
territory, now confined to the Igbo heartland, stalled along the
stiffened Biafran defense perimeter.

A stalemate developed as federal attacks on key towns broke down
in the face of stubborn Biafran resistance. Ill-armed and trained
under fire, rebel troops nonetheless had the benefit of superior
leadership and superb morale. Although vastly outnumbered and
outgunned, the Biafrans probed weak points in the federal lines,
making lightning tactical gains, cutting off and encircling advanc-
ing columns, and launching commando raids behind federal lines.
Biafran strikes across the Niger managed to pin down large concentrations of federal troops on the west bank.

In September 1968, Owerri was captured by federal troops ad-
vancing from the south, and early in 1969 the federal army, expanded to nearly 250,000 men, opened three fronts in what Gowon
touted as the "final offensive." Although federal forces flanked the
rebels by crossing the Niger at Onitsha, they failed to break through.
The Biafrans subsequently retook Owerri in fierce fighting and
threatened to push on to Port Harcourt until thwarted by a renewed
federal offensive in the south. That offensive tightened the noose
around the rebel enclave without choking it into submission.

Biafran propaganda, which stressed the threat of genocide to the
Igbo people, was extremely effective abroad in winning sympathy

for the secessionist movement. Food and medical supplies were scarce in Biafra. Humanitarian aid, as well as arms and munitions, reached the embattled region from international relief organizations and from private and religious groups in the United States and Western Europe by way of nighttime airlifts over the war zone. The bulk of Biafra's military supplies was purchased on the international arms market, with unofficial assistance provided by France through former West African colonies. In one of the most dramatic episodes of the civil war, Carl Gustav von Rosen, a Swedish count who at one time commanded the Ethiopian air force, and several other Swedish pilots flew five jet trainers modified for combat in successful strikes against Nigerian military installations.

Biafra's independence was recognized by Tanzania, Zambia, Gabon, and the Ivory Coast, but it was compromised in the eyes of most African states by the approval of South Africa, Southern Rhodesia, and Portugal. Britain extended diplomatic support and limited military assistance to the federal government. The Soviet Union became an important source of military equipment for Nigeria. Modern Soviet-built warplanes, flown by Egyptian and British pilots, interdicted supply flights and inflicted heavy casualties during raids on Biafran urban centers. In line with its policy of noninvolvement, the United States prohibited the sale of military goods to either side while continuing to recognize the FMG.

In October 1969, Ojukwu appealed for United Nations (UN) mediation for a cease-fire as a prelude to peace negotiations. But the federal government insisted on Biafra's surrender, and Gowon observed that ''rebel leaders had made it clear that this is a fight to the finish and that no concession will ever satisfy them.'' In December federal forces opened a four-pronged offensive, involving 120,000 troops, that sliced Biafra in half. When Owerri fell on January 6, 1970, Biafran resistance collapsed. Ojukwu fled to the Ivory Coast, leaving his chief of staff, Philip Effiong, behind as ''officer administering the government.'' Effiong called for an immediate, unconditional cease-fire January 12 and submitted to the authority of the federal government at ceremonies in Lagos.

Estimates in the former Eastern Region of the number of dead from hostilities, disease, and starvation during the thirty-month civil war are estimated at between 1 million and 3 million. The end of the fighting found more than 3 million Igbo refugees crowded into a 2,500-square-kilometer enclave. Prospects for the survival of many of them and for the future of the region were dim. There were severe shortages of food, medicine, clothing, and housing. The economy of the region was shattered. Cities were in ruins; schools, hospitals, utilities, and transportation facilities were destroyed or inoperative. Overseas groups instituted a major relief effort, but the FMG insisted on directing all assistance and recovery operations and barred some agencies that had supplied aid to Biafra.

Because charges of genocide had fueled international sympathy for Biafra, the FMG allowed a team of international experts to observe the surrender and to look for evidence. Subsequently, the observers testified that they found no evidence of genocide or systematic destruction of property, although there was considerable evidence of famine and death as a result of the war. Furthermore, under Gowon's close supervision, the federal government ensured that Igbo civilians would not be treated as defeated enemies. A program was launched to reintegrate the Biafran rebels into a unified Nigeria. A number of public officials who had "actively counselled, aided, or abetted" secession were dismissed, but a clear distinction was made between them and those who had simply carried out their duties. Igbo personnel soon were being reenlisted in the federal armed forces. There were no trials and few people were imprisoned. Ojukwu, in exile, was made the scapegoat, but efforts to have him extradited failed.

An Igbo official, Ukapi "Tony" Asika, was named administrator of the new East Central State, comprising the Igbo heartland. Asika had remained loyal to the federal government during the civil war, but as a further act of conciliation, his all-Igbo cabinet included members who had served under the secessionist regime. Asika was unpopular with many Igbo, who considered him a traitor, and his administration was characterized as inept and corrupt. In three years under his direction, however, the state government achieved the rehabilitation of 70 percent of the industry incapacitated during the war. The federal government granted funds to cover the state's operating expenses for an interim period, and much of the war damage was repaired. Social services and public utilities were slowly reinstituted, although not to the prewar levels.

The Federal Military Government in the Postwar Era

In the postwar period, all significant political power remained concentrated in the FMG. None of the three major ethnic groups had a powerful voice in its executive element, which was disproportionately composed of representatives of middle belt minorities and to a lesser extent of Muslim Yoruba and of Ijaw and Ibibio from the Eastern Region. The Northern Region had been divided into six states in 1967, which left the area without its former power base in the federation. The decision was accepted by northerners in part because of the military government's relative strength in comparison with earlier civilian governments. Acceptance also was motivated by the fact that northerners were less fearful of the Igbo or a southern coalition. Only the Yoruba power base in the west retained its prewar characteristics. The 1967 administrative structure also made national unity attractive to the westerners because, with the creation of a Yoruba state (Kwara) in the north, their position seemed stronger relative to the northerners. Remaining points of conflict included the number of civil service posts to be allotted to each ethnic group and the assignment of civil servants from former regional services to states other than their own.

The Gowon Regime

Gowon's influence depended upon his position as chairman of the Supreme Military Council, which had come into existence in March 1967. The council included top-ranking staff officers, service and police heads, state military governors, and the civilian administrator of the East Central State. Gowon also chaired the Federal Executive Council, the cabinet of ministers composed of military officers and civilian technocrats. The regime ruled by decree, although the concurrence of state military governors was sought before decrees were issued.

In October 1970, Gowon announced his intention to stay in power until 1976, which was set as the target year for completion of the military's political program and the return to an elected civilian government. Gowon outlined a nine-point program that would enable the military to relinquish control. Included in the package were reorganization of the armed forces; implementation of a national economic development plan, including reconstruction of war-damaged areas; eradication of corruption; establishment of more states; adoption of a new constitution; introduction of a formula for allocating revenue; completion of a national census; organization of national political parties; and elections at federal and state levels. Criticism of the six-year plan was widespread because the agenda was so broad. Many Nigerians feared that the military planned to retain power indefinitely. The reaction of civilian politicians was particularly negative. Muslim traditionalists also expressed concerns that military rule, with its modernizing tendencies, would erode the authority of the emirates.

Foreign Policy

Gowon reaffirmed the priorities in foreign policy established at independence. These included active participation in the UN, advocacy of pan-African solidarity through the Organization of African Unity (OAU), regional cooperation, support for anti-colonial and liberation movements—particularly those in southern

*Railroad construction project in 1963 to open market for
agricultural produce in northeastern Nigeria
Courtesy World Bank*

Africa—and nonalignment in the East-West conflict. The role of
Nigeria in world affairs, outside its African concerns, was insig-
nificant, however.

Nigeria was admitted to the UN within a week of independence
in 1960. It was represented on the committees of specialized agencies and took its turn as a nonpermanent member of the Security
Council. One of Nigeria's earliest and most significant contributions to the UN was to furnish troops for the peacekeeping operation in Zaire in the early 1960s. By 1964 Nigerian army units, under
Ironsi's command, formed the backbone of the UN force. The
FMG was committed to eliminating white-minority rule in Africa, and it channeled financial and military aid to liberation movements through the OAU.

Although there was considerable African criticism of Nigeria during the civil war, the military government resisted this pressure
as interference in the country's internal affairs. An OAU statement in 1967 backing the federal position on national unity assuaged
Nigerian feelings to some extent, but Lagos protested subsequent
OAU efforts to bring about a cease-fire. When the war ended,
Nigeria's participation in OAU activities returned to normal.

63

There were minor problems relating to border demarcations with neighboring countries, but these were resolved to the satisfaction of the parties involved. Relations also were mended with African states that had recognized Biafra. Particularly close ties were developed with the military regime in Ghana, which gave full support to the federal government during the civil war. In 1975 Nigeria joined other West African countries in creating the Economic Community of West African States (ECOWAS), whose mandate was the reduction of trade barriers among countries in the region. Sponsored by Gowon, the agreement was indicative of the government's concern with improving intraregional economic ties.

Nigeria played an active role in the Commonwealth, which linked Nigeria to developing countries outside Africa and complemented regional ties through ECOWAS and the OAU. Financial and technical assistance was channeled to Nigeria through the Commonwealth. The aid came from Britain, Canada, and Australia, with which Nigeria had advantageous trade relations. Nigeria's interaction with Britain continued to be cooperative, although the renewal of arms sales to South Africa, permitted by the Conservative British government in the early 1970s, caused some strain in Nigeria. Relations cooled even more because of Nigeria's apprehension over Britain's application for entry into the European Economic Community (EEC). Nigeria feared that it would suffer economically as a result of British membership in the EEC.

The FMG was committed to the principle of nonalignment, a policy initially established in the early years of independence. Acceptance of Western aid—including US$225 million from the United States in the early years of independence—tended to undermine this position. Nigeria had begun to move toward a more autonomous position in 1962, when the Anglo-Nigerian Defense Pact was abrogated. With this step, Nigeria affirmed its independence of British foreign policy to which it had adhered since achieving nationhood. The abrogation of the pact was a clear message of nonalignment. During the war, the federal government accepted assistance from both East and West. Aircraft and heavy equipment were purchased from the Soviet Union, for example, because Britain and the United States refused to supply heavy armaments. Nigeria's relations with the United States were good, largely because the United States provided financial aid and recognized the FMG during the civil war. United States ties with South Africa and Portugal caused some friction on the official level, and there was considerable criticism in the Nigerian press. The Nigerian version of nonalignment had a slightly pro-Western tilt.

Economic Development

After the civil war, the FMG moved to resurrect the six-year development plan inaugurated in 1962. The First National Development Plan charted Nigeria's transition from an essentially agricultural economy to a mixed economy based on agricultural expansion and limited industrial growth. Government was heavily involved in the economy because locally generated private investment was unable to generate sufficient capital for development. New development plans were instituted in 1970 and 1975, but the goals set in all three plans proved unrealistic (see Planning, ch. 3).

By the late 1960s, oil had replaced cocoa, peanuts, and palm products as the country's biggest foreign exchange earner. In 1971 Nigeria—by then the world's seventh-largest petroleum producer—became a member of the Organization of the Petroleum Exporting Countries (OPEC). The dramatic rise in world oil prices in 1974 caused a sudden flood of wealth that can be described as "dynamic chaos." Much of the revenue was intended for investment to diversify the economy, but it also spurred inflation and, coming in the midst of widespread unemployment, underscored inequities in distribution. In 1975 production fell sharply as a result of the sudden decrease in world demand, and prices moved downward until late in the year when OPEC intervened to raise prices. Nigeria fully supported OPEC policies.

In 1972 the government issued an indigenization decree, the first of a number of Nigerian Enterprises Promotion decrees that barred aliens from investing in specified enterprises and reserved participation in certain trades to Nigerians. At the time, about 70 percent of commercial firms operating in Nigeria were foreign-owned. In 1975 the federal government bought 60 percent of the equity in the marketing operations of the major oil companies in Nigeria, but full nationalization was rejected as a means of furthering its program of indigenization.

Unemployment constituted an increasingly serious problem. Large numbers of farm workers who had gone to urban areas in search of higher wages remained in the cities even if they failed to find jobs, while school graduates and dropouts flooded the labor market at a rate of 600,000 a year in the mid-1970s. Unemployment reached its highest levels in the crowded Igbo areas in the east, where the economy still was recovering from the effects of the war. Skilled workers were reluctant to leave the east in search of work, although eventually the shortage of skilled workers in other parts of the country began to have its effect in overcoming Igbo fears. The dangers involved in discharging large numbers of soldiers who had no job prospects made demobilization of the costly military establishment undesirable. Substantial increases in public-sector employment promised to absorb some of the soldiers, but they lacked training. These economic problems assumed an imposing political dimension. To some extent, they reflected a pattern in the world economic situation, but the popular imagination blamed corruption and mismanagement and held the Gowon regime responsible.

The regime also had to deal with a severe drought that struck the northern states between 1972 and 1974. The drought was the most serious since that of 1913–14. The drought and resulting famine affected the Sahel countries to the west, north, and east far more than Nigeria, but considerable numbers of refugees poured into Nigeria from Niger. Famine conditions also prevailed in some parts of the north of Nigeria. In the long run, however, Nigerian agriculture benefited from the rise in prices that resulted from crop failures in other parts of the Sahel. In the short run, the drought influenced policy decisions about the necessity of promoting irrigation schemes and reforestation.

Crime, Corruption, and Political Turbulence

In 1972 Gowon partially lifted the ban on political activity that had been in force since 1966 in order to permit a discussion of a new constitution that would prepare the way for civilian rule. The debate that followed was ideologically charged. Awolowo's call for a transition to "democratic socialism" made the military particularly nervous. The press, trade unions, and universities demanded a quick return to the democratic process. The call for new states was loud, but there was no agreement over how many there should be. Gowon abruptly ended public discussion, explaining that "peace is more important than politics."

The decennial census was scheduled for 1973. Under the banner "Prepare to be Counted," the military government conducted a public campaign that emphasized the technical rather than political dimensions of the exercise. The procedure was to be supervised by a committee whose members were selected carefully for geographical and ethnic balance, and computers were to be used for processing the returns. Despite measures taken to ensure a more accurate count than had been possible before, the results once again confounded demographers: the census found that Nigeria's population had increased by nearly 44 percent in 10 years, a rate of growth unprecedented in any developing country. According to the returns submitted, the north contained 64 percent of the total population, compared with 53.7 percent in 1963, a figure even then believed to be exaggerated. The 1973 census, on which representation in a new, elected parliament would be based, revived fears that one ethnic group would permanently dominate the others. It also meant that a considerable share of oil revenues would flow to the northern states under the existing system of allocation. The government failed in its efforts to sell the census as a technical exercise because the political implications were widely understood and hotly debated, despite the ban on political discussion.

The Gowon regime came under fire because of widespread and obvious corruption at every level of national life. Graft, bribery, and nepotism were an integral part of a complex system of patronage and "gift" giving through which influence and authority were asserted. Although the military had pledged to rid the government of corruption, the public became increasingly aware of abuses, primarily because of daily exposés in the press. In 1973 the federal government established a special anticorruption police force— the "X-Squad"—whose subsequent investigations revealed ingenious forms of extortion and fraud—not only in government and public corporations but also in private business and in the professions.

A major scandal that had international implications and reached the highest levels of government and the business community took place in the mid-1970s; it involved the purchase abroad of construction materials by state agents at prices well above market values. Rake-offs were pocketed by public officials and private contractors. Other scandals in hospitals and orphanages shocked the populace, and corruption in importing medical drugs whose effective dates long since had expired revealed that even the health of Nigerians was at risk.

Inefficiencies compounded the impact of corruption. In mid-1975, 400 cargo ships—250 of them carrying 1.5 million tons of cement—clogged the harbor of Lagos, which had been paralyzed for fifteen months with vessels waiting to be unloaded. To compound the error, spoiled and inferior-grade cement was concealed by mixing it with acceptable material for use in public building projects. Later, buildings collapsed or had to be dismantled because of the inferior product. New roads washed away because of bad construction and inadequate controls. In these scandals, as in others, the culprits were a combination of Nigerian businessmen, government officials, and foreign companies. Few people and few projects seemed exempt from the scourge.

Crime posed a threat to internal security and had a seriously negative impact on efforts to bring about economic development. Armed gangs, often composed of former soldiers, roamed the countryside engaging in robbery, extortion, and kidnapping. The gangs sometimes operated with the connivance of the police or included moonlighting soldiers. Pirates raided cargo ships awaiting entry to ports or unloaded them at the piers ahead of the stevedores. Drug trafficking and smuggling were prevalent. Punishment was meted out to large batches of convicted and suspected criminals, who were dispatched by firing squads in public executions meant to impress spectators with the seriousness of the offenses and with the government's concern to curb crime. These measures had no noticeable effect on the crime rate, however, but seemed rather to provoke a callous public attitude toward violence.

In January 1975, Gowon revamped the membership of the Federal Executive Council, increasing the number of military ministers. He depended more and more on a small group of advisers and became increasingly inaccessible to his military colleagues. Without broad consultation, he backed off from the 1976 date set for a return to civilian rule, explaining that to adhere rigidly to it would ''amount to a betrayal of a trust'' and ''certainly throw the nation back into confusion.'' Public employees staged protest strikes in May and June that brought essential services to a standstill. The government responded by granting retroactive wage increases that averaged 30 percent; the action fed inflation and led to industrial strikes as union members demanded parallel raises.

The political atmosphere deteriorated to the point that Gowon was deposed in a bloodless coup d'état July 29, 1975—the ninth anniversary of the revolt that had brought him to power. At the time, Gowon was at an OAU summit meeting in Kampala, Uganda. The perpetrators of the coup included many of the officers who had participated in the July 1966 coup. Even the officers responsible for Gowon's security were involved. Gowon pledged his full loyalty to the new regime and left for exile in Britain, where he received a pension from the Nigerian government.

The Regime of Murtala Muhammad, 1975–76

The armed forces chose thirty-eight-year-old Brigadier (later General) Murtala Ramat Muhammad, a Muslim northerner, to succeed Gowon. A Hausa, trained at the British military academy at Sandhurst, Murtala Muhammad had command of federal field forces in the final phase of the civil war, including being responsible for the abortive efforts to cross the Niger River. He was not directly involved in the coup d'état that brought him to power, but he had played a prominent role in rallying northern officers behind the July 1966 coup that felled Ironsi. In a short time, Murtala Muhammad's policies won him broad popular support, and his decisiveness elevated him to the status of a national hero.

One of his first acts was to scrap the 1973 census, which was weighted in favor of the north, and to revert to the 1963 count for official purposes. Murtala Muhammad removed top federal and state officials to break links with the Gowon regime and to restore public confidence in the federal government. More than 10,000 public officials and employees were dismissed without benefits, on account of age, health, incompetence, or malpractice. The purge affected the civil service, judiciary, police and armed forces, diplomatic service, public corporations, and universities. Some officials were brought to trial on charges of corruption, and one former military state governor was executed for gross misconduct in office. Murtala Muhammad also began the demobilization of 100,000 troops from the swollen ranks of the armed forces.

Twelve of the twenty-five ministerial posts on the new Federal Executive Council went to civilians, but the cabinet was secondary to the executive Supreme Military Council. Murtala Muhammad imposed the authority of the federal government in areas formerly reserved for the states, restricting the latitude exercised by state governments and their governors in determining and executing policy. Newly appointed military governors of the states were not given seats on the Supreme Military Couicl, but instead were expected to administer federal policies handed down by Murtala Muhammad through the military coucil. The federal government took over the operation of the country's two largest newspapers, made broadcasting a federal monopoly, and brought remaining state-run universities under federal control.

Murtala Muhammad initiated a comprehensive review of the Third National Development Plan. Singling out inflation as the greatest danger to the economy, he was determined to reduce the money supply that had been swollen by government expenditures on public works. Murtala Muhammad also announced that his government would encourage the rapid expansion of the private sector into areas dominated by public corporations. He reappraised foreign policy, stressing a "Nigeria first" orientation in line with OPEC price guidelines that was to the disadvantage of other African countries. Nigeria became "neutral" rather than "nonaligned" in international affairs. The shift in orientation became apparent with respect to Angola. Nigeria had worked with the OAU to bring about a negotiated reconciliation of the warring factions in the former Portuguese colony, but late in 1975 Murtala Muhammad announced Nigeria's support for the Soviet-backed Popular Movement for the Liberation of Angola (Movimento Popular de Libertação de Angola—MPLA), citing South Africa's armed intervention on the side of the rival National Union for the Total Independence of

Angola (Unição Nacional para a Indepêndencia Total de Angola—
UNITA). The realignment strained relations with the United
States, which argued for the withdrawal of Cuban troops and Soviet
advisers from Angola. In October the Nigerian air force took delivery of Soviet-built aircraft that had been ordered under Gowon.

Preparation for the Return to Civilian Rule

Murtala Muhammad set in motion the stalled machinery of devolution to civilian rule with a commitment to hand over power to
a democratically elected government by October 1979. The transition, as outlined by Murtala Muhammad, would take place in
successive stages. In August 1975, he appointed a five-member
panel to study Gowon's plan for a nineteen-state federation that
would "help to erase memories of past political ties and emotional
attachments." The plan, reaffirmed by the panel, assaulted ethnic power by recommending that the predominantly Yoruba
Western State be divided into three states, the Igbo East Central
State into two, and the six states of the north into nine states, only
three of which would be predominantly Hausa-Fulani. Murtala
Muhammad claimed that he wanted to avoid the "proliferation
of states" that would highlight the problems of minorities and
warned petitioners that no further demands for new states would
be tolerated. In the end, seven more states were created. In 1976
Nigeria came to have nineteen states.

In October 1975, Murtala Muhammad named a blue-ribbon
committee, drawn from business, the professions, universities, and
the civil service, as well as from prominent civilian political leaders, to draft a constitution that would be put before a constituent
assembly for approval. Awolowo, the spokesman for the Nigerian
left, was excluded from the committee. Murtala Muhammad cau-
tioned the drafting committee against opening old wounds. He favored consensus politics that avoided the institutionalized opposition
of the former constitution. Rather than a British parliamentary system, he wanted executive and legislative functions clearly defined,
preferring a strong executive on the United States model. In his
instructions to the committee, Murtala Muhammad said he
preferred the elimination of all political parties, and failing that,
he suggested that parties be limited in number to those with a
genuinely national constituency.

Murtala Muhammad was assassinated during an unsuccessful
coup d'état in February 1976, and the country went into deep
mourning. In less than a year, this man had captured the hearts
of many Nigerians. The political shake-up and the decisive leadership in the midst of rapid economic growth seemed to promise a

bright future. In fact, there was considerable opposition to Murtala Muhammad that would have become more pronounced in the succeeding months, but this opposition was stifled under the outpouring of national loss.

The attempted coup reflected dissatisfaction within the military that was unconnected with the larger currents of opposition in the country. Two groups of conspirators were involved in the coup. The first, composed of middle-grade officers, was led by Lieutenant Colonel Bukar Dimka, who was related to Gowon by marriage. Dimka's opposition to Murtala Muhammad was both professional and political. Dimka's group protested demobilization and alleged that the FMG was "going communist." A group of colonels answering to Major General I.D. Bisalla, the minister of defense, waited in the wings for Dimka's group to overthrow the government, and then planned to seize power. Dimka, Bisalla, and thirty-eight other conspirators were convicted after a secret trial before a military tribunal and were executed publicly by a firing squad. Evidence published by the FMG implied that both groups of conspirators had been in communication with Gowon, who was accused of complicity in the plot against Murtala Muhammad. The British government refused to accede to Nigerian demands for Gowon's extradition, however, and protests against the decision forced Britain to recall its high commissioner from Lagos.

The Obasanjo Regime, 1976–79

Lieutenant General Olusegun Obasanjo, a Yoruba, succeeded Murtala Muhammad. As chief of staff of Supreme Headquarters, Obasanjo was Murtala Muhammad's deputy and had the support of the military. He had commanded the federal division that took Owerri, effectively bringing an end to the civil war. Keeping the chain of command established by Murtala Muhammad in place, Obasanjo pledged to continue the program for the restoration of civilian government in 1979 and to carry forward the reform program to improve the quality of public service.

The draft constitution was published in October 1976, anticipating the seating of a constituent assembly in 1977. Debates during sessions of the drafting committee were frequently ideological in nature, but divisive proposals, such as the attempt to define Nigeria as a "socialist" state, were decisively rejected. Committee members discarded Murtala Muhammad's recommendations for a nonparty system, but they insisted that parties applying for registration had to have national objectives and executive boards whose members represented at least two-thirds of the states. The model for the constitution, which was adopted in 1979, was based on the

Constitution of the United States, with provision for a president, Senate, and House of Representatives. The country was now ready for local elections, to be followed by national elections, that would return Nigeria to civilian rule.

The military regimes of Murtala Muhammad and Obasanjo benefited from a tremendous influx of oil revenue that increased 350 percent between 1973 and 1974, when oil prices skyrocketed, to 1979, when the military stepped down. Increased revenues permitted massive spending that, unfortunately, was poorly planned and concentrated in urban areas. The oil boom was marred by a minor recession in 1978-79, but revenues rebounded until mid-1981. The increase in revenues made possible a rapid rise in income, especially for the urban middle class. There was a corresponding inflation, particularly in the price of food, that promoted both industrialization and the expansion of agricultural production. As a result of the shift to food crops, the traditional export earners—peanuts, cotton, cocoa, and palm products—declined in significance and then ceased to be important at all. Nigeria's exports became dominated by oil.

Industrialization, which had grown slowly after World War II through the civil war, boomed in the 1970s, despite many infrastructure constraints. Growth was particularly pronounced in the production and assembly of consumer goods, including vehicle assembly and the manufacture of soap and detergents, soft drinks, pharmaceuticals, beer, paint, and building materials. Furthermore, there was extensive investment in infrastructure from 1975 to 1980, and the number of parastatals—jointly government- and privately owned companies—proliferated. The Nigerian Enterprises Promotion decrees of 1972 and 1977 further encouraged the growth of an indigenous middle class.

Plans were undertaken for the movement of the federal capital from Lagos to a more central location in the interior at Abuja. Such a step was seen as a means of encouraging the spread of industrial development inland and of relieving the congestion that threatened to choke Lagos. Abuja also was chosen because it was not identified with any particular ethnic group.

Heavy investment was planned in steel production. With Soviet assistance, a steel mill was developed at Ajaokuta in Kwara State, not far from Abuja. The most significant negative sign was the decline of industry associated with agriculture, but large-scale irrigation projects were launched in the states of Borno, Kano, Sokoto, and Bauchi under World Bank (see Glossary) auspices.

Education also expanded rapidly. At the start of the civil war, there were only five universities, but by 1975 the number had

General Olusegun Obasanjo,
president 1976–79,
at Obasanjo Farms,
Ogun State, 1989
Courtesy Orlando E. Pacheco

increased to thirteen, with seven more established over the next several years. In 1975 there were 53,000 university students. There were similar advances in primary and secondary school education, particularly in those northern states that had lagged behind.

The Second Republic, 1979–83

The first elections under the 1979 constitution were held on schedule in July and August 1979, and the FMG handed over power to a new civilian government under President Shehu Shagari on October 1, 1979. Nigeria's Second Republic was born amid great expectations. Oil prices were high, and revenues were on the increase. It appeared that unlimited development was possible. Unfortunately, the euphoria was short-lived, and the Second Republic did not survive its infancy.

Five major parties competed for power in the first elections in 1979. As might be expected, there was some continuity between the old parties of the First Republic and the new parties of the Second Republic. The National Party of Nigeria (NPN), for example, inherited the mantle of the Northern People's Congress, although the NPN differed from the NPC in that it obtained significant support in the non-Igbo states of southeastern Nigeria. The United Party of Nigeria (UPN) was the successor to the Action Group, with Awolowo as its head. Its support was almost entirely in the Yoruba states. The Nigerian People's Party (NPP), the

73

successor to the NCNC, was predominantly Igbo and had Azikiwe as its leader. An attempt to forge an alliance with non-Hausa-Fulani northern elements collapsed in the end, and a breakaway party with strong support in parts of the north emerged from the failed alliance. This northern party was known as the Great Nigerian People's Party under the leadership of Waziri Ibrahim of Borno. Finally, the People's Redemption Party was the successor to the Northern Elements Progressive Union and had Aminu Kano as its head.

Just as the NPC dominated the First Republic, its successor, the NPN, dominated the Second Republic. Shagari won the presidency, defeating Azikiwe in a close and controversial vote. The NPN also took 36 of 95 Senate seats, 165 of 443 House of Representatives seats and won control of seven states (Sokoto, Niger, Bauchi, Benue, Cross River, Kwara, and Rivers). The NPN lost the governorship of Kaduna State but secured control of the Kaduna legislature. The NPN failed to take Kano and lacked a majority in either the Senate or House of Representatives. It was forced to form a shaky coalition with the NPP, the successor of the NCNC, the old coalition partner of the NPC. The NPP took three states (Anambra, Imo, and Plateau), sixteen Senate seats and seventy-eight House of Representatives seats, so that in combination with the NPN the coalition had a majority in both the House of Representatives and the Senate. Nonetheless, the interests of the two parties were often in conflict; hence the NPN was forced to operate alone in most situations. Even though the presidential form of constitution was intended to create a stronger central government, the weakness of the coalition undermined effective central authority.

The UPN came in with the second largest number of seats and effectively formed the official opposition, just as the Action Group had done in the First Republic. The UPN took five states (Lagos, Oyo, Ogun, Ondo, and Bendel), 28 Senate seats, and 111 House seats. Awolowo continued as spokesman for the left of center. The Great Nigerian People's Party managed to win two states (Borno and Gongola), eight Senate seats, and forty-three House of Representatives seats. The People's Redemption Party, which was the most radical of the parties, won Kano and the governorship of Kaduna, seven Senate seats, and forty-nine House of Representatives seats.

A number of weaknesses beset the Second Republic. First, the coalition that dominated federal politics was not strong, and in effect the NPN governed as a minority because no coalition formed to challenge its supremacy. Second, there was lack of cooperation between the NPN-dominated federal government and the twelve states controlled by opposition parties. Third, and perhaps most important, the oil boom ended in mid-1981, precisely when expectations of continuous growth and prosperity were at a height.

There were many signs of tension in the country. The Bakalori Project, an irrigation scheme in Sokoto, for example, became the focus of serious unrest in the late 1970s when thousands of farmers protested the loss of their land, and police retaliated by burning villages and killing or wounding hundreds of people. Widespread dissatisfaction became apparent with the Maitatsine, or Yan Tatsine (followers of the Maitatsine), a quasi-Muslim fringe group that sparked religious riots in Kano in 1980 and Kaduna and Maiduguri in 1982 after police tried to control their activities (see Islam, ch. 2). The disturbance in Kano alone resulted in the deaths of 4,177 people between December 18 and 29, 1980. In 1981 teachers staged a strike because they had not been paid. As the political situation deteriorated, the federal government looked for scapegoats and found them in the large number of foreign workers who had come to Nigeria in response to the jobs created by the oil boom. In the crackdown on illegal immigration, an estimated 2 million foreigners were expelled in January and February 1983, of whom 1 million were from Ghana and 150,000 to 200,000 from Niger.

The recession that set in with the fall in oil prices after the middle of 1981 put severe strains on the Second Republic. For political reasons, government spending continued to accelerate, and the frictions among the political parties and between the federal government and the states only reinforced financial irresponsibility. Nigeria's foreign debt increased from N3.3 billion (for value of the naira—see Glossary) in 1978 to N14.7 billion in 1982. By 1983 the nineteen state governments had run up a combined debt of N13.3 billion. Heavy investment in economic development continued unabated. A steel mill at Ajaokuta in Kwara State was finished, for example, and a second plant opened at Aladje, near Warri, in 1982. Steel rolling mills also were built at Jos, Oshogbo, and Katsina—sites chosen for political reasons. By 1987 N5 billion had been spent on the steel industry alone, most of this committed under the Second Republic, even though the economics of steel development were questionable.

Corruption once again was rampant under the Second Republic. It had been a serious problem since the civil war, when wartime contracts often were awarded under dubious circumstances. Corruption became more serious after the war, most notably in connection with the cement scandal of the early 1970s, the Second World Black and African Festival of Arts and Culture (FESTAC) in Lagos, and the development of Abuja as the new federal capital. Corruption under the Second Republic was even greater. Major scandals involved the Federal Housing Scheme, the National Youth Service Corps, the Nigerian External Telecommunications, the Federal Mortgage Bank, the Federal Capital Territory Administration, the Central Bank of Nigeria, and the Nigerian National Supply Company. In addition, the halfhearted attempts to license imports and to control inflation encouraged smuggling, which became a major crime that went virtually unchecked. Umaru Dikko came to the attention of the international community because of an abortive plot to kidnap him in London and return him to Nigeria to stand trial for corruption. British authorities found him in a shipping crate on a runway moments before he was to be sent to Nigeria. Dikko was involved in many scandals, including the issuance of licenses to import rice—rice imports had risen from 50,000 tons in 1976 to 651,000 tons in 1982.

As elections approached in August 1983, an economic decline that reflected low oil prices, widespread corruption, and continued government spending at record levels was proof to many that the Second Republic was in sad shape. The lack of confidence was evident in the massive flight of capital—estimated at US$14 billion between 1979 and 1983. The second elections under the Second Republic were to be its last. When the results were tallied in 1983, it was clear that there had been fraud (see The Second Republic, ch. 4). The NPN increased its control of states from seven to twelve, including Kano and Kaduna. Shagari was reelected president, and the NPN gained 61 of 95 Senate seats and 307 of 450 House of Representatives seats. Not even the supporters of the NPN expected such results. Considering the state of the economy and the public outcry over the rigged election, the Shagari government stayed in power for a surprisingly long time.

Return to Military Rule

On December 31, 1983, the military seized power once again, primarily because there was virtually no confidence in the civilian regime. The fraudulent election was used as an excuse for the takeover, although the military was in fact closely associated with the ousted government. More serious still, the economy was in chaos. The true cost of the failure to use earlier revenues and foreign reserves to good effect now became apparent.

The leader of the coup d'état was Major General Muhammadu Buhari of Katsina, whose background and political loyalties tied him closely to the Muslim north and the deposed government. Buhari had been director of supply and services in the early 1970s, military governor of Northeast State at the time it was divided into three states, and federal commissioner for petroleum and mines (1976–78) during the height of the oil boom. At the time of the coup, he was commander of the Third Armored Division in Jos.

Buhari tried to restore public accountability and to reestablish a dynamic economy without altering the basic power structure of the country. The military had become impatient with the civilian government. Corruption in particular was out of control, and the fraudulent election had been too obvious. Because the civilians in the NPN could not control the situation, the military would try its hand. Nonetheless, Buhari's political and economic aims were almost identical to those of the NPN (see The Buhari Regime, ch. 4).

The military regime conducted tribunals to curb corruption, and many scandals were revealed. Once again the civil service was cleansed, although on a smaller scale than in the purge of 1975. This time, however, the military tried to achieve two aims. First, it attempted to secure public support by reducing the level of corruption; second, it demonstrated its commitment to austerity by trimming the federal budget. As a further attempt to mobilize the country, Buhari launched a War Against Indiscipline in the spring of 1984. This national campaign, which lasted fifteen months, preached the work ethic, emphasized patriotism, decried corruption, and promoted environmental sanitation.

The campaign was a military program for reform and mobilization that achieved few of its aims. Unemployment was on the rise as the recession worsened, so that speeches about working hard seemed out of place. The appeal to Nigerian nationalism had the negative effect of restricting the flexibility of the government in international negotiations over the debt. The campaign was enforced haphazardly; some people were executed or given long jail terms while others were allowed off if they were well-connected. Environmental sanitation meant that the state capitals had to be cleaned up, and the principal target was the petty bourgeoisie who eked a living out of selling services or retailing commodities on a small scale. Their "illegal structures"—market stalls and workshops along the streets—were destroyed, and as a consequence there was widespread resentment among the small traders, repairmen, and others in the self-employed service sector.

The regime attempted to stifle criticism. Journalists were harassed, and many critics were arrested. Symbolically, the arrest of the popular musician, Fela Ransome-Kuti, personified the crackdown. Ransome-Kuti's lyrics sharply mocked the government's inability to deal with national problems. The National Security Organisation (NSO) became the principal instrument of repression.

The NSO, created in 1976, had played only a marginal role in Nigerian politics until the Buhari regime. Buhari appointed Rafindadi, a civilian, as head of the NSO, and under Rafindadi, Nigeria experienced the harassment and insecurity of a secret police force for the first time. Fortunately, the NSO proved to be inefficient, and subsequent reaction to its operations led to its reorganization.

Buhari's biggest problem was Nigeria's foreign debt. Negotiations with the International Monetary Fund (IMF—see Glossary) dragged on, and in the end efforts to reschedule the debt failed (see The Debt Overhang, ch. 3). Although Buhari was committed to austerity, the IMF insisted on even more drastic measures to cut spending, devalue the currency, and otherwise restructure the economy than most Nigerians were willing to accept. Buhari had to accede to the strong and vocal opposition to the IMF terms. Nigerian nationalism won out over economic necessity, at least in the short run. Furthermore, by the end of 1985 there was considerable frustration within the army. The army had been reduced in size steadily since the end of the civil war, from a total of about 275,000 in 1969 to about 80,000 by the end of the 1980s (see Demographic Factors and the Defense Budget, ch. 5). The economic crisis, the campaign against corruption, and civilian criticism of the military undermined Buhari's position, and in August 1985 a group of officers under Major General Ibrahim Babangida removed Buhari from power.

The officers who staged the coup were mostly from the north, but unlike Buhari (of Hausa origin), they were mostly from minority ethnic groups. Babangida, for example, was of Gwari origin from Niger State. He was a member of the Supreme Military Council under the Murtala Muhammad, Obasanjo, and Buhari regimes and had been involved in the 1975 and 1984 coups. Lieutenant General Domkat Bali became chairman of the Joint Chiefs of Staff. The Armed Forces Ruling Council (which succeeded the Supreme Military Council) was dominated by minority groups from the north. Some radicals and technocrats were appointed to ministerial positions.

The new regime was committed to a return to civilian rule and supported the 1979 constitution. Babangida assumed the title of president, which he justified in terms of the constitution. Furthermore, he tried to assuage the unrest in the country by correcting the excesses of the Buhari regime. The NSO was abolished in 1986, and its duties were reassigned to less threatening bodies. The freewheeling press was allowed fuller rein again, although there was still occasional harassment. Trials of former politicians were ended, and many former officials who had been convicted were

released from jail. In 1987 the regime decreed that all politicians who had held office since 1960 and who had been convicted of criminal offenses were banned from politics.

The Babangida regime had a rocky start. A countercoup in December 1985 failed but made it clear that not everyone in the military sided with the Armed Forces Ruling Council. The most serious opposition centered in the labor movement and on the university campuses. In May 1986, students at Ahmadu Bello University and Kaduna Polytechnic staged demonstrations that led to military occupation of those campuses and to the deaths of a number of students. The student movement had considerable support at other universities. On June 4, 1986, the Nigerian Labour Congress in alliance with students and university teachers organized a national day of sympathy, which led to the arrest of many union leaders. There was also considerable controversy over Nigeria's entry into the Organization of the Islamic Conference, an international body of Muslim states, in 1986. Buhari's regime had made the application, which Babangida allowed to stand. The strong reaction among many Christians, led by the Christian Association of Nigeria (formed in 1976), proved to be an embarrassment to the regime.

Babangida addressed the worsening recession through the structural adjustment program of 1986. By 1986, 44 percent of export earnings was being used to service the foreign debt. Austerity was not enough; rescheduling the foreign debt was essential, but public opinion was against an IMF loan. The government already was committed to many of the conditions for the IMF loan, including even more austere measures. However, it resisted pressures to reduce the petroleum subsidy, to allow trade liberalization, and to devalue the naira. Although negotiations with the IMF were suspended, the federal budget of 1986 still imposed many of the IMF conditions. On October 1, 1986, the government declared a National Economic Emergency, which lasted for fifteen months. Under the emergency, the government de-emphasized large-scale agricultural projects and introduced salary and wage reductions for armed forces and for public- and private-sector employees. Import restrictions were intensified, including a 30-percent surcharge on imports. Officially, the government now encouraged foreign investment and promoted privatization. Finally, the petroleum subsidy was cut back. Despite these drastic moves, efforts to reschedule the foreign debt without an IMF loan failed, and a drop in world oil prices further compounded Nigeria's situation.

Eventually the World Bank stepped into the breach and provided US$4.2 billion over three years to support the structural adjustment program. The eligible debt finally was rescheduled in early

1988. There was heavy devaluation of the naira in 1986, followed by even more drastic reductions in 1989 and early 1990. As a result of the recession, there was a drop in real income, especially for urban dwellers, and unemployment rose steadily from a low in 1980 to almost 12 percent in 1986. The situation in the second half of the 1980s was even worse, with per capita income falling below US$300 in 1988.

The Babangida regime appointed a new body, the Political Bureau, in January 1986 to make recommendations on the return to civilian rule. Its report, submitted in March 1987, was decidedly at odds with the government's structural adjustment program. The Political Bureau, composed of academics and civil servants, wanted to maintain a strong state presence in the economy, whereas the military regime was steadily moving away from that position. The bureau also favored creation of a two-party political system that would be broadly social democratic in ideology, as a means of escaping from the ethnic-based political parties of the past. The Political Bureau also recommended creation of at least two new states, Katsina and Akwa Ibom; this was accomplished in 1987. Although the Babangida regime did not like many of the Political Bureau's recommendations, a Constitution Review Committee was formed in September 1987.

This process of review and discussion convinced the military regime that the transition to civilian rule should be gradual. The perceived mistakes of 1979 and the creation of the Second Republic would not be repeated, it was hoped. The military would stay in power through 1989 to oversee the transition. The first stage was local elections, held in December 1987. No political parties were allowed, and in many districts, especially in Lagos, the results were overturned and new elections held. In 1990 the military continued in power but still promised a return to civilian rule.

* * *

The best introductions to Nigeria are Obaro Ikime's *Groundwork of Nigerian History* and the relevant chapters in J.F. Ade Ajayi and Michael Crowder's *History of West Africa*. For the impact of slavery and the slave trade on Nigeria, see Paul E. Lovejoy's *Transformations in Slavery*. Regional studies include Elizabeth Isichei's *A History of the Igbo People;* A. Afigbo's *Ropes of Sand: Studies in Igbo History and Culture;* Robert S. Smith's *Kingdoms of the Yoruba;* Yusufu Bala Usman's *Studies in the History of the Sokoto Caliphate;* and Michael Watts's *Silent Violence: Food, Famine and Peasantry in Northern Nigeria.* John Flint's *Sir George Goldie and the Making of Nigeria* provides a readable and excellent introduction to British imperialism along the Niger River. For recent history, see Toyin Falola and J.O. Ihonvbere's *The Rise and Fall of Nigeria's Second Republic, 1979–1984* and Thomas Forrest's *Politics, Policy, and Capitalist Development in Nigeria, 1970-1990.* (For further information and complete citations, see Bibliography.)

Chapter 2. The Society and Its Environment

Statue of Oya, traditional goddess of rivers and the wife of Shango, Yoruba god of thunder

NIGERIA, THE MOST POPULOUS country in Africa and the tenth largest country by population in the world, is located at the eastern terminus of the bulge of West Africa. As with many of the other nations of Africa, Nigeria's national boundaries result from its colonial history and cut across a number of cultural and physical boundaries. Nigeria has a total area of 923,768 square kilometers, it is about 60 percent the size of the state of Alaska, and has the greatest area of the nations along the coast of West Africa (although in Africa as a whole, it is only the fourteenth largest country by area). The maximum north-south distance within the country is about 1,040 kilometers, whereas the maximum east-west distance is about 1,120 kilometers. Although it represents only about 3 percent of the surface area of Africa, Nigeria contains about 20 percent of sub-Saharan African population. In this and other respects, it is arguably the single most important country on the continent.

Physical Setting

Relief and Main Physical Features

Much of Nigeria's surface consists of ancient crystalline rocks of the African Shield. Having been subject to weathering and erosion for long periods, the landscape of this area is characterized by extensive level plains interrupted by occasional granite mountains. These features are a major landscape type in Nigeria and in West Africa as a whole. Smaller areas of younger granites are also found, for example, on the Jos Plateau (see fig. 8).

Sedimentary strata dating from various periods overlay the older rocks in many areas. The sedimentary areas typically consist of flat-topped ridges and dissected plateaus and a characteristic landscape of extensive plains with no major rocky outcrops. This landscape is generally found in the basins of the Niger and Benue rivers as well as the depressions of the Chad and Sokoto basins in the far northeast and northwest of the country, respectively. The most dramatic of the sedimentary landscapes are in southeastern Nigeria, where thick sedimentary beds from the Abakaliki Uplift to the Anambra Basin have been tilted and eroded. This process has resulted in a rugged scarp land topography with east-facing cliffs in the Udi Hills, north of Enugu, and in the area around Nanka and Agulu.

Although relatively little of the Nigerian landscape has been shaped by volcanic episodes, there are two main areas of volcanic

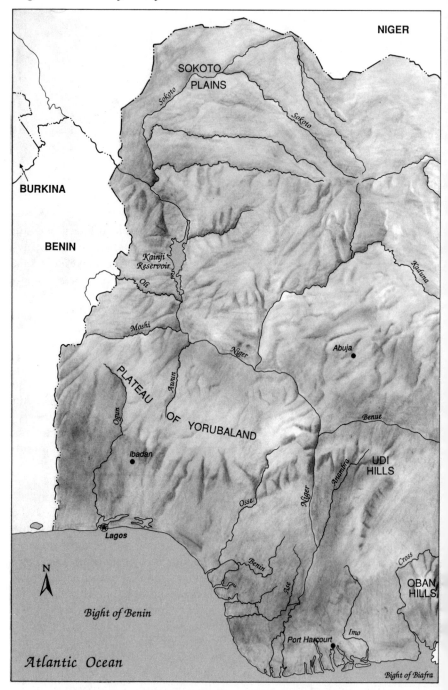

Figure 8. Topography and Drainage

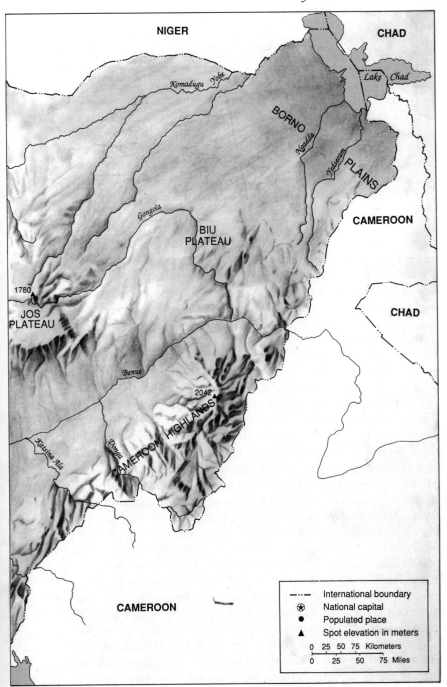

rock. They are found on the Biu Plateau in the northeast, extending into some localized volcanic areas along the eastern border with Cameroon, and on the Jos Plateau in the northern center of the country.

The elevational pattern of most of Nigeria consists of a gradual rise from the coastal plains to the northern savanna regions, generally reaching an elevation of 600 to 700 meters. Higher altitudes, reaching more than 1,200 meters in elevation, are found only in isolated areas of the Jos Plateau and in parts of the eastern highlands along the Cameroon border. The coastal plain extends inland for about ten kilometers and rises to an elevation of forty to fifty meters above sea level at its northern boundary. The eastern and western sections of the coastal plain are separated by the Niger Delta, which extends over an area of about 10,000 square kilometers. Much of this area is swampland, separated by numerous islands. The coastal plain region penetrates inland about seventy-five kilometers in the west but extends farther in the east. This region is gently undulating, with elevation increasing northward and a mean elevation of about 150 meters above sea level. Much of the population of southern Nigeria is located in these eastern and western coastal plains and, as well, in some of the contiguous areas of the coast and the lower Niger Basin.

Separating the two segments of the coastal plain and extending to the northeast and northwest are the broad river basins of the Niger and Benue rivers. The upper reaches of these rivers form narrow valleys and contain falls and rapids. Most of the lower portions, however, are free from rapids and have extensive floodplains and braided stream channels. To the north of the Niger and Benue basins are the broad, stepped plateau and granite mountains that characterize much of northern Nigeria. Such mountains are also found in the southwest, in the region between the western coastal plains and the upper Niger Basin. The western wedge between Abeokuta and Ibadan and the Niger Basin reaches elevations of 600 meters or more, whereas the extensive northern savanna region, stretching from Kontagora to Gombe and east to the border, includes extensive areas with elevations of more than 1,200 meters at its center. The mountainous zone along the middle part of the eastern border, the Cameroon Highlands, includes the country's highest point (2,042 meters). In the far northeast and northwest, elevation falls again to below 300 meters in the Chad Basin in the far northeast and the Sokoto Basin in the northwest.

Climate

As in most of West Africa, Nigeria's climate is characterized by strong latitudinal zones, becoming progressively drier as one moves north from the coast. Rainfall is the key climatic variable, and there is a marked alternation of wet and dry seasons in most areas. Two air masses control rainfall—moist northward-moving maritime air coming from the Atlantic Ocean and dry continental air coming south from the African landmass. Topographic relief plays a significant role in local climate only around the Jos Plateau and along the eastern border highlands. In the coastal and southeastern portions of Nigeria, the rainy season usually begins in February or March as moist Atlantic air, known as the southwest monsoon, invades the country. The beginning of the rains is usually marked by the incidence of high winds and heavy but scattered squalls. The scattered quality of this rainfall is especially noticeable in the north in dry years, when rain may be abundant in some small areas while other contiguous places are completely dry. By April or early May in most years, the rainy season is under way throughout most of the area south of the Niger and Benue river valleys. Farther north, the rains do not usually commence before June or July. Through most of northern Nigeria, the peak of the rainy season occurs in August, when air from the Atlantic covers the entire country. In southern regions, this period marks the August dip in precipitation. Although rarely completely dry, this dip in rainfall, which is especially marked in the southwest, can be useful agriculturally because it allows a brief dry period for grain harvesting.

From September through November, the northeast trade winds generally bring a season of clear skies, moderate temperatures, and lower humidity for most of the country. From December through February, however, the northeast trade winds blow strongly and often bring with them a load of fine dust from the Sahara. These dust-laden winds, known locally as the harmattan, often appear as a dense fog and cover everything with a layer of fine particles. The harmattan is more common in the north but affects the entire country except for a narrow strip along the southwest coast. An occasional strong harmattan, however, can sweep as far south as Lagos, providing relief from high humidities in the capital and pushing clouds of dust out to sea.

Given this climatological cycle and the size of the country, there is a considerable range in total annual rainfall across Nigeria, both from south to north and, in some regions, from east to west. The greatest total precipitation is generally in the southeast, along the coast around Bonny (south of Port Harcourt) and east of Calabar, where mean annual rainfall is more than 4,000 millimeters. Most of the rest of the southeast receives between 2,000 and 3,000 millimeters of rain per year, and the southwest (lying farther north) receives lower total rainfall, generally between 1,250 and 2,500 millimeters per year. Mean annual precipitation at Lagos is about 1,900 millimeters; at Ibadan, only about 140 kilometers north of Lagos, mean annual rainfall drops to around 1,250 millimeters. Moving north from Ibadan, mean annual rainfall in the west is in the range of 1,200 to 1,300 millimeters.

North of Kaduna, through the northern Guinea savanna and then the Sudan (see Glossary) savanna zones, the total rainfall and the length of the rainy season decline steadily. The Guinea savanna starts in the middle belt, or southern part of northern Nigeria. It is distinguished from the Sudan savanna because it has a number of trees whereas the Sudan has few trees. Rainy seasons decline correspondingly in length as one moves north, with Kano having an average rainy period of 120 to 130 days, and Katsina and Sokoto having rainy seasons 10 to 20 days shorter. Average annual rainfall in the north is in the range of 500 to 750 millimeters.

The regularity of drought periods has been among the most notable aspects of Nigerian climate in recent years, particularly in the drier regions in the north. Experts regard the twentieth century as having been among the driest periods of the last several centuries; the well publicized droughts of the 1970s and 1980s were only the latest of several significant such episodes to affect West Africa in this century. At least two of these droughts have severely affected large areas of northern Nigeria and the Sahel region farther north. These drought periods are indications of the great variability of climate across tropical Africa, the most serious effects of which are usually felt at the drier margins of agricultural zones or in the regions occupied primarily by pastoral groups.

Temperatures throughout Nigeria are generally high; diurnal variations are more pronounced than seasonal ones. Highest temperatures occur during the dry season; rains moderate afternoon highs during the wet season. Average highs and lows for Lagos are 31°C and 23°C in January and 28°C and 23°C in June. Although average temperatures vary little from coastal to inland areas, inland areas, especially in the northeast, have greater extremes. There, temperatures reach as high as 44°C before the onset of the rains or drop as low as 6°C during an intrusion of cool air from the north from December to February.

Population

The size of its population is one of Nigeria's most significant and distinctive features. With probably more than 100 million people in 1990—the precise figure is uncertain because there has been no accepted census since 1963, although a census was scheduled for the fall of 1991—Nigeria's population is about twice the size of that of the next largest country in Africa, Egypt, which had an estimated population of 52 million in mid-1989. Nigeria represents about 20 percent of the total population of sub-Saharan Africa. The population is unevenly distributed, however; a large percentage of the total number live within several hundred kilometers of the coast, but population is also dense along the northern river basin areas such as Kano and Sokoto. Population densities, especially in the southwest near Lagos and the rich agricultural regions around Enugu and Owerri, exceed 400 inhabitants per kilometer (see table 2, Appendix). None of the neighboring states of West or Central Africa approaches the total level of Nigerian population or the densities found in the areas of greatest concentration in Nigeria. Several of Nigeria's twenty-one states have more people than a number of other countries in West Africa, and some of the Igbo areas of the southeast have the highest rural densities in sub-Saharan Africa. In contrast, other areas of Nigeria are sparsely populated and have apparently remained so for a considerable time. This pattern of population distribution has major implications for the country's development and has had great impact on the nation's postindependence history.

Migration from rural to urban areas has accelerated in recent decades. Estimates of urban dwellers reveal this shift. In 1952, 11 percent of the total population was classified as urban; in 1985, 28 percent. One-sixth of the urban population, or approximately 6 million people, lived in Lagos, and in 1985 eight other cities had populations of more than 500,000.

Census History

Although numerous estimates of the Nigerian population were made during the colonial period, the first attempt at a nationwide census was during 1952–53. This attempt yielded a total population figure of 31.6 million within the current boundaries of the country. This census has usually been considered an undercount for a number of reasons: apprehension that the census was related to tax collection; political tension at the time in eastern Nigeria; logistical difficulties in reaching many remote areas; and inadequate training of enumerators in some areas. The extent of undercounting has been estimated at 10 percent or less, although accuracy probably varied among the regions. Despite its difficulties, the 1952–53 census has generally been seen as less problematic than any of its successors.

Subsequent attempts to conduct a reliable postindependence census have been mired in controversy, and only one was officially accepted. The first attempt, in mid-1962, was canceled after much controversy and allegations of overcounting in many areas. A second attempt in 1963, which was officially accepted, also was encumbered with charges of inaccuracy and manipulation for regional and local political purposes. Indeed, the official 1963 figure of 55.6 million as total national population is inconsistent with the census of a decade earlier because it implies a virtually impossible annual growth rate of 5.8 percent. In addition to likely inflation of the aggregate figure, significant intraregional anomalies emerge from a close comparison of the 1953 and 1963 figures. In portions of the southeast, for example, the two sets of data imply that some nonurban local government areas (LGAs) had increased at a rate of almost 13 percent per year, whereas other neighboring areas experienced a minute growth rate of 0.5 percent per year. Despite the controversy, the results of the 1963 census were eventually accepted.

After the civil war of 1967-70, an attempt was made to hold a census in 1973, but the results were canceled in the face of repeated controversy. No subsequent nationwide census had been held as of 1990, although there have been various attempts to derive population estimates at a state or local level. Most official national population estimates are based on projections from the 1963 census.

The great improvements in transport and accessibility of most areas, in technological capability, and in the level of education throughout the country, as well as the generalized acceptance of national coherence and legitimacy, favored the success of the fall 1991 census. It was to be conducted in about 250,000 enumeration areas by the National Population Commission, with offices in each of the country's LGAs. To reduce possible controversy, religious and ethnic identification would be excluded from the census forms, and verification of state results would be handled by supervisors from outside the state. Some analysts believe that the effort to carry out a reliable census with perceived legitimacy might become an unexpectedly positive exercise, reinforcing a sense of shared nationhood and providing a model for the attempt to overcome regional and ethnic differences.

Population Estimates and the Demographic Transition

The absence of virtually any reliable current demographic data has not prevented national and international bodies from generating estimates and projections of population and population growth in Nigeria. The World Bank (see Glossary) estimate of Nigeria's 1990 population was 119 million, with an estimated annual growth rate of 3.3 percent. Although other sources differed on the exact figure, virtually all sources agreed that the annual rate of population

Cattle grazing in the hilly terrain of northern Nigeria
Courtesy Embassy of Nigeria, Washington

growth in the country had increased from the 1950s through most of the 1980s. The government estimated a 2 percent rate of population growth for most of the country between 1953 and 1962. For the period between 1965 and 1973, the World Bank estimated Nigeria's growth rate at 2.5 percent, increasing to 2.7 percent between 1973 and 1983. Projections about the population growth rate were uncertain, however, in view of questions concerning the accuracy of Nigerian census statistics.

This increase was typical of most of sub-Saharan Africa, where growth rates increased steadily throughout the post-World War II period. The key to decelerating the rate of population growth would be a sharp decline in the fertility rate, which is defined as the average number of children a woman will bear in her lifetime. Considered the second stage of the demographic transition process, this decline was well under way in 1990 in most other developing regions of the world, except for the Islamic nations of the Middle East. Few African countries, however, had experienced any substantial fertility decline, and the overall fertility rate for sub-Saharan Africa was estimated as 6.5 in 1983.

Any decline in the population growth rate in Nigeria or the rest of sub-Saharan Africa was expected to depend on the balance between the demand for smaller families and the supply of birth control technology. Urbanization (especially when full households, rather than just males, are involved) was likely to be the most powerful factor leading to a decline in fertility because it induced the most radical shifts in the relative costs and benefits of having large numbers of children. Other important factors were likely to include the availability of health care and of birth control information and equipment in both rural and urban areas, the rate of expansion of education, and the general pace of economic development. If the pattern of change in Africa were to follow that in other parts of the world, urbanization, economic development, education, improved health care, increased availability of birth control, and declining infant mortality would eventually lead to a marked decline in fertility rates.

Between 1970 and 1987, life expectancy in Nigeria was estimated to have increased from forty to fifty-one years. Much of this rise resulted from a sharp decline in mortality among infants younger than one year and children ages one to four. Infant mortality was estimated to have declined 25 percent from 152 per 1,000 live births in 1965 to 113 in 1983, and child mortality declined almost 50 percent from 33 to 17 per 1,000 in the same period. These levels were likely to continue to fall, thereby exerting continuing upward pressure on the population growth rate. As of 1990, maternity deaths exceeded 75,000 per year, excluding deaths resulting from illegal abortions, and both were estimated to have risen during the 1980s.

Despite the probable decline in fertility in the 1990s, given the country's age structure, Nigeria's 1990 population was expected at least to double before the middle of the next century. Somewhat less than half of Nigeria's 1990 population was younger than fifteen. As a result, even if population growth were to drop immediately to a replacement rate and remain there, the 1990 population would double before stabilizing. Nigeria, thus, could expect to deal with a population of more than 200 million probably within the next twenty-five years.

These projections suggested that population growth would be an issue of central concern for Nigeria for some time to come. Merely to remain at current per capita levels, agricultural production, industrial and other economic output, and provision of health and other social services would all need to double within twenty-five years. This situation was a challenge of historic proportions for Nigeria, and one faced by many other nations of Africa.

Ethnicity

Ethnicity is one of the keys to understanding Nigeria's pluralistic society. It distinguishes groupings of peoples who for historical reasons have come to be seen as distinctive—by themselves and others—on the basis of locational origins and a series of other cultural markers. Experience in the postindependence period fostered a widespread belief that modern ethnicity affects members' life chances. In Nigerian colloquial usage, these collectivities were commonly called "tribes." In the emergent Nigerian national culture, this topic was discussed widely as "tribalism," a morally reprehensible term whose connotations were similar to American terms such as "discrimination," "racism," or "prejudice." Nigerian national policies have usually fostered tolerance and appreciation for cultural differences, while trying at the same time to suppress unfair treatment based on ethnic prejudice. This long-term campaign involved widespread support in educated circles to replace the term "tribe" or "tribal" with the more universally applicable concept of ethnicity. Nevertheless, the older beliefs died slowly, and ethnic identities were still a vital part of national life in 1990.

The ethnic variety was dazzling and confusing. Estimates of the number of distinct ethnic groupings varied from 250 to as many as 400. The most widely used marker was that of language. In most cases, people who spoke a distinct language that had a separate term for the language and/or its speakers saw themselves, or were viewed by others, as ethnically different. Language groupings were numbered in the 1970s at nearly 400, depending upon disagreements over whether or not closely related languages were mutually intelligible. Language groupings sometimes shifted their distinctiveness rather than displaying clear boundaries. Manga and Kanuri speakers in northeastern Nigeria spoke easily to one another. But in the major Kanuri city of Maiduguri, 160 kilometers south of Manga-speaking areas, Manga was considered a separate language. Kanuri and Manga who lived near each other saw themselves as members of the same ethnic group; others farther away did not.

Markers other than language were also used to define ethnicity. Speakers of Bura (a Chadic language closely related to Marghi) saw themselves traditionally as two ethnic groups, Bura and Pabir, a view not necessarily shared by others. Bura mostly adhered to Christianity or to a local indigenous religion, and a few were Muslims. They lived originally in small, autonomous villages of 100 to 500 persons that expanded and split as the population grew. The Pabir had the same local economy as the Bura, but they were Muslim, they lived in larger (originally walled) villages of 400 to 3,000 with more northerly architectural styles, they resisted splitting up into subgroups, and they recognized a central ruler (emir) in a capital town (Biu). There was a strong movement in the 1980s among many Bura speakers to unite the two groups based on their common

97

language, location, and interests in the wider society. Given long-standing conflicts that separated them as late as 1990, however, their common ethnicity was open to question.

The official language of the country is English, which is taught in primary schools and used for instruction in secondary schools and universities. All officials with education to secondary school level or beyond spoke English and used it across language barriers formed by Nigeria's ethnic diversity. Many in the university-trained elite used English as one of the languages in their homes and/or sent their children to preschools that provided a head start in English-language instruction. In addition to English, pidgin has been used as a lingua franca in the south (and in adjoining Cameroon) for more than a century among the nonschool population. In 1990 it was used in popular songs, radio and television dramas, novels, and even newspaper cartoons. In the north, southerners spoke pidgin to one another, but Hausa was the lingua franca of the region and was spreading rapidly as communications and travel provided a need for increased intelligibility. Counting English, the use of which was expanding as rapidly as Hausa, many Nigerians were at least trilingual. This language facility usually included a local vernacular, a wider African lingua franca, and English. Given the long history of trade and markets that stimulated contacts across local ethnic units, multilingualism was a very old and established adaptation. Such multilingualism enabled communication among different ethnic groups in the country.

Regional Groupings

The broadest groupings of linked ethnic units are regional. Britain ruled most of the area of present-day Nigeria as two protectorates from 1900 to 1914, the southern and northern protectorates each having separate regional administrations. These portions were joined finally under a single Nigerian colonial government in 1914. But they retained their regionally based authorities, divided after 1914 into three regional units. The announcement of their imminent demise by the first postcoup military government in 1966 helped to set off violent reactions in the north against southerners who had settled in their midst, contributing to the outbreak of civil war.

Within each of the major northern and southern regions, there were significant subregions that combined ethnicity, geography, and history. What is generally referred to historically as the south included a western Yoruba-speaking area, an eastern Igbo area (the "g" is softly pronounced), a midsection of related but different groups, and a set of Niger Delta peoples on the eastern and central coastal areas. The north was widely associated with the

Hausa-speaking groups that occupied most of the region, but the Kanuri predominated in the northeast, with a belt of peoples between the two. There were also important pastoral nomadic groups (mostly Fulani) that lived throughout the same region. In the middle belt (see Glossary) were congeries of peoples in an area running east-west in the hills, along the southern rim of the north, dividing it from the larger region of Nigeria's south. On its northern side, the middle belt shaded culturally into the Muslim north. In contrast, on the southern side, its peoples were more similar to those of the south.

The Northern Area

The best known of the northern peoples, often spoken of as coterminous with the north, are the Hausa. The term refers also to a language spoken indigenously by savanna peoples spread across the far north from Nigeria's western boundary eastward to Borno State and into much of the territory of southern Niger. The core area lies in the region in the north and northwest where about 30 percent of all Hausa could be found. It also includes a common set of cultural practices and, with some notable exceptions, Islamic emirates that originally comprised a series of centralized governments and their surrounding subject towns and villages.

These precolonial emirates were still major features of local government in 1990. Each had a central citadel town that housed its ruling group of nobles and royalty and served as the administrative, judicial, and military center of these states. Traditionally, the major towns were also trading centers; some such as Kano, Zaria, or Katsina were urban conglomerations with populations of 25,000 to 100,000 in the nineteenth century. They had central markets, special wards for foreign traders, complex organizations of craft specialists, and religious leaders and organizations. They administered a hinterland of subject settlements through a hierarchy of officials, and they interacted with other states and ethnic groups in the region by links of warfare, raiding, trade, tribute, and alliances.

The rural areas remained in 1990 fundamentally small to medium-sized settlements of farmers ranging from 2,000 to 12,000 persons. Both within and spread outward from the settlements, one-third to one-half the population lived in hamlet-sized farm settlements of patrilocal extended families, or *gandu,* an economic kin-based unit under the authority and direction of the household head. Farm production was used for both cash and subsistence, and as many as two-thirds of the adults also engaged in off-farm occupations.

99

Throughout the north, but especially in the Hausa areas, over the past several centuries Fulani cattle-raising nomads have migrated westward, sometimes settling into semisedentary villages. Their relations with local agriculturalists generally involved the symbiotic trading of cattle for agricultural products and access to pasturage. Conflicts arose, however, especially in times of drought or when population built up and interethnic relations created pressures on resources. These pressures peaked at the beginning of the nineteenth century and were contributing factors in a Fulani-led intra-Muslim holy war and the founding of the Sokoto Caliphate (see Usman dan Fodio and the Sokoto Caliphate, ch. 1). Fulani leaders took power over the Hausa states, intermarried with the ruling families and settled into the ruling households of Hausaland and many adjacent societies. By the twentieth century, the ruling elements of Hausaland were often referred to as Hausa-Fulani. Thoroughly assimilated into urban Hausa culture and language but intensely proud of their Fulani heritage, many of the leading ''Hausa'' families in 1990 claimed such mixed origins. In terms of local traditions, this inheritance was expressed as a link to the conquering founders of Sokoto and a zealous commitment to Islamic law and custom.

Centralized government in the urban citadels along the southern rim of the desert has encouraged long-distance trade over the centuries, both across the Sahara and into coastal West Africa after colonial rule moved forcefully to cut the trans-Saharan trade, forcing the north to use Nigerian ports. Ultimately, this action resulted in enclaves of Hausa traders in all major cities of West Africa, linked socially and economically to their home areas.

In summary, Hausa is both an ethnic group and a language; in contemporary usage the term refers primarily to the language. Linked culturally to Islam, Hausa are characterized by centralized emirate governments, Fulani rulers since the early nineteenth century, extended households and agricultural villages, trade and markets, and strong assimilative capacities. For these reasons, Hausa cultural borders have been constantly expanding. Given modern communications, transportation, and the accelerating need for a lingua franca, Hausa was rapidly becoming either the first or second language of the entire northern area of the country.

The other major ethnic grouping of the north is that of the Kanuri of Borno. They entered Nigeria from the central Sahara as Muslim conquerors in the fifteenth century, set up a capital, and subdued and assimilated the local Chadic speakers. By the sixteenth century, they had developed a great empire that at times included many of the Hausa states and large areas of the central Sahara (see

The Savanna States, 1500–1800, ch. 1). Attacked in the nineteenth century by the Fulani, they resisted successfully, although the conflict resulted in a new capital closer to Lake Chad, a new ruling dynasty, and a balance of power between the Hausa-Fulani of the more westerly areas and the Kanuri speakers of the central sub-Saharan rim.

Even though Kanuri language, culture, and history are distinctive, other elements are similar to those of the Hausa. Similar elements include the general ecology of the area, Islamic law and politics, the extended households, and rural-urban distinctions. There was, however, a distinctive Kanuri tradition of a U-shaped town plan open to the west. The town's political leader or founder was housed at the head of the plaza, in an area formed by the arms of the U. The people remained intensely proud of their ancient traditions of Islamic statehood. Among many ancient traits were their long chronicles of kings, wars, and hegemony in the region and their specific Kanuri cultural identity, which was reflected in the hairstyles of the women, the complex cuisine, and the identification with ruling dynasties whose names and exploits were still fresh.

Things have been changing, however. Maiduguri, the central city of Kanuri influence in the twentieth century, was chosen as the capital of an enlarged Northeast State during the civil war. Because this state encompassed large sections of Hausa-Fulani areas, many of these ethnic groups came to the capital. This sudden incorporation, together with mass communications, interstate commerce, and intensification of travel and regional contacts brought increased contacts with Hausa culture. By the 1970s, and increasingly during the 1980s and into the 1990s, Kanuri speakers found it best to get along in Hausa, certainly outside their home region and even inside Borno State. By 1990 women were adopting Hausa dress and hairstyles, and all schoolchildren learned to speak Hausa. Almost all Bornoans in the larger towns could speak Hausa, and many Hausa administrators and businesspeople were settling in Borno. Just as Hausa had incorporated its Fulani conquerors 175 years earlier, in 1990 it was spreading into Borno, assimilating as it went. Its probable eventual triumph as the universal northern language was reinforced by its utility, although the ethnically proud Kanuri would retain much of their language and culture for many years.

Along the border, dividing northern from southern Nigeria lies an east-west belt of peoples and languages, generally known as the middle belt. The area runs from the Cameroon Highlands on the east to the Niger River valley on the west and contains 50 to 100

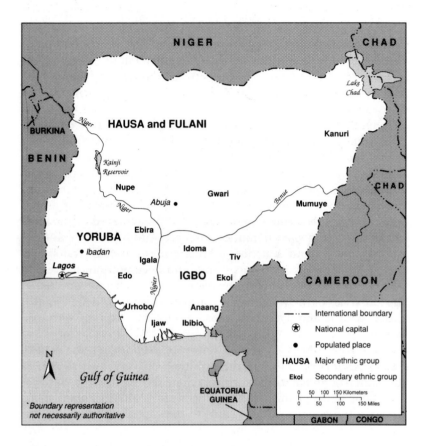

Figure 9. Distribution of Principal Ethnic Groups, 1990

separate language and ethnic groups (see fig. 9). These groups varied from the Nupe and Tiv, comprising more than half a million each, to a few hundred speakers of a distinct language in small highland valleys in the Jos Plateau. On the east, languages were of the Chadic group, out of which Hausa differentiated, and the Niger-Congo family, indicating links to eastern and central African languages. In the west, the language groupings indicated historical relations to Mende-speaking peoples farther west. Cultural and historical evidence supports the conclusion that these western groups were marginal remnants of an earlier substratum of cultures that occupied the entire north before the emergence of large centralized Islamic emirates.

In time three distinct kinds of organized groups emerged. The largest and most centralized groups, such as the Nupe, under colonial administration became smaller versions of the emirates. A few of these peoples, such as the Tiv, were of the classic "segmentary" variety, in which strongly organized patrilineages link large portions of the ethnic group into named nonlocal segments based on real and putative concepts of descent. Local organization, land tenure, inheritance, religious beliefs, law, and allegiances are all related to this sense of segmentary lineage relationship. During the 1960s, some Tiv segments allied with the southern political parties, and others linked with the northern parties. Like the larger groups, they demanded, and by 1960 had been granted, a central "chief" and local administration of their own.

The most common groupings in the middle belt were small localized villages and their outlying hamlets and households; they were autonomous in precolonial times but were absorbed into wider administrative units under British rule. Most often they were patrilineal, with in-marrying wives, sons, unmarried daughters, and possibly parents or parents' siblings living together. Crops separated this residence grouping from similar ones spread out over a small area. They cultivated local fields and prayed to local spirits and the ghosts of departed lineage elders. Descendants of founders were often village heads or priests of the village shrine, whereas leading members of the other lineages formed an eldership that governed the place and a few outlying areas, consisting of those who were moving toward open lands as the population increased.

The missionaries and party politics influenced, but did not obliterate, these older units. Missionaries arrived in the 1910s and 1920s and were allowed into non-Muslim areas. They set up schools using United States or British staff to teach English and helped to create a sense of separateness and educational disparity between the Christianized groups and Muslim ones. From the 1920s to current times, both religions competed for adherents. Political parties representing both southern and northern interests have always found supporters in this border area, making its participation in national life more unpredictable. Attempts in the 1960s and 1970s to create a separate region, or develop a political party representing middle belt peoples, were quickly cauterized by northern Muslim-based political parties whose dominance at the national level could have been weakened by losing administrative control over the middle belt.

At the same time, possibly the greatest influence on the area was that of Hausaization. The emergent dominance of the Hausa language, dress patterns, residential arrangements, and other cultural features was clear as one traveled from the far north into the middle belt area. Local councils that only a few years previously

103

had dressed differently and had spoken in local vernaculars looked and acted in 1990 as if they were parts of more northerly areas. Although Hausaization was weaker in the more remote areas and in Jos, the largest middle belt city, it was progressing rapidly everywhere else and constituted a unifying factor throughout the region.

The Southern Area

In general, the southern groups of peoples are fragmented. In 1990 the two most important groupings were the Igbo and the Yoruba—both linguistic communities rather than single ethnic units. History, language, and membership in the modern nation-state, however, had led to their identity as ethnic groups. In addition, although not as clearly differentiated, two subunits had strong traditions of ethnic separateness. These were the peoples of the Niger River delta area and those on the border between the Igbo and Yoruba.

Yorubaland takes in most of southwestern Nigeria and the peoples directly west of the Nigerian border in the independent country of Benin. In Nigeria alone, Yorubaland included 20 million to 30 million people in 1990 (about double the 1963 census figures). Each of its subunits was originally a small to medium-sized state whose major town provided the name of the subgrouping. Over time seven subareas—Oyo, Kabba, Ekiti, Egba, Ife, Ondo, and Ijebu—became separate hegemonies that differentiated culturally and competed for dominance in Yorubaland. Early nineteenth-century travelers noted that northern Oyo people had difficulty understanding the southern Ijebu, and these dialect differences remained in 1990. The language is that of the Kwa group of the Niger-Congo family, related to the Idoma and Igala of the southern grouping of middle belt chieftaincies south of the Benue River. The population has expanded in a generally westerly and southwesterly direction over the past several centuries. In the twentieth century, this migration brought Yoruba into countries to the west and northwest as far as northern Ghana.

The Yoruba kingdoms were essentially unstable, even when defended by Portuguese guns and later by cavalry (in Ilorin and Kabba), because the central government had insufficient power constitutionally or militarily to stabilize the subordinate chiefs in the outlying centers. This separatist tendency has governed Yoruba contemporary history and has weakened traditional rulers and strengthened the hands of local chiefs and elected councils. Ilorin, like Nupe to the north, was an exception, an extension of Fulani imperial expansion; in 1990 it was ethnically Yoruba, yet more closely allied through its traditional rulers to the Islamic societies to the north. It thus formed a bridge between north and south.

The region has had the longest and most penetrating contacts with the outside world of any area in Nigeria. Returned Yoruba slaves, the early nineteenth-century establishment of the Anglican Church, and Yoruba churchmen, such as Bishop Samuel Adjai Crowther (active in the 1820s), made the region's religious life, its formal education, and its elites among the most Westernized in the country (see Christianity, this ch.). The first university, founded in 1948, was at Ibadan in the heart of Yorubaland, as were the first elite secondary schools; the first research institutes for agriculture, economics, African studies, and foreign affairs; the first publishing houses; and the first radio and television stations. Wole Soyinka, Africa's first Nobel prizewinner in literature, claims Yoruba ethnicity. The entry port of Lagos, predominantly Yoruba, is the largest and economically dominant city in the country (and its first capital).

In relation to other Nigerian peoples, the Yoruba have a strong sense of ethnic identity and of region, history, and leadership. In relation to each other, the seven subgroups have inherited prejudices and behavior that could exacerbate animosities should other factors such as access to education or prominent positions create conflict among the subdivisions. At the same time, the longer contacts of the Yoruba with Westernizing influences have created some dedicated nationalists who see their Yoruba identity as a contributing factor in their loyalty to the wider concept of a Nigerian nation-state.

The other major group of the south are the Igbo. The Igbo are found primarily in the southeast and speak a Kwa language of the Niger-Congo family. This language ties them, historically, to regions east and south of their contemporary locations. In 1990 it was hard to find any major town in Nigeria without an Igbo minority, often in an ethnic enclave. As communities they have traditionally been segmented into more than 200 named groupings, each originally a locally autonomous polity. These groupings vary from a single village to as many as two or three dozen nucleated settlements that over time have expanded outward from an original core town. Most of these central villages ranged from 1,000 to 3,000 persons in the nineteenth century. In 1990 they were as much as five to ten times larger, making severe land shortages and overused farmland a widespread problem. Precolonial trade up the Niger River from the coast stimulated the early development of a few larger towns, such as Onitsha, that in 1990 contained a population of several hundred thousand. Igbo culture, however, unlike the emirates and the Yoruba city-states, does not count urban living among the traditional ways of life.

For the Igbo as an ethnic group, personal advancement and participation in local affairs are matters of individual initiative and skill. Villages are run by a council of the most respected elders of the locality. Colonial administration created local headmen, or "warrant chiefs," who were never fully accepted and were finally replaced by locally elected councils.

This development does not mean that Igbo culture is exclusively dedicated to egalitarianism. Rank and wealth differences have been part of the society from early times and have been highly prized. Success, eldership, wealth, a good modern education, political power, and influence have all been recognized as ways by which people, especially adult males, could distinguish themselves. As with all Nigerian societies, Igbo life is complex, and the organization of local and regional society is stratified into more and less affluent and successful groups, families, individuals, and even neighborhoods. Graduates of secondary schools form "old boy associations," some of which have as members wealthy men linked to one another as local boosters and mutual supporters. Comparatively speaking, Igbo are most unlike other Nigerians in their strong positive evaluation of open competition for success. Children are encouraged to succeed; if they do so skillfully, rewards of high status await them. It is no accident that the first American-style land-grant university, linked for guidance during its founding to Michigan State University, was at Nsukka in Igboland, whereas the first universities in Yorubaland and in the north looked to Britain and its elitist traditions of higher education for their models of university life.

Psychological tests of "achievement motivation" that measure American-style individual competitiveness against standards of excellence given to comparable Nigerian groups resulted in Igbo people placing highest, followed by Yoruba, and then Hausa. This stress on individual achievement has made Igbo people seem "pushy" to fellow Nigerians, whose own ethnic traditions foster individual contributions to collective achievements within close-knit kin and patron-client groups that are more hierarchically arranged. In these latter groups, achievements are obtained through loyalty, disciplined membership in a large organization, and social skills that employ such memberships for personal advancement.

The impressive openness of Igbo culture is what first strikes the outsider, but closer inspection produces several caveats. Besides differences of wealth and rank achieved in one's lifetime or inherited, there is a much older tendency for people who trace their descent from the original settler-founders of a village to have higher status as "owners of the land." Generally, they provide the men who act as priests of the local shrines, and often they provide more local leaders than descendants of later arrivals. At the other end of the scale are known descendants of people, especially women, who were originally slaves. They are akin to Indian "untouchables," low in status and avoided as marriage partners.

As with all Nigerian ethnic groups, there are internal divisions. Generally, these have to do with town area of origin. More northerly areas have had a feeling of separateness, as do larger towns along the Niger River. Beyond Igboland, people from the region are treated as a single unit, live in separate enclaves, and even face restrictions against ownership of local property in some northern towns. Once they had suffered and fought together in the civil war of Biafran secession in the 1960s, these people developed a much stronger sense of Igbo identity that has since been expressed politically. Nevertheless, localized distinctions remain and in 1990 were significant internally.

The peoples of the Atlantic Coast and the Niger River delta are linguistically and culturally related to the Igbo. But the ecological demands of coastal life and the separate history of contact with coastal trade and its effects have produced ethnic differences that are strong enough to have made these people resist the Biafra secession movement when it was promulgated by Igbo leadership. Ijaw, Ibibio, Anang, and Efik live partly from agriculture and partly from fishing and shrimping in the coastal waters. Religion, social organization, village life, local leadership, and gender relations have been deeply affected by this ecology-based differentiation. Although there has been a natural and historical pull of migration to Lagos, especially by young Ijaw men who went to the city to find work and send home remittances, the area boasts its own coastal town of Port Harcourt in Efik country that is, in a sense, the headquarters of this subgrouping.

To a lesser extent, the peoples of the western bank of the Niger River—and the western delta—especially the Bini speakers and Urhobo—are culturally close to those around them but have a sufficient sense of linguistic and historical separateness to see themselves as unique. These differences have been partly buttressed by the past glory of the kingdom of Benin, of which a much diminished remnant survived in 1990. Benin had been used to provide the south first with an extra region, then with extra states when the regional level of government was abandoned in 1967.

Ethnic Relations

Relations between ethnic groups remained a major problem for such a large and pluralistic society in 1990. In precolonial times, interethnic relations were often mistrustful, or discriminatory, and sometimes violent. At the same time, there were relationships, such as trade, that required peaceful communications. The most widespread communication was in the north between pastoral and agricultural peoples, who traded cattle for farm products and pasturage rights for manuring. Farmers might also buy a few cattle and have them cared for by pastoralists. Emirate rulers who normally raided and pillaged among non-Muslim village groups often established peaceful ''trust'' relations with residents of one or two villages; those residents then acted as hosts and guides for the raiders in exchange for immunity for themselves. More subtle and peaceful exchanges involved smaller ethnic groups in the middle belt, each of which specialized in one or more commodities. In towns and along trade routes, occupations such as smithing, producing cotton, selling cattle, weaving, house building, and beer making were often confined to, or correlated with, ethnically defined units. Thus, ecological and economic specializations promoted peaceful interethnic relations. Conversely, promulgating conflict, mistrust, and stereotypes in ethnic relations were droughts; competition for control over trade routes or allies; resistance to, or the creation and maintenance of, exploitative relations; and other factors.

The civil war taught Nigerians that ethnic conflicts were among the most destructive forces in the life of the nation. By 1990 ethnic conflict was suppressed and carefully controlled so that any outbreak or seriously publicized discrimination on ethnic grounds was considered a matter of national security. In the few outbreaks that had occurred since the war, the federal government acted swiftly to gain control and stop the conflict. Nevertheless, the way in which ethnic relations might threaten the security of individuals and groups was one of the most serious issues in national life, especially for the millions of Nigerians who had to live and work in interethnic contexts.

Even in the more cosmopolitan cities, in 1990 more than 90 percent of marriages were within rather than between ethnic units, or at least within identical regions and language groups. Marriages between subgroups of Igbo, Yoruba, Hausa, Fulani, or Kanuri occurred without stigma and had done so for many decades. But in the south, Yoruba-Igbo unions were uncommon, and north-south marriages were even rarer, especially between Hausa-Fulani or Kanuri and any person from southern Nigeria. Northern Muslim intermarriage was not uncommon, nor was intermarriage among peoples of the middle belt. But unions between middle belters and Muslims from emirates farther north remained rare. Migrants who could not find a spouse from their own ethnic group within the

Village elder from Gusau in highlands of eastern Nigeria
Courtesy World Bank (Josef Hadad)

local enclave obtained a mate from the home community. Social pressure for ethnic endogamy was intense and persisted even among elites in business, universities, the military, religion, and politics. In the late 1980s and early 1990s, however, it appeared that marriages within the Christian and Muslim communities were increasingly transethnic.

The conjunction of location, language, religion, and common and differentiating customs has created a strong sense of shared fate among coethnics and has formed a constant basis for organizing ethnically related groupings into political constituencies. Thus, when political parties emerged, they represented the northern Muslim peoples, the Yoruba, and the Igbo; middle belters and others in between were courted from several directions (see The Second Republic, ch. 4). Given the shortage of government jobs and the expanding numbers of qualified applicants coming out of the education system, ethnic rivalry for government posts exacerbated ethnic competition. It was also a driving force in the establishment of more states, with more state capitals and more locally controlled jobs. Such jobs were likely to be less competitive ethnically because the boundaries of local governments tended to correlate with ethnic units. Under such conditions, would-be leaders stimulated the fears of their ethnic constituents. Ethnic organizations and university students wrote letters to newspapers pressuring for greater representation, more development resources, and separate states or districts for their particular group. Countering this practice, after the civil war the new constitution of 1979 provided that no political party could be legalized unless it obtained support in all parts of the country. This attempt to crosscut ethnicity with rules of political party competition has gone far toward alleviating the problem.

People first looked for relatives when migrating into one of the country's many large cities, as an increasing number of Nigerians were doing. If they found none, they looked for coethnics from their own rural area who shared a network of friends, neighbors, and relations. They spoke the same language, went to the same church or mosque and helped one another to find a job and housing and to join ethnic associations. In the textile mills of Kaduna in the north, studies of "class formation" among workers indicated that ethnic groupings were far stronger and used more frequently by workers than were trade unions, unless working conditions became extremely bad. It was only then that union membership, interaction, strength, and unity rose. Otherwise, ethnicity was the primary dimension for worker relations and mutual aid. Studies elsewhere in the country produced similar results. The trade union movement in Nigeria was well established and strong, especially at times of severe economic downturn, such as the late 1980s and early 1990s, when the structural adjustment program (SAP) severely decreased real wages (see Labor Unions; Structural Adjustment, ch. 3). Rivalry within unions, however, and worker associations for mutual aid, as well as normal social life at work and afterward, were strongly influenced by formal and informal ethnic affiliations. Ethnic stereotypes remained strong. Each of the main groups had disparaging stories and sayings about the others that were discussed openly when a foreigner was alone with members of a single ethnic group. Such prejudices died slowly, especially when ethnic groups lived in enclaves, knew little of each other's customs, and often attended different schools. It was official policy, however, to protect the rights of minorities, and in several instances the will to do so was ably demonstrated. Thus, Igbo property abandoned in the north at the time of the civil war was maintained by local governments and later returned. Although there were problems, this property restitution, the attempt to ensure that Igbo were accepted at all major universities, and the placement of Igbo in civil service posts has helped to create a sense of nationhood and trust in the rule of law and in the good intentions of the federal government.

Contemporary Society

Nigerian history has provided an extraordinary set of pressures and events as a context for modern nation building: the imposition of colonial rule, independence, interethnic and interregional competition or even violence, military coups, a civil war, an oil boom that had government and individuals spending recklessly and often with corrupt intentions, droughts, and a debt crisis that led to a drastic recession and lowered standards of living. Under such circumstances, people tended to cleave to what they knew. That is to say, they adhered to regional loyalties, ethnicity, kin, and to patron-client relations that protected them in an unstable and insecure environment. Meanwhile, other factors and processes stimulated by education, jobs, politics, and urban and industrial development created crosscutting ties that linked people in new, more broadly national ways.

By 1990 both sets of distinctions operated at once and gave no sign of weakening. For example, from time to time labor unions were able to call widespread, even general, strikes. At other times, unorganized workers or farmers rioted over long-held or sudden grievances. Nevertheless, attempts to create national movements or political parties out of such momentary flare-ups failed. Instead, once the outburst was over, older linkages reasserted themselves.

111

In effect, the structure of society in 1990 was the result of these two processes—historical, locational, and ethnic on the one hand and socioeconomic on the other. In Nigeria the latter context referred primarily to occupation, rural-urban residence, and formal education. Together these factors accounted for similarities and differences that were common across ethnic and regional groupings.

Social Structure

About 70 percent of all Nigerians were still living in farming villages in 1990, although the rural dwellers formed a shrinking proportion of the labor force. It was among these people that ways of life remained deeply consistent with the past. People lived in small, modest households whose members farmed, sold some cash crops, and performed various kinds of nonfarm work for cash income. With the steady decline of export crop prices since the 1960s and the price rise in locally grown foods after the early 1970s, farmers shifted from export crops to local foods for their own subsistence and for sale to city consumers through middlemen. Most farmers used traditional hand tools in smallholdings outside the rural village. Houses in 1990 might have tin roofs instead of grass, and the village water supply might be a standpipe, or a hand pump. New practices included the widespread acceptance of fertilizers; a few new crops, especially corn; the use of rented tractors; the increased dependence on paid labor; and the development of larger commercial farms. Absentee city-based farmers also had started to buy up agricultural land.

Paved roads, better marketing procedures, and increased extension services in 1990 were producing a change in the rural areas that was missing during the first decades of independence. Surveys indicated that improved transportation (paved or dirt roads and cheap, private minibus services) was felt to be the most important change, bringing almost all rural areas into touch with nearby cities and larger market towns. Still, for most of the 70 to 80 percent of the people who remained involved in agriculture, life was hard, and income levels averaged among the lowest in the country.

Western-style education was a necessary, albeit not always sufficient, means to gain better income and rank. Under colonial rule, literacy and educational qualifications were required for access to more powerful, better paying jobs. Education in 1990 was one of the most widely accepted criteria for job recruitment. Older education systems, especially in the Islamic north, had always produced clerics and judges and some training for the populace. Long years of Quranic learning continued to give one high status in religious occupations, but to qualify for secular jobs in the upper salary scale required at least secondary and, increasingly, postsecondary schooling. Most rural families tried to get at least one child through six years of elementary school and into secondary school, if possible. In the cities, if a family had any stable income, all of the children attended school, tried for secondary level and even went on to university or other postsecondary education if the youngsters could successfully compete for places. For the wealthy, there were private preschools in all major cities that provided a head start in academic work and private boarding schools that generally followed the British model (see Education, this ch.).

By the 1980s, the education system was turning out an increasing surplus of graduates. Dozens of university graduates lined up for a single opening and many more for less specialized positions. Under such conditions, nepotism, ethnic favoritism, and bribery flourished in employment decisions.

Education requirements for work were known and widely discussed. Job descriptions for government posts, commercial companies, and even factory work required set levels of schooling for applicants. Large factories and international corporations had training programs for future managers. In the 1980s, however, the vast majority of workers still learned their skills from the family or on the job. Outside the home, systems of apprenticeship produced cheap labor for the teacher and gave the trainee skills, along with a potential future network of customers or employers. Thus, truck drivers took on trainees, who worked as apprentice-assistants and general laborers for several years before they took a license test and hired out as drivers themselves. During that time, they learned about roads, maps, truck parks, markets, and vehicle servicing; they became acquainted with customers and vehicle owners, who in turn learned about their trustworthiness and efficiency.

In contemporary Nigeria as elsewhere, occupation differentiated people, incomes, and life-styles. In rural areas, smallholder farmers were the rule, but farmers often had a nonfarm occupation in order to produce income during the nongrowing season. The size of the farm depended on family size, farming skills, inherited wealth, and access to nonfarm income to provide money for laborers. Some nonfarm work, such as trade, was prestigious; some, such as butchering, was less so. The most prestigious work in rural areas was in public administration, either as local traditional headmen and chiefs or as rural representatives of government departments—such as teachers, district officers, veterinarians, extension workers, public works foremen, postal officials, and the like. Such offices required formal educational qualifications. The offices offered steady salaries and the possibility of government housing, or housing and vehicle allowances. Unlike farming, such work also meant protection against the vagaries of climate and economic conditions. This situation lasted well into the late 1980s, at which point inflation, recession, and government cutbacks destroyed these advantages.

In 1990 a growing number of medium-sized towns (with more than 10,000 people) were spreading out across the country. They contained branch banks; branches of larger urban-based trading companies; smaller stores; and trade, building, and transport enterprises whose owner-managers formed a rural middle class of semiurbanized households. Often such individuals owned and operated nearby commercial farms as part of their diversified business interests. Their incomes were higher than those of usual farm families; their education level was quite low, ranging up to completion of primary school; and they were often active as local political party representatives with links to more important men and organizations in nearby cities.

In a number of special situations, the government had invested in a rural area, creating peri-urban conditions surrounding a large town. Government involvement might result in a state university or a large irrigation project, for example, or, on a smaller scale, the building of a secondary school that had been sited with appropriate housing, electrification, and transportation links to a nearby urban center. In some instances, such as the Tiga Dam in Kano State or the massive irrigation project on Lake Chad, entire communities had sprung up to provide housing for the technical staff; new schools and markets also were built to meet the increased consumer needs of the farmers whose incomes rose as the project went into production.

Because of high inflation and sluggish salary increases throughout the 1980s and into 1990, rural officials were obliged to moonlight, usually by farming, to maintain real wage levels. Extension workers had been observed spending their days in a nearby city on a second job and carrying out visits to farmers in the evenings and on weekends. The wives of officials set up poultry sheds behind their houses and raised chickens and eggs for local and nearby city markets. By contrast, traditional chiefs, who had less formal education and often received much lower salaries than government representatives, were able to sell services, especially access to land purchases; to adjudicate disputes; and to keep a small portion of taxes. This shadowy income allowed them to maintain or even increase consumption levels more easily and set the pattern for the sale of public services that was quickly picked up by other officials

Migration of Fulani people in northern Nigeria
Courtesy Embassy of Nigeria, Washington

living in rural areas. In the late 1980s, these well-established "corrupt" practices were viewed widely as essential for rural officials because real incomes had fallen so drastically.

In the cities, occupations were highly differentiated. Unskilled traditional work was more common in the northern cities but not yet extinct in southern areas. Unskilled workers in the traditional sector included water carriers, servants, women and young girls selling cooked foods on the streets, and hawkers of all kinds linked to patrons who supplied them and took part of the proceeds. The move to cities involved vast numbers of unemployed, who sought any type of work. In the modern sector, the unskilled were taken on by manufacturing plants, wholesale or retail establishments, hotels, and government departments. Such people lived in crowded rented rooms, often several families in a room with a curtain down the middle. They cooked in a common courtyard and used a latrine that might serve a number of families; the compound might or might not have a source of water. They barely managed even when their wives and children also sought work daily.

Lower-level skilled workers in the traditional sector were employed in house building and a variety of crafts from pottery to iron and brass smithing, leather work, tanning, and butchery. They generally had better incomes, lived in several rooms or even a small house or compound, practiced their craft in the household itself, and sent children to school. Their counterparts in the modern sector were clerks, store attendants, mechanics, carpenters, and factory workers who had some schooling and had managed to get into the lower levels of the wage system. The two groups often lived in the same neighborhoods, although the education of those in the modern sector set them somewhat apart. Their incomes, however, provided them with similar amenities: a standpipe for household water; electricity; a latrine or even a flush toilet; a bicycle or motor scooter, or a motorcycle for the slightly better off; a radio; and, for a few, a small black and white television set and a bank account. Such households often had an extra kin member or two from the country who had come to seek their fortunes.

The middle-level income groups in traditional jobs consisted of higher-level skilled workers and entrepreneurs. They included dye pit owners with a small work force, middlemen who with financing from larger traders bought food and export crops in rural areas for sale and storage in the cities, and wholesalers and retailers of traditional goods and services, as well as transporters of such items as kola nuts, craft goods, specialty crops, and cattle for sale in southern markets. This group was larger in the north than the south because of the larger traditional economic sector in the region. Skilled workers in the modern sector ranged from machine operators and skilled craftsmen to accountants; teachers; lower-level managers of service stations; small to medium-sized storekeepers, who owned or rented and operated a canteen; owners of a truck or two, or of a small minibus used as transport for people and goods; and workers in the middle ranks of the vast public services that, until the shrinkage of the 1980s, accounted for more than half of the salaried jobs in Nigeria.

This group lived in small to medium-sized houses with Western-style furniture, a refrigerator, and electronic receivers; the better-off had color television sets. Housing was sometimes owned by the worker but more often rented. Younger members had motorcycles; more mature ones, cars; and entrepreneurs, a pickup truck. Modern-sector middle-level people generally had some secondary education, which allowed them to spend time filling out applications and to dream of someday attending a university or other postsecondary institution to qualify for higher paid jobs.

At the middle-income level, a number of factors began to separate traditional and modern households. Traditional work did not demand literacy in English, but most jobs at the modern middle level did. The amount of Western-style education and acculturation to more international tastes affected the life-styles of modern-sector workers, although ethnicity, kin, and possible patrons in the more traditional sector meant that connections were not severed. At the same time, both groups had connections upward and downward in both the city and rural areas. For members of the traditional middle group, this meant the possibility of someday becoming wealthier and diversifying their economic activities; for members of the modern group, it most often meant more education, better jobs, and, ideally, entry into the elite level of society in either the public or the private sector. By the late 1980s, a number of middle-income workers and small businessmen in both north and south were putting greater effort into farming in natal or nearby villages, as food prices escalated in the cities and as government policies favored the private acquisition of land and provided farm credits to would-be commercial farmers.

Above the middle rank were the elites. Traditional chiefs in the south had been losing power to business and government leaders for decades. In 1990 they still received respect and officiated at ceremonial occasions, but unless they had taken positions in business or government, their status declined. This situation was less true in the north, where emirs and other titled officials continued to have considerable power and authority. Even there, however, the modern sector produced city and township governments that were eroding the power of local officials. State governments were becoming more important as centralized federal functions carried out by parastatals were being sold off to the private business sector during the 1980s. In the rural areas of the north, however, traditional district and village chiefs remained influential. In the modern sector, public service jobs and incoming top management in corporations required university degrees. Wealthy business leaders might lack formal education, although more and more business leaders, especially in the south, were university graduates. Entry-level salaries for elite jobs were fifteen to twenty times those of the bottom salary scale (compared with two to three times in more developed economies). Added to the basic salary was hidden income in the form of car loans and allowances. Housing often was subsidized to such an extent that only 7 percent of salary was charged for rents and maintenance was free. Housing for holders of elite jobs was generally of the standard of the middle class in a developed country, but ranged up to huge mansions in exclusive housing estates for the very rich.

In the late 1980s, inflation and wage controls had drastically eroded the incomes of the salaried elites, and, in most cases, they had to moonlight in the private sector through farming, trade, consultancy, or business. It was not unusual to find a professor's campus

117

garage used as a warehouse for his trucks and the equipment used in his construction business; behind his house might be pens where his wife conducted a poultry business. Others sought to emigrate, especially highly skilled people, such as doctors, lawyers, and professors, who realized that they could do much better abroad. The sudden decline in the income of the elites resulted from Nigeria's belt-tightening policies. Business people, especially those in trade, were less affected by inflation, but the recessionary effects of the SAP had cut into their incomes, as well, by lowering demand or by controlling imports and exports more tightly. By the late 1980s, many of the elite and even the middle classes were being obliged to adjust to a lower standard of living.

Women's Roles

As with other aspects of society, in the early 1990s women's roles were primarily governed by regional and ethnic differences. In the north, Islamic practices were still common. This process meant, generally, less formal education; early teenage marriages, especially in rural areas; and confinement to the household, which was often polygynous, except for visits to kin, ceremonies, and the workplace, if employment were available and permitted by a girl's family or husband. For the most part, Hausa women did not work in the fields, whereas Kanuri women did; both helped with harvesting and were responsible for all household food processing. Urban women sold cooked foods, usually by sending young girls out onto the streets or operating small stands. Research indicated that this practice was one of the main reasons city women gave for opposing schooling for their daughters. Even in elite houses with educated wives, women's presence at social gatherings was either nonexistent or very restricted. In the modern sector, a few women were appearing at all levels in offices, banks, social services, nursing, radio, television, and the professions (teaching, engineering, environmental design, law, pharmacy, medicine, and even agriculture and veterinary medicine). This trend resulted from women's attendance at women's secondary schools and teachers' colleges, and in the 1980s from women holding approximately one-fifth of university places—double the proportion of the 1970s. Research in the 1980s indicated that, for the Muslim north, education beyond primary school was restricted to the daughters of the business and professional elites, and in almost all cases, courses and professions were chosen by the family, not the women themselves.

In the south, women traditionally had held economically important positions in interregional trade and the markets, had worked on farms as major labor sources, and had had influential positions

A family preparing gari, *cassava porridge*
Courtesy UNICEF (Maggie Black)

in traditional systems of local organization. The south, like the
north, however, had been polygynous; in 1990 it still was for many
households, including those professing Christianity. Women in the
south, especially among the Yoruba peoples, had received Western-
style education since the nineteenth century, and hence they occupied positions in the professions and to some extent in politics. In
addition, women headed households, something not seriously considered in Nigeria's development plans. Such households were more
numerous in the south, but they were on the rise everywhere.

Generally, Nigerian development planning referred to "adult
males," "households," or "families." Women were included in
such units but not as a separate category. Up until the 1980s, the
term "farmer" was assumed to be exclusively male, even though
in some areas of the south women did most of the farm work. In
Nigerian terms, a woman was almost always defined as someone's
daughter, wife, mother, or widow. Single women were suspect,
although they constituted a large category, especially in the cities,
because of the high divorce rate. Traditionally, and to some extent this remained true in popular culture, single adult women were
seen as available sexual partners should they try for some independence and as easy victims for economic exploitation. In Kaduna
State, for example, investigations into illegal land expropriations

119

noted that women's farms were confiscated almost unthinkingly by local chiefs wishing to sell to urban-based speculators and would-be commercial farmers.

A national feminist movement was inaugurated in 1982, and a national conference held at Ahmadu Bello University. The papers presented there indicated a growing awareness by Nigeria's university-educated women that the place of women in society required a concerted effort and a place on the national agenda; the public perception, however, remained far behind. For example, a feminist meeting in Ibadan came out against polygyny and then was soundly criticized by market women, who said they supported the practice because it allowed them to pursue their trading activities and have the household looked after at the same time. Research in the north, however, indicated that many women opposed the practice and tried to keep bearing children to stave off a second wife's entry into the household. Although women's status would undoubtedly rise, for the foreseeable future Nigerian women lacked the opportunities of men.

Religion

Several religions coexisted in Nigeria, helping to accentuate regional and ethnic distinctions. All religions represented in Nigeria were practiced in every major city in 1990. But Islam dominated in the north, Protestantism and local syncretic Christianity were most in evidence in Yoruba areas, and Catholicism predominated in the Igbo and closely related areas. The 1963 census indicated that 47 percent of Nigerians were Muslim, 35 percent Christian, and 18 percent members of local indigenous congregations. If accurate, these figures indicated a sharp increase in the number of Christians (up 13 percent); a slight decline among those professing indigenous beliefs, compared with 20 percent in 1953; and only a modest (4 percent) rise of Muslims. This surge was partly a result of the recognized value of education provided by the missions, especially in the previously non-Christian middle belt. It also resulted from 1963 census irregularities that artificially increased the proportion of southern Christians to northern Muslims. Since then two more forces have been operating. There has been the growth of the Aladura Church, an Africanized Christian sect that was especially strong in the Yoruba areas, and of evangelical churches, in general, spilling over into adjacent and southern areas of the middle belt. At the same time, Islam has been spreading southward into the northern reaches of the middle belt, especially among the upwardly mobile, who saw it as a necessary attribute for full acceptance in northern business and political circles. In general, however, the country should be seen as having a predominantly Muslim north and a non-Muslim, primarily Christian south, with each as a minority faith in the other's region; the middle belt was more heterogeneous.

Indigenous Beliefs

Alongside most Nigerian religious beliefs were systems of belief that had ancient roots in the area. These beliefs tied family ghosts to the primordial spirits of a particular site. In effect the rights of a group defined by common genealogical descent were linked to a particular place and the settlements within it. The primary function of such beliefs was to provide supernatural sanctions and legitimacy to the relationship between, and the regulations governing, claims on resources, especially agricultural land and house sites. Access rights to resources, political offices, economic activities, or social relations were defined and legitimized by these same religious beliefs.

The theology expressing and protecting these relationships centered, first, on the souls of the recently dead, ghosts who continued their interest in the living as they had when they were alive. That is to say, authoritative elders demanded conformity to rules governing access to, and inheritance of, rights to resources. Indigenous theology also comprised all of the duties of the living to one another and to their customs, including their obligations to the dead ancestors whose spirits demanded adherence to the moral rules governing all human actions. The second pantheon were the supernatural residents of the land. These spirits of place (trees, rock outcroppings, a river, snakes, or other animals and objects) were discovered and placated by the original founders, who had migrated to the new site from a previous one. Spirits of the land might vary with each place or be so closely identified with a group's welfare that they were carried to a new place as part of the continuity of a group to its former home. In the new place, these spiritual migrants joined the local spirit population. Such deities developed from an original covenant created by the founders of a settlement between themselves and the local spirits. This covenant legitimized their arrival. In return for regular rites and prayers to these spirits, the founders could claim perpetual access to local resources. In doing so, they became the lineage in charge of the hereditary local priesthood and village headship and were recognized as "owners of the place" by later human arrivals. Both sets of spirits, those of family and those of place, demanded loyalty to communal virtues and to the authority of the elders in defending ancient beliefs and practices.

121

In addition to ensuring access to, and the continual fertility of, both land and people, the spiritual entities protected their adherents from misfortune, adjudicated disputes through trials by ordeal or through messages divined by special seers, and punished personal or communal immorality through personal and group failures, sickness, drought, fires, and other catastrophes. Special practitioners were in control of supernatural forces to heal illnesses, counter malevolent intentions by others and the ghostly entities, and diagnose witchcraft—the effects of malefactors whose personal spirits might cause harm, sometimes without the actual knowledge of the evildoer. Protection against misfortune was strengthened by charms, amulets, and medicinal products sold by the practitioners. In everyday life, misfortune, sickness, political rivalries, inheritance disputes, and even marital choices or the clearing of a new field could be incorporated and explained within this religious framework. Given these beliefs, causal relations were stipulated and explained through the actions of supernatural entities, whose relations to the living involved interventions that enforced morality and traditional values.

As with many peoples around the world, especially in Africa, the adult men were organized into secret societies that imitated the activity of the spirits in maintaining the moral order. In the 1980s in Igboland and in similar societies in neighboring areas, social control and conformity to moral order was still enforced by secret societies. In the 1970s, this pattern was observed spreading into small, originally autonomous communities of the southern middle belt at the northern rim of Igboland. Generally, adult men received some training and were then initiated into membership. In 1990 memberships were more selective, and in some places such organizations had died out. Specifically, these societies enforced community morality through rituals and masked dances. During these performances, secret society members imitated the spirits. They preached and expressed displeasure with and gave warnings about individual and communal morality, attributing accusations and threats to spirits of place and family who were displeased with their human charges.

Sorcery and even witchcraft beliefs persisted and were discussed as forms of medicine, or as coming from "bad people" whose spirits or souls were diagnosed as the cause of misfortune. There also were special ways in which the outcomes of stressful future activity, long trips, lingering illnesses, family and other problems could be examined. Soothsayers provided both therapy and divinatory foreknowledge in stressful situations.

In the city-states of Yorubaland and its neighbors, a more complex religion evolved that expressed the subjugation of village life within larger polities. These city-states produced a theology that linked local beliefs to a central citadel government and its sovereignty over a hinterland of villages through the monarch. The king (*oba*) and his ancestors were responsible for the welfare of the entire state, in return for confirmation of the legitimacy of the *oba*'s rule over his subjects (see Early States Before 1500, ch. 1). In Oyo, for example, there were a number of national cults, each with its own priests who performed rituals under the authority of the king (*alafin*) in the public interest. Shango, god of thunder, symbolized the power of the king and of central government; Ogboni represented the fertility of the land and the monarch's role in ensuring the well-being of the kingdom.

In 1990 these indigenous beliefs were more or less openly practiced and adhered to among many Christians and Muslims in various parts of the country. Thus, in a number of the northern Muslim emirates, the emir led prayers for the welfare of the state at the graves of royal ancestors. In many Muslim and Christian households and villages, a number of the older religious practices and beliefs also survived. On the other hand, research indicated that many, especially younger people, believed the older traditions to be apostasy so that it was common, particularly in rural areas, to see mixtures of local beliefs with either Christianity or Islam. And in some instances, although the overall trend was away from indigenous religions and toward monotheism, older people suffered such mental and physical anguish over denouncing inherited beliefs that they abandoned the newer one.

Islam

Islam is a traditional religion in West Africa. It came to northern Nigeria as early as the eleventh century and was well established in the state capitals of the region by the sixteenth century, spreading into the countryside and toward the middle belt uplands. There, Islam's advance was stopped by the resistance of local peoples to incorporation into the emirate states. The Fulani-led jihad in the nineteenth century pushed Islam into Nupe and across the Niger River into northern Yoruba-speaking areas. The colonial conquest established a rule that active Christian proselytizing could not occur in the northern Muslim region, although in 1990 the two religions continued to compete for converts in the middle belt, where ethnic groups and even families had adherents of each persuasion.

The origins of Islam date to Muhammad (the Prophet), a prosperous merchant of the town of Mecca in Arabia. He began in A.D. 610 to preach the first of a series of revelations granted him by God (Allah) through the agency of the archangel Gabriel. The divine messages, received during solitary visits into the desert, continued during the remainder of his life.

Muhammad denounced the polytheistic paganism of his fellow Meccans; his vigorous and continuing censure ultimately earned him their bitter enmity. In 622 he and a group of followers accepted an invitation to settle in Yathrib, which became known as Medina (the city) through its association with him. The hijra (known in the West as the hegira), or journey to Medina, marked the beginning of the Islamic calendar in the year 622. In Medina Muhammad continued his preaching, ultimately defeated his detractors in battle, and had consolidated the temporal as well as spiritual leadership of most Arabs before his death in 632.

After Muhammad's death, his followers compiled his words that were regarded as coming directly from God in a document known as the Quran, the holy scripture of Islam. Other sayings and teachings of the Prophet, as well as the precedents of his personal behavior as recalled by those who had known him, became the hadith (''sayings''). From these sources, the faithful have constructed the Prophet's customary practice, or sunna, which they endeavor to emulate. Together, these documents form a comprehensive guide to the spiritual, ethical, and social life of the faithful in most Muslim countries.

The *shahada* (profession of faith, or testimony) states succinctly the central belief, ''There is no God but Allah, and Muhammad is his Prophet.'' The faithful repeat this simple profession on ritual occasions, and its recital designates the speaker as a Muslim. The term *islam* means submission to God, and the one who submits is a Muslim.

The God preached by Muhammad was previously known to his countrymen, for *Allah* is the general Arabic term for the supreme being rather than the name of a particular deity. Rather than introducing a new deity, Muhammad denied the existence of the pantheon of gods and spirits worshipped before his prophethood and declared the omnipotence of God, the unique creator. Muhammad is the ''Seal of the Prophets,'' the last of the prophetic line. His revelations are said to complete for all time the series of revelations that had been given earlier to Jews and Christians. God is believed to have remained one and the same throughout time, but humans are seen as having misunderstood or strayed from God's true teachings until set aright by Muhammad. Prophets and sages of the biblical tradition, such as Abraham, Moses, and Jesus, are recognized as inspired vehicles of God's will. Islam, however, reveres as sacred only the message. It accepts the concepts of guardian angels, the Day of Judgment, resurrection, and the eternal life of the soul.

The duties of the Muslim form the "five pillars" of the faith. These are *shahada, salat* (daily prayer), *zakat* (almsgiving), *sawm* (fasting), and hajj (pilgrimage). The believer prays facing Mecca at five specified times during the day. Whenever possible, men observe their prayers in congregation at a mosque under direction of an imam, or prayer leader, and on Fridays are obliged to do so. Women are permitted to attend public worship at the mosque, where they are segregated from men, but their attendance tends to be discouraged, and more frequently they pray in the seclusion of their homes.

In the early days of Islam, a tax for charitable purposes was imposed on personal property in proportion to the owner's wealth. The collection of this tax and its distribution to the needy were originally functions of the state. But with the breakdown of Muslim religiopolitical authority, alms became an individual responsibility.

The ninth month of the Muslim calendar is Ramadan, a period of obligatory fasting in commemoration of Muhammad's receipt of God's revelation. Throughout the month, all but the sick and the weak, pregnant or lactating women, soldiers on duty, travelers on necessary journeys, and young children are enjoined from eating, drinking, smoking, or sexual intercourse during daylight hours. Those adults excused are obliged to endure an equivalent fast at their earliest opportunity. A festive meal breaks the daily fast and inaugurates a night of feasting and celebration. Well-to-do believers usually do little or no work during this period, and some businesses close for all or part of the day. Because the months of the lunar year revolve through the solar year, Ramadan falls at various seasons in different years. A considerable test of discipline at any time of the year, a fast that falls in summertime imposes severe hardship on those who must do physical work.

Finally, at least once during their lifetime all Muslims should make the hajj, or pilgrimage, to the holy city of Mecca to participate in the special rites that occur during the twelfth month of the lunar calendar. For most well-to-do Nigerian traders and business people, the trip was so common that the honorific *hajji* (fem., *hajjia*), signifying a pilgrim, was routinely used to refer to successful traders.

Two features of Islam are essential to understanding its place in Nigerian society. They are the degree to which Islam permeates other institutions in the society and its contribution to Nigerian pluralism. As an institution in emirate society, Islam includes

125

daily and annual ritual obligations; the pilgrimage to Mecca; the sharia, or religious law; and an establishment view of politics, family life, communal order, and appropriate modes of personal conduct in most situations. Thus, even in 1990, Islam pervaded daily life. Public meetings began and ended with Muslim prayer, and everyone knew at least the minimum Arabic prayers and the five pillars of the religion required for full participation. Public adjudication (by local leaders with the help of religious experts, or Alkali courts) provided widespread knowledge of the basic tenets of sharia law—the Sunni school of law according to Malik ibn Anas, the jurist from Medina, was that primarily followed. Sunni (from sunna), or orthodox Islam, is the dominant sect in Nigeria and most of the Muslim world. The other sect is Shia Islam, which holds that the caliphs or successors to the Prophet should have been his relatives rather than elected individuals.

Every settlement had at least one place set aside for communal prayers. In the larger settlements, mosques were well attended, especially on Fridays when the local administrative and chiefly elites led the way, and the populace prayed with its leaders in a demonstration of communal and religious solidarity. Gaining increased knowledge of the religion, one or more pilgrimages to Mecca for oneself or one's wife, and a reputation as a devout and honorable Muslim all provided prestige. Those able to suffuse their everyday lives with the beliefs and practices of Islam were deeply respected.

Air transport had made the hajj more widely available, and the red cap wound with a white cloth, signifying its wearer's pilgrimage, was much more common in 1990 than twenty years previously. Upper-income groups went several times and sent or took their wives as well. The ancient custom of spending years walking across Africa to reach Mecca was still practiced, however, and groups of such pilgrims could be seen receiving charity at Friday prayers outside major mosques in the north.

Nigerian Islam was not highly organized. Reflecting the aristocratic nature of the traditional ruling groups, there were families of clerics whose male heirs trained locally and abroad in theology and jurisprudence and filled major positions in the mosques and the judiciary. These ulama, or learned scholars, had for centuries been the religious and legal advisers of emirs, the titled nobility, and the wealthy trading families in the major cities. Ordinary people could consult the myriads of would-be and practicing clerics in various stages of training, who studied with local experts, functioned at rites of passage, or simply used their religious education to gain increased "blessedness" for their efforts. Sufi brotherhoods (from *suf,* or wool; the wearing of a woolen robe indicated devotion to a mystic life), a form of religious order based on more personal or mystical relations to the supernatural, were widespread, especially in the major cities. There the two predominant ones, Qadiriyah and Tijaniyah, had separate mosques and, in a number of instances, a parochial school system receiving grants from the state. The brotherhoods played a major role in the spread of Islam in the northern area and the middle belt.

Islam both united and divided. It provided a rallying force in the north and into the middle belt, where it was spreading. The wide scope of Islamic beliefs and practices created a leveling force that caused Muslims in the north to feel that they were part of a common set of cultural traditions affecting family life, dress, food, manners, and personal qualities linking them to one another and a wider Islamic world. At the constitutional conference of 1978, Muslim delegates walked out as a unit over the issue of a separate Islamic supreme court, a demand they lost but which in 1990 remained a Muslim goal. To adapt fully to northern life, non-Muslims had to remain in an enclave, living quasi-segregated lives in their churches, their social clubs, and even their work. In contrast, becoming a convert to Islam was the doorway to full participation in the society. Middle belt people, especially those with ambitions in politics and business, generally adopted Islam. The main exception to this rule was Plateau State, where the capital, Jos, was as much a Christian as a Muslim community, and a greater accommodation between the two sets of beliefs and their adherents had occurred.

Divisions within the Muslim community existed, however. The nineteenth-century jihad that founded the Sokoto Caliphate was a regenerative and proselytizing movement within the community of the faithful. In major centers in 1990, the Sufi brotherhoods supported their own candidates for both religious and traditional emirate offices. These differences were generally not disruptive. Islamic activist preachers and student leaders who spread ideas about a return to extreme orthodoxy also existed. In addition, a fringe Islamic cult, known as the Maitatsine, started in the late 1970s and operated throughout the 1980s, springing up in Kano around a mystical leader (since deceased) from Cameroon who claimed to have had divine revelations superseding those of the Prophet. The cult had its own mosques and preached a doctrine antagonistic to established Islamic and societal leadership. Its main appeal was to marginal and poverty-stricken urban migrants, whose rejection by the more established urban groups fostered this religious opposition. These disaffected adherents ultimately lashed

out at the more traditional mosques and congregations, resulting
in violent outbreaks in several cities of the north (see Domestic Security, ch. 5).

Christianity

The majority of Christians were found in the south. A few isolated mission stations and mission bookstores, along with churches
serving southern enclaves in the northern cities and larger towns,
dotted the Muslim north. The Yoruba area traditionally has been
Protestant and Anglican, whereas Igboland has always been the
area of greatest activity by the Roman Catholic Church. Other
denominations abounded as well. Presbyterians arrived in the early
twentieth century in the Ibibio Niger Delta area and had missions
in the middle belt as well. This latter area was an open one. Small
missionary movements were allowed to start up, generally in the
1920s, after the middle belt was considered pacified. Each denomi-
nation set up rural networks by providing schooling and health facilities. Most such facilities remained in 1990, although in many
cases schools had been taken over by the local state government
in order to standardize curricula and indigenize the teaching staff.
Pentecostals arrived mostly as indigenous workers in the postindependence period and in 1990 Pentecostalism was spreading
rapidly throughout the middle belt, having some success in Roman
Catholic and Protestant towns of the south as well. There were also
breakaway, or Africanized, churches that blended traditional Christian symbols with indigenous symbols. Among these was the
Aladura movement that was spreading rapidly throughout Yorubaland and into the non-Muslim middle belt areas.

Apart from Benin and Warri, which had come in contact with
Christianity through the Portuguese as early as the fifteenth century, most missionaries arrived by sea in the nineteenth century.
As with other areas in Africa, Roman Catholics and Anglicans each
tended to establish areas of hegemony in southern Nigeria. After
World War I, smaller sects such as the Brethren, Seventh Day Ad-
ventists, Jehovah's Witnesses, and others worked in interstitial
areas, trying not to compete. Although less well-known, African-
American churches entered the missionary field in the nineteenth
century and created contacts with Nigeria that lasted well into the
colonial period.

African churches were founded by small groups breaking off from
the European denominations, especially in Yorubaland, where such
independence movements started as early as the late nineteenth
century. They were for the most part ritually and doctrinally identical to the parent church, although more African music, and later

dance, entered and mixed with the imported church services. A number also used biblical references to support polygyny. With political independence came African priests in both Roman Catholic and Protestant denominations, although ritual and forms of worship were strictly those of the home country of the original missionaries. By the 1980s, however, African music and even dancing were being introduced quietly into church services, albeit altered to fit into rituals of European origin. Southern Christians living in the north, especially in larger cities, had congregations and churches founded as early as the 1920s. Even medium-sized towns (20,000 persons or more) with an established southern enclave had local churches, especially in the middle belt, where both major religions had a strong foothold. The exodus of Igbo from the north in the late 1960s left Roman Catholic churches poorly attended, but by the 1980s adherents were back in even greater numbers, and a number of new churches had been built.

The Aladura, like several other breakaway churches, stress healing and fulfillment of life goals for oneself and one's family. African beliefs that sorcery and witchcraft are malevolent forces against which protection is required are accepted; rituals are warm and emotional, stressing personal involvement and acceptance of spirit possession. Theology is biblical, but some sects add costumed processions and some accept polygyny.

Major congregations of the larger Anglican and Roman Catholic missions represented elite families of their respective areas, although each of these churches had members from all levels and many quite humble church buildings. Nevertheless, a wedding in the Anglican cathedral in Lagos was usually a gathering of the elite of the entire country, and of Lagos and Yorubaland in particular. Such families had connections to their churches going back to the nineteenth century and were generally not attracted to the breakaway churches. All major urban centers, all universities, and the new capital of Abuja had areas set aside for the major religions to build mosques and churches and for burial grounds.

Interethnic conflict generally has had a religious element. Riots against Igbo in 1953 and in the 1960s in the north were said to be fired by religious conflict. The riots against Igbo in the north in 1966 were said to have been inspired by radio reports of mistreatment of Muslims in the south. In the 1980s, serious outbreaks between Christians and Muslims occurred in Kafanchan in southern Kaduna State in a border area between the two religions.

Urbanization

Throughout Africa societies that had been predominantly rural for most of their history were experiencing a rapid and profound reorientation of their social and economic lives toward cities and urbanism. As ever greater numbers of people moved to a small number of rapidly expanding cities (or, as was often the case, a single main city), the fabric of life in both urban and rural areas changed in massive, often unforeseen ways. Having the largest and one of the most rapidly growing cities in sub-Saharan Africa, Nigeria has experienced the phenomenon of urbanization as thoroughly as any African nation, but its experience has also been unique—in scale, in pervasiveness, and in historical antecedents.

Modern urbanization in most African countries has been dominated by the growth of a single primary city, the political and commercial center of the nation; its emergence was, more often than not, linked to the shaping of the country during the colonial era. In countries with a coastline, this was often a coastal port, and in Nigeria, Lagos fitted well into this pattern. Unlike most other nations, however, Nigeria has not just one or two but several other cities of major size and importance, a number of which are larger than most other national capitals in Africa. In two areas, the Yoruba region in the southwest and the Hausa-Fulani and Kanuri areas of the north, there are numbers of cities with historical roots stretching back considerably before the advent of British colonizers, giving them distinctive physical and cultural identities. Moreover, in areas such as the Igbo region in the southeast, which had few urban centers before the colonial period and was not highly urbanized even at independence, there has been a massive growth of newer cities since the 1970s, so that these areas in 1990 were also highly urban.

Cities are not only independent centers of concentrated human population and activity; they also exert a potent influence on the rural landscape. What is distinctive about the growth of cities in Nigeria is the long history of urban growth and the presence of urban areas in many parts of the country.

Historical Development of Urban Centers

Nigerian urbanism, as in other parts of the world, is a function primarily of trade and politics. In the north, the great urban centers of Kano, Katsina, Zaria, Sokoto, the early Borno capitals (Gazargamo and Kuka), and other cities served as entrepôts to the Saharan and trans-Saharan trade, and as central citadels and political capitals for the expanding states of the northern savanna. They attracted large numbers of traders and migrants from their own hinterlands and generally also included ''stranger quarters'' for migrants of other regions and nations. In the south, the rise of the

Yoruba expansionist city-states and of Benin and others was stimulated by trade to the coast and by competition among these growing urban centers for the control of their hinterlands and of the trade from the interior to the Atlantic (including the slave trade). The activities of European traders also attracted people to such coastal cities as Lagos, Badagri, Brass, and Bonny, and later Calabar and Port Harcourt. Overlying the original features of the earlier cities were those generated by colonial and postcolonial rule, which created new urban centers while also drastically altering the older ones. All these cities and peri-urban areas generally tended to have high population densities in the early 1990s.

The northern savanna cities grew within city walls, at the center of which were the main market, government buildings, and the central mosque. Around them clustered the houses of the rich and powerful. Smaller markets and denser housing were found away from this core, along with little markets at the gates and some cleared land within the gates that was needed especially for siege agriculture. Groups of specialized craft manufacturers (cloth dyers, weavers, potters, and the like) were organized into special quarters, the enterprises often being family-based and inherited. Roads from the gates ran into the central market and the administrative headquarters. Cemeteries were outside the city gates.

The concentration of wealth, prestige, political power, and religious learning in the cities attracted large numbers of migrants, both from the neighboring countryside and from distant regions. This influx occasioned the building of additional sections of the city to accommodate these strangers. In many of the northern cities, these areas were separated between sections for the distant, often non-Muslim migrants not subject to the religious and other prohibitions of the emir, and for those who came from the local region and were subjects of the emir. The former area was designated the "Sabon Gari," or new town (which in southern cities, such as Ibadan, has often been shortened to "Sabo"), whereas the latter was often known as the "Tudun Wada," an area often quite wealthy and elaborately laid out. To the precolonial sections of the town was often added a government area for expatriate administrators. As a result, many of the northern cities have grown from a single centralized core to being polynucleated cities, with areas whose distinctive character reflects their origins and the roles and position of their inhabitants.

Surrounding many of the large, older northern cities, including Kano, Sokoto, and Katsina, there developed regions of relatively dense rural settlement where increasingly intensive agriculture was practiced to supply food and other products to the urban population.

These areas have come to be known as close settled zones, and they remain of major importance to the agricultural economies of the north. By 1990 the inner close settled zone around Kano, the largest of its kind, extended to a radius of about thirty kilometers, essentially the limit of a day trip to the city on foot or by donkey. Within this inner zone, there has long been a tradition of intensive interaction between the rural and urban populations, involving not just food but also wood for fuel, manure, and a range of trade goods. There has also been much land investment and speculation in this zone. The full range of Kano's outer close settled zone in 1990 was considered to extend sixty-five to ninety-five kilometers from the city, and the rural-urban interactions had extended in distance and increased in intensity because of the great improvements in roads and in the availability of motorized transport. Within this zone, the great majority of usable land was under annual rainy season or continuous irrigated cultivation, making it one of the most intensively cultivated regions in sub-Saharan Africa.

In the south, there were some similarities of origin and design in the forest and southern savanna cities of Yorubaland, but culture, landscape, and history generated a very different character for most of these cities. As in the north, the earlier Yoruba towns often centered around the palace of a ruler, or *afin*, which was surrounded by a large open space and a market. This arrangement was still evident in older cities such as Ife. However, many of the most important contemporary Yoruba cities, including the largest, Ibadan, were founded during the period of the Yoruba wars in the first half of the nineteenth century. Reflecting their origins as war camps, they usually contained multiple centers of power without a single central palace. Instead, the main market often assumed the central position in the original town, and there were several separate areas of important compounds established by the major original factions. Abeokuta, for example, had three leading families from the Egba clan, all of whom were headed by chiefs, who had broken away from and become important rivals of Ibadan. Besides these divisions were the separate areas built for stranger migrants, such as Sabo in Ibadan, where many of the Hausa migrants resided; the sections added during the colonial era, often as government reserve areas (GRAs); and the numerous areas of postcolonial expansion, generally having little or no planning.

The high population densities typically found in Yoruba cities—and even in rural villages in Yorubaland—were among the striking features of the region. This culturally based pattern was probably reinforced during the period of intense intercity warfare, but it persisted in most areas through the colonial and independence periods. The distinctive Yoruba pattern of densification involved filling in compounds with additional rooms, then adding a second, third, or sometimes even a fourth story. Eventually, hundreds of people might live in a space that had been occupied by only one extended family two or three generations earlier. Fueling this process of densification were the close connections between rural and urban dwellers, and the tendency for any Yoruba who could afford it to maintain both urban and rural residences.

The colonial government, in addition to adding sections to existing cities, also created important new urban centers in areas where there previously had been none. Among the most important were Kaduna, the colonial capital of the Protectorate of Northern Nigeria, and Jos in the central highlands, which was the center of the tin mining industry on the plateau and a recreational town for expatriates and the Nigerian elite. These new cities lacked walls but had centrally located administrative buildings and major road and rail transport routes, along which the main markets developed. These routes became one of the main forces for the cities' growth. The result was usually a basically linear city, rather than the circular pattern largely based on defensive needs, which characterized the earlier indigenous urban centers.

The other ubiquitous colonial addition was the segregated GRA, consisting of European-style housing, a hospital or nursing station, and educational, recreational, and religious facilities for the British colonials and the more prominent European trading community. The whole formed an expatriate enclave, which was deliberately separated from the indigenous Nigerian areas, ostensibly to control sanitation and limit the spread of diseases such as malaria. After independence, these areas generally became upper income suburbs, which sometimes spread outward into surrounding farmlands as well as inward to fill in the space that formerly separated the GRA from the rest of the city. New institutions, such as university campuses, government office complexes, hospitals, and hotels, were often located outside or on the fringes of the city in the 1980s. The space that originally separated them from the denser areas was then filled in as further growth occurred.

Urbanization since Independence

Spurred by the oil boom prosperity of the 1970s and the massive improvements in roads and the availability of vehicles, Nigeria since independence has become an increasingly urbanized and urban-oriented society. During the 1970s Nigeria had possibly the fastest urbanization growth rate in the world. Because of the great influx of people into urban areas, the growth rate of urban population in Nigeria in 1986 was estimated to be close to 6 percent per year, more than twice that of the rural population. Between 1970 and 1980, the proportion of Nigerians living in urban areas was estimated to have grown from 16 to more than 20 percent, and by 2010, urban population was expected to be more than 40 percent of the nation's total. Although Nigeria did not have the highest proportion of urban population in sub-Saharan Africa (in several of the countries of francophone Central Africa, for example, close to 50 percent of the population was in the major city or cities), it had more large cities and the highest total urban population of any sub-Saharan African country.

In 1990 there were twenty-one state capitals in Nigeria, each estimated to have more than 100,000 inhabitants; fifteen of these, plus a number of other cities, probably had populations exceeding 200,000. Virtually all of these were growing at a rate that doubled their size every fifteen years. These statistics did not include the new national capital, Abuja, which was planned to have more than 1 million inhabitants by early in the twenty-first century, although that milestone might be delayed as construction there stretched out. In 1990 the government was still in the process of moving from Lagos, the historical capital, to Abuja in the middle belt, and most sections of the government were still operating from Lagos. Since 1976 there had been dual capitals in both Lagos and Abuja. If one added the hundreds of smaller towns with more than 20,000 inhabitants, which resembled the larger centers more than the many smaller villages throughout the country, the extent of Nigerian urbanization was probably more widespread than anywhere else in sub-Saharan Africa.

Many of the major cities had growing manufacturing sectors, including, for example, textile mills, steel plants, car assembly plants, large construction companies, trading corporations, and financial institutions. They also included government service centers, large office and apartment complexes, along with a great variety of small business enterprises, many in the "informal sector," and vast slum areas. All postsecondary education installations were in urban centers, and the vast majority of salaried jobs remained urban rather than rural.

Although cities varied, there was a Third World urban approach that distinguished life in the city from that in the countryside. It emerged from the density and variety of housing—enormous poverty and overcrowding for most and exorbitantly wealthy suburbs and guarded enclaves for the upper classes. It also emerged from the rhythm of life set by masses of people going to work each day; the teeming central market areas; the large trading

*Students at recess in a
Lagos primary school
Courtesy Embassy of Nigeria,
Washington*

*Outdoor class at a Quran
school in Lagos in the
early 1960s
Courtesy Embassy of Nigeria,
Washington*

and department stores; the traffic, especially at rush hours; the filth that resulted from inadequate housing and public services; the destitution indicated by myriads of beggars and unemployed; the fear of rising crime; and the excitement of night life that was nonexistent in most rural areas. All these factors, plus the increased opportunity to connect with the rich and powerful through chains of patron-client relations, made the city attractive, lively, and dangerous. Urban people might farm, indeed many were trying to do so as food prices soared in the 1980s, but urban life differed vastly from the slow and seasonally defined rhythm of life in rural areas. Generally, even with all its drawbacks, it was seen as more desirable, especially by young people with more than a primary education.

The most notorious example of urban growth in Nigeria has undoubtedly been Lagos, its most important commercial center. The city has shot up in size since the 1960s; its annual growth rate was estimated at almost 14 percent during the 1970s, when the massive extent of new construction was exceeded only by the influx of migrants attracted by the booming prosperity. Acknowledged to be the largest city in sub-Saharan Africa (although an accurate count of its population must await census results), Lagos has become legendary for its congestion and other urban problems. Built for the most part on poorly drained marshlands, the city commonly had flooding during the rainy season, and there was frequent sewage backup, especially in the poorer lowland sections. As in other Nigerian cities, garbage and waste disposal was a constant problem. Housing construction had boomed but rarely seemed to keep pace with demand. The city's main fame, however, came from the scale of its traffic jams. Spanning several islands as well as a large and expanding mainland area, the city never seemed to have enough bridges or arteries. The profusion of vehicles that came with the prosperity of the 1970s seemed often to be arranged in a massive standstill, which became the site for urban peddling of an amazing variety of goods, as well as for entertainment, exasperation, innovation, and occasionally crime. By 1990 Lagos had made some progress in managing its traffic problems both through road and bridge construction and traffic control regulations. This progress was aided by the economic downturn of the late 1980s, which slowed urban migration and even led some people to return to rural areas.

Aside from Lagos, the most rapid recent rates of urbanization in the 1980s were around Port Harcourt in the Niger Delta region, which was at the heart of the oil boom, and generally throughout the Igbo and other areas of the southeast. These regions historically had few urban centers, but numerous large cities, including Onitsha, Owerri, Enugu, Aba, and Calabar, grew very rapidly as commercial and administrative centers. The Yoruba southwest was by 1990 still the most highly urbanized part of the country, whereas the middle belt was the least urbanized. The problems of Lagos, as well as the desire for a more centrally located capital that would be more of a force for national unity, led to the designation in 1976 of a site for a new national capital at Abuja.

Rural-Urban Linkages

Cities in Nigeria, as elsewhere, have historically exerted potent influences on the countryside. The northern city-states played a major role in the distribution of human population and economic activity throughout the savanna region. As citadels and centers of power and conquest, they caused depopulation in some regions, notably those subject to conquest and raiding, and population concentration in other areas. The low populations of the middle belt savanna probably resulted from the raiding and the conquests of the Hausa and Fulani city-states. The subsequent regrowth of bush land is thought to have led to a resurgence of tsetse flies and other disease vectors, which inhibited attempts to repopulate the region. The complementary effect was to increase population in zones of relative security, either areas under the protection of the dominant political states or areas of refuge, such as hill masses, which were difficult for armed horsemen to conquer.

The areas under the control or influence of major city-states would have been economically oriented toward those centers, both through the coercive exaction of taxes or tribute and through the production of food and manufactured products for the court and urban population. Many of these economic factors were replicated in the modern experience of urbanization, although one major change, dating from the imposition of British colonialism in the north, was the removal of the insecurity caused by warring polities.

Although there are similarities to this northern savanna pattern in the historical impact of Yoruba urbanization, the very different nature of the Yoruba cities led to a distinctive pattern of rural interaction. Yoruba cities traditionally had attached to them satellite villages or hamlets, the inhabitants of which considered themselves as belonging to that city, although most of their lives were spent outside the cities and their livelihoods derived from farming or other rural activities. The resulting close connection between urban dwellers and the surrounding farmers, indeed the fact that they were often identical in that urban dwellers also had farms in which they lived for much of the year, was noted by early European travelers to Yorubaland. Even in 1990, many Yoruba urban dwellers owned farms within a reasonable distance from the city and worked

137

them regularly. Moreover, many villagers owned houses, rooms, or partly completed structures in nearby towns or cities and divided their time, investments, and activities between urban and rural settings. Thus, the traditional pattern of urban-rural interconnections continued to be a deeply rooted facet of Yoruba culture.

Among the most important interactions between rural and urban areas through the 1980s in Nigeria and most other parts of Africa were the demographic impacts of urban migration on rural areas. Because the great majority of migrants were men of working age, the rural areas from which they came were left with a demographically unbalanced population of women, younger children, and older people. This phenomenon was not new to Nigeria and had been evident in parts of the country since long before independence. The 1953 census showed that the crowded rural regions of Igboland, among other areas, had already experienced a substantial migration of men, leaving a large preponderance of women in the prime working ages. In what is today Imo State, for example, the sex ratio (that is, the ratio of men to women, multiplied by 100) for the zero to fourteen age-group in 1953 was 100.2, but for ages fifteen to forty-nine, it fell to 79.1, indicating a large surplus of females. Many of the male Igbo migrants left to work in the cities of the north and southwest. Although the civil war subsequently caused many Igbos to return to the southeast, the overall scale and geographic extent of rural-urban migration in the country had increased steadily after the war. Migration was strongly stimulated by the oil boom of the 1970s, with all of the opportunities that era brought for making one's fortune in cities such as Lagos, Port Harcourt, and Warri, as well as others that were indirectly affected by the oil economy. Since then, migration has waxed and waned with the state of the economy. In the late 1980s, many young people were compelled by the sharp downturn of the economy and the shortage of urban employment to return to their home villages. As a longer-term phenomenon, however, migration from the rural areas, especially by young men, was expected to be an accelerating and largely irreversible social process.

This process affected the rural economy in the areas of migration by creating marked changes in the gender division of labor. In most of Africa, agricultural labor was traditionally specified by gender: men had certain tasks and women had others, although the specific divisions varied by culture and ethnic group. As working-age men left the rural areas, the resulting labor gap was met by others, usually wives or children, or by hired labor—or the tasks were modified or not performed. The departure of men helped to generate a lively market for rural wage labor. In many areas in 1990, male and female laborers were commonly hired to perform agricultural tasks such as land preparation, weeding, and harvesting, which in the past had been done by either household labor or traditional work parties. In turn, the growth in demand for hired labor fostered an increase of seasonal and longer term intrarural migration. The improvement of roads was also extremely important in stimulating the scale of seasonal labor migration. It became feasible, for example, for Hausa and other northern workers to come south to work as hired laborers in the cocoa belt and elsewhere at the onset of the rains and later to return to their home villages in time to plant their own crops.

In more remote areas, however, finding hired workers was often difficult. The absence of men led to neglect of such tasks as land clearing and heavy soil conservation work, which they generally performed. Thus, in forest areas from which there was much male migration, thickly overgrown land that had been left fallow for extended periods would not be cleared for cultivation; instead, the same parcels were used repeatedly, leading to rapid declines in soil fertility and yields. As a result, land degradation also occurred in these low density areas.

Some of the most profound impacts of urban areas on the rural economy derived from the vast increase in food demand generated by the growth of cities. Both the amounts and types of foods consumed by urban populations helped to transform agricultural systems and practices. Cassava, corn, and fresh vegetable production especially benefited from the expansion of urban demand. Cassava tubers can be processed by fermenting, grating, and drying to produce a powdered product known as *gari*, which can be stored and is very suitable for cooking in urban settings. Especially throughout the southern parts of the country, *gari* demand grew rapidly with the expansion of urban populations, causing a large increase in cassava planting and processing, largely done by women as a cottage industry. Demand for and production of corn also increased significantly. In the early portion of the harvest season, fresh corn sold as roadside "fast food" became a highly profitable endeavor, especially in cities. Throughout the northern areas of the country, corn production for dried grain—most of which was grown for sale to urban areas—also expanded rapidly through the 1980s, supplementing or replacing some of the traditional sorghum and millet production. The expansion of commercial chicken and egg production, also largely for the urban market, further raised demand for corn as feed.

The expansion and improvement of the transport network in the 1970s and 1980s played a key role in tying urban markets to rural producing regions. This linkage was most critical for fresh vegetable production, which previously had been very limited in geographical extent but became feasible and profitable in many areas once efficient transport connections to urban areas were established. The continued growth of urbanization and expansion of transport capacity were likely to be the major driving forces of agricultural production and modernization through the 1990s.

Education

There were three fundamentally distinct education systems in Nigeria in 1990: the indigenous system, Quranic schools, and formal European-style education institutions. In the rural areas where the majority lived, children learned the skills of farming and other work, as well as the duties of adulthood, from participation in the community. This process was often supplemented by age-based schools in which groups of young boys were instructed in community responsibilities by mature men. Apprentice systems were widespread throughout all occupations; the trainee provided service to the teacher over a period of years and eventually struck out on his own. Truck driving, building trades, and all indigenous crafts and services from leather work to medicine were passed down in families and acquired through apprenticeship training as well. In 1990 this indigenous system included more than 50 percent of the school-age population and operated almost entirely in the private sector; there was virtually no regulation by the government unless training included the need for a license. By the 1970s, education experts were asking how the system could be integrated into the more formal schooling of the young, but the question remained unresolved by 1990.

Islamic education was part of religious duty. Children learned up to one or two chapters of the Quran by rote from a local *mallam,* or religious teacher, before they were five or six years old. Religious learning included the Arabic alphabet and the ability to read and copy texts in the language, along with those texts required for daily prayers. Any Islamic community provided such instruction in a *mallam*'s house, under a tree on a thoroughfare, or in a local mosque. This primary level was the most widespread. A smaller number of those young Muslims who wished, or who came from wealthier or more educated homes, went on to examine the meanings of the Arabic texts. Later, grammar, syntax, arithmetic, algebra, logic, rhetoric, jurisprudence, and theology were added; these subjects required specialist teachers at the advanced level. After this level, students traditionally went on to one of the famous Islamic centers of learning.

For the vast majority, Muslim education was delivered informally under the tutelage of *mallams* or ulama, scholars who specialized in religious learning and teaching. Throughout the colonial period, a series of formal Muslim schools were set up and run on European lines. These schools were established in almost all major Nigerian cities but were notable in Kano, where Islamic brotherhoods developed an impressive number of schools. They catered to the children of the devout and the well-to-do who wished to have their children educated in the new and necessary European learning, but within a firmly religious context. Such schools were influential as a form of local private school that retained the predominance of religious values within a modernized school system. Because the government took over all private and parochial schools in the mid-1970s and only allowed such schools to exist again independently in 1990, data are lacking concerning numbers of students enrolled.

Western-style education came to Nigeria with the missionaries in the mid-nineteenth century. Although the first mission school was founded in 1843 by Methodists, it was the Anglican Church Missionary Society that pushed forward in the early 1850s to found a chain of missions and schools, followed quickly in the late 1850s by the Roman Catholics. In 1887 in what is now southern Nigeria, an education department was founded that began setting curricula requirements and administering grants to the mission societies. By 1914, when north and south were united into one colony, there were fifty-nine government and ninety-one mission primary schools in the south; all eleven secondary schools, except for King's College in Lagos, were run by the missions. The missions got a foothold in the middle belt; a mission school for the sons of chiefs was opened in Zaria in 1907 but lasted only two years. In 1909 Hans Vischer, an ex-Anglican missionary, was asked to organize the education system of the Protectorate of Northern Nigeria. Schools were set up and grants given to missions in the middle belt. In 1914 there were 1,100 primary school pupils in the north, compared with 35,700 in the south; the north had no secondary schools, compared with eleven in the south. By the 1920s, the pressure for school places in the south led to increased numbers of independent schools financed by local efforts and to the sending of favorite sons overseas for more advanced training.

The education system focused strongly on examinations. In 1916 Frederick Lugard, first governor of the unified colony, set up a school inspectorate. Discipline, buildings, and adequacy of teaching staff were to be inspected, but the most points given to a school's performance went to the numbers and rankings of its examination results. This stress on examinations was still used in 1990 to judge educational results and to obtain qualifications for jobs in government and the private sector.

Progress in education was slow but steady throughout the colonial era until the end of World War II. By 1950 the country had developed a three-tiered system of primary, secondary, and higher education based on the British model of wide participation at the bottom, sorting into academic and vocational training at the secondary level, and higher education for a small elite destined for leadership. On the eve of independence in the late 1950s, Nigeria had gone through a decade of exceptional educational growth leading to a movement for universal primary education in the Western Region. In the north, primary school enrollments went from 66,000 in 1947 to 206,000 in 1957, in the west (mostly Yoruba areas) from 240,000 to 983,000 in the same period, and in the east from 320,000 to 1,209,000. Secondary level enrollments went from 10,000 for the country as a whole in 1947 to 36,000 in 1957; 90 percent of these, however, were in the south.

Given the central importance of formal education, it soon became "the largest social programme of all governments of the federation," absorbing as much as 40 percent of the budgets of some state governments. Thus, by 1984–85 more than 13 million pupils attended almost 35,000 public primary schools. At the secondary level, approximately 3.7 million students were attending 6,500 schools (these numbers probably included enrollment in private schools), and about 125,000 postsecondary level students were attending 35 colleges and universities. The pressure on the system remained intense in 1990, so much so that one education researcher predicted 800,000 higher level students by the end of the 1990s, with a correlated growth in numbers and size of all education institutions to match this estimate.

Universal primary education became official policy for the federation in the 1970s. The goal has not been reached despite pressure throughout the 1980s to do so. In percentage terms, accomplishments have been impressive. Given an approximate population of 49.3 million in 1957 with 23 percent in the primary school age-group (ages five to fourteen), the country had 21 percent of its school-age population attending in the period just prior to independence, after what was probably a tripling of the age-group in the preceding decade. By 1985 with an estimated population of 23 million between ages five and fourteen, approximately 47 percent of the age-group attended school (see table 3, Appendix). Although growth slowed and actually decreased in some rural areas in the late 1980s, it was projected that by the early part of the next century universal primary education would be achieved.

Secondary and postsecondary level growth was much more dramatic. The secondary level age-group (ages fifteen to twenty-four) represented approximately 16 percent of the entire population in 1985. Secondary level education was available for approximately 0.5 percent of the age-group in 1957, and for 22 percent of the age-group in 1985 (see table 4, Appendix). In the early 1960s, there were approximately 4,000 students at six institutions (Ibadan, Ife, Lagos, Ahmadu Bello University, the University of Nigeria at Nsukka, and the Institute of Technology at Benin), rising to 19,000 by 1971 and to 30,000 by 1975 (see table 5, Appendix). In 1990 there were thirty-five polytechnic institutes, military colleges, and state and federal universities, plus colleges of education and of agriculture; they had an estimated enrollment of 150,000 to 200,000, representing less than 1 percent of the twenty-one to twenty-nine-year-old age-group.

Such growth was impossible without incurring a host of problems, several of which were so severe as to endanger the entire system of education. As long as the country was growing apace in terms of jobs for the educated minority through investment in expanded government agencies and services and the private sector, the growing numbers of graduates could be absorbed. But the criterion of examination results as the primary sorting device for access to schools and universities led to widespread corruption and cheating among faculty and students at all levels, but especially secondary and postsecondary. Most Nigerian universities had followed the British higher education system of "final examinations" as the basis for granting degrees, but by 1990 many were shifting to the United States system of course credits. Economic hardship among teaching staffs produced increased engagement in nonacademic moonlighting activities. Added to these difficulties were such factors as the lack of books and materials, no incentive for research and writing, the use of outdated notes and materials, and the deficiency of replacement laboratory equipment. One researcher noted that in the 1980s Nigeria had among the lowest number of indigenous engineers per capita of any Third World country. Unfortunately, nothing was done to rectify the situation. The teaching of English, which was the language of instruction beyond primary school, had reached such poor levels that university faculty complained they could not understand the written work of their students. By 1990 the crisis in education was such that it was predicted that by the end of the decade, there would be insufficient personnel to run essential services of the country. It was hoped that

143

the publication of critical works and international attention to this crisis might reverse the situation before Nigeria lost an entire generation or more of its skilled labor force.

Health

Whereas traditional medicine continued to play an important role in Nigeria in 1990, the country had made great strides in the provision of modern health care to its population in the years since World War II, particularly in the period after independence, especially the 1960s and 1970s. Among the most notable accomplishments were the expansion of medical education, the improvement of public health care, the control of many contagious diseases and disease vectors, and the provision of primary health care in many urban and rural areas. In the late 1980s, a large increase in vaccination against major childhood diseases and a significant expansion of primary health care became the cornerstones of the government's health policies.

Nonetheless, many problems remained in 1990. Sharp disparities persisted in the availability of medical facilities among the regions, rural and urban areas, and socioeconomic classes. The severe economic stresses of the late 1980s had serious impacts throughout the country on the availability of medical supplies, drugs, equipment, and personnel. In the rapidly growing cities, inadequate sanitation and water supply increased the threat of infectious disease, and health care facilities were generally not able to keep pace with the rate of urban population growth. There were several serious outbreaks of infectious diseases during the 1980s, including cerebrospinal meningitis and yellow fever, for which, especially in rural areas, treatment or preventive immunization was often difficult to obtain. Chronic diseases, such as malaria and guinea worm, continued to resist efforts to reduce their incidence in many areas. The presence of acquired immune deficiency syndrome (AIDS) in Nigeria was confirmed by 1987 and appeared to be growing.

History of Modern Medical Services

Western medicine was not formally introduced into Nigeria until the 1860s, when the Sacred Heart Hospital was established by Roman Catholic missionaries in Abeokuta. Throughout the ensuing colonial period, the religious missions played a major role in the supply of modern health care facilities in Nigeria. The Roman Catholic missions predominated, accounting for about 40 percent of the total number of mission-based hospital beds by 1960. By that time, mission hospitals somewhat exceeded government hospitals

University education has a high priority. Main library, University of Lagos
Arts block, University of Ibadan
Courtesy Orlando E. Pacheco

in number; there were 118 mission hospitals, compared with 101 government hospitals.

Mission-based facilities were concentrated in certain areas, depending on the religious and other activities of the missions. Roman Catholic hospitals in particular were concentrated in the southeastern and midwestern areas. By 1954 almost all the hospitals in the midwestern part of the country were operated by Roman Catholic missions. The next largest sponsors of mission hospitals were, respectively, the Sudan United Mission, which concentrated on middle belt areas, and the Sudan Interior Mission, which worked in the Islamic north. Together they operated twenty-five hospitals or other facilities in the northern half of the country. Many of the mission hospitals remained important components of the health care network in the north in 1990.

The missions also played an important role in medical training and education, providing training for nurses and paramedical personnel and sponsoring basic education as well as advanced medical training, often in Europe, for many of the first generation of Western-educated Nigerian doctors. In addition, the general education provided by the missions for many Nigerians helped to lay the groundwork for a wider distribution and acceptance of modern medical care.

The British colonial government began providing formal medical services with the construction of several clinics and hospitals in Lagos, Calabar, and other coastal trading centers in the 1870s. Unlike the missionary facilities, these were, at least initially, solely for the use of Europeans. Services were later extended to African employees of European concerns. Government hospitals and clinics expanded to other areas of the country as European activity increased there. The hospital in Jos, for example, was founded in 1912 after the initiation there of tin mining.

World War I had a strong detrimental effect on medical services in Nigeria because of the large number of medical personnel, both European and African, who were pulled out to serve in Europe. After the war, medical facilities were expanded substantially, and a number of government-sponsored schools for the training of Nigerian medical assistants were established. Nigerian physicians, even if trained in Europe, were, however, generally prohibited from practicing in government hospitals unless they were serving African patients. This practice led to protests and to frequent involvement by doctors and other medical personnel in the nationalist movements of the period.

After World War II, partly in response to nationalist agitation, the colonial government tried to extend modern health and education facilities to much of the Nigerian population. A ten-year health development plan was announced in 1946. The University of Ibadan was founded in 1948; it included the country's first full faculty of medicine and university hospital, still known as University College Hospital. A number of nursing schools were established, as were two schools of pharmacy; by 1960 there were sixty-five government nursing or midwifery training schools. The 1946 health plan established the Ministry of Health to coordinate health services throughout the country, including those provided by the government, by private companies, and by the missions. The plan also budgeted funds for hospitals and clinics, most of which were concentrated in the main cities; little funding was allocated for rural health centers. There was also a strong imbalance between the appropriation of facilities to southern areas, compared with those in the north.

By 1979 there were 562 general hospitals, supplemented by 16 maternity and/or pediatric hospitals, 11 armed forces hospitals, 6 teaching hospitals, and 3 prison hospitals. Altogether they accounted for about 44,600 hospital beds. In addition, general health centers were estimated to total slightly less than 600; general clinics 2,740; maternity homes 930; and maternal health centers 1,240.

Ownership of health establishments was divided among federal, state, and local governments, and there were privately owned facilities. Whereas the great majority of health establishments were government owned, the number of private institutions grew through the 1980s. By 1985 there were 84 health establishments owned by the federal government (accounting for 13 percent of hospital beds); 3,023 owned by state governments (47 percent of hospital beds); 6,331 owned by local governments (11 percent of hospital beds); and 1,436 privately owned establishments (providing 14 percent of hospital beds) (see table 6, Appendix).

The problems of geographic maldistribution of medical facilities among the regions and of the inadequacy of rural facilities persisted. By 1980 the ratios were an estimated 3,800 people per hospital bed in the north (Borno, Kaduna, Kano, Niger, and Sokoto states); 2,200 per bed in the middle belt (Bauchi, Benue, Gongola, Kwara, and Plateau states); 1,300 per bed in the southeast (Anambra, Cross River, Imo, and Rivers states); and 800 per bed in the southwest (Bendel, Lagos, Ogun, Ondo, and Oyo states). There were also significant disparities within each of the regions. For example, in 1980 there were an estimated 2,600 people per physician in Lagos State, compared with 38,000 per physician in the much more rural Ondo State.

In a comparison of the distribution of hospitals between urban and rural areas in 1980, Dennis Ityavyar found that whereas approximately 80 percent of the population of those states lived in rural regions, only 42 percent of hospitals were located in those areas. The maldistribution of physicians was even more marked because few trained doctors who had a choice wanted to live in rural areas. Many of the doctors who did work in rural areas were there as part of their required service in the National Youth Service Corps, established in 1973. Few, however, remained in remote areas beyond their required term.

Hospitals were divided into general wards, which provided both outpatient and inpatient care for a small fee, and amenity wards, which charged higher fees but provided better conditions. The general wards were usually very crowded, and there were long waits for registration as well as for treatment. Patients frequently did not see a doctor, but only a nurse or other practitioner. Many types of drugs were not available at the hospital pharmacy; those that were available were usually dispensed without containers, which meant that the patients had to provide their own containers. The inpatient wards were extremely crowded; beds were in corridors and even consisted of mattresses on floors. Food was free for very poor patients who had no one to provide for them. Most, however, had relatives or friends present, who prepared or brought food and often stayed in the hospital with the patient. By contrast, in the amenity wards available to wealthier or elite patients, food and better care were provided, and drug availability was greater. The highest level of the Nigerian elite frequently traveled abroad for medical care, particularly when a serious medical problem existed.

In the early 1980s, because of shortages of fuel and spare parts, much expensive medical equipment could not be operated. Currency devaluation and structural adjustment beginning in 1986 exacerbated these conditions. Imported goods of all types doubled or tripled in price, and government and public health care facilities were severely affected by rising costs, government budget cuts, and materials shortages of the late 1980s. Partly as a result of these problems, privately owned health care facilities became increasingly important in the late 1980s. The demand for modern medical care far outstripped its availability. Medical personnel, drugs, and equipment were increasingly diverted to the private sector as government hospitals deteriorated.

Government health policies increasingly had become an issue of policy debate and public contention in the late 1980s. The issue emerged during the Constituent Assembly held in 1989 to draft a proposed constitution. The original draft reported by the assembly included a clause specifying that free and adequate health care was to be available as a matter of right to all Nigerians within certain categories. The categories included all children younger than eighteen; all people sixty-five and older; and all those physically disabled or handicapped. This provision was, however, deleted by the president and the governing council when they reviewed the draft constitution.

Primary Health Care Policies

In August 1987, the federal government launched its Primary Health Care plan (PHC), which President Ibrahim Babangida announced as the cornerstone of health policy. Intended to affect the entire national population, its main stated objectives included accelerated health care personnel development; improved collection and monitoring of health data; ensured availability of essential drugs in all areas of the country; implementation of an Expanded Programme on Immunization (EPI); improved nutrition throughout the country; promotion of health awareness; development of a national family health program; and widespread promotion of oral rehydration therapy for treatment of diarrheal disease in infants and children. Implementation of these programs was intended to take place mainly through collaboration between the Ministry of Health and participating local government councils, which received direct grants from the federal government.

Of these objectives, the EPI was the most concrete and probably made the greatest progress initially. The immunization program focused on four major childhood diseases: pertussis, diphtheria, measles, and polio, as well as tetanus and tuberculosis. Its aim was to increase dramatically the proportion of immunized children younger than two from about 20 percent to 50 percent initially, and to 90 percent by the end of 1990. Launched in March 1988, the program by August 1989 was said to have been established in more than 300 of 449 LGAs. Although the program was said to have made much progress, its goal of 90 percent coverage was probably excessively ambitious, especially in view of the economic strains of structural adjustment that permeated the Nigerian economy throughout the late 1980s.

The government's population control program also came partially under the PHC. By the late 1980s, the official policy was strongly to encourage women to have no more than four children, which would represent a substantial reduction from the estimated fertility rate of almost seven children per woman in 1987. No official sanctions were attached to the government's population policy, but birth control information and contraceptive supplies were available in many health facilities.

The federal government also sought to improve the availability of pharmaceutical drugs. Foreign exchange had to be released for essential drug imports; hence the government attempted to encourage local drug manufacture. Because raw materials for local drug manufacture had to be imported, however, costs were reduced only partially. In order for Nigeria both to limit its foreign exchange expenditures and to simultaneously implement massive expansion in primary health care, foreign assistance would probably be needed. Despite advances against many infectious diseases, Nigeria's population continued through the 1980s to be subject to several major diseases, some of which occurred in acute outbreaks causing hundreds or thousands of deaths, while others recurred chronically, causing large-scale infection and debilitation. Among the former were cerebrospinal meningitis, yellow fever, Lassa fever and, most recently, AIDS; the latter included malaria, guinea worm, schistosomiasis (bilharzia), and onchocerciasis (river blindness). Malnutrition and its attendant diseases also continued to be a problem among infants and children in many areas, despite the nation's economic and agricultural advances.

Among the worst of the acute diseases was cerebrospinal meningitis, a potentially fatal inflammation of the membranes of the brain and spinal cord, which can recur in periodic epidemic outbreaks. Northern Nigeria is one of the most heavily populated regions in what is considered the meningitis belt of Africa, an area stretching from Senegal to Sudan that has a long dry season and low humidity between December and April. The disease plagued the northern and middle belt areas in 1986 and 1989, generally appearing during the cool, dry harmattan season when people spend more time indoors, promoting contagious spread. Paralysis, and often death, can occur within forty-eight hours of the first symptoms.

In response to the outbreaks, the federal and state governments in 1989 attempted mass immunization in the affected regions. Authorities pointed, however, to the difficulty of storing vaccines in the harsh conditions of northern areas, many of which also had poor roads and inadequate medical facilities.

Beginning in November 1986 and for several months thereafter, a large outbreak of yellow fever occurred in scattered areas. The most heavily affected were the states of Oyo, Imo, Anambra, and Cross River in the south, Benue and Niger in the middle belt, and Kaduna and Sokoto in the north. There were at least several hundred deaths. Fourteen million doses of vaccine were distributed with international assistance, and the outbreak was brought under control.

Lassa fever, a highly contagious and virulent viral disease, appeared periodically in the 1980s in various areas. The disease was first identified in 1969 in the northeast Nigerian town of Lassa. It is believed that rats and other rodents are reservoirs of the virus, and that transmission to humans can occur through droppings or food contamination in and around homes. Mortality rates can be high, and there is no known treatment.

The presence of AIDS in Nigeria was officially confirmed in 1987, considerably later than its appearance and wide dispersion in much of East and Central Africa. In March 1987, the minister of health announced that tests of a pool of blood samples collected from high risk groups had turned up two confirmed cases of AIDS, both human immunodeficiency virus (HIV) type-1 strains. Subsequently, HIV type-2, a somewhat less virulent strain found mainly in West Africa, was also confirmed. In 1990 the infection rate for either virus in Nigeria was thought to be below 1 percent of the population.

Less dramatic than the acute infectious diseases were a host of chronic diseases that were serious and widespread but only occasionally resulted in death. Of these the most common was malaria, including cerebral malaria, which can be fatal. The guinea worm parasite, which is spread through ingestion of contaminated water, is endemic in many rural areas, causing recurring illness and occasionally permanently crippling its victims. The World Health Organization (WHO) in 1987 estimated that there were 3 million cases of guinea worm in Nigeria—about 2 percent of the world total of 140 million cases—making Nigeria the nation with the highest number of guinea worm cases. In affected areas, guinea worm and related complications were estimated to be the major cause of work and school absenteeism. Virtually all affected states had campaigns under way to eradicate the disease through education and provision of pure drinking water supplies to rural villages. The government has set an ambitious target of full eradication by 1995, with extensive assistance from the Japanese government, Global 2000, and numerous other international donors.

The parasitic diseases onchocerciasis and schistosomiasis, both associated with bodies of water, were found in parts of Nigeria. Onchocerciasis is caused by filarial worms transmitted by small black flies that typically live and breed near rapidly flowing water. The worms can damage the eyes and optic nerve and can cause blindness by young adulthood or later. In some villages near the Volta River tributaries where the disease is endemic, up to 20 percent of adults older than thirty are blind because of the disease. Most control efforts have focused on a dual strategy of treating the

151

sufferers and trying to eliminate the flies, usually with insecticide sprays. The flies and the disease are most common in the lowland savanna areas of the middle belt.

Schistosomiasis is caused by blood flukes, which use freshwater snails as an intermediate host and invade humans when the larvae penetrate the skin of people entering a pond, lake, or stream in which the snails live. Most often, schistosomiasis results in chronic debilitation rather than acute illness.

Welfare

Welfare concerns in Nigeria were primarily related to its general lack of development and the effects on the society of the economic stringency of the 1980s. Given the steady population growth and the decline in urban services and incomes since 1980, it was difficult not to conclude that for the mass of the people at the lower income level, malnutrition, poor health, and overcrowded housing were perpetual problems.

Nigeria had no social security system in 1990. Less than 1 percent of the population older than sixty years received pensions. Because of the younger age of urban migrants, there were fewer older people per family unit in urban areas. Official statistics were questionable, however, because at least one survey indicated a number of elderly living alone in northern cities or homeless persons living on the streets and begging. There was some evidence that the traditional practice of caring for parents was beginning to erode under harsh conditions of scarcity in urban areas. In rural Nigeria, it was still the rule that older people were cared for by their children, grandchildren, spouses, siblings, or even ex-spouses. The ubiquity of this tradition left open, however, the possibility of real hardship for urban elderly whose families had moved away or abandoned them.

Traditionally, family problems with spouses or children were handled by extended kinship groups and local authorities. For the most part, this practice continued in the rural areas. In urban settings, social services were either absent or rare for family conflict, for abandoned or runaway children, for foster children, or for children under the care of religious instructors.

As with many other developing nations, Nigeria had many social welfare problems that needed attention. The existence of a relatively free press combined with a history of self-criticism—in journalism, the arts, the social sciences, and by religious and political leaders—were promising indications of the awareness and public debate required for change and adaptive response to its social problems.

* * *

The literature on Nigeria is voluminous and includes several classic works on Nigeria's major ethnic groups. Among these are the chapters by M.G. Smith (Hausa), Paul and Laura Bohannan (Tiv), and Phoebe Ottenberg (Igbo) in James L. Gibbs, Jr., (ed.), *Peoples of Africa*. Urban Hausa life and its religious and political nature are explored in John N. Paden's *Religion and Political Culture in Kano*. Possibly the fullest account of a northern emirate society is S.F. Nadel's *A Black Byzantium on the Nupe*. Kanuri culture is the subject of Ronald Cohen's *The Kanuri of Bornu,* and Derrick J. Stenning's *Savannah Nomads* is the best work available on the Fulani. Simon Ottenberg's *Leadership and Authority in an African Society* and Victor C. Uchendu's brief but readable *The Igbo of Southeast Nigeria* are recommended on the Igbo. The classic work on the Yoruba is N.A. Fadipe, *The Sociology of the Yoruba*. This work, together with Robert S. Smith's *Kingdoms of the Yoruba,* is the best general work on Yoruba political society.

Understanding Islam in Nigeria still requires looking at John Spencer Trimingham's classic, *Islam in West Africa,* and Islamization is well-treated in *African Religion Meets Islam* by Dean S. Gilliland. Possibly the most important discussion on the synthesis of Christianity and Yoruba religion is that by John D.Y. Peel in *Aladura: A Religious Movement among the Yoruba.*

Perhaps the best recent analysis of drought and climatic variation in northern Nigeria is Michael Mortimore's *Adapting to Drought.* For a general overview of population growth in Africa, including Nigeria, the World Bank study, *Population Growth and Policies in Sub-Saharan Africa,* is extremely useful, as are other standard World Bank and United Nations sources on current population trends.

Finally, much useful information on health and education can be found in the annual *Social Statistics in Nigeria,* published by the Nigerian Office of Statistics. (For further information and complete citations, see Bibliography.)

Chapter 3. The Economy

Ife bronze head said to represent Olorun, god of sea and wealth

A MAJOR FEATURE of Nigeria's economy in the 1980s, as in the 1970s, was its dependence on petroleum, which accounted for 87 percent of export receipts and 77 percent of the federal government's current revenue in 1988. Falling oil output and prices contributed to another noteworthy aspect of the economy in the 1980s—a decline in per capita real gross national product (GNP—see Glossary) that persisted until oil prices began to rise in 1990. Indeed, GNP per capita per year decreased 4.8 percent from 1980 to 1987, a decrease that led in 1989 to Nigeria's classification by the World Bank (see Glossary) as a low-income country (based on 1987 data) for the first time since the annual *World Development Report* was instituted in 1978. In 1989 the World Bank also declared Nigeria poor enough to be eligible (along with countries such as Bangladesh, Ethiopia, Chad, and Mali) for concessional aid from an affiliate, the International Development Association (IDA).

Another relevant feature of the Nigerian economy was a series of abrupt changes in the government's share of expenditures. As a percentage of gross domestic product (GDP—see Glossary), national government expenditures rose from 9 percent in 1962 to 44 percent in 1979, but fell to 17 percent in 1988. In the aftermath of the 1967–70 civil war, Nigeria's government became more centralized. The oil boom of the 1970s provided the tax revenue to strengthen the central government further. Expansion of the government's share of the economy did little to enhance its political and administrative capacity, but did increase incomes and the number of jobs that the governing elites could distribute to their clients.

The economic collapse in the late 1970s and early 1980s contributed to substantial discontent and conflict among ethnic communities and nationalities, adding to the political pressure to expel more than 2 million illegal workers (mostly from Ghana, Niger, Cameroon, and Chad) in early 1983 and May 1985.

The lower spending of the 1980s was partly the result of the structural adjustment program (SAP) in effect from 1986 to 1990. SAP was mooted by the International Monetary Fund (IMF—see Glossary) and carried out under the auspices of the World Bank, which emphasized privatization, market prices, and reduced government expenditures. This program was based on the principle that, as GDP per capita falls, people demand relatively fewer social goods (produced in the government sector) and relatively more private

157

goods, which tend to be essential items such as food, clothing, and shelter.

The Colonial Economic Legacy

Early British Imperialism

The European struggle to establish forts and trading posts on the West African coast from about the mid-1600s to the mid-1700s was part of the wider competition for trade and empire in the Atlantic. The British, like other newcomers to the slave trade, found they could compete with the Dutch in West Africa only by forming national trading companies. The first such effective English enterprise was the Company of the Royal Adventurers, chartered in 1660 and succeeded in 1672 by the Royal African Company. Only a monopoly company could afford to build and maintain the forts considered essential to hold stocks of slaves and trade goods. In the early eighteenth century, Britain and France destroyed the Dutch hold on West African trade; and by the end of the French Revolution and the subsequent Napoleonic Wars (1799–1815), Britain had become the dominant commercial power in West Africa (see European Slave Trade in West Africa, ch. 1).

The slave trade was one of the major causes of the devastating internecine strife in southern Nigeria during the three centuries prior to the mid-1800s, when abolition actually occurred. In the nineteenth century, Britain was interested primarily in opening markets for its manufactured goods in West Africa and expanding commerce in palm oil. Securing the oil and ivory trade required that Britain usurp the power of coastal chiefs in what became Nigeria.

Formal "protection" and—eventually—colonization of Nigeria resulted not only from the desire to safeguard Britain's expanding trade interests in the Nigerian hinterland, but also from an interest in forestalling formal claims by other colonial powers, such as France and Germany. By 1850 British trading interests were concentrating in Lagos and the Niger River delta. British administration in Nigeria formally began in 1861, when Lagos became a crown colony, a step taken in response to factors such as the now-illegal activities of slave traders, the disruption of trade by the Yoruba civil wars, and fears that the French would take over Lagos (see The Nineteenth Century: Revolution and Radical Adjustment, ch. 1). Through a series of steps designed to facilitate trade, by 1906 present-day Nigeria was under British control.

The Colonial Period

Colonies such as Nigeria became part of British imperial expansion that focused on exploiting raw materials, minerals, and foodstuffs important to Western industrial development. Britain tried to encourage tropical export crops in Nigeria and to stimulate demand there for British manufactured goods. The colonies built a railroad network between the 1890s and World War II and constructed roads at an accelerating rate after the 1930s. These developments, along with the introduction of the pound sterling as the universal medium of exchange, encouraged export trade in tin, cotton, cocoa, peanuts, and palm oil. Britain maintained its economic hegemony over the colonies through military power, strategic alliances, and the collaboration of indigenous rulers.

Development of National Economic Interests to World War II

British rule exacerbated differences of class, region, and community in Nigeria. The emergent nationalist movement in the 1930s was spearheaded by a new elite of businesspeople and professionals and promoted mainly by persons who expected to gain economically and politically from independence (see Emergence of Nigerian Nationalism, ch. 1). The movement first became multiethnic—although limited to the south—between 1930 and 1944, when the real incomes of many participants in Nigeria's money economy fell as a result of a deterioration in the net barter terms of trade (the ratio between average export and import prices). During the same period, the Great Depression and, later, World War II, reduced Britain's investment, imports, and government spending in Nigeria.

Once the wartime colonial government assumed complete control of the local economy, it would issue trade licenses only to established firms, a practice that formalized the competitive advantage of foreign companies. Also, wartime marketing boards pegged the prices of agricultural commodities below the world market rate, workers faced wage ceilings, traders encountered price controls, and Nigerian consumers experienced shortages of import goods.

Labor activity grew during the war in reaction to the heavy-handed policies of the colonial government (see Labor Unions, this ch.). Among the expressions of labor unrest was a strike by 43,000 workers in mid-1945 that lasted more than forty days. Aspiring Nigerian entrepreneurs, deprived of new economic opportunities, and union leaders, politicized by the strike's eventual success, channeled their sense of grievance into nationalist agitation. Educated persons, whose economic opportunities were limited largely to private business and professional activity, began to demand more participation in the colonial government.

National Economic Interests in the Postwar Period

Starting in 1949, when Nigeria's recently emergent labor, commercial, and professional elites were first consulted by the British as part of a constitutional review, the peoples of Nigeria engaged in ongoing debate over the processes of decolonization, independence, and modernization. The two coups d'état of 1966 and the civil war of 1967-70 reflected economic as well as political elements.

Between 1951 and 1960, the major political parties played leading roles in unifying and locally mobilizing the economic elite (see Politics in the Crisis Years, ch. 1). Elites from majority parties in the regional assemblies who cooperated with the ruling federal coalition dispensed a wide range of rewards and sanctions, thus retaining their own positions and power and keeping the masses subordinated. Positions in government services and public corporations, licenses for market stalls, permits for agricultural export production, rights to establish enterprises, roads, electrical service, running water, and scholarships were allocated by the governing group to its supporters. Each major party was backed by a bank, which assisted in the transfer of substantial public funds to the party.

At all levels—local and regional after 1951 and federal after 1954—political leaders could use a range of controls, extending over local councils, district administration, police, and courts, to subdue any dissident minority, especially in the far north, where clientage was the social adhesive of the emirate system. Political superiors offered protection, patronage, and economic security in exchange for loyalty and the obedience of inferiors.

The elites attracted clients and socially inferior groups not only in the far north, where Islam legitimized the traditional hierarchy, but even in Igboland, an area of southeastern Nigeria where power had been widely dispersed before the twentieth century. The elites of the three regions preferred to close ranks to share the fruits of office and to prevent challenges to their positions, but by the time independence was achieved in 1960, policies designed to enhance the security of one regional elite threatened the security of others.

The Role of Government

Some of Nigeria's political leaders have advocated African socialism, an ideology that does not necessarily coincide with the Western socialist concept of the ownership of most capital and land by the state. Instead, the African variety usually has included the following: a substantial level of state ownership in modern industry, transportation, and commerce; a penchant for public control of resource allocation in key sectors; a priority on production for domestic consumption; and an emphasis on the rapid Africanization of high-level jobs. Despite the socialist rhetoric of some politicians, in practice Nigeria worked toward a mixed economy, with the directly productive sector dominated by private enterprise, the state investing in infrastructure as a foundation for private activity, and government providing programs and policies to stimulate private (especially indigenous) enterprise.

None of the major Nigerian political parties controlling national or regional governments from 1951 to 1966 (or 1979 to 1983) was a socialist party or a party strongly committed to egalitarianism. Even the Action Group, led during the First Republic by the ostensibly anticapitalist Chief Obafemi Awolowo, had as its foundation the rising new class of professionals, businesspeople, and traders.

After Nigeria's 1967–70 civil war, petroleum output and prices increased rapidly. The government's control of the extraction, refining, and distribution of oil meant that the state became the dominant source of capital. By the mid-1970s, petroleum accounted for about three-fourths of total federal revenue. To the most vigorous, resourceful, and well-connected venture capitalists (often politicians, bureaucrats, army officers, and their clients), productive economic activity lost appeal. Manipulating government spending became the means to fortune. Because of the rapid growth of the state bureaucracy and the establishment of numerous federally funded parastatals, the size of the government sector relative to the rest of the national economy hit a peak in the late 1970s.

In an effort that culminated in the 1970s, the Nigerian government gradually expanded its controls over the private sector, levying differential taxes and subsidies, increasing industrial prices relative to farm prices, favoring investment in key sectors, providing tariff and tax incentives to vital sectors, protecting favored industrial establishments from foreign competition, awarding import licenses to selected firms and industries, and providing foreign exchange to priority enterprises at below-market exchange rates. While the ostensible reasons for this policy of favoritism were to transfer resources to modern industry, expand high-priority businesses and sectors, encourage profitable enterprises, and discourage unprofitable ones, in practice the government often favored urban areas by promoting production that used socially expensive inputs of capital, foreign exchange, and high technology. Market intervention helped political and bureaucratic leaders protect their positions, expand their power, and implement their policies. Project- or enterprise-based policies (unlike reliance on the market) allowed benefits to be apportioned selectively, for maximum political advantage. Government made it in the private interest of numerous individuals to cooperate in programs that were harmful to the interests of producers as a whole. However, market-clearing prices (for farm commodities or foreign exchange), whose benefits were distributed indiscriminately, inspired little or no political support among farmers and businesspeople.

Beginning in 1979, the policy prescription of the World Bank (and IMF) was for African countries to refrain from interfering in foreign exchange and interest rates, wages, and farm prices; to privatize state-owned enterprises (especially agro-processing, farm input distribution, insurance, and retail and wholesale trade); to relax restrictions on foreign capital; and to encourage indigenous business ventures. By the early 1980s, Nigeria faced substantial international payments deficits in the midst of declining export prices and rising import prices, rising external debt payments, and negative economic growth. In 1986 the government consequently undertook its own SAP. It was patterned along World Bank guidelines, with World Bank conditions that included devaluation of the naira (N, for value of the naira—see Glossary), reductions in real government spending, abolition of official agricultural marketing boards, the sale of public enterprises, liberalized trade, and reduced quotas and licenses (see Planning, this ch.).

Planning

Before 1945 the colonial government had undertaken no serious comprehensive planning. Nigeria's earliest national plans, the 1946–55 Ten-Year Plan of Development and Welfare (with plan revisions, 1951–55) and the 1955–60 plan (later extended to 1962), were framed by colonial administrators. As the authors of the First National Development Plan, 1962–68 (henceforth, first plan) wrote, these "were not 'plans,' in the truest sense of the word . . . [but] a series of projects which had not been coordinated or related to any overall economic target." After 1960, however, development planning had a broad scope, encompassing government policies to achieve national economic objectives, such as accelerated growth and higher levels of average material welfare. This planning affected the policies of such agencies as the central bank, state-owned enterprises, the Ministry of Education, marketing boards, state-level departments, and extension services.

Nigerian plans included economic forecasts, policies toward the private sector, and a list of proposed public expenditures. Plans did not constitute commitments by public departments to spend funds. Although Nigerian political leaders made decisions about general objectives and priorities for the first plan, foreign economists were the main authors of the actual document. Its authors favored decentralized decision making by private units, disregard of major discrepancies between financial and social profitability, and high economic payoffs from directly productive investments (as opposed to indirect returns from social overheads). They discouraged increased taxes on the wealthy (out of a fear of dampening private incentive) and advocated a conservative monetary and fiscal policy emphasizing a relatively small plan, openness to foreign trade and investment, and reliance on overseas assistance. Foreign aid was set at one-half of public sector investment.

Nobel economist W. Arthur Lewis has suggested that the main weaknesses of the 1962–68 plan were incomplete feasibility studies and inadequate evaluation of projects, meager public participation, and excessive political intervention in economic decisions. Moreover, insufficient attention was paid to the small indigenous sector, and the machinery for implementing developments in the public sector was unsatisfactory. Lewis noted that the most important aspects of Nigeria's 1962–68 plan were ''how the government proposes to raise the money and to recruit the personnel to carry out its objectives.''

Postwar reconstruction, restoring productive capacity, overcoming critical bottlenecks, and achieving self-reliance were major goals of the Second National Development Plan (1970–74). The replacement cost of physical assets damaged and destroyed in the civil war with the secessionist Igbo area in the southeast, then known as Biafra, was estimated to exceed N600 million (then about US$900 million).

The United Nations (UN) Center for Development Planning, Projections, and Policies observed that Nigeria's real growth in GDP between 1970 and 1974 was 12.3 percent per year. The annual target had been only 6.2 percent. Nigerian growth could be explained by factors largely outside the planners' purview—rapid oil industry growth and sharply increasing oil prices.

Announced in March 1975, the Third National Development Plan (1975–80) envisioned a twelvefold increase in the annual rate of public capital expenditures over the previous plan period. This document included the statement, ''There will be no savings and foreign exchange constraints during the third plan period and beyond.'' The document outlined ambitious plans to expand agriculture, industry, transport, housing, water supplies, health facilities, education, rural electrification, community development, and state programs. The third plan also designated substantial funds for prestige projects, such as the Second World Black and African Festival of Arts and Culture (FESTAC) in Lagos.

163

Amid the euphoria of the 1974 oil price boom, the Ministry of Economic Development approved and added numerous projects for other ministries not supported by a proper appraisal of technical feasibility, costs and benefits, or the technical and administrative arrangements required to establish and operate the projects. According to Sayre P. Schatz, who advised the Ministry of Transport while it prepared feasibility studies for the plan in 1974, "Economic reasoning gave way before economic enthusiasm," and the necessary coordination and implementation were ignored.

Inflationary minimum wage and administrative salary increases after October 1974, in combination with the slowing of the economy, made budget shortfalls inevitable. In June 1975, several state and local governments did not receive their monthly subsidies from the federal government. Just before the July 29, 1975 coup in which head of state General Yakubu Gowon was toppled, government workers in several areas threatened to impair vital services unless their June wages were paid.

In March 1976, in response to an economy overheated by demands for new programs and higher wages, General Olusegun Obasanjo, then head of state, pointed out that petroleum revenue was not a cure-all. Many projects had to be postponed, scaled down, or canceled when oil-revenue-based projections made in 1974–75 later proved too optimistic. Projects tended to be retained for political reasons, not because they were considered socially or economically useful by the Central Planning Office of the Supreme Military Council.

The civilian government that took office on October 1, 1979, postponed the beginning of the fourth plan (1981–85) for nine months. Whereas the plan's guidelines indicated that local governments were to be involved in planning and execution, such involvement was not feasible because local governments lacked the staff and expertise to accept this responsibility. The plan was also threatened by falling oil revenues and an increased need for imported food that had resulted from delays in agricultural modernization. Projected to rise 12.1 percent annually, exports actually fell 5.9 percent yearly during the plan, as a recession among the nations of the Organisation for Economic Co-operation and Development reduced demand for Third World imports. As exports declined, the capacity to import construction materials and related capital goods also fell, reducing growth in the construction, transport, communications, utilities, and housing sectors.

Nigeria was heavily dependent on agriculture, with the sector accounting for more than 40 percent of pre-1973 GDP. But in the decade up to 1983, agricultural output in Nigeria declined 1.9

Mechanized farm in northern Nigeria
Young farmers making vegetable beds at Esa-Oke agricultural settlement
Courtesy Embassy of Nigeria, Washington

percent and exports fell 7.9 percent yearly. Agricultural imports as a share of total imports rose from 3 percent in the late 1960s to 7 percent in the early 1980s. Nigeria's unfavorable agricultural development resulted from the loss of competitiveness among farm exports as the real value of the Nigerian naira appreciated substantially from 1970 to 1972 and from 1982 to 1983.

Thanks in large part to the overthrow at the end of 1983 of Nigeria's second civilian administration, the Second Republic headed by President Shehu Shagari, and of the military government of General Muhammadu Buhari in 1985, the Fifth National Development Plan was postponed until 1988–92. Continuing the emphases of the SAP, the fifth plan's objectives were to devalue the naira, remove import licenses, reduce tariffs, open the economy to foreign trade, promote nonoil exports through incentives, and achieve national self-sufficiency in food production. The drafters of the fifth plan sought to improve labor productivity through incentives, privatization of many public enterprises, and various government measures to create employment opportunities.

In late 1989, the administration of General Ibrahim Babangida abandoned the concept of a fixed five-year plan. Instead, a three-year ''rolling plan'' was introduced for 1990–92 in the context of more comprehensive fifteen- to twenty-year plans. A rolling plan, considered more suitable for an economy facing uncertainty and rapid change, is revised at the end of each year, at which point estimates, targets, and projects are added for an additional year. Thus, planners would revise the 1990–92 three-year rolling plan at the end of 1990, issuing a new plan for 1991–93. In effect, a plan is renewed at the end of each year, but the number of years remains the same as the plan rolls forward. In Nigeria, the objectives of the rolling plan were to reduce inflation and exchange rate instability, maintain infrastructure, achieve agricultural self-sufficiency, and reduce the burden of structural adjustment on the most vulnerable social groups.

Government Finance

A major cause of political conflict in Nigeria since independence has been the changing formula for allocating revenue by region or state. Before 1959 all revenues from mineral and agricultural products were retained by the producing region. But after 1959, the region retained only a fraction of the revenue from mineral production. This policy was a major source of dissatisfaction in the Eastern Region, which seceded in May 1967 as the would-be state of Biafra. By contrast, the revenue from agricultural exports was retained by regional marketing boards after 1959, but the agricultural exports of eastern Nigeria were smaller than those of the other major regions.

The rapid growth of petroleum revenue in the 1970s removed most of the severe constraints placed on federal and regional or state budgets in the 1960s. Total federal revenue grew from N306.4 million in 1966 to N7.791 billion in 1977, a twenty-fivefold increase in current income in eleven years. Petroleum revenue as a percentage of the total went from 26.3 percent in 1970 to more than 70 percent by 1974-77.

During the civil war, most of the twelve new states created in 1967 faced a revenue crisis. But a 1970 decree brought the states closer to fiscal parity by decreasing the producing state's share of export, import, and excise duties, and of mining rents and royalties, and by increasing the share allocated to all states and the federal government. Also, in 1973 the commodity export marketing boards, which had been a source of political power for the states, were brought under federal control. Other changes later in the 1970s further reduced claims to revenue based on place of origin. In the 1970s, the federal government was freed to distribute more to the states, thus strengthening federal power as well as the states' fiscal positions. Statutory appropriations from the federal government to the states, only about N128 million in FY1966, increased to N1,040 million in 1975 with the oil boom, but dropped to N502.2 million in 1976, as oil revenues declined.

The burgeoning revenues of the oil boom had encouraged profligacy among the federal ministries. Government deficits were a major factor in accelerated inflation in the late 1970s and the early 1980s. In 1978 the federal government, compelled to cut spending for the third plan, returned much of the financial responsibility for housing and primary education to state and local governments. Federal government finances, especially, drifted into acute disequilibrium between 1981 and 1983, at the end of President Shagari's civilian administration. The 1983 federal government deficit rose to N5.3 billion (9.5 percent of GDP) at the same time that external debt was increasing rapidly. The state governments' deficit compounded the problem, with the states collectively budgeting for a deficit of N6.8 billion in 1983.

Falling export prices caused the military governments between 1983 and 1988 to continue cutting real spending, especially for capital, imports, civil service and armed forces salaries and consumer subsidies. Many parastatals also had their subsidies cut, and others were sold off entirely. The result of these actions was a substantial reduction in the federal deficit. The announcement of the spending reductions that would be part of the fifth plan coincided with the military coup of August 1985. Unlike earlier plans, the fifth plan (put back to 1988–92 partly because of the coup) allocated the largest amounts of capital to agriculture and stressed the importance of private investment.

In 1988 the federal budget was still highly dependent on oil revenues (taxes on petroleum profits, mining rents and royalties, and Nigerian National Petroleum Corporation earnings). Altogether, oil receipts accounted for 77 percent of total federal current revenue in 1988 (see table 7, Appendix). The federal government retained 62 percent of the revenue it collected in 1988, and the rest of the funds were distributed to the state and local governments by a formula based on population, need, and, to a very limited extent, derivation.

International aid designated for domestic Nigerian development constituted a minor source of government revenue. In 1988 such official assistance amounted to US$408 million, or US$1.09 per capita, which placed Nigeria lowest among low-income and lower-middle-income aid recipients. This aid represented 0.4 percent of Nigeria's GNP, far less than the average of 2.4 percent received by all low-income countries, a group that included such states as China, India, and Zambia.

Economic Development

The reliability of Nigeria's national income statistics was limited by meager industry-wide information (especially for domestically consumed commodities), the questionable validity of data, and quantification based on subjective judgments by state officials. Despite deficiencies in aggregate economic statistics, a few general tendencies concerning growth, income distribution, prices, wages, and the employment rate could be discerned. The Office of Statistics indicated that GDP grew 6.0 percent annually (adjusted for inflation) between FY (fiscal year—see Glossary) 1959 and FY 1967. GDP shrank at an inflation-adjusted annual rate of 1.1 percent between FY 1967 (which ended two months before the secession of the Eastern Region) and FY 1970 (which ended three months after the war). However, because capital destruction such as occurs during wartime is not reflected in annual measures of GDP, the decline in net domestic production was probably severely understated.

Income Distribution

Annual population growth estimates vary considerably, but it is generally held that growth was roughly 2 percent in the late 1950s and early 1960s, 2.5 to 3.0 percent from the mid-1960s to the late

1970s, and 3.0 to 3.5 percent in the 1980s (see Population, ch. 2). Accordingly, annual GDP growth per person can be estimated at 4.0 percent in the late 1950s and early 1960s, 3.0 to 3.5 percent in the mid 1960s, – 3.5 to – 4.0 percent during the civil war, roughly 7 percent in the early to late 1970s, – 6.0 percent from the late 1970s to the early 1980s, and – 2.5 percent for the balance of the 1980s.

Nigeria's decline in real GNP per capita to US$290 by 1988 relegated the nation to low-income status below India, Pakistan, and Ghana. Other indicators of development—life expectancy, for which Nigeria ranked 155th out of the world's 177 countries, and infant mortality, for which Nigeria ranked 148th among 173 countries—were consistent with Nigeria's low ranking in income per capita.

The authors of the first plan had argued that a "very good case can be made that premature preoccupation with equity problems will backfire and prevent any development from taking place." Thus, Nigeria's first plan stressed production and profitability, not distribution. Yet people who already own property, hold influential positions, and have good educations are best situated to profit once growth begins. Thus, a society with initial income inequality that begins to expand economically is likely to remain unequal, or even become more so.

Although wealth appeared to be highly concentrated in Nigeria, the government had no comprehensive income-distribution estimates. From 1960 to 1978, the number of rural poor remained constant, but the rural poverty rate declined. During the same period, the urban poor roughly doubled in number, although the rate of urban poverty also probably declined. Federal civil service studies indicating a substantial increase in income concentration from 1969 to 1976 may have reflected a trend toward overall income inequality, exacerbated perhaps by the large raises given to high-ranking administrators by the Udoji Commission on wages and salaries in 1975. But this inequality probably eased from 1976 to the end of the decade, thanks to increased salaries for low-income workers, the abolition of subsidized automobile allowances for the wealthy, and a decline in economic activity, especially in the oil sector.

During the 1960s and 1970s, Nigeria's degree of income concentration was average for sub-Saharan Africa, which, after Latin America, had the highest income inequality of any region in the world. Income concentration in Nigeria was probably higher than in Niger or Ivory Coast, about the same as in Tanzania, and lower than in Kenya and Cameroon.

Because the rural masses were politically weak, official income distribution policies focused on interurban redistribution. More than 80 percent of Nigeria's second plan (1970–74) investment was in urban areas. The third plan (1975–80) emphasized more even distribution, but did not mention urban-rural imbalances (see Federalism and Intragovernmental Relations).

The ratio of industrial to agricultural labor productivity, 2.5:1 in 1966, increased to 2.7:1 in 1970 and 7.2:1 in 1975. (Urban-rural per capita income ratios showed greater differentials for succeeding years, largely because incomes from capital, property, and entrepreneurial activity were far larger for city dwellers than for rural residents.) The sharp rise in industrial productivity between 1970 and 1975 was caused largely by phenomenal increases in oil output, prices, and tax revenues rather than by technical changes or improved skills. Without oil, 1975's labor productivity ratio would have been 3.0:1, as the terms of trade shifted away from agriculture. Moreover, emigration drained the rural areas of the most able young people, attracted by the Udoji Commission's doubling of government minimum wages. The loss of the superior education and skills of these rural-to-urban migrants resulted in a decline in inflation-adjusted agricultural productivity between 1970 and 1975. Average rural income was so low by 1975 that the richest rural quartile was poor by urban standards.

Rising debt and falling average income in the 1980s had a particularly severe effect on the poor. Consumption per capita fell 7 percent annually during that decade, material standards of living were lower in the mid-1980s than in the 1950s, and calorie and protein intake per capita were no greater in 1985 than in 1952. In effect, the economic crisis of the 1980s canceled out the progress of the previous two decades.

Wages and Prices

Urban real wages fell rapidly between 1982 and 1989 as a result of a minimum wage freeze in the formal sector. Rural real wages also fell, but more slowly because few employers had previously paid as much as the minimum wage on the farm. Beginning in 1986, the liberalizing effect of the SAP on agricultural prices and the exchange rate also redistributed income from urban to rural areas, especially in the agricultural export sector. In the 1980s, the urban self-employed, a group that included many in the low-income informal sector (e.g., cottage industries, crafts, petty trade, and repair work), had lower incomes than urban wage earners. Even the rural self-employed (smallholder farmers, sharecroppers, and tenants, as well as a few commercial farmers) had lower incomes than rural wage earners, who ranged from unskilled, landless workers to plantation workers.

During the 1980s, the urban-rural gap narrowed—a result of rising urban poverty rather than of growing rural affluence. A World Bank-International Finance Corporation study estimated that 64 percent of urban households and 61 percent of rural households lived in poverty in FY 1984. Because 70 percent of Nigeria's population was rural, most of the poor were to be found in rural areas. By the late 1980s, with structural adjustment and agricultural price decontrol, the average income of all rural households exceeded the average for urban households. Ironically, rural household income levels in the late 1980s only improved relative to levels for city households, as real income in both urban and rural areas had fallen throughout the 1980s. As a result, for the first time since independence, more Nigerians migrated to the country than to urban areas.

Rapid inflation, 20 percent yearly between 1973 and 1980 and more than 20 percent per year between 1980 and 1984 (as measured by the consumer price index), dropped to 5.5 percent in 1985, 5.4 percent in 1986 (years of good harvests), and 10.2 percent in 1987, before rising to 38.3 percent in 1988 and 47.5 percent in 1989. Under a World Bank SAP, 1986 and 1987 were years of tight-money financial policy. But a poor harvest in 1987 put pressure on 1988 food prices, and authorities lifted the wage freeze and eased fiscal policies in 1988 in the face of rising political opposition to austerity. Inflation abated somewhat in late 1989, as food supplies grew and the Central Bank of Nigeria tightened monetary policy.

Real wages fell significantly in the 1980s following a statutory wage freeze (1982–88), salary cuts in the public sector in 1985, and a constant nominal minimum wage that started in 1981. From 1986 to 1989, real wages fell almost 60 percent.

Labor

The size of Nigeria's labor force was difficult to calculate because of the absence of accurate census data. The labor force increased from 18.3 million in 1963 to 29.4 million in 1983. Census data apparently understated the number of self-employed peasants and farmers, but estimated that the proportion of Nigerians employed in agriculture, livestock, forestry, and fishing fell from 56.8 percent in 1963 to 33.5 percent in 1983. The percentage of the labor force employed in mining rose from 0.1 percent in 1963 to 0.4 percent in 1983. Exactly comparable data were lacking on manufacturing, but from 1965 to 1980 industry's share of the labor force rose from 10 percent to 12 percent whereas the services sector grew from 18 percent to 20 percent of the labor force (see table 8, Appendix).

Unemployment

The national unemployment rate, estimated by the Office of Statistics as 4.3 percent of the labor force in 1985, increased to 5.3 percent in 1986 and 7.0 percent in 1987, before falling to 5.1 percent in 1988 as a result of measures taken under the SAP. Most of the unemployed were city dwellers, as indicated by urban jobless rates of 8.7 percent in 1985, 9.1 percent in 1986, 9.8 percent in 1987, and 7.3 percent in 1988. Underemployed farm labor, often referred to as disguised unemployed, continued to be supported by the family or village, and therefore rural unemployment figures were less accurate than those for urban unemployment. Among the openly unemployed rural population, almost two-thirds were secondary-school graduates.

Consistently, the largest proportion of the unemployed were secondary-school graduates. There was also a 40-percent unemployment rate among urban youth aged twenty to twenty-four and a 31-percent rate among those aged fifteen to nineteen. Two-thirds of the urban unemployed were fifteen to twenty-four years old. Moreover, the educated unemployed tended to be young males with few dependents. There were relatively few secondary-school graduates, and the lowered job expectations of primary-school graduates in the urban formal sector kept the urban unemployment rate for these groups to 3 to 6 percent in the 1980s.

Labor Unions

Labor unions have been a part of Nigerian industry since 1912, when government employees formed a civil service union. In 1914 this organization became the Nigerian Union of Civil Servants after the merger of the protectorates of Northern Nigeria and Southern Nigeria. In 1931 two other major unions were founded— the Nigerian Railway Workers Union and the Nigerian Union of Teachers (which included private-school teachers). Legalization of unions in 1938 was followed by rapid labor organization during World War II as a result of passage by the British government of the Colonial Development and Welfare Act of 1940, which encouraged the establishment of unions in the colonies. The defense regulation of October 1942 made strikes and lockouts illegal for the duration of the war and denied African workers the cost-of-living allowances that European civil servants received. In addition, the colonial government increased wages only modestly, although the cost of living rose 74 percent from September 1939 to October 1943. In June and July of 1945, 43,000 workers, most of whom were performing services indispensable to the country's economic and administrative life, went on a strike that lasted more than forty days. In large part as a result of the strike's success, the labor movement grew steadily, and by 1950 there were 144 unions with more than 144,000 members.

Although the labor movement was federated in 1941, the period from the end of World War II to 1964 was characterized by numerous splits, regroupings, and further fragmentation. Factionalism was rampant, engendered by the reluctance of the Colonial Office to strengthen union rights, dependence on foreign financial support, the thwarting of labor's political objectives by nationalist leaders, and intramural ideological differences. The most visible manifestation of labor problems was the dispute over whether to affiliate with the East European socialist-oriented World Federation of Trade Unions, based in Prague, or the more capitalist-oriented International Confederation of Free Trade Unions, headquartered in Brussels.

In 1963 union members numbered 300,000, or 1.6 percent of the labor force. Despite this low level of organization, labor discontent worsened as the gap widened between the wages of white-collar and those of blue-collar workers. In FY 1964, supervisors were paid thirty-three times as much as daily-wage workers and semiskilled workers in public service. After independence, many workers had begun to feel that the political leadership was making no effort to reduce the inequalities of the colonial wage and benefit structure. Corruption and conspicuous consumption were perceived to be widespread among politicians. An April 1963 pay raise for ministers and members of parliament further fueled labor resentment because rank-and-file civil servants had been doing without raises since 1960. The five superordinate central labor organizations consequently formed the Joint Action Committee (JAC) to pressure the government to raise wages. Numerous delays in the publication of a government commission report on wages and salaries provided partial impetus for a JAC-mobilized general strike of 800,000 supporters, most of them nonunionists, which lasted twelve days in June 1964. Although the strike demonstrated the government's fragility, the JAC could not translate its victory into permanent political strength; labor unity disintegrated in the face of overtures by political parties to segments of organized labor as the federal elections of December 1964 neared.

Political parties and communal associations were banned during the military rule of the late 1960s, so labor unions posed a potential organized threat to the government. The military government's decree in 1969 forbidding strikes was repeatedly defied during the next four years, most notably in 1973, when the regime gave in to demands by striking postal and telecommunications workers, about one-fifth of the federal civil service. Labor activities and internal strife among four central labor organizations continued up to 1975, when the military government attempted, unsuccessfully at first, to merge the four bodies into one unit, the Nigerian Labour Congress (NLC). The government dissolved the four central unions, prohibited union affiliations with international labor organizations, and in 1977 banned eleven labor leaders from further union activity. Under terms of a 1978 labor decree amendment, the more than 1,000 previously existing unions were reorganized into 70 registered industrial unions under the NLC, now the sole central labor organization.

In the early 1980s, the civilian government found itself losing control of organized labor. Numerous wildcat strikes occurred in 1980–81, and in May 1981, the NLC mobilized 700,000 of 1 million unionized Nigerian workers for a two-day strike, despite the opposition of a government-supported faction.

Working days lost through strikes declined from 9.6 million in 1982 to 200,000 in 1985 in the midst of a decline in national income that had begun in 1983. Industrial unrest resulted, however, in demands by larger number of workers for payments of salary arrears and fringe benefits as real wages fell by almost 60 percent. The causes of the decline in real wages were the World Bank-advised SAP and the unfavorable terms of trade that resulted from the collapse of the world oil market between 1986 and 1989.

Agriculture, Forestry, and Fishing

As economic development occurs, the relative size of the agricultural sector usually decreases. Accordingly, Nigerian GDP originating in the agricultural sector shrank from 65.7 percent in FY 1959 to 30.9 percent by 1976. The overall economic decline reversed this trend, and by 1988, 39.1 percent of GDP was derived from agricultural activity (see table 9, Appendix).

The contribution of the agricultural sector increased 3.8 percent yearly between 1983 and 1988, and the percentage of export value in agriculture grew from 3 percent in 1983 to 9 percent in 1988, although much of this growth resulted from the fall in oil export receipts (see table 10, Appendix). Food production also increased rapidly during the 1980s, especially after exchange-rate reform restricted food imports in 1986.

Cocoa House in Ibadan,
the cocoa marketing center
Courtesy Embassy of Nigeria,
Washington

Spraying cacao plants;
cocoa is a major export
Courtesy Embassy of Nigeria,
Washington

Land Use, Soils, and Land Tenure

In 1990 estimates indicated that 82 million hectares out of Nigeria's total land area of about 91 million hectares were arable. However, only about 34 million hectares (or 42 percent of the cultivable area) were being cultivated at the time. Much of this land was farmed under bush fallow, a technique whereby an area much larger than that under cultivation is left idle for varying periods to allow natural regeneration of soil fertility. Another 18 million hectares were classified as permanent pasture, but much of this land had the potential to support crops. About 20 million hectares were covered by forests and woodlands. Most of this land also had agricultural potential. The country's remaining 19 million hectares were covered by buildings or roads, or were considered wasteland.

Nigeria's soil is rated from low to medium in productivity. However, the Food and Agriculture Organization of the United Nations (FAO) concluded that most of the country's soil would have medium to good productivity if this resource were managed properly.

Traditional land tenure throughout Nigeria was based on customary laws under which land was considered community property. An individual had usufructuary rights to the land he farmed in his lineage or community area. He could possess the land as long as he used it to his family's or society's benefit, and could pass the land on to heirs and pledge its use to satisfy a debt, but could not sell or mortgage it. The right of disposal belonged only to the community, which, acting through traditional authorities, exercised this right in accordance with customary law.

The Fulani conquest of much of northern Nigeria in the early 1800s brought a change in land tenure in areas under Fulani control. The conquerors bestowed fiefs on certain individuals, who sometimes appointed overseers with the power to allocate unused land without regard for local community interests. One result was a growing number of grants to strangers during the nineteenth century because overseers sought to increase the revenue from their landlords' holdings. This practice gradually reduced the extent of bush land and encouraged the migration of farmers to urban areas that began toward the end of the nineteenth century.

In the early 1900s, the British established hegemony over the Fulani and declared all land in the former Fulani fiefs to be public property. Subsequently, in contrast to southern Nigeria, where the community owned land, in the north the government required occupancy permits. However, at the same time the northern authorities were charged with supervision and protection of the indigenous population's traditional rights, and a general reversion to customary land-tenure practices occurred. In predominantly Muslim areas, traditional land inheritance laws were allowed to remain in force. As a result of the government's support of local customary laws, encroachment by outsiders appears largely to have been halted. In 1962 the government of the Northern Region placed formal restrictions on landholding by individuals who were not members of a northern community.

In the south, colonial authorities introduced the concept of individual ownership of property and authorized the legal conveyance of land that could be registered with the government. Various laws and ordinances gave government the power to expropriate statutory landholdings in return for compensation. Expansion of the money economy and the resulting emphasis on commercial crops encouraged farmers to seek private ownership of land. Nonetheless, customary tenure remained the principal form of landholding throughout Nigeria as late as the early 1970s. During the 1970s, however, individuals and business enterprises drove up land prices, especially in newly urbanized areas, by investing heavily in real estate. In the south, customary owners turned from land sales to more profitable high-rent leasing arrangements. In the north, where land was held only by permit, farmers on the outskirts of cities became victims of developmental rezoning. Their permits were revoked, and, only minimally compensated, they moved to other areas. The land was then subdivided and sold at high prices.

In response to a potential crisis in land distribution, the Federal Military Government promulgated the Land Use Decree of March 1978, establishing a uniform tenure system for all of Nigeria. Subsequently incorporated in the constitution of 1979, the decree effectively nationalized all land by requiring certificates of occupancy from the government for land held under customary and statutory rights and the payment of rent to the government. However, the decree stipulated that anyone in a rural or urban area who normally occupied land and developed it would continue to enjoy the right of occupancy and could sell or transfer his interest in the development of the land.

The main purpose of the 1978 decree was to open land to development by individuals, corporations, institutions, and governments. The decree gave state and local governments authority to take over and assign any undeveloped land. Occupancy or possession of undeveloped land by individuals was restricted. To prevent fragmentation, the statutory right of occupancy could be passed on only to one person or heir.

Crops

Nigeria's climate permits the cultivation of a variety of crops in a pattern that emerged in earlier centuries in response to local conditions. As in other West Africa states, rainfall is heaviest in the south, where the forests and savannas benefit from abundant precipitation and relatively short dry seasons. The staples are root crops, including cassava, yams, taro (cocoyams), and sweet potatoes. Tree crops—cacao, oil palm, and rubber—constitute the area's main commercial produce (see table 11, Appendix). Cacao, from which cocoa is made, grows mostly in the southwest. Oil palms (whose kernels can be made into palm wine) predominate in the southeast and are numerous in the south-central area. Rubber stands are common in south-central and southeastern Nigeria.

Smallholder farmers, who use simple production techniques and bush-fallow cultivation and cultivate areas of one-half to two hectares each, contribute two-thirds of farm production. In most areas, some noncash crops are grown, such as sorghum, yams, cassava, cowpeas, millet, corn, cocoyams, sweet potatoes, and rice.

The northern third of Nigeria, which experiences a dry season of five to seven months, during which less than twenty-five millimeters of rain falls, lies mostly in the Sudan (see Glossary) savanna and the arid Sahel (see Glossary) zone. There, the staples are millet, cowpeas, and a drought-resistant variety of sorghum known as guinea corn. Corn is also cultivated, as well as rice in suitable lowland areas. The north's principal commercial crops are cotton and peanuts.

Between the arid north and the moist south lies a Guinea savanna region sometimes referred to as the middle belt (see Glossary). This area produces staples such as yams, sorghum, millet, cassava, cowpeas, and corn, with rice an important crop in some places. The middle belt's southern edge represents the lower limits of the northern grain-dominated economy. The most significant commercial crop of the middle belt is sesame (or benniseed).

Most Nigerians eat grains, but the production and consumption of sorghum (guinea corn) and millet are heavily concentrated in the savanna north. In 1980 the two grains accounted for 80 percent of Nigeria's total grain production. Corn production in the savanna middle belt benefits from heavier rainfall, which frequently permits two crops a year. The demand for rice, much of it imported, increased dramatically during the affluent 1970s, but had to be cut back during the foreign exchange shortages of the 1980s.

Cocoa and peanuts were Nigeria's two major exports until petroleum surpassed both in 1965. Cocoa, cotton, peanuts, oil palm products, and rubber were the principal export crops in the 1960s and early 1970s, but with export reorientation, only cocoa remained of any importance after 1975. Although Nigeria was the world's largest exporter of peanuts in the early 1970s, peanuts fell from the export list by the end of the 1970s as a result of the severe Sahel drought of 1972–74 and a viral disease in 1975. With assistance from the World Bank, the government restored cocoa production in the late 1970s and 1980s through replanting programs and producer price supports. The resulting increase in cocoa output (to 200,000 tons in 1988) kept Nigeria in third place among world cocoa producers, after Ivory Coast and Ghana.

Although the devaluation of the naira and the abolition of agricultural marketing boards in FY 1986 were intended to increase cash-crop output, the results were disappointing. The failure to significantly increase output was caused partly by the lack of incentives for producers to invest in maintenance.

In the late 1980s, Nigeria reduced the structural bias against agricultural activity by decontrolling farm prices, maintaining subsidies on fertilizer and farm exports, and maintaining import bans on some food items. Despite the granting of increased incentives to the domestic farming industry, agricultural output rose slowly because of inadequate transportation and power networks, a lack of appropriate technology, and the ineffective application of rural credit. Although the domestic production of food did not decline, on a per capita basis food became less available during this period.

Irrigation

Traditional cultivators throughout Nigeria used elemental irrigation systems long before the colonial period. These systems included seasonally inundated depressions in upland areas of the south and parts of the middle belt that received heavy rainfall, shallow swamps, and seasonally flooded riverine land. In the north, shadoof irrigation was also used along rivers, and some use was made of wells. Smallholders were using traditional methods to irrigate about 120,000 hectares in the 1950s and about 800,000 hectares in the late 1970s.

In 1949 the Northern Region established the first government irrigation agency. By the end of the 1960s, government projects—all relatively small—brought 9,000 hectares under irrigation. The severe Sahel drought of 1972–74 resulted in the expenditure of large sums for irrigation development by the federal government and by some state governments during the third plan, 1975–80. In 1975 the federal government established the Ministry of Water Resources and in 1976 created eleven river basin development authorities with responsibility for irrigation and the comprehensive development of water resources. Major irrigation projects after the mid-1970s included the South Chad Irrigation Project in Borno State, the Bakolori Project in Sokoto State, and the Kano River Project.

Livestock

Reliable statistics on livestock holdings did not exist, but careful estimates suggested a total of 10 to 11 million cattle in the early 1970s and, after the severe drought, 8.5 million in the late 1970s. Although an epidemic of rinderpest killed more than a million cattle in 1983, production recovered by the end of the 1980s. The UN FAO estimated that in 1987 there were 12.2 million cattle, 13.2 million sheep, 26.0 million goats, 1.3 million pigs, 700,000 donkeys, 250,000 horses, 18,000 camels (found mostly in the Sahel savanna around Lake Chad), and 175 million poultry nationally. This livestock was owned mostly by villages rather than by commercial operators. The livestock subsector accounted for about 2 percent of GDP in the 1980s.

Until the 1990s, cattle-raising was limited largely to the northern fifth of the country that was free of the tsetse fly. A program of tsetse-fly research and eradication was somewhat successful during the 1970s and 1980s, but 90 percent of the national cattle herd was still found in the northern states in 1990. About 96 percent of these animals were zebu-type cattle, most of which were tended by Fulani pastoralists. Traditionally, the Fulani moved their herds during the dry season to pasture in the moister Guinea savanna, returning northward when the rains began and danger from the tsetse fly increased. During the 1970s and 1980s, the expansion of cultivated areas and irrigation seriously obstructed this migration by cutting off access to usual travel routes.

Most of Nigeria's remaining cattle, 3 to 4 percent, are smaller than the zebu type and less valuable as draft animals. However, they possess a resistance to trypanosomiasis that makes it possible to raise them in the tsetse-infested humid forest zone. The government improved these herds in early 1980 by importing breeding stock of a particularly disease-resistant strain from The Gambia.

By the early 1970s, as the general standard of living improved, the demand for meat in Nigeria exceeded the domestic supply. As a result, 30 to 40 percent of the beef consumed in Nigeria was imported from Niger, Chad, and other neighboring countries. In the mid-1970s, Nigeria began importing frozen beef in response to export restrictions initiated by its neighbors. The National Livestock Production Company established domestic commercial cattle ranches in the late 1970s, but with poor results.

Drilling a water well in Okposi region of southern Nigeria, east of Niger River
Courtesy UNICEF (Maggie Black)

Most of Nigeria's sheep and goats are in the north, where the Fulani maintained an approximate ratio of 30 percent sheep and goats to 70 percent cattle. About 40 percent of northern non-Fulani farming households are estimated to keep sheep and goats. Most pigs are raised in the south, where the Muslim proscription against eating pork is not a significant factor.

Almost all rural households raise poultry as a subsistence meat. Chickens are predominantly of indigenous origin, and there is some crossbreeding with foreign stock. Egg production is low. Private commercial poultry operations increased rapidly during the 1970s and 1980s near urban areas, providing a growing source of eggs for the cities. But commercial operations remained largely dependent on corn and other feeds imported from the United States.

Forestry

Nigeria's forests can be divided into two principal categories: woodlands and forests of the savanna regions (four-fifths of the country's forest area) that are sources of fuel and poles, and rainforests of the southern humid zone that supply almost all domestic timber and lumber, with fuelwood as a byproduct. Nigeria's forests have gradually shrunk over the centuries, especially in the north, where uncontrolled commercial exploitation of privately owned forests began in the late nineteenth century. Toward the end of the 1800s, the colonial government began establishing forest reserves.

By 1900 more than 970 square kilometers had been set aside. By 1930 this reserve had grown to almost 30,000 square kilometers, and by 1970 to 93,420 square kilometers, mostly in the savanna regions.

Through the 1950s, forest regeneration was largely by natural reseeding, although the government established some small plantations near larger towns for fuelwood and poles. In the early 1960s, the government began emphasizing the development of forest plantations, especially ones planted with fast-growing, exotic species, such as teak and gmelina (an Australian hardwood). By 1976 about 115,000 hectares had been planted. During the late 1970s and 1980s, state plantations became an important source of timber, paper pulp, poles, and fuelwood. Despite these developments, forestry's share of Nigeria's expanding GDP declined from 6 percent in the late 1950s to 2 percent in the late 1970s and 1980s. Earnings from the export of timber and wood products—6 percent of export income in 1960—declined to 1 percent of export income in 1970 and virtually nothing in the late 1970s and 1980s, as domestic needs increased rapidly. The oil boom of the 1970s slowed exports further, as more and more wood was diverted to the domestic construction industry.

In the 1980s, Nigeria's demand for commercial wood products (excluding paper pulp and paper) threatened to exhaust reserves before the year 2000. To reverse this process, especially in the northern savanna, the government needed to double the rate of annual plantings it set in the 1980s. In June 1989, the government announced receipt of a World Bank loan for afforestation to stabilize wood product output and forest reserves.

Fisheries

Data on fisheries output were meager in 1990. In the mid-1960s, estimates indicated that Nigerian fisheries brought in 120,000 tons of fish per year and imported 180,000 tons, mostly air-dried fish. Domestic production through the 1970s ranged from 600,000 to 700,000 tons annually.

Nigeria has declared an exclusive economic zone extending 200 nautical miles from its coast. These waters include the continental shelf along more than 800 kilometers of coastline, a large area of brackish lagoons and creeks, and freshwater rivers and inland lakes, including fish-rich Lake Chad and Kainji Reservoir, among other artificial bodies of water. In the early 1980s, the bulk of the catch was taken by small businesses using large canoes (some motorized) along the coast, smaller canoes in the creeks and lagoons, and similar small boats in freshwater areas. The modern commercial fishing

Fishing on Lake Chad
Courtesy Embassy of Nigeria,
Washington

Fish being examined at
Baga Experimental Centre
Courtesy Embassy of Nigeria,
Washington

fleet consisted of about 300 licensed craft ranging in size from 20 tons to more than 6,000 tons; about one-third were vessels under 265 tons that engaged in inshore fishing and shrimping. In the mid-1970s, the government set up the Nigerian National Fish Company jointly with foreign interests to operate a deep-sea fishing fleet. In 1975 the Nigerian National Shrimp Company was established in partnership with a North American firm. But deep-sea fisheries were, and in 1990 continued to be, dominated by foreign-owned trawlers, despite substantial investment in fisheries development, including the provision of fishing supplies and outboard motors to small local enterprises in the late 1970s.

Manufacturing

While agriculture's relative share of GDP was falling, manufacturing's contribution rose from 4.4 percent in FY 1959 to 9.4 percent in 1970, before falling during the oil boom to 7.0 percent in 1973, increasing to 11.4 percent in 1981, and declining to 10.0 percent in 1988. Whereas manufacturing increased rapidly during the 1970s, tariff manipulations encouraged the expansion of assembly activities dependent on imported inputs. These activities contributed little to indigenous value added, or to employment, and reduced subsequent industrial growth. The manufacturing sector produced a range of goods that included milled grain, vegetable oil, meat products, dairy products, refined sugar, soft drinks, beer, cigarettes, textiles, footwear, wood, paper products, soap, paint, pharmaceutical goods, ceramics, chemical products, tires, tubes, plastics, cement, glass, bricks, tiles, metal goods, agricultural machinery, household electrical appliances, radios, motor vehicles, and jewelry.

From 1982 to 1986, Nigeria's value added in manufacturing fell 25 percent, partly as a result of inefficient resource allocation caused by distorted prices (especially for exports and import substitutes) and prohibitive import restrictions. Between 1986 and 1988, World Bank structural adjustment program (SAP) measures contributed to larger increases in manufacturing's contribution to GDP, which grew 8 percent in 1988. These measures included liberalized regulations governing the import of capital, raw materials, and components; the creation of import-substitution industries; and, beginning in 1988, privatization. The SAP increased production efficiency, cut into the black market, and reduced factory closures resulting from import bans on essential inputs.

The Nigerian Enterprises Promotion decrees of 1972, 1977, and 1981, by limiting foreign ownership shares in various industries, shifted the manufacturing sector from foreign majority ownership in the 1960s to indigenous majority ownership in the mid-1970s and late 1970s. Businesspeople participated in economic policymaking, influencing the government's implementation of indigenization. "Nigerianization," in which foreigners were obligated to sell ownership shares to Nigerians, became an instrument by which a few civil servants, military leaders, businesspeople, and professionals amassed considerable wealth. In 1985 the government selectively relaxed the indigenization decrees to encourage foreign investment in neglected areas, such as large-scale agrobusiness and manufacturing that used local resources. After March 1988, foreign investors were allowed to increase their holdings in a number of other sectors.

Mining, Petroleum, and Energy Resources

Petroleum products accounted for two-thirds of the energy consumed in 1990, but Nigeria also had substantial resources in the form of hydroelectricity, wood, subbituminous coal, charcoal, and lignite. In the 1980s, most cooking was done with wood fuels, although in urban areas petroleum use increased. Coal, originally mined as fuel for railroads, largely had been replaced by diesel oil except in a few industrial establishments. Coal production fell from 940,000 tons in 1958 to 73,000 tons in 1986, only a fraction of 1 percent of Nigeria's commercially produced energy.

Tin and columbite output fell from the 1960s through the 1980s as high-grade ore reserves became exhausted. A fraction of the extensive deposits of iron ore began to be mined in the mid-1980s, and uranium was discovered but not exploited. Almost none of these minerals left the country, however, as petroleum continued to account for virtually all of Nigeria's mineral exports.

Mining contributed 1.0 percent of GDP in FY 1959, on the eve of independence. This sector's share (including petroleum) stood at more than 14 percent in 1988. Mining's general upward trend since 1959, as well as the fluctuations in the size of its contribution to GDP, can be attributed to the expansion and instability of the world oil market since 1973.

Oil and Gas

Nigeria's first oil refinery, at Alesa Eleme near Port Harcourt, began operations in late 1965 with a capacity of 38,000 barrels per day, enough to meet domestic requirements at the time. The refinery expanded production to 60,000 barrels per day after the civil war but failed to satisfy the demands of a rapidly growing economy. An additional refinery, delayed by political maneuvering over its location, was constructed at Warri, opening in 1978 with a capacity of 100,000 barrels per day. This plant was entirely owned

185

by a parastatal, the Nigerian National Petroleum Company (NNPC), which starting in 1979 also held an 80 percent interest in the earlier plant. Technical problems and shutdowns for routine maintenance reduced production, and the combined total of petroleum processed by the two plants in 1979 averaged 89,000 barrels per day—about 83 percent of the domestic requirement.

In the late 1970s and early 1980s, the NNPC had substantial amounts of oil refined abroad (mostly by Shell) to make up the shortfall, and some oil was also processed in Cameroon, Ghana, and Ivory Coast. In October 1980, a third refinery, with a capacity of 100,000 barrels per day, began operations at Kaduna, but did not become fully productive until the mid-1980s. A fourth refinery was completed in March 1989 at Alesa Eleme, increasing Nigeria's refining capacity to 445,000 barrels per day. Domestic petroleum demand stood at 250,000 barrels per day; hence a portion of the output of the four refineries could now be exported. However, by the early 1990s gasoline output was sufficiently short of the growing domestic demand to require that the NNPC still refine some gasoline abroad.

In 1988 about 96 percent of the oil Nigeria produced came from companies in which the NNPC held at least 60 percent of the equity. The NNPC also was responsible for 75 percent of total investment in petroleum. In the late 1980s, the major Western oil companies exploring oil resources in Nigeria (primarily in midwestern, southeastern, and nearby offshore wells) were (in descending order of importance) Shell, Chevron, Mobil, Agip, Elf Aquitaine, Phillips, Texaco, and Ashland. In 1985–88 11 percent of all extracted oil (about 66 percent of domestic requirements) was refined in Nigerian refineries, where the NNPC owned majority equity shares.

From 1974 to 1981, while real oil prices remained high, lending to major oil exporting countries, such as Nigeria, was considered very safe. Indeed, Nigeria did not borrow extensively abroad until 1978, when a fall in the price of oil required Lagos to borrow US$16 million on world capital markets. Thereafter, Nigeria continued international borrowing for an ambitious investment program, anticipating an oil-price recovery. The world's sixth largest oil exporter and the leader in oil exports in sub-Saharan Africa, Nigeria nonetheless experienced an external trade surplus only from 1973 to 1975 and 1979 to 1980, during two oil price peaks, and in the late 1980s, when debt-servicing burdens forced import reductions, especially in services.

Besides oil, Nigeria had substantial reserves of natural gas. Although the consumption of natural gas increased steadily in the

Punch press with operators
Courtesy Embassy of Nigeria,
Washington

late 1970s and 1980s, and in 1990 constituted more than 20 percent of Nigeria's total energy from commercial sources, the quantity of gas used was only a fraction of what was available. In 1988, with the largest natural gas reserves in Africa, Nigeria produced 21.2 billion cubic meters per day, with 2.9 billion cubic meters used by the National Electric Power Authority (NEPA) and other domestic customers, 2.6 billion cubic meters used by foreign oil companies, and 15.7 billion cubic meters (77 percent) wasted through flaring. Small amounts of gas were also consumed by petroleum producers to furnish power for their own operations and as fuel for some equipment. Domestically, there remained a large potential market for bottled liquid petroleum gas (LPG), which was produced primarily at the Kaduna refinery.

In the early 1990s, Nigeria was undertaking a major project to market liquefied natural gas (LNG) instead of flaring gas produced in the oil fields by building a gas liquefaction plant on the Bonny River. Four companies signed an agreement in May 1989 to implement this plan: NNPC (60 percent share), Shell (20 percent), Agip (Azienda generale italiana dei petroli—10 percent), and Elf Aquitaine (10 percent), with plant construction scheduled to begin in 1991. Other aspects of the project involved Nigerian government construction of gas pipelines for distribution to domestic residential and commercial users and a supply of gas to the NNPC chemical complex at Port Harcourt. Much of the gas was intended

187

for export, however, and the first LNG tanker was launched in October 1990 through the cooperative efforts of Nigeria and Japan.

Electric Power

Hydroelectric power furnished about 14 percent of the energy consumed by Nigerians in the 1980s. Total energy used in the form of electricity was considerably larger, however, because much of the energy provided by petroleum products and gas was converted into electricity. In 1990 most electricity was supplied by NEPA. This agency had been established in 1972 as a semiautonomous government activity through the merger of the Electric Corporation of Nigeria (ECN—created by the government in 1950 to generate and transmit power nationally) and the Niger Dam Authority (NDA—set up in 1962 to develop the economic potential of the Niger River). As part of its mandate, the NDA had constructed the Kainji Dam and an associated hydroelectric plant, which began operations in 1968. Until the late 1970s, the plant was the principal source of Nigeria's electrical power.

The demand for power grew at an average annual rate estimated at 15 to 20 percent after the start of the 1973-74 oil boom. NEPA's total generating plant, having an installed capacity of 881 megawatts in FY 1976—almost half of which was located at the Kainji hydroelectric plant—was unable to meet the rapidly growing requirement. By FY 1978 an additional 250 megawatts had been installed, of which 200 megawatts were at Kainji, but a drought in 1977 and 1978 significantly lowered the level of Kainji Reservoir and thus reduced the plant's output. During the drought, blackouts were frequent, verging on the catastrophic for major industrial establishments. Goods in the process of assembly had to be destroyed, and interruptions in machine operations substantially reduced productivity. The situation improved in the 1980s: two 120-megawatt units were added to the Kainji hydroelectric station, ten units of 120 megawatts each installed in Sapele, new hydroelectric stations built at Shiroro on the Kaduna River and Jebba downstream from Kainji Reservoir, and another 200 megawatts added at various smaller plants.

Power was distributed through a national grid that linked many of the large towns, some of which had been previously served by local diesel power stations. Yet the power sector, lacking spare parts, had neglected maintenance to the point that generating capacity was rapidly declining.

Transportation and Communications

Transportation

Nigeria's transportation network was potentially one of the best

in Africa in 1990, featuring an extensive system of paved high-ways, railroads, airports, and ports (see fig. 10). During the oil boom of the 1970s, however, most government funds earmarked for transportation were applied to the construction of new roads, and maintenance of existing facilities was ignored. As a result, the transportation system was plagued with congestion and a deteriorating infrastructure.

Roads

The road system began in the early 1900s essentially as a feeder network for the new railroads. In the 1920s, the government established a basic grid of two north-south trunk roads from Lagos and Port Harcourt to Kano, and several east-west roads, two north and two south of the natural division created by the Niger and Benue rivers. In later decades, this system was expanded until most state capitals and large towns were accessible by paved road. In 1978 an expressway was constructed from Lagos to Ibadan, and a branch from this route was later extended east to Benin City. Another expressway connected Port Harcourt with Enugu. In 1990 Nigeria had 108,000 kilometers of roads, of which 30,000 kilometers were paved, 25,000 kilometers were gravel, and the rest were unimproved earth. Carrying 95 percent of all the nation's goods and passengers, the roads constituted by far the most important element in the transportation network.

The poor maintenance of past years forced the government to shift its emphasis in the 1980s from constructing new roads to repairing existing ones. Massive traffic jams were reported in most large cities, and there were long delays in the movement of goods. Safety standards were low; in 1988 more than 30,000 accidents and 8,000 highway deaths were reported.

Railroads

In 1990 the rail system consisted of 3,500 kilometers of narrow-gauge (1.067-meter) track. The system's basic elements were two main lines running inland from the coast: one, in the west from Lagos to Kano, opened in 1912, and the other, in the east from Port Harcourt to a conjunction with the western line at Kaduna, opened in 1926. Three major extensions were subsequently constructed. One was a branch line from Zaria to Kaura Namoda, an important agricultural area in the northwest, completed in 1929. The second was a branch from Kano to Nguru, a cattle-raising region in the northeast, completed in 1930. The third, a 645-kilometer branch from the eastern line to Maiduguri, was completed

191

in 1964. A short spur to the mining area at Jos and two short branches from Lagos and Kaduna rounded out the system.

Poor maintenance, inadequate government funding, and declining traffic all contributed to a deterioration of the rail system. A plan to convert the entire system to standard gauge (1.435-meter) by laying new track parallel to the old was shelved in the early 1980s for lack of funds. Construction of a new line from Oturkpo to the steelworks at Ajaokuta was also halted in the mid-1980s. In 1988 the Nigerian Railway Corporation (NRC), operator of the system, declared bankruptcy. In an attempt to cut an inefficient and over-sized staff, the government laid off one-quarter of NRC's workforce. The remainder responded by shutting down the entire system for six months. In 1989 some trains were reported running again, but the system still was reportedly tottering on the verge of total breakdown.

Airports

In 1990 Nigeria had thirty-two airports with paved runways, three of which—Murtala Muhammad International at Lagos, Aminu Kano International at Kano, and Port Harcourt—offered regularly scheduled international flights. The parastatal Nigeria Airways provided domestic service between these three airports and fields in ten other Nigerian cities. Schedule irregularities and passenger complaints were common, and the government put increasing pressure on Nigeria Airways to improve its standard of service and reduce its financial losses. Despite the problems, the number of passengers on domestic flights increased throughout the 1980s, in part because of the poor state of other modes of transportation.

Ports

Nigeria's port system consisted of three complexes—Lagos, Rivers, and Delta—and the port of Calabar. The Lagos port complex was by far the most important, handling most of Nigeria's cargo. In addition to the cargo ports, two specialized tanker terminals handled crude oil exports.

The Lagos port complex consisted of the large quays at Apapa and new, smaller facilities at Tin Can Island west of Apapa. Apapa was Nigeria's principal cargo port and had direct rail connections to the national system. Docking facilities at Warri, Sapele, and several smaller towns near the mouth of the Niger River comprised the Delta complex. The main element in the Rivers ports complex was Port Harcourt, starting point for the eastern line of the Nigerian railroads and located sixty-six kilometers from the sea on the Bonny River. Calabar, eighty-three kilometers up the Cross

River, served as eastern Nigeria's main port. Nigeria's crude oil was exported through modern facilities at Bonny, near Port Harcourt, and Burutu, near Warri.

Import restrictions imposed in 1982, a soft worldwide crude oil market, and a decline in the country's crude oil exports throughout the 1980s caused a sharp decrease in oceangoing trade. In addition, the government shifted development funds in the last half of the 1980s from improving deepwater ports to building river ports in the hope that increased passenger traffic on the nation's inland waterways would relieve the strained highway system.

Communications

Already one of the best in sub-Saharan Africa, the domestic telecommunication system was undergoing a major expansion in 1990. At the end of the 1980s, there were about 155,000 telephones in Nigeria. About one-third of them were in the capital. A domestic satellite system with nineteen ground stations, along with coaxial cable and a microwave network, linked all major urban areas. Most localities could receive at least one of the sixty-five amplitude-modulation (AM) radio stations. More than a dozen cities had frequency-modulation (FM) radio stations. Shortwave broadcasts from six transmitters were directed at remote rural areas; broadcasts were in English, Yoruba, Hausa, Igbo, and twelve other languages. Most urban areas also had television service. In 1990 the country had an estimated 10 million radios and 10 million television sets.

International telecommunications were modern and provided high-quality links to the rest of the world. In coordination with International Telecommunications Satellite Corporation (Intelsat) Atlantic Ocean and Indian Ocean satellites, three ground stations made live television broadcasts; and direct telephone dialing was possible between Nigeria and the rest of the world. Lagos was the terminus of an undersea coaxial cable linking the West African countries with France and capable of carrying 960 simultaneous long-distance telephone calls.

Banking, Finance, and Other Services

In 1892 Nigeria's first bank, the African Banking Corporation, was established. No banking legislation existed until 1952, at which point Nigeria had three foreign banks (the Bank of British West Africa, Barclays Bank, and the British and French Bank) and two indigenous banks (the National Bank of Nigeria and the African Continental Bank) with a collective total of forty branches. A 1952 ordinance set standards, required reserve funds, established bank examinations, and provided for assistance to indigenous banks. Yet for decades after 1952, the growth of demand deposits was slowed by the Nigerian propensity to prefer cash and to distrust checks for debt settlements.

British colonial officials established the West African Currency Board in 1912 to help finance the export trade of foreign firms in West Africa and to issue a West African currency convertible to British pounds sterling. But colonial policies barred local investment of reserves, discouraged deposit expansion, precluded discretion for monetary management, and did nothing to train Africans in developing indigenous financial institutions. In 1952 several Nigerian members of the federal House of Assembly called for the establishment of a central bank to facilitate economic development. Although the motion was defeated, the colonial administration appointed a Bank of England official to study the issue. He advised against a central bank, questioning such a bank's effectiveness in an undeveloped capital market. In 1957 the Colonial Office sponsored another study that resulted in the establishment of a Nigerian central bank and the introduction of a Nigerian currency. The Nigerian pound (see Glossary), on a par with the pound sterling until the British currency's devaluation in 1967, was converted in 1973 to a decimal currency, the naira (N), equivalent to two old Nigerian pounds. The smallest unit of the new currency was the kobo, 100 of which equaled 1 naira. The naira, which exchanged for US$1.52 in January 1973 and again in March 1982 (or N0.67 = US$1), despite the floating exchange rate, depreciated relative to the United States dollar in the 1980s. The average exchange rate in 1990 was N8.04 = US$1. Depreciation accelerated after the creation of a second-tier foreign exchange market under the SAP in September 1986.

The Central Bank of Nigeria, which was statutorily independent of the federal government until 1968, began operations on July 1, 1959. Following a decade of struggle over the relationship between the government and the Central Bank, a 1968 military decree granted authority over banking and monetary policy to the Federal Executive Council. The role of the Central Bank, similar to that of central banks in North America and Western Europe, was to establish the Nigerian currency, control and regulate the banking system, serve as banker to other banks in Nigeria, and carry out the government's economic policy in the monetary field. This policy included control of bank credit growth, credit distribution by sector, cash reserve requirements for commercial banks, discount rates—interest rates the Central Bank charged commercial and merchant banks—and the ratio of banks' long-term assets to deposits. Changes in Central Bank restrictions on credit and monetary expansion affected total demand and income. For example, in 1988, as inflation accelerated, the Central Bank tried to restrain monetary growth.

During the civil war, the government limited and later suspended repatriation of dividends and profits, reduced foreign travel allowances for Nigerian citizens, limited the size of allowances to overseas public offices, required official permission for all foreign payments, and, in January 1968, issued new currency notes to replace those in circulation. Although in 1970 the Central Bank advised against dismantling of import and financial constraints too soon after the war, the oil boom soon permitted Nigeria to relax restrictions.

The three largest commercial banks held about one-third of total bank deposits. In 1973 the federal government undertook to acquirea 40-percent equity ownership of the three largest foreign banks. In 1976, under the second Nigerian Enterprises Promotion Decree requiring 60-percent indigenous holdings, the federal government acquired an additional 20-percent holding in the three largest foreign banks and 60-percent ownership in the other foreign banks. Yet indigenization did not change the management, control, and lending orientation toward international trade, particularly of foreign companies and their Nigerian subsidiaries of foreign banks.

At the end of 1988, the banking system consisted of the Central Bank of Nigeria, forty-two commercial banks, and twenty-four merchant banks, a substantial increase since 1986. Merchant banks were allowed to open checking accounts for corporations only and could not accept deposits below N50,000. Commercial and merchant banks together had 1,500 branches in 1988, up from 1,000 in 1984. In 1988 commercial banks had assets of N52.2 billion compared to N12.6 billion for merchant banks in early 1988. In FY 1990 the government put N503 million into establishing community banks to encourage community development associations, cooperative societies, farmers' groups, patriotic unions, trade groups, and other local organizations, especially in rural areas.

Other financial institutions included government-owned specialized development banks: the Nigerian Industrial Development Bank, the Nigerian Bank for Commerce and Industry, and the Nigerian Agricultural Bank, as well as the Federal Savings Banks and the Federal Mortgage Bank. Also active in Nigeria were numerous insurance companies, pension funds, and finance and leasing companies. Nigeria also had a stock exchange (established in Lagos in 1961) and a number of stockbrokerage firms. The Securities and Exchange Commission (SEC) Decree of 1988 gave the

Nigerian SEC powers to regulate and supervise the capital market. These powers included the right to revoke stockbroker registrations and approve or disapprove any new stock exchange. Established in 1988, the Nigerian Deposit Insurance Corporation increased confidence in the banks by protecting depositors against bank failures in licensed banks up to N50,000 in return for an annual bank premium of nearly 1 percent of total deposit liabilities.

Finance and insurance services represented more than 3 percent of Nigeria's GDP in 1988. Economists agree that services, consisting disproportionately of nonessential items, tend to expand as a share of national income as a national economy grows. However, Nigeria lacked comparable statistics over an extended period, preventing generalizations about the service sector. Statistics indicate, nevertheless, that services went from 28.9 percent of GDP in 1981 to 31.1 percent in 1988, a period of no economic growth. In 1988 services comprised the following percentages of GDP: wholesale and retail trade, 17.1 percent; hotels and restaurants, less than 1 percent; housing, 2.0 percent; government services, 6.0 percent; real estate and business services, less than 1 percent; and other services, less than 1 percent.

Foreign Trade and Balance of Payments

Foreign Trade

Until the mid-1950s, agricultural commodity exports—mainly cocoa, peanuts, palm oil, and palm kernels—earned more than the cost of merchandise imports. The demand for imports remained limited by the country's low income, lack of industrialization, negligible use of foreign inputs in agriculture, and sterling bloc restrictions. Nigeria had continued to specialize in primary products (food, raw materials, minerals, and organic oils and fats) and to import secondary products, such as chemicals, machinery, transportation equipment, and manufactures, used in Nigeria's development (see table 12, Appendix). Primary commodities comprised 98 percent of exports and 21 percent of imports in 1955, 92 percent of exports and 19 percent of imports in 1975, and 98 percent of exports and 24 percent of imports in 1985.

Minerals (largely petroleum) accounted for an increasing proportion of exports through the 1970s, increasing from 13 percent in 1955 to 35 percent in 1965, to 93 percent in 1975, and then to 96 percent in 1985 (see table 13, Appendix). The dependence on oil and a few other export commodities made Nigeria particularly vulnerable to world price fluctuations. Nigeria's overall commodity terms of trade (price of exports divided by price of imports) fell substantially, from a base of 100 (1980) to 83.8 (1984) and 35.5 (1986), before rising to 42.6 (1987) and then falling to 34.6 (1988). Meanwhile, export purchasing power (quantity of exports multiplied by the commodity terms of trade) declined from 100 (1980) to 48.3 (1984), 23.0 (1986), 23.1 (1987), and 20.4 (1988), a 79.6 percent reduction in the purchasing power of exports in eight years.

Nigeria traded worldwide with about 100 countries, but the composition of trade by country had changed since the colonial period. During the colonial era, Britain was Nigeria's dominant trading partner. As late as 1955, 70 percent of Nigeria's exports were to Britain and 47 percent of its imports were from Britain. However, by 1976 Britain's share of Nigerian exports and imports had dropped to 38 percent and 32 percent respectively. In the 1970s, Britain was replaced by the United States as Nigeria's chief trading partner. In 1988 the United States was Nigeria's best customer, buying more than 36 percent of its exports (primarily petroleum products); Britain was Nigeria's leading vendor, selling the nation more than 14 percent of its imports.

In 1990 Nigeria had associate status, including some export preferences, with the European Economic Community (EEC). As a result, it had a number of major EEC trading partners, including Germany, France, Italy, Spain, and the Netherlands. Nigeria also had an active trade relationship with some members of the Organisation for Economic Co-operation and Development, notably the United States, Canada, and Japan (see table 14, Appendix). Trade with African countries, mainly neighboring countries within the Economic Community of West African States (ECOWAS— created in 1975), comprised only 3 to 4 percent of total trade. In the 1980s, trade with Eastern Europe and the Soviet Union constituted less than 1 percent of Nigeria's total.

Balance of Payments

Nearly all of Nigeria's foreign exchange assets before the 1970s were held in British pounds sterling. Under the post-World War II IMF- modified gold exchange standard, which lasted until 1973, sterling was a key currency in international trade. A country that accumulated sterling, as Nigeria did in the twenty years before 1955, mostly years of restrictions on sterling convertibility, essentially extended credit to Britain. During this period, Nigeria restricted nonsterling imports, strengthening the balance-of-payments positions of the sterling area and Britain's international financial position.

From 1956 to 1965, Nigeria had a persistent merchandise trade deficit, which changed to a surplus in the period between 1966 and

1977 (including the 1967–70 civil war) with petroleum's rapid growth as an export commodity (see table 15, Appendix). In late 1977 and 1978, demand for Nigeria's low-sulfur crude decreased as oil became available from the North Sea, Alaska, and Mexico, and as global oil companies reacted to the less favorable participation terms offered by the Nigerian government. Except for the period from 1979 to 1980, when oil shortages and prices increased, demand for Nigerian crude remained sluggish until 1990. From 1978 through 1983 the trade deficit continued. In April 1984, the Nigerian government closed Nigeria's land borders and international airports for several days, replaced all old naira notes with new currency bills, and introduced tough exchange-control regulations designed to reduce the repatriation of naira smuggled abroad and prevent future convertibility to other currencies.

From 1984 through 1986 and in 1990, Nigeria had surpluses. These came, however, not because of export expansion but because an economic breakdown forced Nigeria to adopt severe import restrictions. Nigeria's structural adjustment under World Bank auspices brought some stability in the domestic and international economy but at the expense of falling real wages and decreased government social spending for much of the late 1980s.

The Debt Overhang

Among less developed countries (LDCs), Nigeria had the eleventh largest external public debt in 1989 (and the largest among sub-Saharan countries.) Its debt had increased from US$9 billion in 1980 to US$33 billion by 1989. The country faced persistent difficulties servicing its debt; in the 1980s, debt rescheduling was almost continuous. The secondary market price of Nigeria's bank debt in mid-1989 was only 24 cents on the dollar, indicating that the markets were heavily discounting the probability that Nigeria would pay its external debt.

Official reluctance to devalue the naira between 1981 and 1983, when inflation was more than 20 percent per year, discouraged foreign direct investment, spurred substantial capital flight, and encouraged firms to build up large inventories of imports (often with overinvoicing and concomitant foreign deposits) or to underprice exports (with the difference placed on deposit abroad). Having exhausted its official reserves and borrowing limits, Nigeria built up its arrears on trade credit to US$6 billion by the end of 1983.

From 1985 to 1986, President Ibrahim Babangida skillfully played the World Bank against the IMF for public relations gains, conducting a year-long dialogue with the Nigerian public that resulted in a rejection of IMF terms for borrowing. Subsequently, the

Outdoor market along the railroad line near Lagos
Shopkeeper's stall in Jos, capital of Plateau State
Courtesy Orlando E. Pacheco

199

military government's agreement to impose similar terms "on its own" was approved by the World Bank, which in October 1986 made available (with Western commercial and central banks) a package of US$1,020 million in quickly disbursed loans and US$4,280 million in three-year project loans.

Nigeria's contractionary fiscal policy in 1986 and 1987 reduced the budget deficit substantially. During early 1988, when the poor 1987 harvest put pressure on food prices and opposition to austerity mounted, authorities eased financial policy, more than doubling the budget deficit. Nigeria also eased monetary and fiscal policy in late 1989. Still, the country had managed to reduce real public spending since the early 1980s.

Despite several debt reschedulings in the 1980s and early 1990s, Nigeria's debt overhang continued to dampen investment and adjustment in the late 1980s and early 1990s. Facing years of austerity and stagnation, Nigeria could not afford to reduce consumption to effect an external transfer; thus a major contributor to adjustment was reduced investment. A lengthy schedule of large loan repayments acted as a tax on investment, since a share of returns had to go to creditors. Substantial debt servicing often meant slowing economic growth to avoid an import surplus. Without concessional funds, rescheduling only postponed an external crisis. Moreover, Nigeria's highly oligopolistic money markets, financial repression of interest rates and exchange rates, and sluggish expansion in response to improved prices in export and import-substitution industries prevented timely adjustments to financial and exchange rate changes.

Structural Adjustment

Under World Bank structural adjustment, the government tried to eliminate inefficient state intervention and obtain budgetary relief by abolishing agricultural commodity marketing boards and liberalizing cash-crop exports. These measures, together with devaluation, increased the naira prices of export crops, especially cocoa. The state also privatized many public enterprises by selling equity to private investors, while restructuring other parastatals to improve efficiency. The federal government encouraged private investment in the late 1980s, allowed foreign ownership in most manufacturing, and liberalized and accelerated administrative procedures for new investment.

The Babangida government, which came to power in August 1985 at a time of depressed oil prices, undertook its structural adjustment program between 1986 and 1988. In September 1986, the government introduced a second-tier foreign exchange market

(SFEM), sold on auction for a near equilibrium price and used for export earnings and import trade requirements. Under SFEM, the naira depreciated 66 percent to N1 = US$0.64 (N1.56 = US$1) and declined further in value through July 1987, when the first and second tiers were merged. When adopting the SFEM, Nigeria abolished the ex-factory price controls set by the Prices, Productivity, and Incomes Board, as well as the 30 percent import surcharge and import licensing system. It reduced its import prohibition list substantially and promoted exports through fiscal and credit incentives and by allowing those selling abroad to retain foreign currency. Although this action opened the way for an IMF agreement and debt rescheduling, the military government declined to use an allocation of Special Drawing Rights (see Glossary) in IMF standby funds.

Meanwhile, the naira continued depreciating, especially after the relaxation of fiscal policy early in 1988. The effect of the SFEM in breaking bottlenecks, together with the slowing of food price increases, dampened inflation in 1986, but the easing of domestic restrictions in 1988 reignited it. Real interest rates were negative, and capital flight and speculative imports resumed. In 1989 the government again unified foreign exchange markets, depreciating—but not stabilizing—the naira and reducing the external deficit. Manufacturing firms increased their reliance on local inputs and raw materials, firms depending on domestic resources grew rapidly, and capacity utilization rose, although it was still below 50 percent. Concurrently, nonoil exports grew from US$200 million in 1986 to US$1 billion in 1988. This amount, however, represented only 13 percent of export value at the level of the 1970s, and cash crops like cocoa dominated the export market. Large firms benefited from the foreign exchange auction and enjoyed higher capacity use than smaller ones. Despite dramatically reduced labor costs, domestic industrial firms undertook little investment or technological improvements.

Structural adjustment was accompanied by falling real wages, the redistribution of income from urban to rural areas, and reduced health, education, and social spending. The decrease in spending on social programs contributed to often vociferous domestic unrest, such as Muslim-Christian riots in Kaduna State in March 1987, urban rioting in April 1988 in response to reduced gasoline subsidies, student-led violence in opposition to government economic policies in May and June 1989, and the second coup attempt against General Babangida in April 1990.

*   *   *

Current reliable information on the Nigerian economy is scarce. Central Bank of Nigeria periodicals, *Annual Report and Statement of Accounts, Economic and Financial Review,* the Economist Intelligence Unit's annual *Country Profile,* and irregularly issued Office of Statistics publications are the major sources, but income and employment statistics are subject to a wide margin of error. The World Bank's annual *World Development Report* and frequent studies on sub-Saharan Africa include Nigerian statistics. *African Business, Financial Times, West Africa, Africa Research Bulletin* (Economic Series), and *Africa Report* include informative articles on the economy. Pius N.C. Okigbo's *National Development Planning in Nigeria* is an excellent update. (For further information and complete citations, see Bibliography.)

Chapter 4. Government and Politics

Brass statue of an oni, an Ife king of the early fourteenth or fifteenth century

THE STORY OF NIGERIA during the postcolonial era has been one of a search for the constitutional and political arrangement that, while allowing for the self-expression of its socially and culturally diverse peoples, would not hinder the construction of a nation out of this mosaic. In this search, the country has experienced cycles of military and civilian rule, civil war, and peaceful reconstruction.

If any nation typified political scientist Richard Sklar's characterization of the African continent as a "workshop of democracy," it would certainly be Nigeria. The country has experimented with different federal, state, and local government systems, learning more about its needs, resources, and constraints with each experiment. Despite the predominance of military regimes during the three postcolonial decades, Nigerian society has retained many of the fundamental building blocks of a democratic polity: vigorous entrepreneurial classes, a broad intelligentsia and numerous centers of higher education, a dynamic legal community and judiciary, diverse and often outspoken media, and, increasingly, courageous human rights organizations.

Despite the differences in character and composition of the successive governments, it is still possible to identify the major threads of Nigeria's institutional evolution. As the nation finds itself once more on the threshold of transition from military to civilian rule, promised for 1992, examination of these threads is essential for understanding the Nigeria that will become the Third Republic.

Nigeria is essentially an artificial creation, which, like most other African states, is a product of colonialism. This fact is central to understanding the country's government and politics, which have been conditioned and bedeviled by the problems of accommodating several diversities: ethnic, linguistic (there are between 250 and 400 distinct languages), geopolitical, religious (there is a deepening cleavage between Christians and Muslims), and class.

Nigeria became politically independent on October 1, 1960, after about seven decades of colonial rule by the British. Prior to colonial rule, most of the groups that today make up the country were often distinguished by differences in history, culture, political development, and religion. The major differences among these precolonial groups pertained to their sociopolitical organization: anthropological and historical studies usually distinguish between societies that were centralized ("state") and those that were noncentralized ("stateless"). To the former category belonged the Sokoto

Caliphate and the emirates of the north that, together with the Kanem-Borno Empire, were advanced Islamic theocracies. Also included in this category were the Benin, Oyo, and other western kingdoms, as well as the Igala Kingdom in the middle belt (see Glossary) or lower north. In these centralized systems, there were clear divisions between the rulers and the ruled, usually based on wealth and ascribed status. Institutions of a distinctly political nature, as well as taxation systems, were already established. Of all the centralized systems, the Sokoto Caliphate with its vassal emirates had the most advanced form of state organization. Not surprisingly, it provided the model for the British colonial policy of indirect rule, i.e., the governance of indigenous peoples through their own institutions and rulers.

By contrast, in noncentralized systems such as those of the Igbo and other eastern and middle-belt groups, there was a diffusion of political, economic, and religious institutions and practices. Also to be found was a large measure of egalitarianism, democracy, and decentralized authority. Under the colonial policy of indirect rule, "traditional" rulers (known as warrant chiefs) were imposed on these stateless societies.

In the immediate precolonial period, a pronounced religious gulf separated the northern from the southern peoples. Islam had been introduced to the Hausa states and other northern parts in the fifteenth century, but it did not dominate until the jihad of 1804, which extended Islamic influence to most parts of the north and even to towns on the southern fringe, such as Oyo and Auchi. The southern peoples were devotees mainly of traditional religions who underwent increasing contact with, and exposure to, Europeans and Christianity. In some areas of the south, such as Benin and Warri, the penetration of Christianity dates to the fifteenth century. When the north experienced contact with Europeans much later, the spread of Christianity and other Western influences was slowed by the strong attachment to Islam. This fact explains in part the uneven rates of economic and educational development between the northern and southern peoples that have persisted to this day, with important consequences for government and politics.

It should not be assumed that the various population groups in precolonial Nigeria were completely separated from one another. Historians have established evidence of various forms of interaction among the peoples, the major ones being trade and superordinate-subordinate relationships. Powerful centralized systems, such as the Sokoto Caliphate and the Benin Empire, dominated several neighboring groups. Where no established group held sway over the others, as was the case among the Yoruba-speaking people in the nineteenth century, a pattern of conflicts and wars prevailed. On balance, there were pronounced differences among the people who later came to comprise Nigeria, especially when the major regional groups are considered. British rule did much to accentuate these differences and, in some cases, created new divisive sentiments. Even the nature of British conquest and the process by which its rule was established encouraged separate identities.

The conquest and colonization of the coastal area of Lagos and its hinterlands took place between 1861 and 1897. The conquest of the eastern region and the declaration of the Niger Coast Protectorate occurred in 1894. Finally, a third wave of penetration led to the declaration of a protectorate over the northern areas in 1900. In 1906 the colony of Lagos and the Protectorate of Southern Nigeria (which included the former Niger Coast Protectorate) were joined together to become the Colony and Protectorate of Southern Nigeria. Finally, in 1914 the northern and southern protectorates were amalgamated to become the Colony and Protectorate of Nigeria, although both parts continued to be administered separately.

During the period extending from amalgamation in 1914 to independence from colonial rule in 1960, Nigeria had four major constitutions, each named after the colonial governor who formulated it: the Clifford Constitution (1922), Richards Constitution (1946), Macpherson Constitution (1951), and Lyttleton Constitution (1954). Although the first two constitutions were virtually imposed on the country, the latter two involved some consultations with representatives of the people through constitutional conferences. At the Ibadan General Conference of 1950, Nigerian leaders agreed that only a federal system that allowed each of the three regions (north, west, and east as created by the Richards Constitution) to progress at its own pace would be acceptable. Until that point, the constitutions had a unitary orientation. In creating three regions and delegating some powers to them, the Richards Constitution was a forerunner of the later federal constitutions.

Although the regional leaders at the Ibadan conference had unequivocally declared their preference for federalism, the subsequent Macpherson Constitution was essentially unitary. It went farther than the Richards Constitution in devolving power to the regions but left the regions subordinate and closely tied to the central government. Because many Nigerian political leaders favored a federal system in which the regions enjoyed wide autonomy, the Macpherson Constitution engendered continuing opposition. Finally, in 1953, this constitution became unworkable.

Rather than self-government for the whole nation, the northerners wanted self-government as soon as practicable and only for any region that was ready for it. They believed that each region should progress politically at its own pace. When a constitutional conference was convened in London in 1953, a federal constitution that gave the regions significant autonomy eventually emerged. This Lyttleton Constitution was the one that remained in force, with slight amendments, until independence in 1960. It enabled the regions to become self-governing at their own pace: the two southern regions in 1956 and the northern region in 1959.

Several important developments that have continued to affect Nigeria's government and politics in the postcolonial period marked the period of colonial rule. First, British colonial rule nurtured north-south separation, which has remained the classic cleavage in the country. In particular, after Lord Frederick Lugard's pact with northern emirs to protect Islamic civilization, the north was shut off from much of the Westernizing influences to which the south was exposed. This protection gave the southern peoples a head start, especially in Western education. During the struggle for independence, northern leaders were afflicted by a constant fear of southern domination. Many of the northern responses to national politics to this day can be attributed to this fear. At the same time, with the creation of three regions that saw the northern region larger in size and population than the two southern regions, there was also a southern fear of northern domination. The image of a homogenous north, although contradicted by the cultural diversity of that region, continued in 1990 to feature prominently in most southerners' perception of national politics.

Second, in creating largely artificial regions, the British fostered the cleavage between ethnic majority and minority groups. Each region contained the nucleus of a majority group that dominated in its respective region: the Hausa-Fulani in the north, the Yoruba in the west, and the Igbo in the east. The major political parties that emerged in the regions and controlled them were based on these groups. With regional autonomy, the major groups became the major ''shareholders'' of the federation. Power-sharing and political calculations have consequently centered on ensuring a balance of power among these groups. The minorities, feeling oppressed and dominated, agitated for separate states in the regions. Although a panel was appointed in 1956 to inquire into the fears of the minorities and to explore ways of allaying them, their requests were not met until after independence.

Third, the uneven rates of development among the groups, which generally coincided with regional boundaries, strengthened the forces of regionalism. The creed became north for northerners, west for westerners, and east for easterners. Despite the periodic creation of more states during the postcolonial period, these regional feelings continued to affect national politics, especially in the distribution of national resources. One manifestation of this tendency was the ceaseless disagreements and rancor over revenue allocation.

Another consequence of these regional and ethnic divisions was the fragmentation of the national elite. Unlike a few other African countries, Nigeria had no fully national leaders at independence. Nnamdi Azikiwe, an Igbo, who had the greatest potential for becoming a national leader, was forced by regionalist pressures to become a sectional leader. The other leaders during the post-independence period—Ahmadu Bello, Abubakar Tafawa Balewa, Obafemi Awolowo, Michael Okpara, Samuel Akintola, and Aminu Kano—are best remembered as sectional leaders, even though they are usually called nationalists. This fractionalization of the political elite in turn reinforced ethnicity, regionalism, and religious conflicts, inasmuch as these sentiments were often aroused in the competition for power, material resources, and privileges.

The colonial heritage, therefore, produced a country that was only weakly united. At some points, the regional leaders threatened to secede from the federation: in the early to mid-1950s northern leaders contemplated separation after their humiliation by southerners because of their refusal to support a motion for achieving self-government in 1956; in 1954 the Western Region threatened to separate itself if the colony of Lagos were not made a part of that region. There were strong countervailing factors that prevented breakup of the federation. First, British colonial rule had held the country together as one unit. Second, the regions had economic complementarity. In particular, given the export orientation of the colonial economy, the landlocked northern region depended greatly on the southern regions that had access to the sea. Third, in the final days of colonial rule, Nigerian leaders recognized the advantages conferred by the country's large size and population.

The First Republic

Nigeria became independent on October 1, 1960. The period between this date and January 15, 1966, when the first military coup d'état took place, is generally referred to as the First Republic, although the country became a republic only on October 1, 1963. After a plebiscite in February 1961, the Northern Cameroons, which before then was administered separately within Nigeria, voted to join Nigeria.

At independence Nigeria had all the trappings of a democratic state and was indeed regarded as a beacon of hope for democracy. It had a federal constitution that guaranteed a large measure of autonomy to three (later four) regions; it operated a parliamentary democracy modeled along British lines that emphasized majority rule; the constitution included an elaborate bill of rights; and, unlike other African states that adopted one-party systems immediately after independence, the country had a functional, albeit regionally based, multiparty system.

These democratic trappings were not enough to guarantee the survival of the republic because of certain fundamental and structural weaknesses. Perhaps the most significant weakness was the disproportionate power of the north in the federation. The departing colonial authority had hoped that the development of national politics would forestall any sectional domination of power, but it underestimated the effects of a regionalized party system in a country where political power depended on population. The major political parties in the republic had emerged in the late 1940s and early 1950s as regional parties whose main aim was to control power in their regions. The Northern People's Congress (NPC) and the Action Group (AG), which controlled the Northern Region and the Western Region, respectively, clearly emerged in this way. The National Council of Nigerian Citizens (NCNC), which controlled the Eastern Region and the Midwestern Region (created in 1963), began as a nationalist party but was forced by the pressures of regionalism to become primarily an eastern party, albeit with strong pockets of support elsewhere in the federation. These regional parties were based upon, and derived their main support from, the major groups in their regions: NPC (Hausa-Fulani), AG (Yoruba), and NCNC (Igbo). A notable and more ideologically based political party that never achieved significant power was Aminu Kano's radical Northern Elements Progressive Union (NEPU), which opposed the NPC in the north from its Kano base.

There were also several political movements formed by minority groups to press their demands for separate states. These minority parties also doubled as opposition parties in the regions and usually aligned themselves with the party in power in another region that supported their demands for a separate state. Ethnic minorities therefore enabled the regional parties to extend their influence beyond their regions.

In the general election of 1959 to determine which parties would rule in the immediate postcolonial period, the major ones won a majority of seats in their regions, but none emerged powerful enough to constitute a national government. A coalition government was formed by the NPC and NCNC, the former having been greatly favored by the departing colonial authority. The coalition provided a measure of north-south consensus that would not have been the case if the NCNC and AG had formed a coalition. Nnamdi Azikiwe (NCNC) became the governor general (and president after the country became a republic in 1963), Abubakar Tafawa Balewa (NPC) was named prime minister, and Obafemi Awolowo (AG) had to settle for leader of the opposition. The regional premiers were Ahmadu Bello (Northern Region, NPC), Samuel Akintola (Western Region, AG), Michael Okpara (Eastern Region, NCNC), and Dennis Osadebey (Midwestern Region, NCNC).

Among the difficulties of the republic were efforts of the NPC, the senior partner in the coalition government, to use the federal government's increasing power in favor of the Northern Region. The balance rested on the premise that the Northern Region had the political advantage because of its preponderant size and population, and the two southern regions (initially the Eastern Region and the Western Region) had the economic advantage because they were the source of most of the exported agricultural products and controlled the federal bureaucracy. The NPC sought to redress northern economic and bureaucratic disadvantages. Under the First National Development Plan, many of the federal government's projects and military establishments were allocated to the north. There was an ''affirmative action'' program by the government to recruit and train northerners, resulting in the appointment of less qualified northerners to federal public service positions, many replacing more qualified southerners. Actions such as these served to estrange the NCNC from its coalition partner. The reactions to the fear of northern dominance, and especially the steps taken by the NCNC to counter the political dominance of the north, accelerated the collapse of the young republic.

The southern parties, especially the embittered NCNC, had hoped that the regional power balance could be shifted if the 1962 census favored the south. Population determined the allocation of parliamentary seats on which the power of every region was based. Because population figures were also used in allocating revenue to the regions and in determining the viability of any proposed new region, the 1962 census was approached by all regions as a key contest for control of the federation. This contest led to various illegalities: inflated figures, electoral violence, falsification of results, manipulation of population figures, and the like. Although the chief census officer found evidence of more inflated figures in the southern regions than in the northern region, the latter region retained its numerical superiority. As could be expected, southern leaders rejected the results. Their response led to the cancellation of the census and to the holding of a fresh census in 1963. This population count was finally accepted after a protracted legal battle by the NCNC and gave the Northern Region a population of 29,758,975 out of the total of 55,620,268. These figures eliminated whatever hope the southerners had of ruling the federation.

Since the 1962–63 exercise, the size and distribution of the population have remained volatile political issues (see Population, ch. 2). In fact, the importance and sensitivity of a census count have increased because of the expanded use of population figures for revenue allocations, constituency delineation, allocations under the quota system of admissions into schools and employment, and the siting of industries and social amenities such as schools, hospitals, and post offices. Another census in 1973 failed, even though it was conducted by a military government that was less politicized than its civilian predecessor. What made the 1973 census particularly volatile was the fact that it was part of a transition plan by the military to hand over power to civilians. The provisional figures showed an increase for the states that were carved out of the former Northern Region with a combined 51.4 million people out of a total 79.8 million people. Old fears of domination were resurrected, and the stability of the federation was again seriously threatened. The provisional results were finally canceled in 1975. As of late 1990, no other census had been undertaken, although one was scheduled for 1991 as part of the transition to civilian rule. In the interim, Nigeria has relied on population projections based on 1963 census figures.

Other events also contributed to the collapse of the First Republic. In 1962, after a split in the leadership of the AG that led to a crisis in the Western Region, a state of emergency was declared in the region, and the federal government invoked its emergency powers to administer the region directly. These actions resulted in removing the AG from regional power. Awolowo, its leader, along with other AG leaders, was convicted of treasonable felony. Awolowo's former deputy and premier of the Western Region formed a new party—the Nigerian National Democratic Party (NNDP)—that took over the government. The federal coalition government also supported agitation of minority groups for a separate state to be excised from the Western Region. In 1963 the Midwestern Region was created.

By the time of the 1964 general elections, the first to be conducted solely by Nigerians, the country's politics had become polarized into a competition between two opposing alliances. One was the Nigerian National Alliance made up of the NPC and NNDP; the other was the United Progressive Grand Alliance (UPGA) composed of the NCNC, the AG, and their allies. Each of the regional parties openly intimidated its opponents in the campaigns. When it became clear that the neutrality of the Federal Electoral Commission

*Preparations for building
bridge over Gongola River,
an infrastructure
development project
Courtesy World Bank*

*Survey team for road construction
Courtesy Embassy of Nigeria,
Washington*

could not be guaranteed, calls were made for the army to supervise the elections. The UPGA resolved to boycott the elections. When elections were finally held under conditions that were not free and were unfair to opponents of the regional parties, the NCNC was returned to power in the east and midwest, whereas the NPC kept control of the north and was also in a position to form a federal government on its own. The Western Region became the "theater of war" between the NNDP (and the NPC) and the AG–UPGA. The rescheduled regional elections late in 1965 were violent. The federal government refused to declare a state of emergency, and the military seized power on January 15, 1966. The First Republic had collapsed.

Scholars have made several attempts to explain the collapse. Some attribute it to the inappropriateness of the political institutions and processes and to their not being adequately entrenched under colonial rule, whereas others hold the elite responsible. Lacking a political culture to sustain democracy, politicians failed to play the political game according to established rules. The failure of the elite appears to have been a symptom rather than the cause of the problem. Because members of the elite lacked a material base for their aspirations, they resorted to control of state offices and resources. At the same time, the uneven rates of development among the various groups and regions invested the struggle for state power with a group character. These factors gave importance to group, ethnic, and regional conflicts that eventually contributed to the collapse of the republic.

The final explanation is closely related to all the foregoing. It holds that the regionalization of politics and, in particular, of party politics made the stability of the republic dependent on each party retaining control of its regional base. As long as this was so, there was a rough balance between the parties, as well as their respective regions. Once the federal government invoked its emergency powers in 1962 and removed the AG from power in the Western Region, the fragile balance on which the federation rested was disturbed. Attempts by the AG and NCNC to create a new equilibrium, or at least to return the status quo ante, only generated stronger opposition and hastened the collapse of the republic.

Military Intervention and Military Rule

In most developing countries, there is a disruption of the civil-military equilibrium usually assumed in liberal democracies. In liberal tradition, the military is insulated from politics and subject to civilian control. In several developing countries, however, the military has not only intervened in the political process and overthrown the constitutional civilian authority, but it also often has established its supremacy over elected politicians. Even in those countries where the military has become almost a permanent feature of politics, military rule is still considered an aberration and symptomatic of a malfunctioning political system. In Nigeria, which typifies the scenario just presented, military rule was usually seen as a "rescue" operation necessary to save the country from civilian ineptitude. Military rule was not expected to last long; once the rescue operation was complete, the military should return to the barracks where they belonged and leave the governing to civilian politicians. The problem, however, was that although military officers accepted this rationale, military rule usually became self-sustaining.

From the onset of independent government in Nigeria in 1960 to the end of 1990, the military had ruled for twenty-one years. Altogether there were five coups d'état involving changes of government: those of January 15, 1966; July 29, 1966; July 29, 1975; December 31, 1983; and August 27, 1985. There was also an unsuccessful coup in which the head of state, General Murtala Muhammad, was killed in February 1976, and another that was nipped in the bud in December 1985. An attempt to overthrow General Ibrahim Babangida was made in April 1990. Of these coups, only those of January 1966 and December 1983 were against civilian governments. Several explanations of military intervention have been added to those given by the coup plotters themselves. Whereas the latter have cited economic mismanagement and corruption, other explanations have ranged from the continuation of ethnoregional politics by military means to the personal ambitions of officers.

The 1966 Coups, Civil War, and Gowon's Government

At the time a disparate group of junior officers struck first in January 1966, the officers were still politically naive and had yet to master the art of coup planning and execution. This inexperience partly explains why Major Kaduna Nzeogwu and others who masterminded the coup failed to take over state power. Instead, Major General Johnson Aguiyi Ironsi, commander in chief of the army, became Nigeria's first military ruler. Some of the remote causes of the coup included the use of soldiers to quell unrest, such as the riots among the Tiv people of the lower northern region, and calls on the military to supervise the 1964 elections. Whereas the latter involvement gave the soldiers a feeling of political efficacy, the beginnings of what came to be known as the "federal character" principle that sought to give each area some parity of representation

215

gave military personnel a sense of being sectional representatives. The coup of January 1966 was seen by many northerners as an attempt by the Igbo people of the east to dominate the federation. A successful countercoup six months later led by northern soldiers demonstrated the degree to which soldiers had become politicians in uniform.

The immediate reasons for the first coup, however, concerned the nationwide disillusionment with the corrupt and selfish politicians, as well as with their inability to maintain law and order and guarantee the safety of lives and property. During the initial stages, Nzeogwu and his collaborators were hailed as national heroes. But the pattern of killings in the coup gave it a partisan appearance: killed were the prime minister, a northerner, the premier of the Northern Region, and the highest ranking northern army officers; only one Igbo officer lost his life. Also killed was the premier of the Western Region who was closely allied with the NPC.

General Ironsi, an Igbo, emerged as the head of state. In his policies and actions, Ironsi did little to allay the fears of Igbo domination. He failed to place the coup plotters on trial as northern leaders demanded, and he appointed Igbos to sensitive governmental positions. Against all advice, Ironsi promulgated Decree Number 34 of 1966, which abrogated the federal system of government and substituted a unitary system; he argued that the military could only govern in this way. Given the already charged atmosphere, this action reinforced northern fears. As the north was less developed than the south, a unitary system could easily lead to southerners "taking over control of everything," as a northern spokesperson put it. It was at the height of northern opposition to unitarism that the countercoup of July 1966 took place. Most top-ranking Igbo officers, including Ironsi, lost their lives; the "status quo" of northern dominance was restored.

Lieutenant Colonel (later General) Yakubu Gowon, a Christian from the middle belt, became the head of state after the coup. His first act was to reinstate the federal system, along with the four regions and their allotted functions. But relations between the federal government and the Eastern Region, led by military governor Colonel Chukwuemeka Odumegwu Ojukwu, were very strained. In addition to the elimination of many Igbo officers during the July coup, a massive pogrom against Igbos occurred in the Northern Region. In September Colonel Gowon summoned an ad hoc constitutional conference to deliberate on the country's political future. Most regional delegates to the conference, with the exception of those from the midwest, recommended a confederal system to replace the federal system. The delegates from the Eastern Region insisted that any region wishing to secede from the federation should be allowed to do so. The conference was ended abruptly by increased killings of Igbos in the north and the heightening of tensions between the federal government and the Eastern Region. A summit of military leaders at Aburi, Ghana, in January 1967 attempted to resolve the disagreements and recommended the establishment of a loose confederation of regions. The Aburi Agreement became a source of contention, however (see Civil War, ch. 1).

In anticipation of eastern secession, Gowon moved quickly to weaken the support base of the region by decreeing the creation of twelve new states to replace the four regions. Six of these states contained minority groups that had demanded state creation since the 1950s. Gowon rightly calculated that the eastern minorities would not actively support the Igbos, given the prospect of having their own states if the secession effort were defeated. Many of the federal troops who fought the civil war, known as the Biafran War, to bring the Eastern Region back to the federation, were members of minority groups.

The war lasted thirty months and ended in January 1970. In accepting Biafra's unconditional cease-fire, Gowon declared that there would be no victor and no vanquished. In this spirit, the years afterward were declared to be a period of rehabilitation, reconstruction, and reconciliation. The oil-price boom, which began as a result of the high price of crude oil (the country's major revenue earner) in the world market in 1973, increased the federal government's ability to undertake these tasks.

The postwar Gowon government issued a nine-point transition program that was to culminate in the handing over of power to a civilian government on October 1, 1976. The agenda of the transition included the reorganization of the armed forces, the completion of the establishment of the twelve states announced in 1967, a census, a new constitution, and elections.

Gowon initiated several nation-building policies, the most notable of which was the National Youth Service Corps (NYSC), a community service institution that required one year of service by each Nigerian immediately after graduation from university or other institution of higher learning. Each member of the corps had to serve in a state other than his or her home state. More than 1 million graduates had served in this program by 1990.

The Gowon years also saw the oil boom and a buoyant economy. The federal government was encouraged to take on some responsibilities formally allocated to the states, especially in the area of education. It embarked on major infrastructural projects to transfer control of the economy from foreigners to Nigerians. The Nigerian

Enterprises Promotion decree of 1972, which was expanded in 1977, stipulated that only Nigerians could participate in certain categories of business. In those in which foreign involvement was permitted, controlling shares had to be owned by Nigerians.

The structure of government under Gowon was basically unitarian. At the apex of government was the all-military Supreme Military Council (SMC), which was the lawmaking body for the entire federation. Its decrees could not be challenged in any law court. Most members of the SMC under Gowon were state governors. There was also a Federal Executive Council composed of military and civilian commissioners. The states also had commissioners appointed by the governor. The states were practically reduced to administrative units of the federal government, which in several domains made uniform laws for the country. This basic structure of military federalism has, with amendments, remained the same during all military governments in the country.

The Muhammad-Obasanjo Government

General Gowon was overthrown in a palace coup in July 1975 and succeeded by General Murtala Muhammad, who was in turn assassinated in an abortive coup on February 13, 1976. He was replaced by Olusegun Obasanjo, formerly his second in command. General Obasanjo basically continued the policies and plans of the Muhammad regime.

Murtala Muhammad, a Hausa from the north (Kano State), ruled for only seven months. Within that short period, he endeared himself to most Nigerians because of his strong leadership and the radical reforms he introduced in domestic and foreign policies. He "purged" the public-service ministries, universities, parastatals, and other government agencies at the federal and state levels of individuals accused of being corrupt, indolent, or inefficient. He set up a panel headed by Justice Ayo Irikefe to advise on the creation of more states. Its report led to the creation of seven additional states in 1976. Murtala Muhammad also set up a panel under Justice Akintola Aguda to consider whether a new federal capital should be created because of the congestion in Lagos. The panel recommended Abuja in the southern part of the former Northern Region as the site of a new capital. In economic matters, Murtala Muhammad introduced the "low-profile" policy, a radical departure from the ostentation of the Gowon era.

Although he retained the framework of military federalism, Murtala Muhammad removed state governors from membership in the SMC and created a new body in which they were included at the center, the National Council of States. Because this body was

chaired by the head of state and subordinate to the SMC, its creation underscored the subordinate position of the state governments.
This arrangement enabled the head of state to exert greater control over the state governors than had been the case under Gowon.
In the area of foreign policy, Murtala Muhammad pursued a
vigorous policy that placed Africa at the center and that involved
active support for liberation movements in the continent.

Of all Murtala Muhammad's actions, however, the one that had
the most lasting consequences was a program of transition to civilian
rule that he initiated before his death. The program was carried
through as planned by his successor, Obasanjo. The stages of the
transition agenda included the creation of more states, the reform
of the local government system, the making of a new constitution,
the formation of parties and, finally, the election of a new government. The transition process was to culminate in the handing over
of power to civilians on October 1, 1979.

In February 1976, Murtala Muhammad was killed in an unsuccessful coup led by Colonel Bukar Dimka and officers from the
middle belt; the coup appeared to be an attempt by middle-belt
officers to bring back Gowon from his self-imposed exile and reinstate him as head of state. Obasanjo, a Yoruba and southerner,
became head of state. Although unfavorably compared with Murtala Muhammad initially, he succeeded in many areas of his administration where the more intransigent Murtala Muhammad
might have failed. Obasanjo became an adept political ruler, determined not to exacerbate north-south and Muslim-Christian
schisms in the country.

In addition to its methodical conduct of all the stages of the transition to civilian government in 1979, the Obasanjo government
initiated numerous reforms in public life. Attempts were made to
introduce greater probity in the activities of civil servants and other
public officials. The main vehicle for this process was the establishment of public complaints commissions in all states of the federation and in the capital. Despite the publicizing of particular cases
of abuse of office and corruption, however, little progress was made
in stopping the spread of this cancer in the society and economy.

The Obasanjo administration expanded the economic indigenization program started under Gowon. It also used the Land Use
Decree of 1978 to rationalize the country's haphazard tenurial systems, to reduce the crippling land speculation, and to curb the frequent litigation over individual and communal property rights. It
was hoped that these reforms would facilitate the acquisition of land
for modern agricultural purposes. In a similar vein, the Obasanjo
regime launched Operation Feed the Nation to counter the rapid

rise in food exports. None of these efforts was successful, but the programs indicated the kind of strategies that Nigeria would have to adopt to alter its economic imbalances.

In view of the complex process of transition to civilian rule and the many reforms introduced in the four years of the Muhammad-Obasanjo governments, those regimes seemed in retrospect to have tried to do too much too soon. In the final year he was in power, Obasanjo introduced many austerity measures and insisted on a ''low profile'' for all government officials. He was aware that Nigeria, despite its oil wealth, was still largely an underdeveloped country and its businesspeople mainly agents or intermediaries for foreign businesses. Such a salutary attitude was soon forgotten, however, as the successor regime rode the crest of a renewed upsurge in oil prices, spent resources faster than they could be realized, and left the country deeply in debt and its economy nearly in shambles when it ended in 1983 (see The Second Republic, this ch.).

The Buhari Regime

On December 31, 1983, the army struck again. This time the brazen corruption, the economic mismanagement, and the inept leadership of civilians provided the grounds for military intervention. Indeed, conditions had deteriorated so much in the Second Republic that when the coup came, it was widely acclaimed. Major General Muhammadu Buhari, a Hausa-Fulani northerner from Katsina State and a former member of the SMC in the Muhammad-Obasanjo governments, became the head of state. Because of the great powers that his second in command, Major General Tunde Idiagbon, chief of staff at Supreme Headquarters, was believed to wield, many commentators refer to this government as the Buhari-Idiagbon regime. In broad outline, the structure of government remained essentially the same as it was under Muhammad and Obasanjo. At the apex was the SMC, and the subordinate bodies were the Federal Executive Council and the National Council of States.

The urgent task before the government was to salvage the country's economy, which had suffered from the mismanagement of the Second Republic and from the rapid drop in the price of crude oil. Nigeria had become heavily indebted to several foreign monetary agencies, and the price of crude oil had begun to slide. Buhari believed that urgent economic problems required equally urgent solutions. He also thought that it was not a pressing issue to prepare to hand power over to civilians; in fact, all of Nigeria's military regimes have ruled without the benefit of democratic checks and balances.

The Buhari government investigated and detained the top political leaders of the Second Republic, holding them responsible for economic excesses of the previous regime. The government also placed constraints on various groups, including the Nigerian Medical Association, which was outlawed, and the National Association of Nigerian Students, and promulgated two decrees that restricted freedom of the press and suppressed criticism of the government. Decree Number 4 forbade any journalist from reporting information considered embarrassing to any government official. Two journalists, Tunde Thompson and Nduka Irabor, were convicted under the decree. Decree Number 2 gave the chief of staff at Supreme Headquarters the power to detain for up to six months without trial anyone considered a security risk. Special military tribunals increasingly replaced law courts, and the state security agency, the National Security Organisation, was given greater powers.

Buhari's controls also extended to his efforts to deal with the problems of "indiscipline" in the areas of environmental sanitation, public decorum, corruption, smuggling, and disloyalty to national symbols such as the flag and the anthem. He declared a War Against Indiscipline and specified acceptable forms of public behavior, such as a requirement to form lines at bus stops. The main concern, however, remained the economy. The government introduced a comprehensive package of austerity measures. It closed the country's land borders for a period to identify and expel illegal alien workers and placed severe restrictions on imports and heavy penalties on smuggling and foreign exchange offenses. The austerity measures made it difficult for local industries to procure essential imported raw materials, leading many of them to close or to operate at greatly reduced capacity. Many workers were laid off, and government itself retrenched many workers to increase its "cost effectiveness." All of these actions were accompanied by high inflation. The price of basic food items rose, and life became increasingly difficult, even for the affluent.

Despite the increased efficiency with which Buhari and his associates tackled the multifaceted national crisis, the regime's inflexibility caused discontent. The latter was the main justification given for the overthrow of Buhari by General Babangida in a palace coup on August 27, 1985, although the personal ambition of Babangida was an important contributing factor.

The Babangida Government

Babangida, of Gwari origins and a middle belt Muslim, was Nigeria's sixth military ruler and, as of 1990, the most powerful. Compared with Buhari, Babangida was a somewhat more methodical ruler, and his style was different. Whereas Buhari was stern and resolute, Babangida was deft and tactical. Babangida was reported to have taken part in all coups in Nigeria, which may explain his confident handling of national affairs. He was, however, unpredictable.

Although Babangida came to power as a champion of human rights, his record in this area deteriorated over time. He gradually released most of the politicians incarcerated by Buhari. Yet, he often hounded opposition interest groups, especially those of labor and students, and detained many radical and anti-establishment persons for various offenses. The infamous Decree Number 2 remained in force in 1990 to facilitate these oppressive acts.

The year after seizing power, the Babangida regime declared a National Economic Emergency. The options open to the country, Babangida said, were either to accept an International Monetary Fund (IMF—see Glossary) loan and the conditions attached or to embark on more austere economic measures that would require great sacrifices. Although the people favored a non-IMF option, they soon discovered that the hardships eventually imposed differed little from the IMF's conditions. The economic recovery program recommended by the World Bank (see Glossary) was instituted as a self-imposed structural adjustment program (SAP) that involved a drastic restructuring of the country's economy. Under SAP, unemployment rates soared, food prices increased significantly, and numerous user fees for education and health services were imposed. These hardships did not dissuade the government from SAP, which it believed to be the only approach to the country's social and economic problems. The benefits of SAP, such as lower inflation and a more balanced budget, began to be seen, but SAP was adhered to less stringently in the late 1980s.

Babangida's government adopted other economic reforms leading to a market system and political reforms leading to democratic processes. Important changes were made in the basic structures of military federalism. For the first time, a military leader was called president, presumably to emphasize the executive power he wielded. The name of the supreme lawmaking body was changed from Supreme Military Council to the Armed Forces Ruling Council (AFRC). There was also a new Armed Forces Consultative Assembly, formed in 1989, which functioned as an intermediate legislative chamber between the AFRC and the rest of the military. In spite of these elaborate structural changes, Babangida adroitly increased the powers of his office. He changed his ministers and state governors frequently. Even supposedly powerful members of the government were not spared, as was demonstrated in 1986 when

View of downtown Jos, a leading northern city
Courtesy Orlando E. Pacheco
Apapa, a major seaport near Lagos
Courtesy Embassy of Nigeria, Washington

he dropped his second in command, Commodore Ebitu Ukiwe. In his place, he appointed Rear Admiral Augustus Aikhomu, former chief of the naval staff. The most dramatic of these changes was made at the end of 1989, when Babangida reassigned several ministers, including General Domkat Bali, the powerful minister of defense and chairman of the Joint Chiefs of Staff (see Constitutional and Political Framework, ch. 5). The changes were perceived by southerners and Christians as resulting in an AFRC that consisted mainly of northern Muslims. The service chiefs of the army, navy, and police were Muslims; only the chief of the air staff was a southerner. The ministries of external affairs, petroleum resources, internal affairs, and defense, considered the most powerful cabinet posts, were held by northern Muslims (the minister of defense being the president himself). These changes generated heated controversy and antigovernment demonstrations by Christians in some northern cities. Babangida emerged from the changes more powerful than before.

Babangida also introduced far-reaching changes in the civil service, the police, the armed and security forces, and the political system. Certain actions of his government exacerbated religious tensions. The religious cleavage in the country had become increasingly politicized, beginning in the debates in 1977 when Muslims began pressing for the extension of sharia law (Muslim religious law) from state courts in the north to the federal courts (see Islam, ch. 2). In the Second Republic, activist Islamic groups emerged in the north, demanding the Islamization of the country. After coming to power in 1985, Babangida adopted several measures that were considered to favor Muslims and to threaten the secular nature of the Nigerian state. In 1986 Nigeria became a member of the Organization of the Islamic Conference (OIC), an international association of Islamic states in which Nigeria had long held observer status; this action was very controversial. In apparent contradiction, Babangida survived several religious crises by reiterating that the federation remained secular. At one point, he set up a religious advisory panel to mediate in the religious crises.

On April 22, 1990, a coup attempt led by Major Gideon Orkar almost toppled the Babangida regime. The presidential residence in Dodan Barracks was extensively damaged by the rebellious soldiers, but the head of state escaped. A unique feature of this coup attempt was the level of involvement of Nigerian civilians, who allegedly helped finance the operation. During the hours when the rebels controlled the radio station in Lagos, they broadcast a critique of the regime that combined attacks on its dictatorial nature and pervasive corruption with threats to expel the far northern states from the federation.

The survival of Babangida and all senior members of the regime enabled the government to continue its policies, especially the planned transition to civilian rule in 1992. The detention of several journalists and other critics of the military regime and the temporary closure of some newspapers, however, indicated the government's awareness that it had overstayed its welcome and would have to govern with even stricter controls than before. The state congresses of the two government-sponsored political parties, the National Republican Convention and the Social Democratic Party, the only legal parties, were held in the summer of 1990, and campaigning began in earnest thereafter.

Political Transitions and Transition Planning

Political transition in Nigeria has been based not only on the military ruler's conviction that civil rule was desirable but also on the expectation of the people that, after the military had performed its rescue operation, it should turn power over to civilians. Gowon and Buhari failed to do so. As a result, their popular support eroded, and they were overthrown. In accepting demilitarization as a necessary process, political transition has been on the agenda of every military government since Ironsi's, with the probable exception of that of Buhari. Ironsi set up a Constitution Review Committee, whose task was overtaken by the promulgation of the unitary decree; Gowon designed a transition plan, which he later aborted; the Muhammad-Obasanjo governments successfully executed a transition program and handed power over to civilians; and Babangida in 1990 was implementing a transition program, designed to culminate in civilian rule in 1992.

The Second Republic

In the program of transition to the Second Republic, the military leaders' primary concern was to prevent the recurrence of the mistakes of the First Republic. They believed that if the structures and processes of government and politics that had proved inappropriate in the First Republic could be changed, a stable and effective civilian government would emerge. The transition was therefore designed to address those fundamental issues, which were historically divisive, and to establish new political institutions, processes, and orientations. Except for the census, which remained problematic, most issues that threatened the stability and survival of the federation were addressed. The revenue allocation process was altered based on the recommendation of a technical committee,

225

despite the politicians' rejection of its recommendation. Local governments were also streamlined and made more powerful by the 1976 reforms.

The second aspect of the transition involved the making of a new constitution and appropriate institutions. A Constitution Drafting Committee (CDC) was appointed in 1975 under the chairmanship of a leading lawyer, Rotimi Williams, and, in 1977, a Constituent Assembly (CA) composed of both elected and appointed officials examined and ratified the draft constitution. After final ratification by the SMC, the constitution was promulgated in 1979. Political parties were formed, and new corrective national bodies, such as the Code of Conduct Bureau, Corrupt Practices Investigation Bureau, and Public Complaints Commission, were established. The most far-reaching changes of the transition were made in the area of institutionalizing a new constitutional and political system.

At the inauguration of the CDC, Murtala Muhammad outlined the objectives of transition as the continuation of a federal system of government with constitutional law guaranteeing fundamental human rights, maximum participation, and orderly succession to political power. To avoid the pitfalls of the First Republic, the new constitution was designed to eliminate political competition based on a system of winner-takes-all, broadening consensus politics to a national base, eliminating overcentralization of power, and ensuring free and fair elections. The SMC suggested that these objectives could be met by recognition of national rather than sectional parties, controls on the proliferation of parties and on the creation of more states, and an executive presidential system similar to that in the United States. In addition, the federal character of the country was to be reflected in the cabinet; an independent judiciary was to be established as well as corrective institutions.

The draft constitution incorporated these elements. When the CA met to ratify the constitution, a few issues were highly volatile. The most notable was the matter of sharia law, which Muslims argued should be given appellate jurisdiction at the federal level. Most Christian members of the assembly vehemently opposed this. Only the intervention of the head of state resolved the situation. Although the sharia clause was deleted from the constitution, the cleavage between Christian and Muslim groups persisted. Other controversial issues included the creation of more states, the determination of an age limit for participation in politics (intended to eliminate most discredited politicians who had actively participated in politics in the First Republic), and the scope of the executive president's powers. After the CA completed its work, the SMC added a few amendments, including use of Hausa, Igbo, and Yoruba as additional official languages in the National Assembly and applying the federal-character principle to the composition of the armed forces' officer corps.

By Decree Number 25 of 1978, the 1979 constitution was enacted. The constitution differed from that of the First Republic in 1963 in that it introduced a United States-type presidential system in place of the parliamentary system. Previously, the executive branch of government derived its powers from the legislature. Under the 1979 constitution, the president and vice president, as well as state governors and their deputies, were elected in separate elections. The elections had the federation and the state, respectively, as constituencies. Furthermore, while the Senate was largely a ceremonial body in the First Republic, the new constitution gave the Senate and House of Representatives coequal powers.

There were other provisions in the 1979 constitution that aimed at eliminating past loopholes. The first was the federal-character principle, which sought to prevent the domination of power by one or a few states, ethnic groups, or sections at the federal center, and by one or more groups in the states and local government areas. The principle required that the composition of the cabinet, boards, and other executive bodies, as well as appointments to top government positions, should reflect the federal character or diversity of the country at the particular level of government. This principle also applied to the composition of the armed forces. The principle was extended to the distribution of national resources, such as the siting of schools and industries.

The question of party politics became a constitutional matter. In view of the need for a limited number of national political parties, the constitution specified certain criteria that parties had to meet in order to be registered: the name, emblem, or motto of the party could not contain any ethnic or religious connotation or give the party the image of a sectional party; membership in the party must be open to all Nigerians irrespective of ethnic or religious affiliation; the party headquarters must be in the federal capital; and the executive committee of the party must reflect the federal character of the country. The task of registering political parties and conducting elections was given to the Federal Electoral Commission (FEDECO). The necessity for national parties resulted from the conviction that the disunity of the First Republic was engendered by the regional parties then operating. When the ban placed on political activities in 1966 was lifted in September 1978, at least fifty-three political associations were formed. Seventeen of them applied for registration, but only five were registered: the National

Party of Nigeria (NPN), the Nigerian People's Party (NPP), the United Party of Nigeria (UPN), the Great Nigeria People's Party (GNPP), and the People's Redemption Party (PRP). In 1981 a sixth party, the Nigeria Advance Party (NAP), was registered. Contrary to the expectations of the drafters of the constitution and the military rulers, most of these parties resembled the ethnoregional ones of the pre-1966 period although legally parties were required to transcend ethnoregional bases. The only exceptions were the NAP, which proclaimed itself a "new breed" party, and the NPN, which despite its regional antecedents, was probably the only national party in Nigeria. The UPN was a resurrection of the AG with its Yoruba core; the NPP was a rejuvenation of the NCNC with its Igbo core and strands of middle-belt support; the PRP recalled Kano's NEPU; and the GNPP, which appeared initially to be a new minorities formation, had its strength within the Kanuri section of the north. Apart from the PRP, which flickered as a radical party, and the populist NAP, the other parties appeared to be parties of the wealthy class or those who aspired to join it, for whom politics was a means of enriching themselves and consolidating their material base. Given this character of the registered parties, it can be argued that the perceived need to balance the power groups in the country rather than the constitutional requirements decided which parties were registered.

In the 1979 presidential election, NPN candidate Shehu Shagari was declared the winner, even though many people thought he did not meet the full requirements. He obtained a simple majority of the total votes cast in the federation but failed to get 25 percent of the total votes cast in thirteen states of the federation. The latter was the generally accepted interpretation of the constitutional requirement that the winner of the presidential election should obtain 25 percent of the total votes cast in two-thirds of the nineteen states of the federation. Shagari obtained 25 percent of the votes in twelve states but got only 19 percent in the thirteenth state. When FEDECO declared Shagari the winner "in the absence of any legal explanation or guidance in the electoral decree," Awolowo, the presidential candidate and leader of the UPN, led other defeated candidates and their parties to challenge the declaration in the electoral tribunal and later in the Supreme Court. But the challenge was to no avail. The controversy led to strong anti-NPN, anti-Shagari sentiments in several states controlled by the other parties. Once the NPN had succeeded in consolidating power at the center, the attraction it held was strong enough to tear the other parties asunder. Consequently, the history of the Second Republic is replete with interparty and intraparty schisms and federal-state conflicts.

At the domestic level, the NPN-controlled federal government embarked on politically expedient but uneconomic projects, such as establishing a federal university in every state, commissioning iron and steel plants that remained unfinished in 1990, and indiscriminately awarding contracts to build the new federal capital at Abuja. To finance these projects, the government relied heavily on foreign loans and aid. While the external debt of the country increased, the lot of the common citizen worsened. The global economic recession in the early 1980s and the collapse of crude oil prices in the world market accelerated the economic decline of the Second Republic (see Oil and Gas, ch. 3). By the time Shagari decided to initiate IMF-inspired austerity measures under the Economic Stabilization Act (1982), the problems of the economy required more drastic measures. This act, however, provided the blueprint for the austerity measures subsequently introduced by Buhari and by Babangida.

The demise of the Second Republic was accelerated by the tension generated by the 1983 general elections, which were similar to those of 1964–65. As in the earlier elections, two major political camps were involved in the contest: the NPN and the Progressive Parties Alliance, comprising the UPN, the NPP, and factions of the PRP and the GNPP. The NPN won landslide victories even in states considered traditional strongholds of the other parties. In several places, violence erupted, and every election was contested in court. A number of the electoral verdicts were rescinded in view of evidence that results were falsified. Under these circumstances, the military intervened in December 1983 (see The Buhari Regime; The Babangida Government, this ch.).

The Third Republic

The transition program of the military rulers toward the establishment of civilian rule in the Third Republic was more elaborate and deliberate than was the process followed in setting up the Second Republic. The goal was to prevent a recurrence of past mistakes. It was recognized that far-reaching changes involving more than the constitution and political institutions must be introduced. Consequently, as much attention was paid to restructuring the economy through the SAP as to fostering a new social order and a political culture through a program of social mobilization. In 1990 the transition program was tightly controlled, based on the assumption that desirable changes must occur through government intervention. It was also the most extended transition thus far, and this protracted schedule contributed to frequent changes in the agenda (see table 16, Appendix). The date of the final handing over of power was shifted from 1990 to 1992, state gubernatorial and assembly elections from 1990 to 1991, and the census from 1990 to 1991. Apart from these changes, major decisions frequently were reversed. Although President Babangida claimed that the transition was "sequential and methodical," it was actually responsive and ad hoc.

The transition to the Third Republic began with the setting up of a seventeen-member Political Bureau in 1986 to formulate a blueprint for the transition, based on ideas collated during a nationwide debate. In its report, the bureau recommended that a socialist ideology be introduced through a process of social mobilization, that local governments be strengthened as an effective third tier of government, and that a two-party system be created. The government accepted the recommendations except for the proposal advocating socialism. Most knowledgeable observers believed, however, that the Political Bureau was largely a facade created by the military, who had little intention of following the advice of the young intellectuals who composed the bureau.

Of all the recommendations, the two-party system was the most significant because it marked a departure from the multiparty system of the past. A majority in the bureau thought that a two-party system was the best way to ensure that the parties would be national and that they be financed largely by the state, as recommended. The bureau argued that in the First Republic and the Second Republic, the electoral alliances pointed to a two-party system. The north-versus-south character of these alliances led many to fear that a two-party system would function along similar lines, especially given the increasing sensitivity of the Muslim-Christian division. The government decreed the formation of two new parties in October 1989, requiring that the parties draw from a national, as opposed to a regional, constituency to prevent such a dichotomy.

Other aspects of the transition included a new Constitution Review Committee, a National Electoral Commission (NEC), strengthened local governments, the creation of local councils through nonpartisan elections, and the setting up of a Constituent Assembly (CA) to ratify the draft constitution, subject to final approval by the AFRC. The government, however, forbade the CA to deliberate on sensitive matters on which decisions had already been made or were to be made by the AFRC: the creation of more states and local government areas, the census, revenue allocation, the two-party system, and sharia (the latter was added to the list after the issue again threatened to tear the assembly apart, as it did in 1978).

In May 1989, after introducing eleven amendments, the AFRC promulgated the new constitution by Decree Number 12. The first amendment covered the deletion of Section 15 of the new constitution that pronounced the country a welfare state and of Sections 42 and 43 that provided for free education to age eighteen and free medical care for persons up to age eighteen or older than sixty-five, the handicapped, and the disabled. The second amendment provided for streamlining the jurisdiction of sharia and customary courts of appeal to make them apply at the state level only to matters relating to the personal status of Muslims. Amendment three described civil service reforms. Amendment four reduced the minimum age requirements for federal and state elective offices from forty to thirty-five for the president, thirty-five to thirty for senators and governors, twenty-five for members of the House of Representatives, and twenty-one for members of state houses of assembly and local government councillors. The fifth amendment replaced the six-year, single-term tenure for the president and governors with a four-year, maximum two-term tenure. Amendment six removed from the National Assembly control over matters of national security because, in the view of the AFRC, it "exposes the chief executives and the nation to clear impotence in the face of threats to security." The seventh amendment made the federal Judicial Service Commission accountable in the hope that this action would enhance the independence of the judiciary. Amendment eight eliminated provisions establishing an armed forces service commission to supervise compliance with provisions of the federal-character principle, i.e., that government bodies, such as the military, the civil service, and university faculties, reflect the various elements of the population. Amendment nine covered the reduction of the number of special advisers to the president from seven to three and alteration of the provisions for gubernatorial advisers. Amendment ten eliminated Section 1 (4) of the draft constitution outlawing coups and making them a criminal offense. The eleventh amendment deleted the provisions forbidding the federal government to obtain external loans without the approval of the National Assembly.

These amendments ensured that some of the changes introduced by the Babangida government would remain binding after the government had handed over power. In spite of those amendments, the 1989 constitution is similar to that of 1979; the presidential system is retained with minor amendments, such as the reduction in the number of senators from each state from five to three. The major difference in the new political arrangement is the two-party system.

Two unique aspects of the transition program since 1989 require emphasis. One was the blanket ban placed on all former politicians and top political officeholders, especially those found guilty of abuse of office. In effect, the new political order was to be built around the "new breed" politicians, namely, those who supposedly had not been affected by corruption, ethnicity, religious fanaticism, and other vices that characterized the "old brigade." A corollary of this ban was the government's opposition to the participation of ideological and religious "radicals" and "extremists." To participate in the Third Republic, each prospective politician needed a clearance certificate from the National Electoral Commission.

The second important factor was the decision to create in October 1989 two parties wholly run and financed by the state. After the ban on political activities was lifted in May 1989, a number of political associations were formed, and thirteen applied for registration. The requirements for registration were very strict and almost impossible to fulfill in the time allotted: the submission of the names, addresses, and passport photographs of all members of the association in the federation was required to facilitate physical confirmation of the claims by the NEC. In its report to the AFRC, the NEC gave low scores to the associations, including the "big four" that were the strongest—the People's Solidarity Party, the Nigerian National Convention, the Patriotic Front of Nigeria, and the Liberal Convention. The report stated that most of the membership claims were found to be false, their manifestos and organization were very weak, and most of the associations were affiliated with banned politicians.

The AFRC's reaction to the report was unanticipated. It dissolved all the political associations and decreed two new parties—the National Republican Convention (NRC) and the Social Democratic Party (SDP). It arranged for constitutions and manifestos of these two parties to be written by the NEC and by specially constituted panels based on a synthesis of those of the dissolved associations. The difference between the two parties was made a supposed ideological divide: "a little to the right" and "a little to the left." The finances of the parties, their secretariats in every local government area of the country, the appointment of their administrative secretaries, and their membership drives were now the responsibility of the federal government. The government described this new system as a "grass-roots democratic model" anchored in the rural and local groups rather than the "moneybags" and city elites that had allegedly hijacked the political process in the past.

A connection has also been made between these political changes and attempts to alter the economic and social realms. The economic transition centered on the SAP, whereas the social component included the process of social mobilization aimed at fostering a new social order and political culture. The general process was coordinated by the Directorate of Social Mobilization; the declared goals were social justice, economic recovery, mass mobilization, and political education under the acronym MAMSER (Mass Mobilization for Self-Reliance). MAMSER has been popularized, but time will be needed to gauge how far its goals have been realized. An emphasis has also been placed on rural development through strengthening of local governments, the Directorate of Rural Development, and improving facilities for the rural women's program.

The transition program toward the establishment of the Third Republic was the most ambitious undertaken in Nigeria. The success and stability of the republic, however, depended on the degree to which inherent structural problems could be overcome. Much depended on the orientations and on the actions of the politicians themselves, as well as on the dispositions of the military. Above all, the republic's success depended on the accompanying economic and social transformations. The stability of the Third Republic, therefore, would rest not only on the operation of the new two-party system but also on the effectiveness of the SAP and MAMSER.

The 1989 constitution provided for more than twenty ministers in the executive branch, in addition to various councils and commissions (see fig. 11). The names and numbers of these ministries and commissions, which, generally speaking, were responsible directly to the president, have changed occasionally since early 1990. Reportedly, Babangida was considering reducing the number of ministries to economize.

Federalism and Intragovernmental Relations

Given the territorially delineated cleavages abounding in Nigeria and the historical legacy of divisions among ethnic groups, regions, and sections, the federal imperative was so fundamental that even military governments—characteristically unitarian, hierarchical, and centralist—attached importance to the continuation of a federal system of government. The federation began as a unitary colonial state but disaggregated into three and later four regions. In 1967 the regions were abrogated and twelve states created in their place. The number of states increased to nineteen in 1976, and to twenty-one in 1987 (see fig. 7). In addition, in 1990 there were 449 local government areas that had functioned as a third tier of government since the late 1980s.

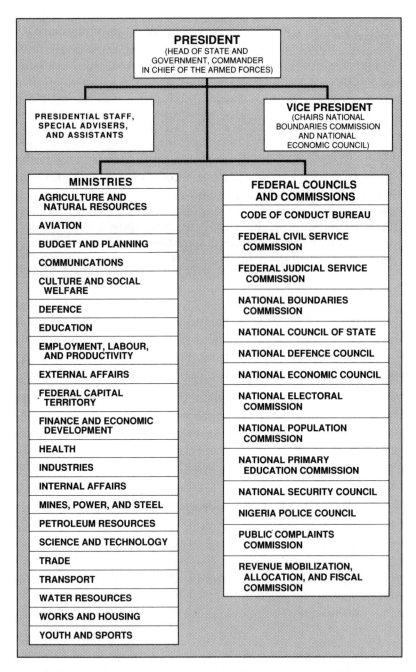

Source: Based on information from *Constitution of Nigeria, 1989*, Abuja, 1989.

Figure 11. Executive Branch, According to 1989 Constitution

In 1990 the Federal Military Government (FMG) included the president, the AFRC, the Federal Executive Council, the civil service, and a federal judiciary made up of federal high courts, courts of appeal, and the Supreme Court. The locus of power was the president and the AFRC, which possessed all law-making powers that could not normally be challenged in any court of law. The Federal Executive Council was an enlarged instrument of the president. The federal judiciary had appellate jurisdiction in appeals emanating from the state judiciaries. It did not have much independence because the government was directly involved in the appointment of judges and in the finances of the federal Judicial Service Commission. The integrity of the judiciary was constantly weakened by the setting up of special tribunals. Some of these tribunals were responsible for conducting trials of politicians of the Second Republic, and a few tried "miscellaneous" cases involving drug, smuggling, or foreign exchange offenses.

The state governments consisted of the military governor, a cabinet, the civil service, and the state judiciary. In most policy matters and in matters of finance, the state governments had to abide by federal directives and were subject to coordination by the National Council of States. The local governments had elected management councils comprising a chairman and councillors until June 1989, when these councils were dissolved. They were replaced by sole administrators, state civil servants appointed by the state governors. New local government elections were held in December 1989. In spite of the increasing powers of local governments, they remained subordinate to the state and federal governments and could be described as administrative agencies of these two higher levels of government.

"Civilian federalism" and "military federalism" corresponded to civilian government and to military government, respectively. According to federal theory, civilian federalism was the true form of federalism. It entailed government based on a constitutional sharing of power between the federal and state governments (and local government as well), using the principle of decentralization of powers. It was marked by party politics, which determined the nature of the federation, the configuration of powers, and the prevalence of the rule of law. The major elements of military federalism included the suspension and modification of the constitution; the omnipotence of the Supreme Military Council (SMC) at the center, and therefore the existence of only one decision-making level of government; and the ban on all (civilian) political activities. Because military federalism had been more common than

235

civilian federalism, this model made the federal government the "master" in relation to the "dependent" state governments.

At independence largely autonomous regions possessed the residual powers in the federation and functioned almost independently. Even before the First Republic collapsed, the federal government was asserting greater powers. In particular, it controlled the national economy and possessed emergency powers to intervene in any region where law and order had broken down, as it did in the Western Region in 1962. Relative to the powers of the states in 1990, however, the regions were very powerful; they had separate constitutions, foreign missions, and independent revenue bases. All this changed under military rule.

The FMG expanded its control over the economy to the extent that in 1990 the states depended on it for up to 90 percent of their revenues. The federal government also took over such matters as education, which formerly had belonged to the states. Because state governors were appointed on military assignment by the president, the states had little autonomy except in deciding how to implement policies formulated by the federal government. Attempts by state governments to reassert their autonomy during the Second Republic were aborted by the return of military rule. Some state governments that were controlled by parties other than the NPN took the NPN-controlled federal government to court on many occasions over matters of jurisdictional competence. This trend was likely to recur during the Third Republic, when the states would seek to regain powers lost under military rule.

Another area in which successive military governments had changed intragovernmental relations was in the bolstering of local governments as a third tier of government. This process began with the 1976 local government reforms, which introduced a uniform local government system; gave local governments jurisdictional competence in matters such as markets, parking lots, and collection of local taxes; and made it statutory for both the federal and state governments to give specified percentages of their revenues to local governments. Although these reforms were embodied in the 1979 constitution, state governments in the Second Republic refused to allow local governments any measure of autonomy, partly because they were themselves struggling to reclaim their autonomy. With the return of military rule, and as part of the transition toward the Third Republic, local governments were further strengthened.

Because the federal government accepted the recommendation of the Political Bureau that local governments should be made an effective tier of government, efforts had been made to reduce their control by state governments. In 1988 state ministries of local government, the major instrument of control, were replaced by directorates of local government in the governors' offices. All local government funds were paid directly to the local governments by the federal government rather than through the state governments. The functions and jurisdiction of local governments were streamlined, and state governments were asked to stay out of local affairs.

These measures increased the importance of local governments and infused in their civilian-elected functionaries a certain stubbornness that led to open conflicts with state governments over matters of jurisdiction. In several cases, these conflicts became the subject of litigation. State governments resisted the loss of jurisdiction, and many underscored the subordinate status of local governments at every opportunity. It would be a mistake, however, to conclude that local governments were sufficiently autonomous to be an effective tier of government.

The allocation of federal revenues was a problematic aspect of fiscal federalism because the states were unequally endowed and were virtually dependent on allocations from the federal government. Several revenue allocation commissions were set up, among them the National Revenue Mobilization, Allocation, and Fiscal Commission established during the 1980s. The major problem arose from disagreements over the criteria that should be used in allocations—derivation, population, need, equality, or minimum government responsibility.

The federal-character principle emerged as a balancing formula in the 1979 constitution to forestall the domination of the government or any of its agencies or resources by persons from one or a few states, ethnic groups, or sections. The uneven rates of development among the states and sections was largely responsible for the tension and controversy associated with the application of this principle, complicated by the pattern of distribution of the major ethnic groups.

The issue of state creation derived from the very nature of the federation. From three regions in 1960, the number of constituent units had increased to twenty-one states and the Federal Capital Territory. It was likely that a few more would be created (see Introduction). The increasing number of states was a direct response to the demands and agitations of groups that were not satisfied with their positions in the federation. Initially, it was the minorities who agitated for more states, but in 1990 the need for states had changed. They were no longer needed to protect group identity and autonomy. Any group that sought a share of the "national cake" or that wanted to maximize its share of the cake demanded more states, although states were not designed to have an ethnic basis. An example of the latter was the Igbo, who constituted the majority in only two states, Anambra and Imo; the other major groups, the Hausa-Fulani and the Yoruba, represented majorities in about five states each. The Igbo had persistently pressed for equality with other major groups by demanding new states. Realizing that the creation of states could go on endlessly, the federal government tried to bolster local governments as another way of meeting the demands. The subordinate status of local governments, however, coupled with the continued use of the states as units for distributing national resources, made demands for more states a recurrent theme in Nigerian federalism.

According to the 1989 constitution, representation in the legislative branch was based both on population (the House of Representatives, with 453 members) and on states (the Senate with 64 members, 3 from each of the 21 states and 1 from the Federal Capital Territory), which together composed the National Assembly (see fig. 12). These figures were subject to change to reflect a possible increase in the number of states and the redistribution of population. The judicial branch consisted of the Federal High Court, the Court of Appeal, and, at the top, the Supreme Court with a chief justice and up to fifteen other justices.

The Civil Service

The civil service in 1990 consisted of the federal civil service, the twenty-one autonomous state civil services, the unified local government service, and several federal and state government agencies, including parastatals and corporations. The federal and state civil services were organized around government departments, or ministries, and extraministerial departments headed by ministers (federal) and commissioners (state), who were appointed by the president and governors, respectively. These political heads were responsible for policy matters. The administrative heads of the ministry were the directors general, formerly called permanent secretaries. The "chief" director general was the secretary to the government and until the Second Republic also doubled as head of the civil service. As chief adviser to the government, the secretary conducted liaison between the government and the civil service.

The major function of the director general, as of all senior civil servants, was to advise the minister or the commissioner directly. In doing so, the director general was expected to be neutral. In the initial periods of military rule, these administrative heads wielded enormous powers. For some time, the military rulers refused to appoint civilian political heads. Even after political heads were appointed, it was years before the era of "superpermanent secretaries" ended. That happened in 1975 when, after Gowon's fall, the civil service was purged to increase its efficiency. Many of the superpermanent secretaries lost their jobs, and the subordinate status of permanent secretaries to their political bosses was reiterated. Another consequence of the purge, reinforced subsequently, was the destruction of the civil service tradition of security of tenure. The destruction was achieved by the retirement or dismissal of many who had not attained retirement age.

Until the 1988 reforms, the civil service was organized strictly according to British traditions: it was apolitical, civil servants were expected to serve every government in a nonpartisan way, and the norms of impersonality and hierarchical authority were well entrenched. As the needs of the society became more complex and the public sector expanded rapidly, there was a corresponding need to reform the civil service. The Adebo Commission (1970) and the Udoji Commission (1972) reviewed the structure and orientations of the civil service to make it more efficient. Although these commissions recommended ways of rationalizing the civil service, the greatest problems of the service remained inefficiency and red tape. Again in 1985, a study group headed by Dotun Phillips looked into the problems. It was believed that the 1988 reforms, the most current measures aimed at dealing with the problems of the service as of 1990, were based on this report.

Compared with the 1960s and 1970s, the civil service by 1990 had changed dramatically. It had been politicized to the extent that most top officials openly supported the government of the day. The introduction of the quota system of recruitment and promotion, adherence to the federal-character principle, and the constant interference of the government in the day-to-day operation of the civil service—especially through frequent changes in top officials and massive purges—meant that political factors rather than merit alone played a major role in the civil service.

The 1988 reforms formally recognized the politicization of the upper echelons of the civil service and brought about major changes in other areas. The main stated objective of the reforms was "to ensure a virile, dynamic and result-oriented civil service." As a result, ministers or commissioners vested with full executive powers were fully accountable for their ministries or commissions. The director general had become a political appointee whose length of tenure was dependent on that of the government of the day; in practice, this fact meant that directors general need not be career civil servants, thereby reducing the latter's career prospects. Each ministry had been professionalized so that every official, whether specialist

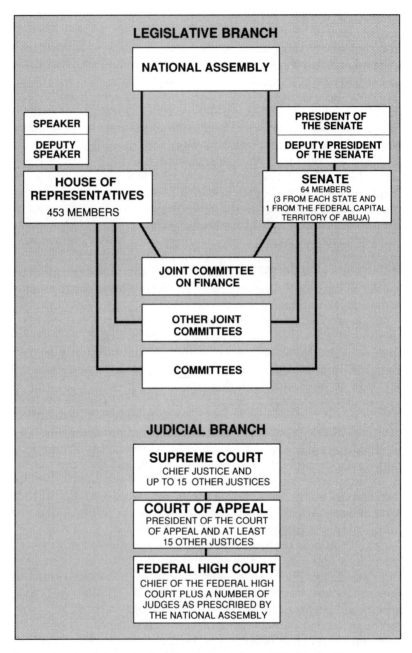

LEGISLATIVE BRANCH

NATIONAL ASSEMBLY

SPEAKER

DEPUTY SPEAKER

PRESIDENT OF THE SENATE

DEPUTY PRESIDENT OF THE SENATE

HOUSE OF REPRESENTATIVES
453 MEMBERS

SENATE
64 MEMBERS
(3 FROM EACH STATE AND 1 FROM THE FEDERAL CAPITAL TERRITORY OF ABUJA)

JOINT COMMITTEE ON FINANCE

OTHER JOINT COMMITTEES

COMMITTEES

JUDICIAL BRANCH

SUPREME COURT
CHIEF JUSTICE AND
UP TO 15 OTHER JUSTICES

COURT OF APPEAL
PRESIDENT OF THE COURT
OF APPEAL AND AT LEAST
15 OTHER JUSTICES

FEDERAL HIGH COURT
CHIEF OF THE FEDERAL HIGH
COURT PLUS A NUMBER OF
JUDGES AS PRESCRIBED BY
THE NATIONAL ASSEMBLY

Source: Based on information from *Constitution of Nigeria, 1989*, Abuja, 1989.

Figure 12. Legislative and Judicial Branches, According to 1989 Constitution

or generalist, made his career entirely in one ministry, whereas previously an official could move among ministries. A new department—the Presidency—comprising top government officials was created at the federal level to coordinate the formulation of policies and monitor their execution, thus making it a clearinghouse between the president and all federal ministries and departments.

The reforms created a new style of civil service, but the structure might change under later governments with different priorities. In the past, the attempt by every government to effect changes in the civil service produced many discontinuities. Ministries have been constantly restructured, new ones created, and existing ones abolished. Nevertheless, the 1988 reforms might solve some of the problems of the civil service because most civil servants tended to remain in their jobs despite reorganizations. Also, the move of the capital from Lagos to Abuja in the early 1990s will provide new opportunities to apply the federal-character principle in replacing Lagosian civil servants unwilling to move.

Interest Groups and National Politics

Organized interest groups played a crucial role in national politics, especially under military regimes when other forms of direct political participation were prohibited.

Professional Associations

Professional associations were the most established interest groups in the country and included the Nigerian Bar Association (NBA), the Nigerian Medical Association (NMA), the Nigerian Society of Engineers, the Nigerian Economic Society, and the Nigerian Political Science Association. Many of these associations were mainly concerned with matters relating to the professional interests of their members. In pursuing professional concerns, however, they articulated and demanded important political actions. Between 1983 and 1985, for example, the NMA called a strike of medical doctors to demand an improvement in health care delivery. Its leaders were detained, and the union banned until 1986. The NBA has been at the forefront of the movement for the observance of the rule of law and human rights in Nigeria. Most other associations held annual conferences at which positions were taken on national issues. The most distinguishing characteristics of professional associations were their elitist and urban base, and the nonviolent pursuit of their interests.

Trade Unions

The central trade union in the country was the Nigerian Labour

Congress (NLC), which was formed in 1975 as the umbrella trade union and recognized by Decree Number 44 of 1976 as the sole representative of all trade unions in the country (see Labor Unions, ch. 3). The NLC had a national executive and secretariat, as well as state councils in all states. It had more than 100 affiliated unions. Although most labor matters were channeled through the NLC, the affiliate unions had engaged individually in union activities, such as strikes and lockouts. In the 1980s, the NLC was torn apart by leadership struggles, ideological differences, and ethnoregional conflicts. The NLC nearly broke up in 1988 after disagreements over elections of its leadership, resulting in the federal government's appointing an administrator for several months. The NLC organized a nationwide workers' strike in 1986 to demand the retention of government subsidies on petroleum products and continued to articulate workers' demands on matters such as minimum wages and improved welfare conditions. Several other trade unions were also active. A few, such as the Academic Staff Union of Universities, were proscribed for alleged antigovernment activities.

The Media

The press was a specialized interest group in Nigeria. As the fourth estate or the "societal watchdog," it was the most vocal and effective interest group in the country, especially because other interest groups channeled their demands and support through the press. The media could act as a watchdog because of the large number of newspapers and radio and television stations, and because of the wide degree of press freedom.

In 1990 Nigeria had more than thirty national and provincial newspapers, more than twenty general magazines and journals, and more than 100 television and radio stations. Although the radio and television stations were owned by the federal and state governments, most of the newspapers and magazines were privately owned and were, in general, seen as instruments of partisan political interests. Thus, the latter could afford to be critical of the government. At some points, newspapers and magazines have been proscribed, as happened to *Newbreed* in 1977, the *Tribune* in 1984, and *Newswatch* in 1988. Individual journalists have been harassed and intimidated by government security agents. In 1971 Minere Amakiri, a *Nigerian Observer* correspondent, was detained and his hair shaved. Since then, numerous editors and reporters have been detained.

The organized interest groups representing the press included the Nigeria Union of Journalists, the Newspaper Proprietors Association, and the Nigerian Guild of Editors. These associations mainly pursued the professional interests of their members but also played active roles on broader social issues.

Student Associations

Since 1962, when students prevented the government from signing the Anglo-Nigerian Defense Pact, they have played an active role in influencing government actions. From the 1970s on, they have engaged in violent protests and riots that have sometimes resulted in fatalities. The grounds for these riots have ranged from narrow concerns, such as unacceptable dining facilities and boarding conditions, to broader national issues, such as the removal of government subsidies on petroleum products, the SAP, and repressive government. Since 1977 no year has passed without one university or other institution of higher learning being closed because of violent student protests. The most dramatic were the 1978 ''Ali must go'' riots, in which all universities in the country protested a rise in the costs of university education; and the 1989 anti-SAP riots, which claimed many lives.

Student activities were coordinated nationally by the National Association of Nigerian Students (NANS), which has operated underground since its proscription in 1986. Every institution of higher learning had a student union. Until 1986, when the Justice Muhammad panel recommended voluntary membership as a way to check student protests, membership in student unions was compulsory. There were several other student associations, such as voluntary groups and religious associations, which also articulated students' interests.

Women's Organizations

Nigeria had several women's organizations, most of them professional and social clubs. The umbrella organization, recognized as the voice of women on national issues, was the National Council of Women's Societies (NCWS). Many of the women's groups were affiliated with the NCWS, which tended to be elitist in organization, membership, and orientation. Another major women's association was Women in Nigeria, composed primarily of university women and inclined toward Western feminist views. Conservative Nigerian Muslim women in the late 1970s began to indicate discontent with the liberal trends of these two organizations and in the mid-1980s created the Federation of Muslim Women's Associations of Nigeria, which had about 400 member bodies throughout the country. In the 1980s, women from lower social strata in the towns, represented mainly by the market women's associations, became militant and organized mass protests and demonstrations in several states. Their major grievances ranged from narrow concerns such as allocation of market stalls to broader issues such as increased school fees.

Other Interest Groups

Other notable interest groups included social clubs and fraternities, old boys' and alumni associations, and various voluntary associations. On the whole, the activities of interest groups and the roles they played in national politics depended on how narrow or broad the group's interests were, the resources available to it, its ties with those in authority, its affiliation with other groups, and the ideological character of its membership. The major interest groups were elitist, but other groups were also active at times.

Foreign Relations

A 1989 publication by the Federal Military Government, *Four Years of the Babangida Administration,* summarized the priority issues of Nigerian foreign policy: the abolition of apartheid in South Africa; the enhancement of Nigeria's relations with member countries of the European Economic Community (EEC), the United States, the Soviet Union, and with other major industrialized countries to increase the flow of foreign investments and capital into Nigeria; and continued support for international organizations, such as the Economic Community of West African States (ECOWAS), the Organization of African Unity (OAU), and the Non-Aligned Movement (NAM). Relations with other African states constituted the cornerstone of Nigerian foreign policy.

The Ministry of External Affairs was directly responsible for foreign policy formulation and implementation. Because matters were usually left in the hands of the minister and his officials, foreign policy positions could change radically from one minister to another, depending on the minister's orientation. In addition to the minister's immediate staff, there was a small foreign policy elite comprising other top government officials, interest group leaders, academicians, top military officers, religious leaders, and journalists. This elite exerted indirect influence through communiqués and press releases, as well as direct pressure on the government. In 1986 a conference—to which every stratum of this elite was invited—was held to review Nigeria's foreign policy and recommend broad policy frameworks for the 1990s and beyond.

Several factors conditioned Nigeria's foreign policy positions. First, the ethnic and religious mix of the country required cautious positions on some issues, such as policy toward Israel. Nigeria found

President Ibrahim Babangida,
1990
Courtesy Embassy of Nigeria,
Washington

it difficult to restore diplomatic ties with Israel and had not done so as of 1990 because of Muslim opposition and sympathy with the rest of the Arab Muslim world. Second, Nigeria's legacy as an ex-British colony, combined with its energy-producing role in the global economy, predisposed Nigeria to be pro-Western on most issues despite the desire to maintain a nonaligned status to avoid neocolonialism. In 1990 this pro-Western posture was reinforced by Nigeria's "economic diplomacy," which involved negotiating trade concessions, attracting foreign investors, and rescheduling debt repayment to Western creditors (see The Debt Overhang, ch. 3). Third, the country's membership in and commitment to several international organizations, such as the United Nations and bodies mentioned earlier, also affected foreign policy positions. Fourth, and most important, as the most populous country in Africa and the entire black world, Nigeria perceived itself as the "giant" of Africa and the potential leader of the black world. Thus, Nigerian external relations have emphasized African issues, which have become the avowed cornerstone of foreign policy.

These factors have caused certain issues to dominate Nigerian foreign policy across various governments, but each government has had distinctive priorities and style. During the 1950s and early 1960s, foreign policy aimed at proper behavior in the international system, and British authorities played a major role in Nigerian foreign relations. Consequently, the Balewa government stressed

245

world peace, respected sovereign equality, and maintained nonalignment based on friendship with any country that took a reciprocal position. After the fall of the First Republic, critics asserted that the government had been too pro-Western and not strong enough on decolonization or integration, and that the low profile had been embarrassing. Nonetheless, Gowon continued to keep a low profile by operating within the consensus of the OAU and by following routes of quiet diplomacy.

The civil war marked a distinct break in Nigerian foreign policy. The actions of various countries and international bodies during the war increased awareness of the alignments within Africa and appreciation of the positive role that the OAU could play in African affairs. Whereas some European countries had supported Biafra, the OAU sided with the federation by voting for unity. The OAU stance proved helpful for Nigerian diplomacy. Nigeria first turned to the Soviet Union for support after the West refused to provide arms to the federation, and after the war, a less pro-Western stance was maintained. At the same time, Africa remained Nigeria's top priority. In the mid- to late 1970s, attention focused on the liberation of southern Africa, on the integration of ECOWAS, and on the need for complete economic independence throughout Africa. These goals were included in the 1979 constitution: promotion of African unity; political, economic, social, and cultural liberation of Africa; international cooperation; and elimination of racial discrimination.

Relations with Neighboring States

Nigeria had cordial relations with all its neighbors—Benin, Niger, Chad, Cameroon, and Equatorial Guinea—as well as with other countries in the West African subregion, with most of which it had bilateral agreements. There had been occasional border disputes with Chad and Cameroon, and military action against these neighbors was contemplated by the civilian government in 1982 and 1983. Another problem arose in the early 1980s, when Nigeria decided to expel many illegal immigrants, mainly Ghanaians, but this dispute also was resolved amicably. The guiding principle of Nigeria's regional foreign policy was that of good neighborliness and friendship. In this spirit, it helped to resolve conflicts between Liberia and Sierra Leone, Burkina Faso and Mali, and Togo and Ghana. Nigeria also tried to make its neighbors "safe" friends, partly to reenforce boundary claims and protect human rights of Nigerian citizens who were migrant-workers and partly to stabilize relations between the immediate neighboring countries. For example, since 1988 it has established a strong presence in Equatorial Guinea.

To pursue its economic interests through foreign relations within West Africa, Nigeria championed the formation of ECOWAS and, in spite of competing allegiances to rival organizations within the subcontinent, continued to support the organization's objectives. Strengthening ECOWAS promoted Nigeria's national interests through encouraging development of the region's economy and discouraging its neighbors' reliance on extra-African countries for military, political, and economic survival. ECOWAS thus served such security interests as weakening colonial divisions within West Africa, ending border disputes, contributing to African unity, and strengthening West Africa's bargaining positions vis-à-vis the EEC.

Relations with the Rest of Africa

The prevailing perception in Nigeria's foreign policy was that, as the predominant African leader, it should play a big-brother role in relations with African states. Nigeria was a founding member of the OAU and often channeled major policy initiatives through that organization. Most of its relations with other African states took place outside the OAU framework but were guided by OAU principles. Nigeria's primary African commitment was to liberate the continent from the last vestiges of colonialism and to eradicate apartheid in South Africa. Promoting liberation had grown from a weak and conservative stance during the 1960s to an increasingly firm push after the civil war. This commitment was pursued most actively after Murtala Muhammad successfully backed the Movimento Popular de Libertação de Angola's ascent to power in Angola in 1975 by providing the swing vote in the OAU decision to recognize the MPLA. Nigeria had played a role in the independence of Zimbabwe and in the late 1980s was active in assisting Namibia to achieve independence. In the latter case, it contributed about US$20 million to assist the South West Africa People's Organization in the 1989 elections and other preparations for Namibian independence. The country also contributed financially to liberation movements in South Africa and to the frontline states of Zambia, Tanzania, Mozambique, and Zimbabwe, which were frequently harassed by South Africa.

Although Nigeria's armed forces were among the largest in black Africa in the early 1990s, sizable military might has rarely been used in foreign policy (see Local and Bilateral Issues; African and Regional Issues, ch. 5). The army participated in peacekeeping forces, either alone or through the OAU and contributed personnel to United Nations peacekeeping missions. In line with its ECOWAS commitment, Nigeria was one of the main contributors of troops to the ECOWAS Cease-fire Monitoring Group (ECOMOG) sent to Liberia August 23, 1990, after the peace talks there failed. Additional forces were sent in late September 1990 under a Nigerian field commander, General Doganyaro. Threats to fight for southern African liberation were made but not acted on, but Nigeria did give military and financial aid to the African National Congress for its efforts against the apartheid regime in South Africa and provided military equipment to Mozambique to help its struggle against South African-backed guerrillas.

In addition, Nigeria gave aid and technical assistance to several African states, often through the African Development Bank of which it was a major benefactor. In 1987 a Technical Aid Corps, operating along the lines of the United States Peace Corps, was established. Under it, young Nigerian professionals served in other African, Caribbean, and Pacific countries where their expertise was needed. Nigeria also provided scholarships and fellowships, training facilities, grants, equipment, and medical supplies, and subsidized oil during the 1970s' oil crisis to African countries under certain conditions.

In July 1974, the Gowon government decided to sell crude oil at concessionary rates to African countries on condition that they had their own refineries and would not re-export to third countries. The decision came after more than two years of deliberations and despite Nigeria's role as a member of the Organization of the Petroleum Exporting Countries (OPEC) that generally favored higher prices. Nigeria acted largely in response to external pressures: international actors attempted to divide Third World countries into OPEC members and nonoil producers; various African countries, especially Liberia, begged for less expensive oil; and both the Organization of the Islamic Conference and the Organization of Arab Petroleum Exporting Countries had established programs to aid poor countries while encouraging other oil producers, especially African nations, to follow suit. Providing subsidies for African countries was a safe move for Nigeria because Africa comprised only a small portion of the country's total oil export market, it enhanced Nigeria's position and influence in Africa while building African solidarity, and it protected security interests by preventing economic decline. Moreover, this example of generosity aided Nigeria in its efforts to create ECOWAS. In November 1990, Babangida suggested that Nigeria might again offer concessionary prices to other African countries as the Middle East crises pushed oil prices upward.

Relations with Major Powers

During the Gulf crisis that began with Iraq's invasion of Kuwait in the summer of 1990 and that marked the end of the Cold War and the beginning of a coalition, Nigeria kept a low profile. It did not send troops to engage in the Persian Gulf war but continued to be an active supporter of UN policy. Buying the bulk of Nigeria's crude oil, the United States was Nigeria's most important trading partner. Until the civil war, Nigeria had had no significant relationship with the Soviet Union and Eastern Europe. Since then, ties with the Soviet Union had increased, although they remained minimal in comparison with ties to the West. Nigeria's other major trading partners were Japan and the EEC, from which it continued to obtain loans and aid.

Although Nigeria has always leaned toward the West, the closeness of the relationship has varied. Nigeria's Western ties were originally strongest with Britain, its former colonial ruler. The special relationship, which lasted until the 1966 coup, led Nigeria to side with Britain on most issues. After the coup and the civil war, the new Nigerian leaders were less favorable toward Britain, especially after Britain took a position of neutrality in the civil war, refused to sell arms to the federation, and ignored the blockade against Biafra. Nigerian leaders also were rankled by Britain's support of white-dominated governments in southern Africa. Several Nigerian groups pressured the new government to weaken ties with Britain as the only way to true independence. To appease popular sentiment, Nigerian leaders at times made statements or took actions of a symbolic nature that made it appear that relations with Britain were more damaged than they were in reality.

Throughout the Cold War, the United States and the Soviet Union were interested in Nigeria because of its size, population, economic and military potential, and, especially for the United States, its oil. From 1966 to 1977, Nigeria was very cool toward the United States. The two countries took opposing positions over southern African liberation. Nigerians were angered by pro-Biafran propaganda in the United States and by the United States refusal to sell arms to the federation during the civil war. United States involvement was even suspected by Nigeria in the assassination of Murtala Muhammad. In 1977 Jimmy Carter became president, and Nigerian relations with the United States suddenly changed. The United States recognized Nigeria as a stabilizing force in Africa and was willing to consult with Nigeria on African issues. The two governments appeared to have similar interests in southern Africa. The special relationship had a weak basis, however, depending mostly upon continuing agreement and cooperation over southern African issues. Once Ronald Reagan replaced Carter as president (1981–89), the countries again had divergent interests in southern Africa.

Just as the balance of trade was not expected to shift dramatically with the opening of Eastern Europe so, too, Nigeria's political position was not expected to change greatly. In a time of shifting world coalitions, a position of nonalignment with a leaning toward the West provided more options for Nigeria than ever. Events in southern Africa, including Namibia's independence and the opening of debate for eliminating apartheid in South Africa, removed the largest obstacles to closer relations with the United States without excluding the Soviet Union or other leading powers.

Relations with International Organizations

Nigeria played active roles in various international organizations and vied for positions in them. For example, Joseph Garba, Nigeria's former permanent representative to the UN, was elected in 1989 to a one-year term as president of the UN General Assembly; Adebayo Adeedji was executive secretary of the Economic Commission for Africa, a UN affiliate; and Emeka Anyaoku became secretary general of the Commonwealth of Nations in 1989. Former military head of state Obasanjo also had become a recognized world statesman and spokesman on African issues. Nigeria contributed personnel to many UN peacekeeping missions, including operations in Congo, Tanzania, and the UN India-Pakistan Observer Mission in the 1960s, the UN Interim Force in Lebanon in 1978, and UN forces observing the Iran-Iraq cease-fire and the Angola-Namibia accords in 1988.

The importance that Nigeria placed on international organizations grew out of a striving for peace and international cooperation. In the cases of the OAU and ECOWAS, these organizations also served to increase African unity, another important Nigerian goal. Nigeria played an initiating role in the creation of both organizations and was active in both thereafter. Although Nigeria's positions on various issues have changed over the years, its level of activity in international organizations has increased.

In 1987 Nigeria initiated a Concert of Medium Powers, more widely known as the Lagos Forum, to facilitate multilateral cooperation and to enable member states to exert greater collective influence on world affairs. Forum members included Sweden, Austria, Zimbabwe, and Egypt. The initiative, which could be seen as an effort preceding the end of the Cold War, seemed to collapse, however, after its initiator, Boleji Akenyemi, was removed as minister for external affairs in 1987.

*　*　*

A wide range of books and articles exists on Nigerian government and politics. On the colonial period and the First Republic

(1960–66), the major studies are those by Eme O. Awa, *Federal Government in Nigeria;* James Smoot Coleman, *Nigeria: Background to Nationalism;* Larry Diamond, *Class, Ethnicity, and Democracy in Nigeria: The Failure of the First Republic;* Billy J. Dudley, *Parties and Politics in Northern Nigeria;* Robin Luckham, *The Nigerian Military: A Sociological Analysis of Authority and Revolt: 1960–67;* J.P. Mackintosh, *Nigerian Government and Politics;* Kenneth W.J. Post, *The Nigerian Federal Election of 1959;* Richard L. Sklar, *Nigerian Political Parties;* and C. Sylvester Whitaker, *The Politics of Tradition: Continuity and Change in Northern Nigeria, 1946–66.*

On the Gowon government (1966–75), there are major studies by Henry Bienen, *Political Conflict and Economic Change in Nigeria;* Billy J. Dudley, *Instability and Political Order;* Oye Oyediran, *Nigerian Government and Politics under Military Rule, 1966–79;* and S.K. Panter-Brick, *Nigerian Politics and Military Rule: Prelude to the Civil War.* A.H.M. Kirk-Greene's two-volume *Crisis and Conflict in Nigeria: A Documentary Sourcebook* is a valuable resource on the civil war period. There are also excellent studies by John J. Stremlau, *The International Politics of the Nigerian Civil War, 1967–1970,* and by John de St. Jorre, *The Nigerian Civil War.*

On the Obasanjo government and the transition to the Second Republic, the central studies are those by J. Bayo Adekson, *Nigeria in Search of a Stable Civil-Military System;* Larry Diamond et al., *Democracy in Developing Countries;* Richard A. Joseph, *Democracy and Prebendal Politics in Nigeria: The Rise and Fall of the Second Republic;* and Shehu Othman, ''Classes, Crises, and Coups: The Demise of Shagari's Regime.''

Overviews on Nigerian politics and government can be found in Peter P. Ekeh and E.E. Osaghae, *Federal Character and Federalism in Nigeria* and William Graf, *The Nigerian State.* (For further information and complete citations, see Bibliography.)

Chapter 5. National Security

Benin bronze statue of warrior chief of the seventeenth century

ON DECEMBER 29, 1989, Nigerian president General Ibrahim Babangida, a Muslim, abruptly executed a major reshuffle of his ministers, the Armed Forces Ruling Council (AFRC), the national security organs, military state governors and important military commands, and took personal control of the Ministry of Defence and the security services. Ten days later, Lieutenant General Domkat Bali, a Christian, the erstwhile minister of defense who had been reassigned as minister of internal affairs, refused to accept his new post and resigned from the army. Nigeria's vice president since 1988 has been Admiral Augustus Aikhomu, a Christian. Babangida and Aikhomu have sought to share responsibilities so as to diffuse the "religious" factor in national politics. Despite these efforts, public protests erupted almost immediately against the president's alleged arbitrary decisions and discrimination against Christian middle belt (see Glossary) officers like Bali who lost their posts to northern Muslims. Then, on April 22, 1990, antinorthern rebel officers launched a bloody abortive coup against Babangida's regime, resulting in the arrest of 14 officers and more than 200 soldiers. After regaining control, Babangida announced his intention to overhaul the security system and to press ahead with his plan to restore civilian rule by October 1, 1992. Forty-two of the military rebels, including ten officers, were executed in July after sentencing by a special military tribunal; an additional twenty-seven were executed in September. Nine others, including three civilians, received prison terms ranging from seven years to life. Reports of army restiveness continued.

This dramatic series of events underscored the instability and uncertainty that have pervaded Nigeria's politico-military system for more than a quarter of a century. It also emphasized the transience of any description of Nigeria's national security apparatus. Indeed, even if the Federal Military Government (FMG) were to achieve its goal of civilian restoration, the new government would almost certainly again restructure the armed forces and national security organs. Notwithstanding such anticipated changes, however, underlying conditions and trends continued to affect Nigeria's security environment into the 1990s.

At the onset of the 1990s, Nigeria was a regional power with a growing sense of self-assurance and a developing capability to demonstrate it. In the three decades since independence, its original Western orientation had shifted toward more neutral, autonomous, and Afrocentric strategic directions. Although still seeking a coherent vision of its role in Africa and the world, Lagos sought and played various roles as regional leader, peacekeeper, mediator, and arbiter. Domestically, the Nigerian polity had endured a civil war (1967–70); frequent political crises punctuated by military coups, attempted coups, and regime reshuffles; and the boom-and-bust cycle of an oil-based economy. As General Babangida's military government prepared to restore elected civilian rule in 1992, the armed forces were being drastically reduced in size and professionalized. External and internal security thus were closely linked.

Nigeria's size, demography, economic strength, and military capabilities set it apart as the dominant regional power. It was surrounded by smaller and weaker states, whose vulnerability to external influence and pressure could adversely affect Nigeria's security. The lack of regional rivals made large-scale conflicts unlikely but did not spare Nigeria border clashes with neighboring Cameroon and Chad, peacekeeping deployments to Chad and Liberia, a leadership role in the Economic Community of West African States (ECOWAS) peacekeeping force in Liberia, or strategic maneuvering against France and South Africa in Equatorial Guinea.

Nigeria's armed forces, estimated to be at least 94,500 in 1990, and among the largest in Africa, were modest in relation to the country's territory, population, and economic resources. The diversity of foreign-origin armaments reduced dependence on any single supplier but imposed significant logistical constraints; a fledgling domestic arms industry had also been established. Nigeria acquired naval, amphibious, and airlift forces and created a rapid deployment force for African contingencies, thus confirming its intention and capacity for power projection abroad. Externally, therefore, Nigeria remained basically secure and its defenses adequate.

The same could not be said, however, about internal security. A political formula for stability continued to elude successive Nigerian governments, economic and social conditions worsened during the 1980s, and the military became entrenched as the ultimate arbiter of power. Indeed, the future role of the military and the fear of coups, resulting especially from radicalization of frustrated junior officers and soldiers, haunted Babangida's regime as it attempted to create a durable constitutional government in a highly uncertain political environment. Ethnic, sectional, and religious cleavages marked the underlying political fault lines, from which the military itself was not immune, and organized labor and students continued to be the agents of public discontent. These internal sources of instability could be incited or intensified by an array of external forces, such as foreign subversion, oil prices, and foreign debt. To make matters worse, the national police and criminal justice system were strained beyond capacity. Crime was increasing, prisons were grossly overpopulated, and military rule by decree bred human rights abuses that were the object of public and international reproach.

On balance, one could find grounds for either optimism or pessimism about Nigeria's national security prospects. Indeed, there was an essential ambivalence among Nigerians and observers alike about the state's increasing autonomy and capability amidst countervailing threat perceptions. An increasing sense of national "manifest destiny" was thus tempered by limited capacity, and Nigeria's international power remained more potential than actual. Whether Nigeria would become more activist, interventionist, or assert overweening regional hegemony remained contingent on many external factors, such as its threat perceptions, the degree of regional stability, and the regional distribution of military capabilities. Much also depended on how well Nigeria coped with its social and economic crises, on the process and outcome of restoration of civilian rule, and, ultimately, on the political disposition and competence of the military.

National Security Issues and Perceptions

Safeguarding the sovereign independence and territorial integrity of the state was the central pillar of Nigerian national security policy. Other guiding principles were African unity and independence, nonintervention in the internal affairs of other states, and regional economic development and security cooperation. Subordinate goals included military self-sufficiency and regional leadership. In pursuing these goals, Nigeria was diplomatic and flexible, but it employed coercive methods or measured force when necessary. Nigeria was an active participant in the United Nations (UN), the Organization of African Unity (OAU), and ECOWAS. In 1990 the leadership seemed intent on retrenchment, according priority to domestic political and economic problems, and displayed a mature and conciliatory approach to foreign policy (see Foreign Relations, ch. 4).

Nigeria's location on the Gulf of Guinea, straddling western and equatorial Africa, its long land and coastal boundaries, and its offshore oil deposits defined the country's regional geostrategic situation (see fig. 1). A British colonial background set it apart from its francophone neighbors, an historical anomaly that affected the local security milieu. Nigeria's relations with the major powers were shaped, in the case of Britain and France, largely by this postcolonial heritage. A short-lived defense pact with Britain after independence was terminated in 1962. In the case of the superpowers, whose interests in the region until the late 1980s were functions of their global rivalry and resource needs, Lagos deliberately balanced its relations with Washington and Moscow.

Nigeria's security concerns and threat perceptions emanated from many quarters. The country's dependence on the production and export of oil was aggravated by naval deployments of the major powers along the maritime transit routes of the South Atlantic and the Gulf of Guinea. Its experience of incursions by neighbors, coupled with fears of foreign influence or of subversion of neighbors by such potential adversaries as France, Libya, and South Africa, heightened Lagos's sensitivities about border security. Regional conditions also produced a sense of isolation and uncertainty, particularly shifts in the balance of power across northern Africa, political instability in West Africa, and encirclement by relatively weak francophone states with residual or formal defense ties to their former colonial power. More generally, conflicts throughout Africa and the related propensity for great power intervention (for example, in Chad, Zaire, Angola, and Ethiopia) and occasional eruptions of radicalization or militant pan-Africanism were inimical to Nigeria's interest. Finally, South Africa's apartheid policy, regional dominance in the continent, and nuclear capability constituted threats to Nigeria's national security goals throughout the 1980s. Broadly speaking, therefore, Nigeria's security conditions and concerns could be grouped into three separate but related categories: local and bilateral, African and regional, and global.

Local and Bilateral Issues

Oil was the most important single factor in Nigerian economic life throughout the 1980s and early 1990s. Consequently, the exploitation and protection of oil deposits and of distribution infrastructure (including about 5,500 kilometers of pipelines), concentrated offshore in the southeast, were inextricably linked to national security. Nigeria's recognition of this vulnerability was magnified by its conflict with Cameroon over contested offshore oil rights. On the other hand, Nigeria could and did use its "oil weapon" against Ghana, Chad, and European companies by cutting off oil supplies to induce compliance with its demands.

Nigeria's 853-kilometer irregular coastline boasted several major port complexes. Such seaward assets served to justify the notable expansion of Nigeria's naval capabilities (see fig. 13; Navy, this ch.).

Border security with each of its neighbors was a constant problem for Nigeria. The Nigeria-Benin Joint Border Commission was reactivated in 1981 to deal with minor incursions by Beninese troops and with increased smuggling into Nigeria. In 1986, in response to increasing clashes between communities along the Benin border, Nigeria decided to establish about 100 additional border posts staffed by customs and immigration officials. A major conference on Nigeria-Benin border cooperation in Lagos in 1988 agreed that proper border demarcation would help control smuggling, illegal aliens, and harassment of people. In September 1988, the presidents of the two nations agreed to relax formalities so that their respective local authorities could establish direct contacts on illegal immigration and on traffic matters. In April 1989, Lagos began a yearlong effort to survey the 773-kilometer border with Benin.

Illegal immigrants and smuggling from Niger, with which Nigeria shared a 1,497-kilometer border, posed perennial problems. In April 1984, Nigeria recalled all its existing currency notes in exchange for new notes. This step was designed to preempt the return of the old currency, much of which had been smuggled out of the country by politicians, and to establish a new baseline for Nigeria's financial system that could more readily be monitored. To prevent the reentry of the smuggled currency, Nigeria closed all its borders. Although gasoline and meat, on which landlocked Niger depended, were excepted, Niger lost nearly one-fourth of its 1984 customs revenue. Nigeria also resorted to mass deportations of illegal aliens in 1983 and 1985, the latter including an estimated 100,000 Nigerois. A clash occurred near the Borno State border in May 1989, when Nigerian soldiers and immigration officials investigated reported crop damage by a cattle herd from Niger. Many regional issues and problems were handled by tripartite meetings of the heads of Katsina State and the Maradi and Zinder regions of Niger.

The approximately eighty-five-kilometer border with Chad through Lake Chad witnessed more serious hostilities. Clashes between Nigerian and Chadian soldiers in April 1983 resulted in more than 100 casualties; the tensions were resolved temporarily by an agreement to revive joint border patrols (which had lapsed) and to have the four-nation Lake Chad Basin Commission take up border security issues and demarcate their common borders. After further clashes, however, Nigerian president Shehu Shagari and Chadian president Hissein Habré agreed to military disengagement, to an exchange of prisoners, to reopening the frontier, to reactivation of joint frontier patrols, and to a special joint commission on border demarcation among the states touching on Lake Chad. Nigeria postponed reopening the Chad border until November 1986, eight months after other borders closed in April 1984 were reopened, to prevent the feared mass influx of refugees from that war-torn country.

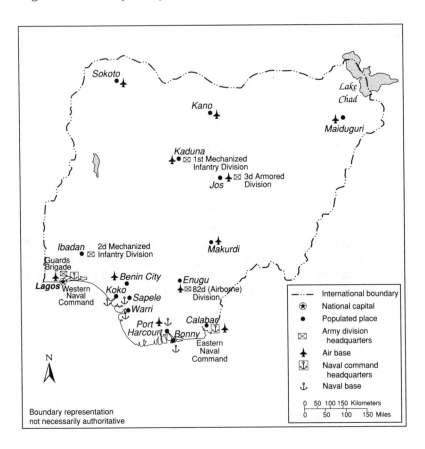

Figure 13. Prinicipal Military Installations, 1990

Nigeria's longest frontier, the 1,690-kilometer border with Cameroon, witnessed several clashes. (Neither Cameroon nor Chad was a signatory of the ECOWAS protocols on the free movement of community citizens and hence greater border tensions existed between these countries and Nigeria.) In 1981 five Nigerian soldiers were killed and three wounded when a Cameroonian patrol boat fired on a Nigerian vessel off the contested Rio-del-Rey area, which was thought to be rich in oil, gas, and uranium deposits. Coming in the wake of an incursion by Beninese troops, this incident provoked public demands for compensation, for punitive measures, and even for war. The crisis was settled peaceably; tensions along the frontier continued, however, and in May 1987, Cameroonian gendarmes allegedly occupied sixteen border villages in Borno State until repulsed by Nigerian army units. Lagos issued orders to state governors "to take military reprisals against any belligerent neighboring country," and tension remained high until Babangida's December visit to Yaoundé, capital of Cameroon, yielded mutual pledges of steps to prevent a recurrence of border clashes, including joint border patrols. In October 1989, Cameroonian gendarmes allegedly abducted four Nigerian customs officials on routine border patrol duties. In mid-1990 boundary demarcation was still in process, and minor clashes between border residents and transients continued. Deeper divisions were apparent when Yaoundé media charged Nigerian agitators with instigating illegal demonstrations in Bamenda and at Yaoundé University in May 1990 and with seeking to incite a popular revolt; the Nigerian media made countercharges that Nigerians were being systematically harassed, detained, tortured, or murdered by Cameroonian security forces.

Nigeria took several measures during the 1980s to improve and to strengthen overall border management. After the 1981 clash with Cameroon, Nigeria decided to fence its entire international boundary, to enclose each border beacon, and to augment its immigration staff by 1,000. In the mid-1980s, Nigeria's 2,100 immigration officers were given a four-week weapons training course, new border posts were established, and modern border-patrol and surveillance equipment was procured. The 1984 border closure was designed to control widespread currency trafficking and smuggling. The borders reopened only after Nigeria set up trade corridors and joint border patrols with its neighbors and began a program to strengthen and expand customs and patrol posts. In late 1986, after signing phase two of the ECOWAS protocols on free movement of community citizens, Nigeria said it would deploy immigration officers to each local government to regulate movement in and out of the country and proposed to open 100 new control posts—there had been 45. In addition, Lagos planned to purchase aircraft, helicopters, boats, vehicles, and communication and surveillance equipment; the initial US$13 million phase included 25 speedboats, more than 1,400 Land Rovers and patrol cars, and 200 motorcycles. After the mid-1987 clash with Cameroon, the Nigerian army intensified its border patrols and considered permanently stationing units on the frontiers.

Finally, in an effort to regularize boundary management, in July 1988 Babangida appointed a nine-member National Boundaries Commission under the chief of General Staff. The commission was empowered to coordinate the activities of all agencies involved in internal and international borders and to inquire into and to resolve any boundary problem or issue between Nigeria and its neighbors, and between states within the federation. The president also announced a five-year plan to demarcate, survey, and map all borders, and the establishment of joint boundary commissions with each of Nigeria's neighbors.

To bolster its influence and prestige, Nigeria also engaged in bilateral military cooperation programs with African states. For example, in 1977 Ghana and Nigeria set up a joint committee for military cooperation under which ten Nigerian officers attended each session of the Ghana Senior Staff College's yearlong course. Nigeria also supplied twelve combat-capable L-39 training aircraft to Ghana in 1990. Likewise, in 1979 Nigeria and Benin concluded an agreement providing for joint border patrols and for Beninese to attend Nigerian military training institutions. Military cooperation with Togo included sending Nigerian army units and jet aircraft to Lomé's national parade in January 1988. Nigeria also participated in the eight-nation Commonwealth of Nations team formed to retrain the Ugandan army in 1982, after President Milton Obote's return to power. Military training was also provided to Zimbabwe and Botswana. Since 1986 military personnel from Equatorial Guinea have attended Nigerian military academies and trained with Nigerian forces, and Nigerians have manned one of the Equatorial Guinea patrol boats.

France was Nigeria's only perceived extracontinental threat. The validity of that perception varied over time and was based on several factors including Nigeria's own strategic vision. Paris disregarded African and world opinion by conducting atomic tests in the Sahara Desert in the early 1960s. Particularly galling to Nigeria was France's recognition of secessionist Biafra, a move joined by francophone Ivory Coast and Gabon, two of France's closest African allies. Nigeria believed that France's close cultural, political, economic, and military ties with its former colonies perpetuated metropolitan loyalties at the expense of inter-African identity and ties. Its pervasive economic ties stymied efforts toward self-reliance and regional economic integration, such as ECOWAS. Furthermore, France maintained defense pacts with several West African states; stationed troops permanently in Senegal, Chad, Ivory Coast, Gabon, and Central African Republic; and intervened directly to make or break local regimes. Paris was also seen as the spearhead of Western security interests and interventions in local African conflicts, such as in Zaire and Chad, thus thwarting the emergence of African collective security arrangements. In short, France's hegemonic interests and regional penetration constrained Nigeria politically and strategically, frustrating its "natural" emergence as the preeminent regional power. The Nigerian government never explicitly articulated this threat assessment, but such concerns underlay its regional policies. However, the convergence of French and Nigerian interests in containing Libya, stabilizing Chad, and expanding economic ties reduced mutual anxieties after the mid-1980s.

Libya and South Africa were the only perceived continental threats. Both were geographically remote, and their threats emanated more from their peculiar regimes than from underlying historical or geopolitical rivalry. In the 1980s, Libya's military intervention in Chad and subversive activities in Nigeria and neighboring states, often through the agency of illegal immigrants, strained relations with Nigeria. Although relations improved after Babangida's visit to Tripoli in mid-1988, Nigeria remained wary of the unpredictable Muammar al Qadhafi.

South Africa was a perpetual security concern until the late 1980s. Its apartheid regime deeply offended African dignity and was seen as the root cause of regional insecurity. In 1985 the Nigerian National Petroleum Corporation stopped selling oil to a Swiss-owned company suspected of diverting oil to South Africa in contravention of UN sanctions. Pretoria also could pose direct threats to Lagos. In 1986 Nigerian army and air force headquarters confirmed reported South African plans to attack Nigeria from an unnamed neighboring state, widely rumored to be Equatorial Guinea. Whether or not such a plot existed, the incident demonstrated Nigeria's extreme suspicions of South Africa's intentions.

Nigeria's handling of the Equatorial Guinea crisis underscored its determination to protect its strategic interests against perceived threats from both South Africa and France. Relations with this small neighboring state had been strained periodically over alleged harassment and maltreatment of Nigerian migrant laborers. In 1976 Nigeria evacuated 10,000 of its nationals and later landed a military transport in Malabo, the capital, to demand compensation for the death of a Nigerian at the hands of Guinean security personnel. In the late 1980s, Nigeria's concerns were heightened by French economic penetration and by reports that South Africa had established an air base in Malabo, within twenty minutes' striking distance of Nigeria. Lagos reacted swiftly to remove these potential threats by using both diplomacy and threats. In January 1987, at Nigeria's request, Equatorial Guinea and Nigeria agreed to conclude several accords to facilitate and to expand bilateral cooperation, reaffirmed their shared strategic interests, and signed a defense pact. In mid-1988, however, reports that South Africa had bought Nigerian oil through Malabo, was upgrading Malabo's airport, and planned secretly to build a satellite tracking station again raised Nigeria's fears. Lagos demanded and achieved the expulsion of

South Africans from Equatorial Guinea, and Babangida's January 1990 state visit concluded an effective campaign using diplomatic pressure and military and economic aid to solidify ties with Malabo at the expense of South African and French interests. However, South Africa's decided shift toward regional peace and domestic reform, including progressive dismantling of apartheid, substantially reduced Nigerian security concerns from that quarter.

African and Regional Issues

Nigeria has been a leading spokesman on African security issues, such as internal and interstate conflicts, foreign intervention, colonialism, and regional defense arrangements. It supported the strengthening of the OAU and the use of diplomacy to resolve intra-African conflicts, and it played an active role in continental security issues. The Nigerian head of state, Lieutenant General Olusegun Obasanjo, and Mali's president, Colonel Moussa Traoré, undertook a mission in 1980 on behalf of the OAU's "committee of wise men" to mediate the Western Sahara dispute. Complaining of Moroccan inflexibility, Nigeria withdrew from the OAU Implementation Committee on Western Sahara and recognized the Sahrawi Arab Democratic Republic in 1984. Obasanjo also accused Tanzania of setting "a dangerous precedent of unimaginable consequences" by overturning Idi Amin's regime in Uganda and by starting the conflict between the two countries. Although Nigeria steadfastly opposed foreign interference in Africa, it acknowledged Zaire's right to call on French and Belgian paratroopers during the 1978 crisis in Shaba Region, Zaire. Obasanjo gave qualified endorsement to Soviet and Cuban intervention in Angola because they had been invited "to assist in the liberation struggle and the consolidation of national independence," but he warned that "they should not overstay their welcome."

Nigeria actively participated in OAU discussions on the formation of a pan-African defense force, to be either a peacekeeping force on the UN model for African interstate conflicts or an African high command to defend African states against outside powers and South African aggression. In 1972 Nigeria proposed formation of a joint African military task force to which all OAU members would contribute. It would be stationed in independent states bordering the Portuguese colonies to defend sanctuaries and rear areas of the liberation movements and to defend independent host states from colonialist attacks. In 1981 Nigeria hosted an emergency summit of the southern Africa frontline states that called on all OAU members to extend urgent assistance, especially military aid, to Angola to repel South African forces. The concept of an

African high command has not gained widespread support, however. Some African states advocated a mission limited to defense against racist and imperialist threats, but not intra-African conflicts or insurgencies within independent African states. Others argued for a continental military command to deter external attacks, to intervene in domestic disorders to prevent or suppress military coups, and to counter South African forces.

Although Africa lacked a continent-wide collective security system, both informal and formal regional mutual defense arrangements have developed. Nigeria participated in the defense pact of the sixteen-nation ECOWAS, the only regional economic organization with such a collective security arrangement.

ECOWAS was established by a treaty ratified by fifteen states in May 1975—Cape Verde joined in 1977—to promote trade, economic development, and cooperation in West Africa. In 1978 ECOWAS adopted a nonaggression protocol, and in 1981 thirteen of its members signed a mutual defense pact providing for collective military response against attack from non-ECOWAS countries, mediation and peacekeeping missions in the event of armed conflict between member states, and defense against external states that initiate or support insurgencies within member states. It also provided for a Defence Council, a Defence Commission, and joint exercises, but no standing regional force or command structure. ECOWAS has a mixed record in mediating disputes between member states, particularly in attempting to resolve the civil war in Liberia. An ECOWAS Cease-fire Monitoring Group (ECOMOG) comprising about 8,000 troops led by Nigeria was dispatched to Liberia in August 1990. It succeeded in implementing a cease-fire agreement between the main rival factions and in appointing an interim president.

In this loosely structured defense system, only Nigeria's armed forces had the size, experience, equipment, and logistical resources to provide or serve as the core of an ECOWAS rapid deployment force. On the other hand, ECOWAS members were wary of Nigeria's aspirations to regional dominance. Many francophone states had long-standing military aid and security agreements with France, and seven of them were already parties to the nonaggression and mutual defense pact of the francophone West African Economic Community (Communauté Économique de l'Afrique de l'Ouest—CEAO). Moreover, many ECOWAS members, including Nigeria, had found bilateral and less formal means to pursue their regional security objectives, sometimes under the auspices of ECOWAS. For example, Nigeria and Guinea were mandated in 1986 to mediate between Liberia and Sierra Leone after Liberia had closed its border in the wake of a coup attempt allegedly launched from Sierra Leone. In mid-1990 Babangida also offered to mediate Liberia's civil war within the ECOWAS framework, but at the same time Nigeria was reportedly arming the armed forces of Liberia that supported President Samuel K. Doe (killed in September 1990) against the rebels. Although Nigeria's creation of a rapid deployment force during 1988–89 suggested its intent to rely on unilateral means to intervene in regional crises, it did not rule out participation in multilateral deployments (see Army, this ch.). Indeed, the history of Nigeria's participation in international peacekeeping missions was second to none among African states.

In the late 1980s, ECOWAS became the focus of regional efforts to deal with emerging environmental and security threats posed by toxic waste, international smuggling, and narcotics trafficking. Two incidents affecting Nigeria attracted international attention. In May 1988, after an Italian ship dumped toxic industrial waste at the port of Koko in Bendel State, Nigerian authorities evacuated the local population and seized the ship until the waste was removed by the Italian government. In October 1989, Nigeria ordered out of its territorial waters a Greek ship allegedly carrying frozen meat contaminated by nuclear fallout from Chernobyl', Soviet Union. At the eleventh ECOWAS summit in June 1988, chaired by Babangida, members agreed to make the dumping of toxic and nuclear waste in the region a criminal offense and approved a Nigerian plan to set up a ''dump watch'' alert and information-sharing system. Babangida also urged ECOWAS members to set up mechanisms to counter smuggling.

Nigeria's most significant regional deployments were its intercession in the complex Chadian and Liberian civil wars, experiences fraught with lessons for future African peacekeeping missions. In 1979 it mediated between rival Chadian factions and Libya at two conferences in Kano and sent an 850-member peacekeeping force to N'Djamena to police the cease-fire. However, within three months Nigeria was asked to evacuate after a dispute about compliance with Chadian government orders. Nigeria hosted a summit in August 1980, at which all eleven rival Chadian groups entered into the Lagos Accord on National Reconciliation in Chad. Conditions continued to deteriorate, however, as Libyan intervention persisted and as French troops pulled out. A summit of four African presidents in May 1981 failed to find a formula for Libyan withdrawal and for introduction of an African peacekeeping force. France urged Nigeria and friendly francophone states to constitute an OAU-sponsored joint force having logistical support from France.

In November 1981, six African states—Nigeria, Senegal, Zaire, Benin, Togo, and Guinea—pledged to form a joint 6,000-member force under a Nigerian commander. Financial constraints prevented half of them from meeting their commitments, and only Senegal, Zaire, and Nigeria provided troops for this second Chadian operation. Lagos had to bear most of the burden, including provision of three of the five army units and the airlift and logistical units the others failed to provide. Worse still, the mission itself failed. The OAU's inability to affect internal Chadian politics, the delayed deployment of the ill-equipped force, and its limited, uncertain mandate left Nigeria in a difficult military situation. Habré's forces entered the capital victoriously in June 1982. This episode undermined military and popular confidence in the government of Shagari and contributed to its downfall. Although stung by this experience, Nigeria continued to pursue its security interests in Chad by active diplomacy, including mediation between Chad and Libya.

In the case of Liberia, when the seven-nation ECOWAS mediation committee failed to end the three-way civil war, ECOWAS decided to send a peacekeeping force, ECOMOG, in August 1990. Nigeria's 5,000 troops, logistical support, and naval and air force units provided the bulk of this five-nation effort. Thousands of Nigerians were evacuated from the war-torn country, but ECOMOG's mission as a neutral peacekeeping force was soon compromised. Nigerian units became embroiled in the conflict, which spilled over into Sierra Leone, staging point for the ECOMOG operation. At least 500 fresh Nigerian troops were then deployed to Sierra Leone to defend the supply lines and assist the Sierra Leone army in fending off Liberian rebel incursions.

Nigeria has been in the vanguard of African support for the liberation of southern Africa and defense of the frontline states. It was one of the most consistent and generous providers of political, financial, and material assistance to the Namibian liberation movement, the South West Africa People's Organization (SWAPO), including substantial support to help organize pre-independence elections. Nigeria donated several million dollars' worth of military and financial aid to the African National Congress in its struggle against South Africa's apartheid regime. Nigeria also sent military equipment to Mozambique, which was attempting to suppress South African-backed Resistência Nacional Moçambicana (Renamo) guerrillas.

Global Interests

Nigeria's global interests and roles were demonstrated in different ways, most notably in its contribution of military units to several

267

UN peacekeeping missions, its leadership in various international fora, and its participation in the global nuclear nonproliferation movement. Nigeria's only foreign military deployments other than its border clashes with Chad and Cameroon have been multilateral missions. Nigerian units took part in operations beyond the colony's borders in both world wars. Since independence, Nigeria has proudly boasted Africa's longest and most distinguished record of participation in UN peacekeeping operations. Nigeria dispatched two infantry divisions under UN command to Congo in the early 1960s, and a battalion to Tanzania after the 1964 mutiny. It also contributed to the UN India-Pakistan Observer Mission (UNIPOM) in 1965, the UN Interim Force in Lebanon (UNIFIL) in 1978, and the UN observer mission to oversee the Iran-Iraq cease-fire and the Angola-Namibia accords in 1988. For reasons of internal politics and security, however, Nigeria did not send troops to participate in the 1990 Persian Gulf war. All told, Nigeria has contributed about 16,000 troops to UN peacekeeping functions. Nigeria also called for a permanent African seat on the UN Security Council.

Nigeria's internationalism also was manifest in its initiative to create a Concert of Medium Powers among nonaligned states in March 1987, at which Nigeria was appointed chair of the group and coordinator of its program. Also known as the Lagos Forum, the group held a September 1987 meeting attended by more than twenty countries. Nigeria also hosted the second meeting of the twenty-three-nation Zone of Peace and Cooperation of the South Atlantic in July 1990.

Nuclear nonproliferation was another important global security issue for Nigeria. Lagos signed the Nuclear Nonproliferation Treaty on the day it was opened for signature in 1968 and has made proposals at the UN for an African nuclear-free zone. Nigeria has made clear, however, that its continued nuclear forbearance is contingent on other signatories honoring their obligations and on the behavior of nonsignatories, such as South Africa. Various Nigerian academicians and officials have spoken in favor of keeping open or even of exercising the military "nuclear option" to enhance Nigeria's power and prestige and to avoid nuclear blackmail by South Africa, Libya, or the superpowers. In early 1988, Nigeria signed a safeguards agreement with the International Atomic Energy Agency, ensuring peaceful uses of its nuclear reactor project.

Armed Forces

Although the military history of the West African region extends back a millennium or more, Nigeria's present-day armed forces, like those of most African states, are the direct descendants of colonial military units. The officer corps was made fully indigenous by the mid-1960s, and in 1990 the Nigerian armed forces were among the largest and most professional in Africa. The military and political functions and international peacekeeping roles of the armed forces have expanded significantly but remained subject to several constraints. Nigeria was still heavily dependent on foreign arms but had embarked on a program of military industrialization. Voluntary military service and a large demographic base made recruitment easy, and training was highly professional. Nigeria's long-term challenge was to define its strategic interests and military missions more precisely and to achieve an appropriate modernized force structure to meet them.

Early Development

The Nigerian army traces its historical origins to three nineteenth-century military formations. The first dates from the establishment in 1862 by Captain John Glover of a small Hausa militia (dubbed Glover's Hausas) to defend the British colony of Lagos. Its mission was expanded to include imperial defense when dispatched to the Gold Coast during the Asante expedition of 1873-74. Enlarged and officially entitled the Hausa Constabulary in 1879, this unit performed both police and military duties until 1895, when an independent Hausa Force was carved out of the constabulary and given exclusively military functions. This demographic recruitment base perpetuated the use of Hausa as the lingua franca of command in Ghana and Nigeria, where it persisted into the 1950s. It also marked the historical origin of the ethnic imbalance that has characterized the Nigerian armed forces to this day (see Regional Groupings, ch. 2).

In addition to the Hausa Constabulary, the Royal Niger Company Constabulary was raised in 1888 to protect British interests in Northern Nigeria. It later provided the nucleus of the Northern Nigeria Regiment of the West African Frontier Force (WAFF). A third formation, the Oil Rivers Irregulars, was created during 1891-92; it was later redesignated the Niger Coast Constabulary and formed the basis of the WAFF's Southern Nigeria Regiment.

In 1897 WAFF was founded under the command of Colonel Frederick (later Lord) Lugard to counter French encroachments from the north. By 1901 WAFF was an interterritorial force composed of the Nigeria and Gold Coast regiments, the Sierra Leone Battalion, and the Gambia Company, and commanded by a small number of British army officers and noncommissioned officers seconded to the force. WAFF was under the Colonial Office in London, but each regiment was commanded by an officer responsible directly to the local colonial governor. The two regiments were consolidated into the Nigeria Regiment of the WAFF when the Northern and Southern Nigeria Protectorates were amalgamated on January 1, 1914 (see Unification of Nigeria, ch. 1). These colonial units fought in World War I, in the German colonies of Cameroons and Togoland, and in German East Africa. In 1928 the WAFF became the Royal West African Frontier Force, and in 1939 control of RWAFF shifted from the Colonial Office to the War Office.

In 1930 the Nigeria Regiment had about 3,500 men. During the 1930s, as part of a RWAFF reorganization, its four battalions were reorganized into six, and the colony was divided into northern and southern commands; major units were at Sokoto, Kano, Zaria, Kaduna, Maiduguri, Yola, Enugu, and Calabar. Although Hausa and their language predominated in the infantry and general support units, specialists were recruited mainly from the south. For example, the signals company required fluency in English, so Yoruba were recruited for that unit.

In World War II, Nigerians saw action in Kenya and the Italian East Africa and Burma campaigns, and Nigeria was the assembly and training site for the two West African divisions dispatched to Burma. In 1941 auxiliary groups, consisting of 630 porters organized into three companies for each infantry brigade, were also formed. After the war, the auxiliaries were disbanded, but some locally recruited carriers continued to be employed. In the 1950s, expansion to a two-brigade army was undertaken, and specialized combat and service units such as light artillery, communications, signals, medical, engineers, and motor transport were formed.

In the postwar years, RWAFF resumed its primary mission of internal security. Nigerian units undertook police actions and punitive expeditions to break strikes, to control local disturbances, to enforce tax collection, and to support police anticrime operations. They also mounted a major internal security operation in the southern part of British Cameroons to counter secessionists rebelling against colonial authority.

In 1956 the Nigeria Regiment was renamed the Nigerian Military Forces, RWAFF, and in April 1958 the colonial government of Nigeria took over from the War Office control of the Nigerian Military Forces. Africanization of the officer corps began slowly but accelerated through the 1950s. The first Nigerian officer was appointed in 1948; by independence in 1960, there were eighty-two Nigerian officers, mostly Igbo from the southeast. This ethnic imbalance within the officer corps contrasted with that in the rank and file, where northerners predominated.

Constitutional and Political Framework

Section 197 of the 1979 constitution provides for establishing, equipping, and maintaining an army, a navy, an air force, and "any other branches of the armed forces" deemed necessary for defending against external aggression, for ensuring territorial integrity and security of the nation's land, sea, and airspace, for suppressing insurrection and aiding civil authorities when so directed by the president, and for performing other such functions as may be legally prescribed. The president, as commander in chief of the armed forces, is empowered to determine their operational use and to appoint the chief of the Defence Staff and the heads of the military services. Section 265 authorizes the president, subject to parliamentary action under certain conditions, to issue a proclamation of emergency only when the federation is at war, in imminent danger of invasion or involvement in war, in cases of natural disaster or an actual or imminent breakdown of public order and public safety.

The regime of General Muhammadu Buhari (which held power for twenty months from December 1983), in Decree Number 1, suspended and modified parts of the constitution to empower the FMG to issue decrees signed with the force of law. It also vested all executive authority in the head of the FMG, who exercised it in consultation with the Supreme Military Council (SMC). The SMC was composed of the head of the FMG as president of the council; the chief of staff, Supreme Headquarters; the minister of defense; the chiefs of the army, navy, and air staffs; the general officers commanding the four army divisions; the commander of the Artillery Command; the attorney general; the inspector general of police; six other appointed senior military officers; and other members that the SMC might appoint. Its principal functions were to determine national policy on major issues and on all constitutional and national security matters and to appoint and to ratify appointments of top government, military, and public officials.

A National Council of States, composed essentially of the same officials as the SMC except for the line military commanders, was also established. Finally, Decree Number 1 provided for a National Defence and Security Council, which, under the direction of the SMC, was responsible for matters of defense and public security. This council, which replaced the National Defence Council of the Second Republic, had as its members the head of the FMG as chairman; the chief of staff, Supreme Headquarters; the ministers of defense, of external affairs, and of internal affairs; the three service chiefs of staff; the director general of the Nigerian Security

271

Organisation; the inspector general of police; and others appointed ad hoc by the head of the FMG.

After ousting Buhari on August 27, 1985, General Babangida issued Decree Number 17, amending Decree Number 1 to establish the institutional basis of his regime. In place of the title head of the FMG, Babangida assumed the new dual title of president and commander in chief of the armed forces. A chief of General Staff, General Staff Headquarters, replaced the chief of staff, Supreme Headquarters; the minister of defense was also chairman, Joint Chiefs of Staff. Buhari's Federal Executive Council was replaced by the Council of Ministers. The Armed Forces Ruling Council (AFRC), which replaced the SMC, originally had an enlarged all-service membership of nearly thirty, consisting of the same functional posts as the SMC plus the flag officers commanding the Eastern Naval Command, the Western Naval Command, and the Naval Training Command; the air officers commanding the Training, Tactical Air, and Logistics commands; and twelve other appointed senior military officers. In February 1989, however, Babangida reconstituted the AFRC with only nineteen members. The National Council of State (thus renamed) and the National Defence Council and National Security Council, separated into two bodies, were retained. In the December 1989 government reorganization, Babangida assumed the defense portfolio but assigned the functions of chairman, Joint Chiefs of Staff, to the chief of army staff (see fig. 14). In September 1990, the Supreme Headquarters was replaced by the Defence Headquarters, and large-scale reassignments and retirements of senior army, navy, and air force officers occurred. Babangida simultaneously relinquished the post of minister of defense to General Sanni Abacha, who also assumed the new position of chief of Defence Staff.

Organization, Mission, and Order of Battle

Nigeria's armed forces, sharply reduced from about 300,000 after the 1967–70 civil war (see Civil War, ch. 1) and undergoing continuing reductions into the 1990s, included the army, the navy (including coast guard), and the air force. Estimates of its size in late 1990 ranged from 94,500 to well over 100,000. In addition to military personnel, the defense establishment employed about 25,000 civilians. The military head of state, as commander in chief, exercised his authority through the AFRC, and operationally through the minister of defense and chief of Defence Staff, and the chiefs of staff of the three armed services. In September 1990, the post of chief of Defence Staff was elevated to full general and the service chiefs were also upgraded. The post of chief of General Staff,

General Staff Headquarters, created after the August 1985 coup, was a political rather than a military post. It was abolished in September 1990, and its incumbent, Vice Admiral Augustus Aikhomu, was appointed to the new position of vice president. The National Defence Council and the National Security Council were responsible for deliberating on strategic national and international issues affecting the political stability or security of Nigeria and the region. Their specific functions were thought to include threat assessment, overall defense planning, coordination of military procurement, and joint operations. In 1989 a 265-member Armed Forces Consultative Assembly consisting of battalion commanders and above, their equivalents in all services, and selected staff officers was inaugurated to discuss military matters, meeting perhaps quarterly (see fig. 15).

The armed forces' missions and roles were to defend the sovereignty and territorial integrity of the nation and other African states against external aggression; and to contribute to international peace and security through service in multilateral peacekeeping operations of the UN, the OAU, ECOWAS, or other prospective pan-African military operations. They also were charged with supporting and reinforcing the border security efforts of the immigration and customs departments, with providing internal security in support of the police and local law enforcement authorities, and with contributing to nation building through inculcation of patriotism and technical skills.

Army

In preparation for the restoration of civilian rule in 1979, specified geographic areas of responsibility defined from north to south were assigned to the army's three infantry divisions. By design these divisional areas cut across ethnic, regional, and state boundaries, thus denying division commanders a ready base for political mobilization. Each division had a mobile brigade as a protective screen for the capital. A fourth formation, composed mostly of logistical units, was deployed around Lagos.

By 1990 the army, which numbered at least 80,000, had been restructured into four divisions to accommodate the formation of an airborne division in 1981. The First Mechanized Infantry Division, headquartered at Kaduna, had brigades at Sokoto, Kano, and Minna. The Second Mechanized Infantry Division was headquartered at Ibadan. The Third Armored Division was based at Jos, with one mechanized and two armored brigades. The Eighty-second (Airborne) Division, stationed at Enugu in the southeast, had three brigades (airborne, airmobile, and amphibious) to defend

273

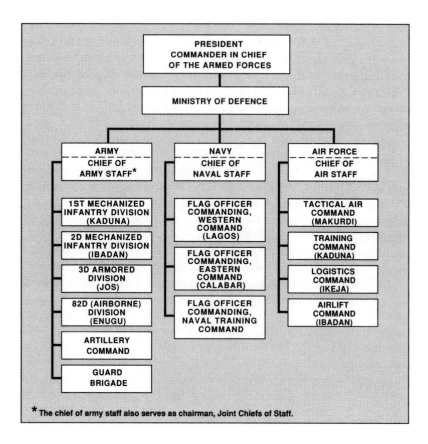

Figure 14. Organization of the Ministry of Defence and of the Armed Forces, 1990

the Cameroon border and for other foreign commitments. Each of the four divisions had an artillery and engineering brigade and a reconnaissance battalion. Finally, a Guard Brigade of three battalions and an armored reconnaissance battalion near Lagos provided security for army logistical units and the seat of government. The guard battalions were rotated periodically, as evidenced by the move of the Sixth Guard Battalion from Lagos to Port Harcourt in mid-1986. The guards thwarted the April 1990 coup attempt, losing five members in defense of Dodan Barracks. The army was equipped with tanks and other armored vehicles, and with artillery of various kinds (see table 17, Appendix).

In October 1986, Nigeria announced a plan to set up a reserve army under the Directorate of Army Recruitment, Resettlement, and Reserve. By 1990, however, the reserve force was still in the planning stage. Also under consideration for several years was the creation of an army light aviation force, for which American Bell 412 helicopters were being considered. It was not clear whether this force was to be part of the new airborne brigade, or another unit.

In 1989 the army established a rapid deployment force to be used for any contingency, particularly in relation to neighboring African countries. This unprecedented formation might have resulted from concern about reported South African attempts to gain a foothold in Nigeria's "soft underbelly" in Equatorial Guinea, to deter such actions in the future, and to ensure combat readiness for any foreign contingency. Nigerian spokesmen stressed that the force was not intended to intimidate Nigeria's neighbors, but to fight external and internal threats.

The Nigerian army and headquarters were undergoing restructuring in late 1990. As part of the continuing reorganization, army headquarters redesignated and upgraded the authority of the officers reporting to the chief of staff. The director of training and operations was renamed chief of operations, and the director of staff duties and plans was retitled chief of policy and plans.

Navy

Nigeria's navy dated to 1914, when the northern and southern marine detachments were merged to form the Nigerian Marine Department. In 1956 eleven small boats and harbor craft and about 200 officers and men were transferred from the then defunct Nigerian Marine to an independent naval force. In 1958 the British Parliament formally reconstituted the colony's small Naval Defence Force as the Royal Nigerian Navy. The term *Royal* was dropped when Nigeria became a republic. The 1964 Navy Act assigned to the navy the tasks of defending territorial waters, of training in naval duties, of conducting hydrographic surveys, of assisting in the enforcement of customs laws, and of undertaking other missions assigned by the government. Its specific tasks in the 1990s included defense against seaborne attack and protection of international shipping, and of offshore oil and sea resources, particularly prevention or prosecution of illegal bunkering and lifting of petroleum.

Administrative and operational control of the navy was vested in the chief of naval staff (CNS), under the broad policy direction of the Navy Board. The latter was composed of the armed forces commander in chief as chairman, the chief of General Staff, the minister of defense, and the CNS as members, and the director general of the Ministry of Defence as secretary. In the late 1980s, naval headquarters at Lagos was organized into five staff branches

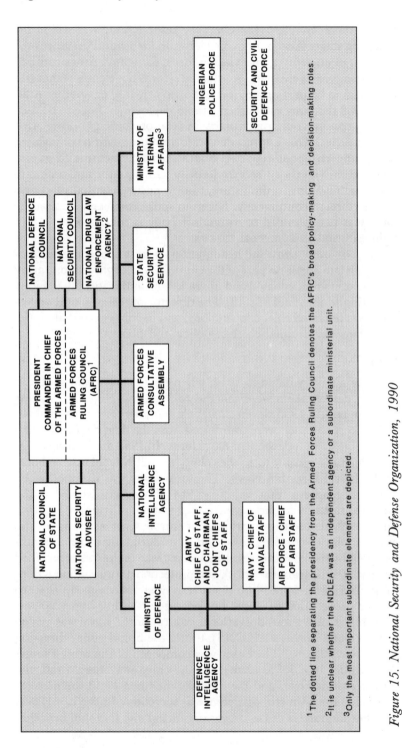

Figure 15. National Security and Defense Organization, 1990

[1] The dotted line separating the presidency from the Armed Forces Ruling Council denotes the AFRC's broad policy-making and decision-making roles.

[2] It is unclear whether the NDLEA was an independent agency or a subordinate ministerial unit.

[3] Only the most important subordinate elements are depicted.

under branch chiefs, who were principal staff officers responsible to the CNS: accounts and budget; logistics (responsible for provisioning, procurement, and maintenance of all equipment and installations, with directorates for supply, ship spares, projects, and armament supply); matériel; operations (responsible for daily operations and training, with directorates for plans, operations, intelligence, hydrography, and weapons and tactics); and personnel. Each directorate was headed by a director whose immediate subordinates were staff officers.

During 1990 naval headquarters was restructured into "corpslike" organizations. By the end of 1990, five such corps had been established: the Fleet Maintenance Corps, the Naval Matériel Supply Corps, the Building and Engineering Service Corps, the Naval Information Management Corps, and the Naval Ordnance Corps. The intent of this reorganization was to make headquarters function in a manner that resembled field formations.

During the 1970s, the navy was organized into three commands: the Western Naval Command and the Flotilla Command headquartered at Apapa near Lagos, and the Eastern Naval Command based in Calabar. The Flotilla Command was responsible for operations and for deployment of warships, the Western Naval Command for most of the logistics and repair facilities, and the Eastern Naval Command for naval bases and training facilities. The defects of this functional type of organization were the vulnerable concentration of ships and command facilities at Apapa, and the lack of warships based in the east where oil resources were concentrated. The naval establishment was therefore reorganized in 1983 by abolishing the Flotilla Command and by regrouping the warships into eastern and western fleets under independent commands.

In 1990 the navy was composed of the two geographical fleet commands and the Naval Training Command (see Training, this ch.). The latter, established in November 1986, included all training facilities, some of which were collocated with fleet commands. The senior Western Naval Command, commanded by a rear admiral, had operational responsibility for the area from the Brass River, in the Niger Delta, to the border with Benin. Its main shore establishments were Nigerian Naval Station (NNS) Olokun; NNS Quorra in Apapa; and the Navy Helicopter Squadron, the Naval Hospital, the Navy Secondary School, and the Navy Diving School, all at Ojo near Lagos. West of the Niger Delta were NNS Umalokum, an operational base in Warri, which was to be expanded with a shipbuilders' workshop and jetties to accommodate ships of up to 2,000 deadweight tons; and NNS Uriapele, commissioned in

277

1986 as a logistics base, and the Navy Technical Training Centre, both at Sapele.

The Eastern Naval Command, usually headed by a commodore, had operational responsibility from the Brass River to the Cameroon border. Its principal shore establishments were the operational base NNS Anansa and the Navy Supply School in Calabar. In the Port Harcourt area were NNS Akaso at Borokiri, a training base; the Nigerian Naval College near Bonny; NNS Okemiri, a naval base commissioned in late 1986 in the Port Harcourt area; the Navy Hydrographic School at Borokiri; and the Basic Seamanship Training School in Port Harcourt. Other naval bases were located at James Town and Bonny, and a special forces base was located on the Escravos River.

The largest maritime force in West Africa, the Nigerian navy had about 500 officers and 4,500 enlisted men and women in 1990. Its balanced fleet of modern warships, auxiliaries, and service craft was acquired from Britain, the Federal Republic of Germany (West Germany), France, Italy, the Netherlands, and the United States. The fleet consisted of two frigates, six missile craft, two corvettes, eight large patrol craft, forty-one coastal patrol craft, two minesweepers, two amphibious vessels, and various support ships (see table 18, Appendix). However, most ships were in disrepair and had not been overhauled since the early 1980s.

A naval aviation arm was inaugurated in May 1986 with three Westland Lynx Mk 89 MR/SR helicopters for maritime reconnaissance, search and rescue, and antisubmarine warfare; the air arm was based at Navytown at Ojo, near Lagos. The first naval air station of its kind in black Africa, Navytown provided ground support for helicopters deployed aboard the multipurpose frigate flagship, *Aradu*. The navy lacked only submarines; negotiations reportedly had begun to acquire one, but fiscal constraints precluded procurement. The small Nigerian Coast Guard of about eighteen patrol craft was controlled and manned by the navy.

Nigeria increasingly asserted its maritime interests and long-range goal of becoming a regional sea power. Although its coastline is only 853 kilometers, the seaward environment is of crucial importance to the nation's economic life: Nigeria's registered merchant marine consisted of about 220 vessels; it accounted for 70 percent of seaborne trade in West Africa and Central Africa; and 70 percent of its petroleum production—oil accounted for about 87 percent of the country's exports in 1988—came from six offshore oil platforms. Two official acts set forth Nigeria's maritime interests and policy. Decree Number 10 of April 1987 promulgated a national shipping policy, and the Navy Board's approval of a maritime

Army Armoured Corps personnel checking vehicles
Army Signal Corps members testing equipment
Courtesy Embassy of Nigeria, Washington

defense strategy, announced in April 1988, shifted Nigeria's strategic focus toward the South Atlantic because of external threats to its economic lifeline to the southeast. Operational preparedness to carry out this new strategy was demonstrated by the first fleet-level exercise involving both the Eastern Naval Command and the Western Naval Command in 1987 after a joint training exercise, including a cruise to neighboring African states. Nigeria also expanded international naval cooperation, hosting visits by Brazilian task forces in 1985 and 1986, and holding joint naval exercises with Brazil in March 1987 to gain experience in antisubmarine warfare.

Nigerian naval strategists conceptualized the navy's maritime mission as defense in depth within three overlapping perimeters. Level One, the highest priority, was coastal defense and inshore operations involving surveillance, early warning, antismuggling and piracy operations; protecting offshore oil installations; search and rescue; and policing out to 100 nautical miles. Level Two encompassed the maintenance of a naval presence in the Exclusive Economic Zone (EEZ) for monitoring, policing, and sea control; and for coordinating regional efforts, such as prevention of poaching, dumping of hazardous materials or toxic waste, and marine research. Level Three, the outer ring, involved surveillance, intelligence-gathering, training and flag-showing cruises; independent and joint exercises; and allied operations.

The navy's maritime defense roles, officially known as the Trident Strategy, comprised three elements contributing toward national military strategy. The first element was subregional sea control to defend Nigeria's national and maritime interests and to execute the national shipping policy by protecting sea-lanes. The second element, coastal defense, included protection of the coastal zone's approaches, territorial waters, and the EEZ. In the third element, the navy was to provide adequate sealift and gunfire support to the army in amphibious operations. This ambitious strategy may require increased resources in the future. In an effort to increase navy appropriations, in 1988 the service began an impressive public relations effort, including a "navy-citizens dialogue" to promote the navy as a cost-effective investment and publications extolling the navy's contributions to national security. It also published in 1989 a book entitled *Sea Power: Agenda for National Survival* and an article on Nigeria's naval roles and aspirations in the *Proceedings* of the United States Naval Institute. In a 1990 article in the *African Defence Journal,* the Nigerian naval information director called for strong naval or coastal surveillance capabilities to combat maritime security threats and to realize "tremendous indirect economic

Naval gunnery exercise at sea
Minister of defense and chairman of Joint Chiefs of Staff
observes first Naval Small Arms Competition at Ibadan, 1989.
Courtesy Embassy of Nigeria, Washington

281

gains'' by defending vital maritime and fisheries interests against unauthorized foreign exploitation.

Air Force

The Nigerian National Assembly approved the creation of an air force in 1962, and the government sought assistance initially from Ethiopia, India, Britain, the United States, Canada, and particularly West Germany. West Germany received a contract in 1963 to create the Nigerian air force from scratch, including designing and setting up its legal and organizational framework; recruiting and training personnel; furnishing equipment, supplies, maintenance, and construction services; and providing the first generation of twenty Dornier Do-27 liaison/transports and fourteen Piaggio 149D primary trainer aircraft. The Nigerian air force (NAF) was officially established by the 1964 Air Act, which also provided for an air force reserve to which officers and enlisted personnel would be transferred on completion of active service. An assistance group provided by the West German air force departed in 1966, at the onset of the disturbances preceding the civil war, leaving behind a fledgling air force of 800 army officers and enlisted personnel seconded to it. The civil war precipitated a period of rapid growth and the first acquisition of combat aircraft, Soviet MiG-17Fs, which played substantial roles in the interdiction of gunrunning and tactical air support to the army. Afterward, the NAF undertook a massive relief effort to the former secessionist region.

From the 1970s onward, the NAF expanded considerably, acquired a large and diversified inventory of combat and support aircraft, and substantially improved its ability to perform its primary missions of defending the country's airspace, of supporting the army and navy, and of conducting rescue operations over land and sea. In 1990 its estimated strength was 9,500 officers and enlisted personnel. Nigeria ranked eighth among African states in the number of combat aircraft, and sixth in total aircraft; among subSaharan states, only the South African air force exceeded Nigeria's combat aircraft assets. In 1989 the NAF unveiled its first locally built trainer aircraft, dubbed the Air Beetle. Training and maintenance deficiencies in the air force, however, resulted in high loss of aircraft and pilots. Long-range needs included adequate communication systems, search and rescue units, improved armament storage facilities, strategic fuel reserves, combat training, and weapons delivery ranges.

The NAF was organized into four specialized air commands: Tactical Air (headquartered in Makurdi), Training (Kaduna), Logistics (Ikeja), and Airlift (Ibadan), which was formed in June

1988. There were fifteen major air bases, the largest located at Benin, Enugu, Kaduna, Kano, Lagos, Makurdi, and Port Harcourt. In December 1986, the Tactical Air Command announced the establishment of a unit of Aermacchi MB–339AN trainers at Calabar to defend the airspace in the region and to support international missions necessitated by Nigeria's prominent role in African defense. The chief of air staff announced in October 1987 that the NAF would build an air base in Sokoto State to check violations of the country's airspace.

In 1990 the NAF had about 260 aircraft, including three squadrons with 69 attack/fighters, one maritime reconnaissance squadron, five transport squadrons, and 51 training aircraft. Budgetary constraints disrupted air force procurements in the last half of the 1980s. A 1985 order for fifty Brazilian Embracer Tucano trainers as part of an oil-for-goods agreement was shelved in late 1986 when barter deals were suspended; apparently no deliveries were made. The purchase of Boeing CH–47 Chinook helicopters was also delayed, and reportedly the NAF was considering disposing of its Aermacchi MB–339AN trainers and Aeritalia G–222 transports (see table 19, Appendix).

In addition to its small naval air arm, the NAF operated a squadron of maritime patrol aircraft and search-and-rescue helicopters in support of the navy. The first combined fleet exercise in late 1987 included air force strike aircraft in flights over the Atlantic. Although the NAF had exclusive responsibility for long-range maritime patrol, this function could be transferred to the navy as the latter service expanded its missions and capabilities.

The NAF's air defense capabilities were limited as a result of incomplete airspace control, of command and communications deficiencies, and of aircraft shortfalls relative to territory. The Selenia radar system installed at Murtala Muhammad International Airport satisfied both civilian and military purposes, including control of nearby air defense units equipped with antiaircraft guns and Roland surface-to-air missiles. Similar systems were in place at Enugu, Kano, and Kaduna. In March 1987, the NAF completed installation of an intercommand communication system.

Arms Procurement and Defense Industries

Like most Third World states, Nigeria depended largely on foreign sources for arms and military matériel. However, its arms acquisitions exhibited two distinctive features. First, Nigeria had one of the most internationally diversified and balanced defense procurement strategies. Nigeria acquired arms from about eight suppliers during 1978–82, tying Zaire as the most diversified sub-Saharan state (see table 20, Appendix). Its largest supplier during that period, West Germany, provided only about one-third of its US$845 million total. This diversified pattern became even more pronounced in the mid-1980s. During 1983–87, Nigeria imported military matériel valued at US$1.5 billion from about ten major suppliers—more than any other African state, and Italy, its largest supplier, accounted for only 23 percent.

Nigeria relied on equally diverse foreign suppliers of military technical services, while making gradual progress toward indigenization. A long-standing, military training arrangement with Britain ended in late 1986 with the Nigerianization of training. West German assistance was engaged to improve the Navy Technical Training Centre at Sapele, which was set up and operated with the help of Dornier (Nigeria). A West German firm also received a contract in late 1987 to upgrade radar and weapons systems for *Aradu,* the German Meko-360H class frigate. The Czechoslovak defense minister visited Nigeria in late 1987 and offered to assist in expanding arms production efforts. Yugoslavia offered to train NAF pilots, and Bulgaria provided equipment maintenance services. In May 1989, Nigeria discussed with Romania cooperation between their air forces and the manufacture and maintenance of tanks, armored personnel carriers, and other military vehicles and possible modernization of Nigeria's T–55 tanks. In October 1989, the chief of army staff made a ten-day official visit to France and China to explore military cooperation.

Defense ties with Third World countries were especially notable. In addition to military cooperation with African countries, Nigeria concluded defense cooperation, military personnel, and exchange agreements with the Republic of Korea (South Korea); Nigeria also discussed naval cooperation, especially officer training, with India (see Local and Bilateral Issues; African and Regional Issues, this ch.). Military ties with Brazil expanded considerably after conclusion of a 1983 military cooperation accord. The two countries established a joint committee in December 1985 to examine military training and exchange programs, and their joint military-naval exercise in December 1987 ended with a pledge to pursue more extensive cooperation.

United States arms transfers and security assistance to Nigeria were modest. During fiscal years (FY) 1972–90, United States Foreign Military Sales deliveries and licensed commercial exports of defense articles and services totaled US$63 million and US$110.8 million, respectively. Previously, during FY 1962–72 the United States had provided International Military Education and Training (IMET) grants valued at US$1.5 million to train 480 Nigerian

Air Force NCO receiving his sergeant's stripes
Courtesy Embassy of Nigeria, Washington

military personnel. After a thirteen-year hiatus, IMET grants were renewed in FY 1986 and have been funded annually since at more than US$90,000 for more than twenty students. A total of 585 Nigerian military students had participated in the IMET program by FY 1990.

Nigeria's fledgling domestic defense industry was the second distinctive source of military matériel, particularly for small arms, ammunition, and maintenance and repair services. The state-owned Defence Industries Corporation (DIC), established in 1964, geared up to produce ammunition during the civil war. By the 1970s, its facilities in Kaduna produced West German-designed HK G-3 rifles, BM-59 and PM-12 handguns, and 7.62mm and 9mm parabellum ammunition. Lack of financial and management support, however, impeded further progress until the DIC was reenergized in 1984 by then army chief of staff Babangida. After becoming president, Babangida expanded the DIC to increase Nigeria's self-reliance.

In 1977 the army decided to standardize its infantry weapons with Belgian FAL assault rifles, Browning GP pistols, and MAG machine guns. In 1978 licensed production rights were acquired, and in 1980 the DIC's facilities in Kaduna were adapted and upgraded by Belgian technicians to assemble these weapons. Production

285

began in 1983; full production capacity was achieved in 1987; and the next year the DIC was reported to be relying entirely on local raw materials and to be producing all the basic rifles and ammunition the army and police used. Its annual production capacity was 15,000 FAL rifles, 9,000 to 10,000 GP pistols, and 1,000 MAG machine guns. The FAL rifle entered service in 1989 as the NR-1.

In addition to the small arms and ammunition factories at Kaduna, newer facilities for the assembly of armored fighting vehicles and light tanks were under development at Bauchi in 1990. Austrian Steyr 680M 4x4 tactical military trucks were reportedly assembled there, and it was also planned to produce Pinzgauer light tracked armored vehicles and Steyr 4K 7FA tracked armored personnel carriers. By 1987 the DIC employed 2,000 to 3,000 people at its Kaduna and Bauchi plants. Indications of a nascent commercial defense industry included a manufacturer in Anambra State whose inexpensive jeeps included military models being tested by the army; a local service industry to supply uniforms, accoutrements, and selected ordnance matériel; and increased domestic sourcing for aircraft and naval ship components and maintenance services. Local assembly of West German MBB Bo-105 helicopters for the air force was also contemplated. Further progress hinged on the availability of foreign capital and technology, joint ventures, and export opportunities, especially for rifles and ammunition.

On its silver anniversary April 22, 1989, the air force unveiled and conducted a test flight of a prototype of Nigeria's first domestically built aircraft, the Air Beetle. Jointly built over two years by the NAF and a West German Kaduna-based firm from the design of the United States Van RV-6 sport aircraft, the Air Beetle had the unique feature of being able to fly on standard automobile fuel. This two-seat, single engine airplane was intended to be the primary trainer for the NAF, replacing the aging British Bulldog trainers. The production program called for sixty units by 1992 and eventual development of an improved version, the Super Air Beetle. In early 1990, the first export orders were reported, and forty aircraft of the first production run were scheduled for delivery to foreign customers.

Under a national aircraft maintenance policy approved in 1987, depots were being set up around the country with the aim of achieving complete overhaul capability for all civil and military aircraft. In July 1988, a task force to implement the national aircraft maintenance center was inaugurated. The center will be a civilian organization with the capability to service, maintain, and overhaul military aircraft and components. In 1989 the air force was directed to indigenize 50 percent of its maintenance work within ten years.

The manufacture of such basic aircraft components and spare parts as hydraulic units and actuators, brakes, and plastic passenger cabin parts had also begun by the late 1980s. These domestic production and technical service industries were intended to save foreign exchange, to foster self-reliance, and to promote a local technological and industrial base.

The navy also turned increasingly to local suppliers for spare parts and maintenance services. In mid-1989 about 40 percent of the spare parts for naval vessels reportedly had been produced in Nigeria, and the navy saved N20 million at that time (for value of the naira—see Glossary) by using locally made parts, including propeller shafts and generator parts. The new navy dockyard, opened at the end of 1990 at Victoria Island near Lagos, will eventually have the capacity to boost domestic production of spare parts for ships to 70 percent of requirements and to permit future modification and even construction of ships.

Recruitment and Conditions of Service

Nigeria's large population and the decreasing size of the armed forces made recruitment relatively easy. More than 15 million men were fit for military service, and each year about 1.2 million reached the military age of eighteen. Military service was voluntary, but Section 200 of Nigeria's 1979 constitution provided for the establishment and maintenance of adequate facilities for carrying out any law requiring compulsory military service or training. Further, until such an act passed, the president was authorized to maintain facilities for military training in any secondary or postsecondary education institution that desired such training. The new draft constitution, promulgated by Decree Number 12 of 1989, to become effective on October 1, 1992, contains identical provisions.

Since 1973 Nigeria has had a National Youth Service Corps (NYSC); graduates of polytechnic schools and universities at home or abroad were obligated to serve one year in the corps in a state other than their native one. The NYSC expanded from about 5,000 men and 1,100 women during 1976–77 to 30,000 men and 13,000 women in 1985. The corps was primarily a technical and education program for national development, and it had no paramilitary functions or relationship to the armed forces.

Military recruitment was highly selective and subject to a constitutional mandate that the composition of both the officer corps and other ranks should reflect Nigeria's "federal character." The minimum educational qualification was a West African School Certificate. Reports that more than 20,000 applicants had sought 1,760 places in the army during one recruitment period underscored its

287

selectivity. Nigerian law required the army to recruit equal quotas from among the states and to mix recruits in units. Northerners were overrepresented, however, especially in the infantry, in which soldiers from the states of Sokoto, Niger, Kaduna, Kano, and Borno predominated. In 1985 it was estimated that 70 percent of senior officers came from the northern or middle belt region, whereas the administrative, technical, and logistic formations were dominated by southerners. The highest ranking women in 1984 were one army colonel, one air force wing commander, and one navy commander, all in the Medical Corps.

In early 1989, the Directorate of Army Recruitment, Resettlement, and Reserve reported that almost 43,000 Nigerians had joined the army during the previous decade: 18,981 between March 1979 and January 1988, and 23,971 between April 1983 and December 1988. Army enrollments were also expected to double from 3,000 to 6,000 as a one-time measure under the revitalization program under which entrants from 1963 or earlier were discharged to make room for younger soldiers who had joined in 1979 or later. To meet targeted force reduction levels, in 1990 the army began discharging soldiers who could not read or write after the four-year literacy campaign (1986–89), strictly enforcing disciplinary codes, and encouraging early retirements. The navy accepted about 500 recruits per year. In 1989 the navy announced that it was suspending recruitment of women, except nurses, until adequate and appropriate conditions of service had been devised, such as accommodations, training, promotions, and authorization for marriages and pregnancies.

Military pay and benefits were generally adequate if not attractive, although their value in real terms eroded during the period of economic austerity in the late 1980s. A new salary and benefits structure for the armed forces was announced in December 1990, to be implemented in January 1991. Benefits included a basic benevolent fund plan that provided immediate but token relief to dependents of deceased service personnel. In 1989 benefits were increased to N4,000 for noncommissioned officers (NCOs), N5,000 for senior NCOs, and N10,000 for commissioned officers; personnel contributed a premium of about N36 yearly. The army introduced an insurance plan in 1988, a benefit soon emulated by the other services. An Air Force Welfare Insurance Scheme was introduced in April 1989 to provide life insurance with death benefits ranging between N10,000 to N80,000 depending on rank. Members' contributions varied by rank, from N10 monthly for airmen to N100 monthly for air commodores. The new plan supplemented the existing benevolent fund and special coverage for pilots and flight technicians. The NAF also announced plans to establish its own bank. In 1989 an impending Nigerian Navy Welfare Insurance Scheme was also announced.

Several problems were apparent, however. During 1986 a census of army personnel and dependents was conducted to determine needs for adequate housing, utilities, and medical care and to identify and eject persons illegally occupying military accommodations. It found uniforms in such short supply that all sorts of irregular attire and accoutrements were in use. Thousands of soldiers and their families lived in *bashas,* shanty-like structures that the army hoped to replace with suitable housing before October 1992. In late 1988, Babangida expressed deep concern about general social malaise and economic crimes, which were aggravated by the use of sophisticated weapons obtained with the connivance of military personnel. In early 1990, the army chief of staff noted the continued problem of service personnel engaged in smuggling, armed robbery, and other antisocial activities.

The most demanding personnel problem was managing the steady demobilization of the armed forces from about 300,000 in the early 1970s to a scheduled number of perhaps 75,000 by 1993. An Armed Forces Rehabilitation Centre was set up in 1972 to resettle disabled soldiers. It has continued to operate with a broader mission and under various names but has lacked direction. It has pensioned off disabled soldiers, discharged police, reenlisted ex-servicemen, and handled voluntary discharges. Most of the voluntary discharges were skilled technicians retained on active duty until 1980. Discharged service personnel experienced massive administrative problems, such as delays or failure to receive pensions and gratuities, whereas other ex-service personnel received discharges or benefits to which they were not entitled. Finally, in January 1989, the government announced a major resettlement program, including guidance and counseling, job placement, and technical and vocational training. Taken together with the new welfare insurance plans, this program promised to improve conditions of service and release.

In 1989 the army announced it would undertake a review of military laws to correct deficiencies. Among measures contemplated were plans to educate lawyers about military laws and to develop better procedures for trying soldiers accused of violations. Existing laws only stated offenses for which a soldier could be charged but did not prescribe procedures. The army also called for inclusion of military law in the teaching curricula of university law faculties.

Training

Nigeria boasted comprehensive and almost completely indigenized professional military training institutions, including the national triservice Nigerian Military University, the Command and Staff College, and the National Institute for Policy and Strategic Studies. In addition, each service maintained extensive training programs for its own needs.

The central pillar of the military training establishment was the Nigerian Military University. Founded in 1964 in Kaduna as the Nigerian Defence Academy, this unique academy for regular commissioned officer candidates in 1983 had a staff of about 1,100. The academy was upgraded and redesignated as the national Nigerian Military University in 1985 and awarded its first degrees in September 1988. By 1989 it had trained about 5,300 officers, including 300 from other countries. In a message to the 104 graduating officers in September 1990, President Babangida announced that the academy would be moved to a permanent site by mid-1992. For prospective army officers, the academy offered a two-and-a-half-year program leading to commissions as second lieutenants. Naval and air force cadets attended an eighteen-month joint training program, after which successful candidates advanced to specialized training with their chosen service before commissioning. During the 1970s, to meet the demand for officers the academy also offered a six-month short service commission course for army and air force personnel selected from the ranks. In June 1980, President Shagari announced plans to establish both a naval and an air force academy, but as of 1990 they had not been implemented.

The need for both a national defense academy and a command and staff college was occasioned by the manpower explosion during the civil war, the acute shortage of officers, the poor quality of professional training, and the diversity of foreign training experiences. In 1975 the Nigerian army sought assistance from Britain in establishing a staff college at Jaji, near Kaduna, the site of the Nigerian Army School of Infantry. The college opened in May 1976 with two senior officers' courses lasting five and one-half months, with a curriculum derived from the British Army Staff College at Camberley but specially tailored to Nigerian circumstances and needs. The first course had forty army officers and the second fifty officers, including two each from the navy and air force.

Concurrently, planning proceeded for an eleven-month course for field-grade officers, which began in September 1977 with 70 officers; this course was increased to the planned 100 the next year. This five-term course covered staff duties, organizations, and logistics; operational staff duties, command, and intelligence; basic tactics; training and counterrevolutionary warfare; advanced counter-revolutionary warfare; and other general subjects. Students from Guyana, Ghana, Kenya, and Tanzania also attended the 1978 course, by which time air and naval wings had been formed.

The junior division of the Army Command and Staff College for senior lieutenants and junior captains opened in April 1978 (it was renamed the Command and Staff College later in 1978). Four ten-week courses were offered annually, initially with thirty students but later increased to forty. By 1987 the course had expanded to eighteen weeks and was run generally along the lines of the junior division of the British Staff College at Warminster. Also at Jaji was a Demonstration Battalion, the Army School of Artillery, and armor support from a composite armored battalion in Kaduna.

The air faculty opened with twenty students in September 1978, the same year the NAF set up a junior division at the air base in Kaduna. At that time, the joint service nature of the college at Jaji resulted in its being redesignated the Command and Staff College. The navy faculty was established in September 1981 with twelve students, and in August 1984 a junior navy division was set up with assistance from the British Royal Navy. The transfer of the junior air faculty from Kaduna to Jaji completed the process of expansion and consolidation of this unique full-fledged staff college, with junior and senior divisions of all three services at the same campus.

In addition to technical military training, the Command and Staff College increased attention to internal security and aid to the civil authority. Students and instructors from the Police Staff College at Jos, Nigerian Prison Service officers, and senior Ministry of Defence civil servants joined the army senior division. Jaji also attracted officers from other African states. Students from Benin, Ethiopia, Ghana, Sierra Leone, Tanzania, Uganda, and Zimbabwe regularly attended, and the first Botswanan officers attended the 1986–87 course. In 1986 it was decided that the training program would be fully indigenized. Henceforth, contracts with expatriate staff were not renewed, and foreign faculty members were accepted only on an exchange basis. At that time, there were forty-seven directing staff—thirty-eight Nigerian, seven British, and two Ghanaian, the latter under a long-standing exchange program. By 1986, 1,172 officers had graduated from Jaji's senior divisions and 1,320 from the junior divisions.

Each service also operated its own training institutions and facilities. The army's Training and Doctrine Command, based at Minna, had overall responsibility for developing, conducting, and evaluating army training and doctrine. It was organized into six directorates and two departments with sixteen training schools, including infantry, intelligence, signals, airborne, and amphibious warfare. Since 1985 it has used the United States-designed Systems Approach to Training, under which each of the army's four divisions prepared and conducted a comprehensive annual training program.

The multiprogram Nigerian Army School of Infantry (NASI) was the largest single-service school. In late 1988, it was announced that 5,040 officers and soldiers and 13 NAF officers had completed instruction at NASI during the previous three years; other graduates included 146 police, 2 civilians from the DIC, and 145 military personnel from other African countries, mainly Zimbabwe. The number of officers in the various courses in 1988 was 273 airborne, 376 young officers course, 112 range management course, 67 quartermaster and direct short commission, 75 company commanders course, 15 unit sappers, and 23 mortar platoon.

The navy's schools for officer and basic seamanship technical training were at the training complex at NNS Quorra, where the curriculum included navigation, diving, communications, and gunnery. Officer training at the Nigerian Naval College, Onura, entailed a two-year military and academic program followed by two years' shipboard and operational experience before commissioning as sublieutenants. The last class of forty-five midshipmen graduated in July 1990, after which the Nigerian Military University took over officers' training.

The Naval Training Command, established in November 1986, included several major subordinate facilities: NNS Onura and NNS Akaso near Port Harcourt; NNS Quorra at Apapa; the Diving School at Navytown in Ojo; the Navy Technical Training Centre, Sapele; the Dockyard Apprentice School near Lagos; and the NNS Logistic Centre. The navy relied primarily on West German and British firms to help establish its technical and professional schools. A new Underwater Warfare School, built by Dornier of Germany, opened in 1990 with more than 600 students. In late 1989, plans to set up a naval military school were still delayed by budgetary limitations, but officer training cooperation was being explored with India. By 1990 about 85 percent of naval training had been localized, resulting in annual savings of N100 million.

For its part, the NAF Training Command operated three flying schools offering comprehensive flight, armaments, helicopter, and paratrooper training, and a Technical Training Group (TTG). The air force had specialized schools for such subjects as primary and advanced flying, helicopter weapons, and tactical training. Primary

*General Babangida and senior armed forces officers
overseeing Exercise Fast Strike
Courtesy Embassy of Nigeria, Washington*

flight training was conducted at the 301 Flying Training School at the Nigerian air base in Kaduna, under the air force Tactical Training Group. British Bulldogs were the primary trainers, and Aermacchi MB–339ANs were used for basic and advanced flight training. In July 1989, the Student Pilot School graduated eleven of the fourteen candidates who had started the course. Since its inception in 1964, more than 600 pilots from the NAF and from other African countries have graduated. In 1987 the Tactical Air Command at Makurdi acquired sophisticated British Aerospace flight simulators to reduce accidental crashes. When fully operational, the NAF helicopter training school at Enugu also planned to train pilots from other African countries.

The TTG at Kaduna comprised officers' schools for engineering, logistics management, communication and electronics, air management, and aircraft maintenance. Its modern aircraft training and maintenance support equipment included electroplating shops, a heat-treatment laboratory, and forging and welding shops, and permitted the NAF to achieve a high degree of self-sufficiency. In 1987 the NAF ceased aircraft maintenance training abroad and began to set up an armament engineering department. The TTG fabricated nearly all the spare parts and components used to maintain the NAF's equipment; by then about 80 percent of NAF training was done locally. In 1989 it was announced that the TTG would be affiliated with the Nigerian Military University in Kaduna and redesignated the NAF Institute of Technology. Comparable to university-level colleges of technology, the new institute would offer degree programs and train air force personnel in automotive and aircraft trades and weapon services.

Finally, the National Institute for Policy and Strategic Studies at Kuru, near Jos, afforded senior officers an opportunity to study and to reflect on domestic and international security affairs. Its programs were similar to those of senior service schools and "war colleges" in other countries. A separate national defense institute was reported to be in planning in 1990.

Military Capabilities

Compared with its neighbors, Nigeria possessed overwhelming military strength. Its sizable and relatively well-equipped armed forces were capable of defending the country against any likely external threat and of projecting power in the region. In fact, as of December 1990, Nigeria was the only country in west-central Africa to mount and sustain military operations abroad. Although the army had been cut by more than one-half since 1970, its firepower and mobility have increased considerably. The other services have grown little, but their combat systems increased in number and sophistication. The navy expanded its mission from coastal defense to sea-lane protection and acquired modest amphibious and antisubmarine warfare capabilities. Likewise, the NAF developed and improved its capacity for ground attack, air support, interdiction, air defense, airlift, and air mobility operations.

Nigeria's military capabilities were subject to several systemic constraints, however. Economic difficulties and budgetary limitations slowed the pace of military modernization, delayed new equipment procurements, hindered defense industrial growth, reduced training, and magnified logistical and maintenance deficiencies. The diversity of equipment of foreign origin precluded standardization and compounded logistics and maintenance deficiencies. Indeed, in the 1980s it was estimated that, at any given time, one-third of Nigeria's major systems was operational, another third could be made operational within a few weeks, and the remainder was indefinitely unserviceable. Moreover, the top military echelons had become politicized, engrossed in government functions, and preoccupied with internal security at the expense of professional military development. Inefficiency and corruption exacerbated these problems, all of which combined to hurt operational readiness and effectiveness. However, the progressive withdrawal of the military from politics during the transition to the Third Republic (expected to begin with the completion of the return to civilian rule in late 1992), the restructuring of the armed forces, and the emphasis on professionalism since the late 1980s were intended to remedy these problems.

Uniforms, Ranks, and Insignia

Each component service fosters allegiance through its own distinctive uniforms and its system of ranks and insignia. In 1963 the Nigerian army discarded the ceremonial dress of the RWAFF in favor of a uniform of indigenous design. Since then a peaked cap, a dark green tunic with patrol collar, and light-colored trousers have comprised the army's ceremonial uniform. The field and service uniforms follow the British pattern, as does the service cap with its use of gold braid. In late 1990, reports indicated that new uniforms were to be introduced in 1991. Badges of rank were patterned on those of the British army, except that the Nigerian eagle had replaced the British crown on the insignia of majors and higher ranking officers (see figs. 16 and 17). Rank titles in the Nigerian navy generally follow those of the Royal Navy. The Nigerian air force originally adopted titles identical to those of the army for officers below the general officer grades. In 1976 this system was discarded in favor of the rank titles used in the Royal Air Force.

Armed Forces and Society

The military has been the dominant institution of the Nigerian polity since the mid-1960s when it became professional. The armed forces cannot rule the country indefinitely. However, no civilian successor regime can ignore the military's institutional demands and ultimate power to remove civilian authority. Long periods of military rule, concomitant claims on national resources, and the proliferation of linkages between the military and the economy have expanded military roles and evoked pronounced public responses.

Attitudes Toward the Military

Attitudes toward the military in Nigeria were ambivalent in the early 1990s. On the one hand, it was well regarded. Despite repeated interventions, the military as an institution has remained intact and not succumbed to radicalization; it has ruled firmly and, with a few notable exceptions, humanely; and it has made the restoration of stable civilian rule a high priority. The repeated turnovers

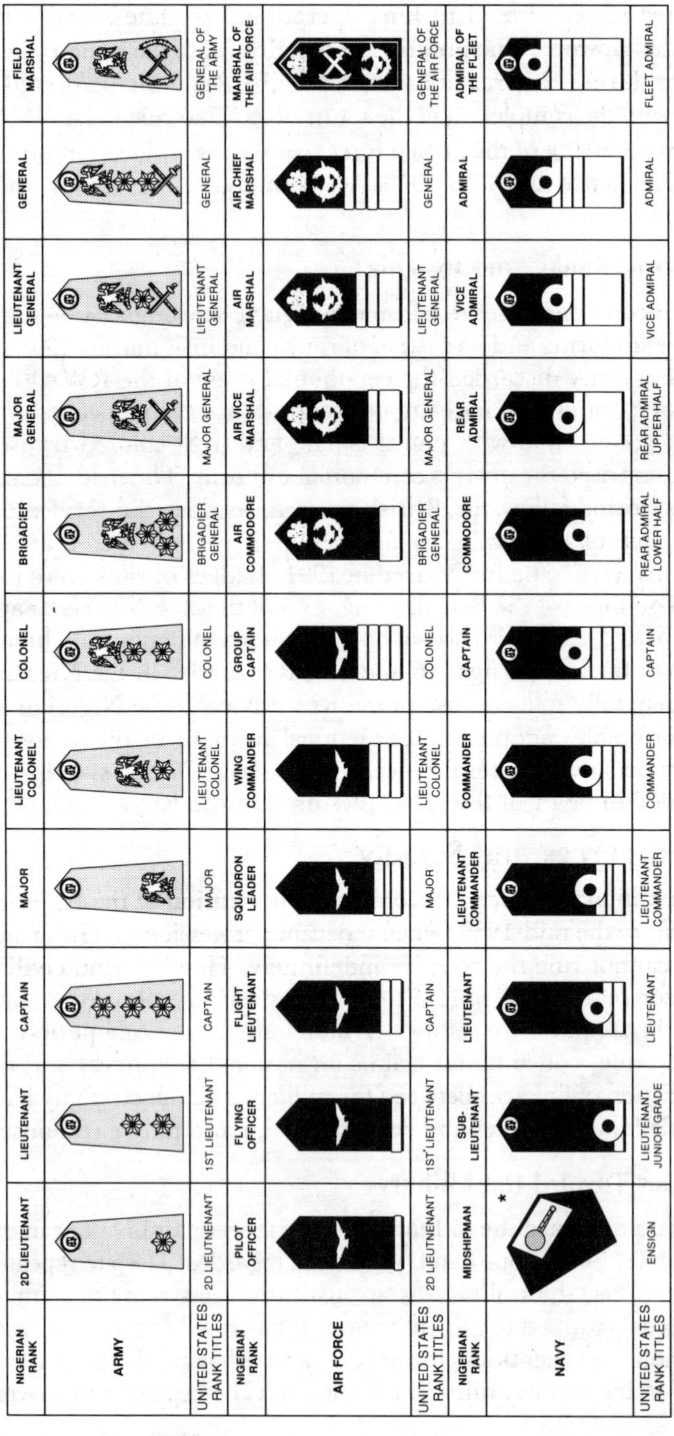

NIGERIAN RANK	2D LIEUTENANT	LIEUTENANT	CAPTAIN	MAJOR	LIEUTENANT COLONEL	COLONEL	BRIGADIER	MAJOR GENERAL	LIEUTENANT GENERAL	GENERAL	FIELD MARSHAL
ARMY											
UNITED STATES RANK TITLES	2D LIEUTNENANT	1ST LIEUTENANT	CAPTAIN	MAJOR	LIEUTENANT COLONEL	COLONEL	BRIGADIER GENERAL	MAJOR GENERAL	LIEUTENANT GENERAL	GENERAL	GENERAL OF THE ARMY
NIGERIAN RANK	PILOT OFFICER	FLYING OFFICER	FLIGHT LIEUTENANT	SQUADRON LEADER	WING COMMANDER	GROUP CAPTAIN	AIR COMMODORE	AIR VICE MARSHAL	AIR MARSHAL	AIR CHIEF MARSHAL	MARSHAL OF THE AIR FORCE
AIR FORCE											
UNITED STATES RANK TITLES	2D LIEUTNENANT	1ST LIEUTENANT	CAPTAIN	MAJOR	LIEUTENANT COLONEL	COLONEL	BRIGADIER GENERAL	MAJOR GENERAL	LIEUTENANT GENERAL	GENERAL	GENERAL OF THE AIR FORCE
NIGERIAN RANK	MIDSHIPMAN	SUB-LIEUTENANT	LIEUTENANT	LIEUTENANT COMMANDER	COMMANDER	CAPTAIN	COMMODORE	REAR ADMIRAL	VICE ADMIRAL	ADMIRAL	ADMIRAL OF THE FLEET
NAVY	*										
UNITED STATES RANK TITLES	ENSIGN	LIEUTENANT JUNIOR GRADE	LIEUTENANT	LIEUTENANT COMMANDER	COMMANDER	CAPTAIN	REAR ADMIRAL LOWER HALF	REAR ADMIRAL UPPER HALF	VICE ADMIRAL	ADMIRAL	FLEET ADMIRAL

* Worn on collar

Figure 16. Officer Ranks and Insignia, 1990

	NO RANK	PRIVATE	LANCE CORPORAL	CORPORAL	SERGEANT	STAFF SERGEANT	WARRANT OFFICER CLASS II	WARRANT OFFICER CLASS I	NO RANK
NIGERIAN RANK — ARMY		NO INSIGNIA							NO INSIGNIA
UNITED STATES RANK TITLES	BASIC PRIVATE	PRIVATE	PRIVATE 1ST CLASS	CORPORAL/ SPECIALIST	SERGEANT	STAFF SERGEANT	SERGEANT 1ST CLASS	MASTER SERGEANT — FIRST SERGEANT	SERGEANT MAJOR — COMMAND SERGEANT MAJOR
NIGERIAN RANK — AIR FORCE	NO RANK	AIRCRAFTSMAN / NO INSIGNIA	LANCE CORPORAL	CORPORAL	SERGEANT	FLIGHT SERGEANT	WARRANT OFFICER	MASTER WARRANT OFFICER	AIR WARRANT OFFICER
UNITED STATES RANK TITLES	AIRMAN BASIC	AIRMAN	AIRMAN 1ST CLASS	SENIOR AIRMAN/ SERGEANT	STAFF SERGEANT	TECHNICAL SERGEANT	MASTER SERGEANT	SENIOR MASTER SERGEANT	CHIEF MASTER SERGEANT
NIGERIAN RANK — NAVY	NO RANK	ORDINARY RATING / NO INSIGNIA	ABLE RATING	LEADING RATING	NO RANK	PETTY OFFICER	NO RANK	CHIEF PETTY OFFICER	WARRANT PETTY OFFICER / NO INSIGNIA
UNITED STATES RANK TITLES	SEAMAN RECRUIT	SEAMAN APPRENTICE	SEAMAN	PETTY OFFICER 3D CLASS	PETTY OFFICER 2D CLASS	PETTY OFFICER 1ST CLASS	CHIEF PETTY OFFICER	SENIOR CHIEF PETTY OFFICER	MASTER CHIEF PETTY OFFICER

Figure 17. Enlisted Ranks and Insignia, 1990

among the generals occasioned by coups and intraregime power realignments accelerated upward mobility for capable officers and attracted high-quality volunteers. In addition, the political and managerial experience acquired by senior officers in government posts during long periods of military rule offered exceptional and lucrative postservice business opportunities. These "up or out" conditions created what critics dubbed a "baby general" boom.

On the other hand, Nigeria's highly charged and pluralistic political culture afforded ample latitude to criticize the military, although with some inhibitions during periods of military rule. Nigerian scholar Ikenna Nzimiro decried the "military psychosis" that beset Nigeria and the class nature of the military as part of a privileged ruling class. In his view, this military oligarchy rewarded itself with sharply increased but socially unproductive military spending. Other human rights advocacy groups and prominent individuals often protested the military regime's incompetence and misuse of power (see Human Rights, this ch.). A July 1990 poll conducted by the Ministry of Information found widespread public dislike of coups and military regimes.

Political Role of the Military

Although Babangida announced in January 1986 that restoration of an elected civilian government would occur by October 1, 1990, he later postponed the changeover by two years. In the interim, the government undertook not only to mobilize the body politic for the transition to democracy, but also to transform the military from ruling institution to loyal servant of the Third Republic. For example, the new constitution will ban any person or group from taking over the government by force. In July 1987, the minister of defense announced a plan to establish a special unit to educate military personnel in their primary role as guardians of national security. In particular, they were to be instructed to tolerate the deficiencies of civilian rule and not to engage in plotting coups. Members of the armed forces were also admonished, under penalty of dismissal, neither to support politicians or political parties nor to canvass or assist any political party in campaigning on military bases. Similarly, the chief of naval staff directed all commands to establish education programs to prepare for the restoration of democracy. The armed forces also planned to assist with logistical arrangements for the elections; both navy and air force units would transport matériel and personnel in remote areas.

As Babangida made clear, however, the military continued to regard itself as the custodian of the polity and the ultimate political arbiter. He justified military intervention to preserve national unity and stability when the conditions for democracy were on the verge of collapse. The armed forces were first and foremost patriots dedicated to the defense of the nation; they had been forced into a governing role, not by design but to prevent anarchy. Above all, the military forces were professionals convinced of their righteous cause. For them, withdrawal from politics must be a strategic move to bring about a true and enduring democratic process. Hence, the military was crucial to the political life of the country, and the primary aim during the transitional period was to achieve the conditions for return to a civilian government whose conduct would obviate future coups.

Whether or not civilian restoration endures, the political landscape has been altered by the large number of retired senior officers who will continue to play leading political and economic roles. According to one observer, no other country has promoted and retired its generals faster than Nigeria, where political imperatives led to pensioning off potential opponents or officers of questionable loyalty. More than forty senior officers were retired or dismissed after Babangida's coup, and thirty-eight army officers were retired in the wake of the foiled coup attempt in December 1985. By 1989 more than 200 generals, many of them "baby generals" only in their forties, had been retired with full pay and with allowances for life. Since the mid-1970s, the military produced more millionaires than any other profession. Many were chairmen or directors of parastatals or private companies and were eagerly sought by business because of their personal ties to the regime. Such conditions increased opportunities for corruption. The prospects for political stability were enhanced, however, to the extent that ambitious military officers who had tasted power were pensioned off and rewarded in the private sector.

Demographic Factors and the Defense Budget

The civil war and extended periods of military rule created conditions that sustained the military's rising claims on national resources. There were few opponents of defense spending, given increasing national security challenges and Nigeria's self-image as regional leader and power broker. The main reason for the sharp rise in defense spending in the 1970s was the large postwar military establishment and the associated costs of foreign arms procurement, military housing construction, substantial salary increases, expansion of the officer corps, and the retirements and self-promotions after the 1975 coup.

During the civil war, Nigeria's armed forces, arms imports, and defense spending swelled, and military personnel levels were maintained at between 200,000 and 300,000 until the late 1970s. Defense spending as a percentage of total federal spending surged from about 6 percent before the war to 43 percent in the last year of the conflict. It remained high—34 percent during 1970–71 and about 20 percent from 1971 to 1974—before beginning a downward trend that continued through the 1980s. The 1970s also featured rapid economic expansion and budget growth driven by oil exports. As a result, absolute levels of military spending rose substantially during peacetime even though the level declined relative to available resources. According to some analysts, such ''militarization'' led to declining gross national product (GNP—see Glossary), to increasing inflation, and to an unfavorable balance of trade (see Foreign Trade and Balance of Payments, ch. 3).

In comparative global terms, however, Nigeria's level of ''militarization'' was remarkably low and had been decreasing since the mid-1970s. According to a survey of 144 countries compiled by the United States Arms Control and Disarmament Agency, Nigeria's ranking on five key measures of ''militarization'' declined sharply between 1975 and 1985. Nigeria's average global ranking on indicators of ''military buildup'' (armed forces per 1,000 population and the ratios of military expenditure to GNP, central government expenditure, population, and armed forces) fell from 47 in 1975, to 88 in 1980, and to 118 in 1985.

The steep downward trends in defense expenditure were apparent across the board. Military spending plunged precipitously from US$906 million to US$180 million (in constant 1987 dollars) between 1977 and 1987—an astounding reduction of 80 percent. Relative to GNP, military spending dropped steadily from 3.5 percent to less that 1 percent in 1987, while as a portion of total government expenditure it fell from more than 14 percent to 2.7 percent in 1987. The value of arms imports (measured in constant 1987 dollars) averaged US$93 million annually between 1977 and 1980, surged to an average of US$434 million annually between 1981 and 1984, dropped to about US$340 million during 1985–86, and fell to US$60 million in 1987. Likewise, the armed forces personnel numbers declined from 3.7 per 1,000 persons in 1977 to 1.3 in 1987.

Defense spending in 1988 and 1989 was about N1.3 billion and N1.7 billion, but high inflation reduced its real value by at least 30 percent. Capital expenditure nominally trebled, from N256.6 million in 1986 and 1987 to N750 million in 1988 and 1989. This increase reflected new investments in equipment, construction, and other long-term capital improvements, although at levels substantially lower than in the early 1980s. The N2.1 billion defense budget for 1990, however, represented a real growth of 16 percent over 1989.

As in most Third World states, Nigeria's military spending was dedicated largely to recurrent costs of salaries, allowances, training, and other personnel-related overhead expenses. Such operating costs had ranged from 55 to 88 percent of the defense budget almost every year since independence. General Staff Headquarters, which operated under a separate account budgeted at N35 to N55 million annually between 1984 and 1987, received N124 million in 1988. The pattern of defense spending during the period 1988–90, particularly the increases in capital investment and equipment procurement relative to personnel-related expenditures, reflected in part determined efforts to modernize and to upgrade capabilities and readiness while completing demobilization. It also represented the military's last opportunities to attend to defense needs on its own terms, in anticipation that the Third Republic might be less generous in allocating scarce budgetary and foreign exchange resources to the armed forces.

Civic Action and Veterans' Groups

As of 1990, army engineers built bridges and roads in rural areas, and consideration was being given to a more vigorous civic action role for the military in general. Agricultural work was excluded, however, because farming was thought to result in loss of military skills.

After World War II a very small number of veterans received vocational training or loans to establish farms; businesses with more than ten workers had to employ a quota of veterans. In the early 1950s, training programs were discontinued. In the early 1960s, plans to establish industries for ex-servicemen foundered. However, an Education Corps was set up to provide rudimentary reading and writing skills in English to recruits during their first six months in uniform. As a result, virtually all ex-servicemen found employment after service. No information was available concerning civilian employment of thousands of veterans since the 1970s.

Internal Security

Threats to internal security in Nigeria have been persistent and chronic. They stemmed from endemic divisions that were aggravated by rapid socioeconomic changes and by deteriorating economic trends. Political and civil disorder, extended periods of military rule, human rights violations, rampant crime, and inadequate security forces and penal institutions defined the internal security environment at the beginning of the 1990s.

Domestic Security

Nigeria has experienced substantial internal insecurity. Mass violence erupted frequently. During the five years immediately preceding the civil war, 124 riots were reported. The civil war between 1967 and 1970 produced about 2 million deaths. Regime instability also came to characterize political life, which was punctuated by a number of coups between 1966 and 1985; several attempted coups, often accompanied or followed by violent retribution; and periodic government reorganizations and leadership changes. Primary sources of potential dissent and opposition were illegal aliens, sectional-ethnic cleavages, religious sectarianism, the labor force and labor unions, and intellectuals. Although none of these groups was capable of overthrowing the government or of offering an alternative political formula, recurring and sometimes widespread violence involving one or more of these interests precipitated major security crises.

Nigeria's relative wealth, particularly during the oil-fueled boom of the 1970s, was a magnet for alien migrant laborers, many of whom entered illegally. Relations with these workers were tense and marked by two large-scale expulsions. In early 1983, Nigeria ordered all foreigners illegally residing and working in the country to leave within a matter of weeks; most had entered under the ECOWAS protocol on free movement of people and goods but had overstayed. At least 1.3 million West Africans—mainly from Ghana, Niger, Chad, and Cameroon—were expelled despite international protests. A second campaign to expel 700,000 illegal aliens took place in May 1985, but it was not clear how many were actually repatriated.

Nigeria's ethnic and religious heterogeneity was the most persistent source of violent conflicts. Although the issue of secession based on regional ethnic nationalism was settled by the unsuccessful Biafran experience and later muted politically by the abolition of the regions in favor of twenty-one states, the assertion or reassertion of the country's primordial "nations" remained a latent threat to national unity.

Religious Sectarianism

Whereas ethnic cleavages generally remained dormant, religious sectarianism emerged as the most potentially explosive social division. Islam and Christianity spread rapidly in the twentieth century at the expense of indigenous religions. About half of all Nigerians were Muslims in 1990, most of whom lived in the northern two-thirds of the country. About 40 percent were Christians, residing predominantly in the south, and particularly in the southeast. Since 1980 there had been several outbreaks of sectarian violence, resulting in thousands of deaths, injuries, and arrests, mostly attributable to sectarian tensions and also to some fringe quasi-Islamic groups.

The first and most dramatic eruption in a series of religious disturbances incited by the Maitatsine, or Yan Tatsine, movement was an eleven-day emergency in Kano in late December 1980 (see Islam, ch. 2). Led by Alhajji Muhammadu Marwa (alias Tatsine or Maitatsine), followers of this heretical Muslim sect of perhaps 3,000 persons opposed secular authority, were willing to use violence if necessary, and demanded absolute obedience to Marwa. The Kano riots were suppressed by the army and the air force after the police failed to restore order. More than 4,000 deaths resulted, including that of Marwa; there were also 1,000 arrests, including arrests of 224 foreigners.

In addition, another Muslim movement known as Yan Izala, which began in Zaria and Kaduna in the 1960s, also caused disturbances. This group, which created unrest in the early 1980s, protested innovations in Islam and was particularly opposed to the Sufi brotherhood movement.

Renewed rioting in Kano in July 1981 that destroyed or damaged several state government buildings was attributed to Muslim extremists opposed to the proposed removal of the emir of Kano.

More riots by Maitatsine followers broke out in Maiduguri in late October 1982 and spread to Kaduna, where thirty-nine sect members were killed by vigilantes. The official death toll was 188 civilians and 18 police (mostly in Maiduguri) and 635 arrested, but the commission of inquiry afterward concluded that deaths probably exceeded 500. The sect was banned in November 1982, and its adherents have been subject to surveillance and arrest.

Nevertheless, in February 1984 members of the proscribed Maitatsine sect struck again, this time in northeastern Nigeria and in Yola, the capital of Gongola State. The army was again obliged to intervene, using artillery to quell the disturbances, but between 1980 and 1985 it was ill-equipped for riot control. As a result, more than 700 persons died, 30,000 were left homeless, and about 2,000 homes were destroyed and 1,500 damaged. In April 1985, riots inspired by Maitatsine adherents in Gombe claimed more than 100 lives and resulted in 146 arrests of suspected sect members.

Another violent incident occurred in November 1988 over the disputed succession of a new sultan of Sokoto. Ten persons died and fifty were arrested.

In 1987, in contrast to previously mentioned intra-Muslim disputes, religious conflict took on new and ominous dimensions when unprecedented violence between members of Nigeria's two largest faiths—Muslims and Christians—erupted at secondary schools and universities. Clashes between Muslim and Christian students in March 1987 at the College of Education in Kafanchan, Kaduna State, left at least twelve dead and several churches burned or damaged. The rioting spread to Zaria, Katsina, and Kano within a few days. Police reportedly arrested 360 in the city of Kaduna alone and about 400 in the university city of Zaria. Army troops again intervened, and the commander warned that the army would shoot anyone committing arson or murder. Bayero University in Kano was closed after about twenty students were injured in Muslim-Christian clashes. In Zaria Muslim students burned the chapel at the College of Advanced Studies and attacked Christian students; the riots spilled over into the town, where more than fifty churches were burned. A curfew was imposed in Kaduna State, and outdoor processions and religious preaching were banned in Bauchi, Bendel, Benue, Borno, and Plateau states. All schools in Kaduna and five in Bauchi State closed. Babangida denounced these outbreaks as "masterminded by evil men . . . to subvert the Federal Military Government." He also issued a Civil Disturbances (Special Tribunal) Decree establishing a special judicial tribunal to identify, arrest, and try those responsible and banned preaching by religious organizations at all institutions of higher learning. In June and July 1987, Kaduna State authorities twice closed the exclusive Queen Amina College girls' high school in Zaria after clashes between Muslim and Christian students.

Relative calm prevailed among religious elements until January 1990, when thousands of Christians in the northern states of Plateau, Kaduna, Bauchi, and Gongola demonstrated against Babangida's cabinet reshuffle, which appeared to penalize Christian officers. Protesters of the Christian Association of Nigeria from all eleven northern states and the Abuja capital district marched on the Kaduna State government to protest the perceived religious imbalance and to present a petition signed by the top Roman Catholic clerics and the archbishop of Kaduna.

Labor Organizations

Nigeria's labor force numbered about 50 million in 1990. About 3.5 million wage earners belonged to forty-two recognized trade unions under the single national labor federation, the Nigerian Labour Congress (NLC). The Socialist Working People's Party reportedly had considerable influence in the NLC, although it was banned along with other parties in 1983. The police prevented the inauguration of the Nigerian Socialist Party in May 1989, citing the ''general insecurity in the country.''

Organized labor has been more a nuisance than a menace to national security. For example, a 1985 strike by public health doctors ended when the FMG arrested its leaders, outlawed the Nigerian Medical Association (NMA) and the National Association of Resident Doctors (NARD), dismissed sixty-four doctors including officers of the NMA and the NARD, and imposed financial penalties on others. Likewise, when the NLC threatened a twenty-four-hour general strike and demonstrations in June 1986 to protest the May killing of more than a dozen Ahmadu Bello University students by police, the police broke up NLC meetings and detained its leaders, and the FMG warned that any strike would be put down with ''all the means at its disposal.'' In May 1987, Babangida lifted the ten-year-old ban on Nigeria's veteran labor leader, Chief Michael Imoudu, and ten others, but in late 1987, thirteen senior NLC officials were detained after union demonstrations, and in February the AFRC dissolved the NLC executive. Serious industrial union demonstrations occurred in April 1988 to protest the government's austerity measures under the structural adjustment program (SAP), especially the increase in gasoline prices and the perceived excessive use of force by police in putting down a strike by students and workers in Jos. In December 1989, the government acceded to NLC demands for a negotiating forum to resolve a long-standing minimum-wage dispute after the union threatened to call a nationwide general strike.

Academic unionists also clashed with the authorities on several occasions in 1986 and 1988. The protests resulted in 1988 in the detention of eight Academic Staff Union of Universities (ASUU) leaders. Finally, the government banned the ASUU, and its intimidations were denounced by human rights monitoring groups and the Nigerian Bar Association. The ban was lifted in August 1990.

Student Organizations

Students were a perpetual source of dissent. During the 1970s, the National Union of Nigerian Students (NUNS), a government-sanctioned federation of all student unions in Nigeria and of Nigerian students abroad, actively opposed government policies on several issues, including students' rights and educational conditions. In April 1978, NUNS instigated or participated in nationwide campus protests against increased university fees, during which police and army units killed or seriously wounded at least twenty students. The FMG responded by closing three universities indefinitely, by banning NUNS, and by appointing a commission of inquiry, after which several senior university officials and students were dismissed.

The next major round of violent student demonstrations occurred in May 1986, when police killed more than a dozen Ahmadu Bello University students protesting disciplinary action against student leaders who had been observing "Ali Must Go" Day (referring to the minister of education), in memory of students killed in the 1978 demonstration. Disorders spread rapidly to other campuses across the country. The government imposed a national ban on demonstrations and closed nine of Nigeria's fifteen universities; they were not reopened until July. The National Association of Nigerian Students (NANS), founded in 1980 to replace the banned NUNS and itself theoretically banned as a result of the May 1986 riots, called for dismissals of government, university, and police officials. Its call was supported by the NLC. After a commission of inquiry, the government accepted some recommendations for removals but dissolved all student unions for the remainder of the academic year. NANS, however, rejected the commission's findings and, in May 1987, five universities were closed in connection with campus incidents involving remembrances of the anniversary of Ahmadu Bello University students' slayings the year before.

In February 1988, the government closed Ahmadu Bello University and the University of Nigeria campuses at Nsukka and Enugu and narrowly averted a NANS-supported nationwide student strike by rescinding a decision to try nine Nsukka students for arson and property damage. Two months later, five universities were shut down after student riots in Jos to protest a 3-percent rise in gasoline prices, during which several persons, including two police officers, died. Between May and July 1989, student riots in several southern states again led to closure of several universities and a secondary school and forced Babangida to cancel an official visit to France. Student rioters in Benin City, joined by townspeople, burned vehicles, government buildings, and two prisons from which about 600 inmates escaped; the riot was put down by police and army units two days later. Rioting soon spread to Ibadan and Lagos where soldiers again were called in to restore order; to Obafemi Awolowo University School of Agriculture's Akure campus near Ibadan, where about seventy students were arrested; and to the College of Agriculture in Yande, near Loko, in Benue State.

The government closed six schools until March 1990 but permitted them to reopen on October 30 after requiring returning students to sign a formal pledge of good behavior. To deter further student unrest, in early 1990 the AFRC issued Decree Number 47. It imposed a five-year jail term and/or a N50,000 fine on any student found guilty of organizing or participating in demonstrations, set up special tribunals to try offenders, and again banned the NANS.

Human Rights

Nigeria was party to several international human rights treaties, including the Convention Relating to the Status of Refugees (1967) and the Protocol Relating to the Status of Refugees, the Convention on the Political Rights of Women (1953) and the International Convention on the Elimination of All Forms of Discrimination against Women (1977), the International Convention on the Elimination of All Forms of Racial Discrimination (1966) and the International Convention on the Suppression and Punishment of the Crime of Apartheid (1981), and the African Charter on Human and Peoples' Rights (1981). Nigeria also ratified the Slavery Convention of 1926, the Supplementary Convention on the Abolition of Slavery of 1956, and the 1949 Geneva Conventions Relative to the Treatment of Prisoners of War and the Protection of Civilian Persons in Time of War. However, it had not signed the Convention on the Prevention and Punishment of the Crime of Genocide (1948); the International Covenant on Civil and Political Rights (1966); the International Covenant on Economic, Social, and Cultural Rights (1966); or the Convention Against Torture and Other Cruel, Inhuman, or Degrading Treatment or Punishment.

The government's human rights record was mixed and generally worse during military rule, when decrees were exempt from legal challenge. Until the late 1970s, when military rulers deprived many citizens of their rights through detention without trial, physical assault, torture, harassment, and intimidation, the issue of human rights was not a major concern. It had been taken for granted that having a bill of rights guaranteed human rights. Thus, the independence (1960), republican (1963), Second Republic (1979), and Third Republic (1989) constitutions had elaborate sections on fundamental human rights. The fact that Nigeria did not become a one-party state as most other African states did immediately after independence forestalled the emergence of repressive measures, such as the preventive detention acts prevalent in Africa.

By the early 1970s, however, the days of "innocence" in relation to human rights were over. As Major General Yakubu Gowon's popularity declined, especially after he reneged on his promise to hand over power to civilians in 1976, criticisms of him and his cohorts increased. He reacted by detaining these critics for indefinite periods. This trend of abuse of the rights of regime opponents continued under the Muhammad-Obasanjo government and, after the creation of the Nigerian Security Organisation (NSO) in 1976, human rights violations became frequent. The return of constitutional government in the Second Republic (1979–83) reduced the violations, although the human rights record was poor because of the increasing powers of the police force and the NSO and the constant harassment of political opponents.

Under the Buhari regime, military security was the criterion for judicial action, often in the form of military tribunals. The government not only gave the NSO greater powers but also promulgated decrees that directly violated human rights. The most notable were State Security (Detention of Persons) Decree Number 2 of 1984, which empowered the chief of staff at Supreme Headquarters to detain indefinitely without trial anyone suspected of being a security risk (detention was for three months initially, and then renewable), and Decree Number 4, which made the publication of any material considered embarrassing to any government official a punishable offense. Under Decree Number 2, many people considered "enemies" of the government were detained in NSO cells and allegedly tortured. Second Republic government officials, whom the Buhari regime held collectively responsible for the economic mess, were detained without trial or were tried by special military tribunals. At these tribunals, the accused was assumed guilty until proved innocent rather than innocent until proved guilty. Journalists and media organizations were regularly harassed by security agents; organized interest groups whose members dared to criticize the government openly or engage in demonstrations or strikes were proscribed.

The most active human rights group in Nigeria in 1990, the Civil Liberties Organisation (CLO), founded by a group of young lawyers led by Olisa Agbakobe, emerged during the Buhari days. Before its emergence, human rights groups included the local branches of Amnesty International, far less effective than the parent organization, and the Nigeria Council for National Awareness, founded after the assassination of Murtala Muhammad to protect a just and humane society. Several other organizations criticized the government's violations of civil rights and urged remedial measures. These groups included NANS, the NBA, the NLC, and the Nigeria Union of Journalists. In 1988 another human rights organization, the Committee for the Defence of Human Rights, was founded by Dr. Beko Ransome-Kuti, the radical deputy chairman of the NMA detained under the Buhari government.

When Babangida toppled Buhari in August 1985, one of his main arguments was the need to restore civil liberties. The new regime prided itself on being a defender of human rights, and many of Babangida's initial acts justified his human rights posture. He scrapped the NSO, threw open its cells and replaced it with the State Security Service (SSS) and other agencies; he released most of the politicians detained without trial and drastically reduced the jail terms of those already convicted; he appointed Bola Ajibola, the NBA president noted for his human rights advocacy, as minister of justice and attorney general; he scrapped Decree Number 4 and reduced the punishment for drug traffickers from public execution to jail terms; he annulled the proscription of "radical" groups such as the NMA and NANS; and he persisted with plans to restore civilian rule by 1992.

In other ways, however, human rights remained substantially circumscribed in 1990. Decree Number 2 remained in place, and numerous citizens had been incarcerated under it, although the allowable period of detention without charge was reduced from six months to six weeks in January 1990. With the aid of this and other decrees that restricted freedom, usually promulgated retrospectively, such radical and outspoken critics of the government as Gani Fawehinmi, Tai Solarin, and Balarabe Musa were regularly detained. Despite having annulled Decree Number 4, the government had several brushes with media organizations. In 1988 *Newswatch* was proscribed for six months, and journalists, academics, and civil rights activists continued to be harassed by state security agents. Although the notorious NSO was dissolved in 1986, the new security establishment in 1990 continued to act arbitrarily and with impunity. The government proscribed radical interest groups like NANS and the Academic Staff Union of Universities, the central body of all university professors and lecturers. Several innocent citizens were subjected to physical assault without government reparations.

Internal Security Forces and Organizations

Between 1976 and 1986, internal security responsibilities in Nigeria were divided among the NSO, a central state security organ reporting to the president; the Ministry of Internal Affairs;

the national police force; and the Ministry of Defence. As noted, the army was called upon to suppress domestic disorders on several occasions.

Intelligence Services

The NSO was the sole intelligence service for both domestic and international security during its ten-year existence. It was charged with the detection and prevention of any crime against the security of the state, with the protection of classified materials, and with carrying out any other security missions assigned by the president. Under the Buhari administration, the NSO engaged in widespread abuses of due process, including detention without charge and trial, arrests without pretext, and wiretapping.

The NSO's performance was bluntly criticized after the 1980 uprisings by the Maitatsine movement. It had penetrated the movement but failed to prevent it from instigating bloody riots.

Fulfilling one of the promises made in his first national address as president, Babangida in June 1986 issued Decree Number 19, dissolving the NSO and restructuring Nigeria's security services into three separate organizations under the Office of the Co-ordinator of National Security. The new State Security Service (SSS) was responsible for intelligence within Nigeria, the National Intelligence Agency (NIA) for foreign intelligence and counterintelligence, and the Defence Intelligence Agency (DIA) for military-related intelligence outside and inside the country. This reorganization followed a formal investigation of the NSO by former director Umaru Shinkafi.

Notwithstanding this rationalization and depoliticization of the national security services, they remained deficient in intelligence collection and analysis capabilities; they also were poorly equipped to counter security threats, such as covert foreign operations, dissident movements, coup plots, and border violations. The integrity of the new agencies also eroded after the prosecution in 1988 of the director of the DIA and the deputy director of the SSS, for the 1986 murder of *Newswatch* publisher Dele Giwa.

In the government reshuffle of December 29, 1989, Vice Admiral Patrick S. Koshoni, chief of naval staff since October 1986, became head of the National Commission for the Reorganisation of Internal Security; the Office of the Co-ordinator of National Security was abolished; and the SSS and NIA remained independent agencies directly responsible to the president.

Ministry of Internal Affairs

The public security functions of the Ministry of Internal Affairs included passport and immigration control, prison administration, fire service, and oversight of compliance with certain commercial and civic regulations. Immigration control was regarded as important and such steps as expulsions, expanded border controls, and acquisition of surveillance and communications equipment, and of weapons for immigration officers had been taken to enforce immigration laws. Immigration officer training schools were located in Kano, in Lagos, and at state headquarters. In 1983 the main ministry staff consisted of about 5,300 persons; the Immigration Department employed about 2,900, the Fire Service Department 900, and the Nigerian Prison Service 23,000. In August 1988, the authority to arrest and detain suspects without trial, formerly assigned to the chief of General Staff and to the inspector general of police, was extended to the Ministry of Internal Affairs. The ministry also had a paramilitary Security and Civil Defence Force, whose size, mission, and organization were unknown. In August 1989, it was announced that this unit was to be reorganized.

Nigeria Police Force

The Nigeria Police Force (NPF) is designated by Section 194 of the 1979 constitution as the national police with exclusive jurisdiction throughout the country. Constitutional provision also exists, however, for the establishment of separate NPF branches "forming part of the armed forces of the Federation or for their protection of harbours, waterways, railways and airfields." One such branch, the Port Security Police, was reported by different sources to have a strength in 1990 of between 1,500 and 12,000.

Nigeria's police began with a thirty-member consular guard formed in Lagos Colony in 1861. In 1879 a 1,200-member armed paramilitary Hausa Constabulary was formed. In 1896 the Lagos Police was established. A similar force, the Niger Coast Constabulary, was formed in Calabar in 1894 under the newly proclaimed Niger Coast Protectorate. Likewise, in the north, the Royal Niger Company set up the Royal Niger Company Constabulary in 1888 with headquarters at Lokoja. When the protectorates of Northern and Southern Nigeria were proclaimed in the early 1900s, part of the Royal Niger Company Constabulary became the Northern Nigeria Police, and part of the Niger Coast Constabulary became the Southern Nigeria Police. Northern and Southern Nigeria were amalgamated in 1914, but their police forces were not merged until 1930, forming the NPF, headquartered in Lagos. During the colonial period, most police were associated with local governments (native authorities). In the 1960s, under the First Republic, these forces were first regionalized and then nationalized.

The NPF performed conventional police functions and was responsible for internal security generally; for supporting the prison, immigration, and customs services; and for performing military duties within or outside Nigeria as directed. Plans were announced in mid-1980 to expand the force to 200,000. By 1983, according to the federal budget, the strength of the NPF was almost 152,000, but other sources estimated it to be between 20,000 and 80,000. Reportedly, there were more than 1,300 police stations nationwide. Police officers were not usually armed but were issued weapons when required for specific missions or circumstances. They were often deployed throughout the country, but in 1989 Babangida announced that a larger number of officers would be posted to their native areas to facilitate police-community relations.

The NPF was under the general operational and administrative control of an inspector general appointed by the president and responsible for the maintenance of law and order. He was supported at headquarters in Lagos by a deputy inspector general and in each state by police commissioners. The 1979 constitution provided for a Police Service Commission that was responsible for NPF policy, organization, administration, and finance (except for pensions), promotion, discipline, and dismissal of police officers. In February 1989, Babangida abolished the Police Service Commission and established the Nigeria Police Council in its stead, under direct presidential control. The new council was chaired by the president; the chief of General Staff, the minister of internal affairs, and the police inspector general were members. As part of the government reorganization in September 1990, Alhajji Sumaila Gwarzo, formerly SSS director, was named to the new post of minister of state, police affairs.

In late 1986, the NPF was reorganized nationwide into seven area commands, which superseded a command structure corresponding to each of Nigeria's states. Each command was under a commissioner of police and was further divided into police provinces and divisions under local officers. NPF headquarters, which was also an area command, supervised and coordinated the other area commands.

The 1986 NPF reorganization was occasioned by a public eruption of tensions between the police and the army. A superintendent was suspended for a time for grumbling that the army had usurped police functions and kept police pay low, and there were fights between police and army officers over border patrol jurisdiction. The armed forces chief of staff announced a thorough reorganization of the NPF into the seven new area commands and five directorates (criminal investigations, logistics, supplies, training, and operations) under deputy inspectors general. About 2,000 constables and 400 senior police officers were dismissed by mid-1987, leaving senior police officers disgruntled.

In mid-1989 another NPF reorganization was announced after the AFRC's acceptance of a report by Rear Admiral Murtala Nyako. In 1989 the NPF also created a Quick Intervention Force in each state, separate from the mobile police units, specifically to monitor political events and to quell unrest during the transition to civil rule. Each state unit of between 160 and 400 police was commanded by an assistant superintendent and equipped with vehicles, communications gear, weapons, and crowd control equipment, including cane shields, batons, and tear gas. Under the new structure, a Federal Investigation and Intelligence Bureau (FIIB) was to be set up as the successor to the Directorate of Intelligence and Investigation; three directorates were established for operations, administration, and logistics, each headed by a deputy inspector general. The Directorate of Operations was subdivided into four units under a deputy director—operations, training, communications, and the police mobile force. The Directorate of Administration was composed of an administration unit headed by an assistant inspector general (AIG), and of budget and personnel units under commissioners. The Directorate of Logistics had four units—procurement, workshop/transport, supply, and work/maintenance—under AIGs. The zonal arrangements were retained. However, AIGs were authorized to transfer officers up to the rank of chief superintendent, to set up provost units, to deploy mobile units, and to promote officers between the ranks of sergeant and inspector.

The NPF operating budget between 1984 and 1988 remained in the N360 million to N380 million range, and in 1988 increased to N521 million. More notable were large capital expenditure infusions of N206 million in 1986 and N260.3 million in 1988, representing 3.5 and 2.5 percent of total federal capital expenditures in those years. These increases were used to acquire new communications equipment, transport, and weapons to combat the rising crime wave, such as 100 British Leyland DAF Comet trucks delivered in 1990 (see Incidence and Trends in Crime, this ch.). Despite these purchases, an NPF study in late 1990 concluded that the force's budget must double to meet its needs.

Although generally considered an attractive career, the NPF experienced endemic problems with recruiting, training, inefficiency, and indiscipline, and it lacked expertise in specialized fields. Corruption and dishonesty were widespread, engendering a low level of public confidence, failure to report crimes, and tendencies to resort to self-help. Police were more adept at paramilitary operations and the exercise of force than at community service functions or crime prevention, detection, and investigation. During the Obasanjo period, an attempt was made to expand the NPF by reducing the recruitment age from nineteen to seventeen and by enrolling demobilized soldiers, but it failed. In mid-1980 the then federal police minister acknowledged that the police had recovered only 14 percent of the US$900 million worth of property reported stolen in the preceding six months and that only 20 percent of the 103,000 persons arrested had been found guilty, a performance record about the same as that reported in the 1960s. The use of excessive violence in quelling student disorders led the AFRC in June 1986 to direct the police to use only rubber bullets in containing student riots. Reports of police collusion with criminals were common, as were official appeals to police officers to change their attitude toward the public, to be fair and honest, and to avoid corrupt practices. In an effort to reduce bribery and to make identification of offenders easier, police officers on beats and at checkpoints were not allowed to carry more than N5 on their person.

Police training was directed from headquarters by a deputy inspector general designated as commander. Recruits were trained at police colleges in Oji River, Maiduguri, Kaduna, and Ikeja, which also offered training to other security personnel, such as armed immigration officers. The Police College at Ikeja trained cadet assistant superintendents and cadet subinspectors. There were also specialized schools for in-service training, including the Police Mobile Force Training School at Guzuo, southwest of Abuja, the Police Detective College at Enugu, the Police Dogs Service Training Centre, and the Mounted Training Centre. The NPF inspector general visited Algeria in January 1988; as a result, new training practices were under consideration.

In August 1989, Babangida laid the foundation stone for a Nigeria Police Academy (NPA) in Kano State. The NPA was to be affiliated with Bayero University until adequate infrastructure was available for independent operation. Admission was to be regulated by merit, by the quota system, and by federal character. The commandant was to be at least an AIG and assisted by a provost who would oversee the academic program. Modeled after the Nigerian Military University in Kaduna, the NPA would offer a five-year academic and professional degree program for new cadets and an eighteen-month intensive course for college graduates aspiring to a police career. Babangida also disclosed plans to obtain technical assistance from Britain to establish a central planning and training program to modernize and upgrade police training.

Finally, mention should be made of the establishment in 1989 of a paramilitary National Guard directly under the president. This new security force, set up by decree to combat crime and terrorism, became controversial because its mission overlapped both the police and the army, and it could be used for political witch-hunting and intimidation. Apparently, only a few police mobile units bore the guard's insignia before the government decided to reconsider its formation. The matter was still under review in 1990.

Crime and Punishment

Nigeria had a dual prison system for more than a half century until the consolidation of the federal and local prisons in 1968. The Nigerian Prison Service, a department of the Ministry of Internal Affairs, was headquartered in Lagos and headed by a director responsible for administering nearly 400 facilities, including regular prisons, special penal institutions, and lockups. All of these facilities since 1975 came under federal control. Each state had its own prison headquarters under the supervision of assistant directors of prisons, and the prisons themselves—depending on type, size, and inmate population—were variously under chief superintendents, superintendents, or assistant superintendents.

In 1989 the prison staff was reported to be 18,000, an apparent decrease from the 23,000 level in 1983. The average daily prison population in 1976 was nearly 26,000, a 25-percent increase from 1975. Ten years later, Nigeria's prison population was about 54,000. Lagos State accounted for the largest number, about 6,400; Anambra, Borno, and Kaduna housed more than 4,000 each; and Kwara, Niger, and Ondo, with fewer than 1,000 each, had the smallest inmate populations. By 1989 the prison population had increased to 58,000.

Prison admissions increased steadily from about 130,000 in 1980 to more than 206,000 in 1984. The most common offenses were theft, assault, traffic violations, and unlawful possession, which together accounted for 53 percent of prison admissions between 1982 and 1984. Thieves represented the largest single category of offenders, accounting for between 37 and 46 percent of prison admissions between 1982 and 1984. Admissions to prisons in Kaduna, Lagos, Borno, Kano, Plateau, Gongola, and Benue exceeded 10,000 in 1983. This figure did not reflect the geographical distribution of crimes, however, because more than 10,000 prisoners each were from Anambra, Benue, Borno, Cross River, Gongola, Imo, Kaduna, Kano, and Sokoto. People between the ages of twenty-six and fifty consistently constituted the largest category of prisoners, ranging between 53 and 78 percent between 1980 and

1984. In 1984 Christians and Muslims accounted for 45 and 37 percent of prison admissions, respectively, and women for almost 4 percent. In the same year, only 32 percent of prisoners admitted were convicted, whereas the rest were on remand or awaiting trial. Among those convicted, about three-fourths served terms of less than two years, while 59 percent were first-time offenders and 41 percent were recidivists. Foreigners constituted an unknown proportion; in 1989, for example, about 2,000 aliens from other West African states were held in Kaduna's federal prisons for illegal emerald mining.

Although prison policy called for provision of legal, religious, educational, vocational, and social welfare services, Nigeria's prison system, as in most Third World countries, was grossly inadequate. There was no systematic classification of prisoners, so that young and old, and suspects for minor offenses—most of whom were pretrial detainees and first-time offenders incarcerated for extended periods and eventually released upon acquittal—were intermixed with dangerous and deranged criminals or repeat offenders. Despite ever-increasing prison admissions and an inmate population more than double the prison system's capacity, after a development project allocation of N50 million in 1983, capital expenditures for prisons between 1985 and 1988 ranged only between N3 million and N11.6 million. Overall, by the late 1980s the overcrowding rate of the prison systems exceeded 200 percent, with 58,000 inmates housed in facilities designed to accommodate 28,000; in some prisons the situation was much worse. Although the government had announced a prison construction program, little progress was evident and conditions were projected to worsen: by the year 2000, Nigeria's prison population was expected to be almost 700,000.

Apparently unable to deal with the prison crisis systematically, the government resorted to periodic amnesties to reduce the inmate population, usually on the occasion of a regime anniversary or a national holiday. General Buhari freed 2,500 prisoners, including 144 political detainees, in early 1985; the AFRC directed state governors to release old, sick, underaged, and handicapped prisoners on independence day in 1989; and the government granted general amnesty in 1990 to more than 5,000 inmates who had served three-fourths of their sentences, been jailed for minor offenses with terms that did not exceed one year, or who had served at least ten years of a life sentence.

The criminal justice system was so backlogged that at least three-fifths of the country's prison population consisted of pretrial detainees rather than convicts. Reform and rehabilitation programs were nominal, and the prisons were aptly dubbed "colleges for criminals" or "breeding grounds for crime." For example, in the late 1980s the majority of the 2,000 inmates awaiting trial at Ikoyi spent nine years in detention for minor offenses, which, on conviction, would have carried prison terms of less than two years. The egregious conditions at the Kirikiri maximum-security facility were highlighted when Chief Ebenezer Babatope's 1989 prison memoir, *Inside Kirikiri*, was published. In mid-1990 the government was considering an advisory committee recommendation to separate detainees from prisoners.

Most prisons had no toilet facilities, and cells lacked water. Medical facilities were severely limited; food, which represented 80 percent of annual prison expenditures, was inadequate, despite a prison agricultural program designed to produce local foodstuffs for the commercial market. Malnutrition and disease were therefore rampant. In March 1990, the minister of justice said that the prisoners' feeding allowance had been increased from N1.5 to N5 and that health and other problems were being studied.

Mistreatment of inmates was common, abuse frequent, and torture occasional. In May 1987 at Benin prison, armed police killed twenty-four inmates rioting over food supplies, and in 1988 a "secret" ten-year-old detention camp on Ita Oko Island, off Lagos, was exposed and closed. Nearly 300 prisoners died of "natural causes" in 1984, and 79 committed suicide, a dramatic increase from the average of 12 suicides per year between 1980 and 1983. Ikoyi alone recorded more than 300 deaths in 1988, and 42 deaths in the first three months of 1989. In June 1989, the Civil Liberties Organisation filed suit on behalf of 1,000 detainees held without trial at Ikoyi, charging the government with mistreatment and urging that the 113-year-old prison be closed.

Incidence and Trends in Crime

In the 1980s, serious crime grew to nearly epidemic proportions, particularly in Lagos and other urbanized areas characterized by rapid growth and change, by stark economic inequality and deprivation, by social disorganization, and by inadequate government service and law enforcement capabilities. Published crime statistics were probably grossly understated because most of the country was virtually unpoliced—the police were concentrated in urban areas where only about 25 percent of the population lived—and public distrust of the police contributed to underreporting of crimes.

Annual crime rates fluctuated around 200 per 100,000 population until the early 1960s and then steadily increased to more than 300 per 100,000 by the mid-1970s. Available data from the 1980s

317

indicated a continuing increase. Total reported crimes rose from almost 211,000 in 1981 to between 330,000 and 355,000 during 1984–85. Although serious crime usually constituted the larger category, minor crimes and offenses accounted for most of the increase. Crimes against property generally accounted for more than half the offenses, with thefts, burglary, and breaking and entering covering 80 to 90 percent in most years. Assaults constituted 70 to 75 percent of all offenses against persons. The British High Commission in Lagos cited more than 3,000 cases of forgeries annually.

In the late 1980s, the crime wave was exacerbated by worsening economic conditions and by the ineffectiveness, inefficiency, and corruption of police, military, and customs personnel who colluded and conspired with criminals or actually engaged in criminal conduct. In 1987 the minister of internal affairs dismissed the director and 23 other senior officials of the customs service and "retired" about 250 other customs officers for connivance in or toleration of smuggling. In October 1988, Babangida threatened to execute publicly any police or military personnel caught selling guns to criminals. Indeed, one criminologist argued that the combination of discriminatory law enforcement and official corruption served to manage rather than reduce crime, by selectively punishing petty offenders while failing to prosecute vigorously major criminals and those guilty of white collar crime.

The public response to official misconduct was to take matters into its own hands. In July 1987, butchers, traders, and unemployed persons in Minna vented their wrath over police harassment, intimidation, and extortion in a six-hour rampage against police and soldiers that was quelled by military units. In November 1989, when a police team raided suspect stores in Katsina market, the merchants feared it was a police robbery and sounded the alarm, attracting a mob that was then dispersed by riot police. As loss of confidence in law enforcement agencies and public insecurity increased, so also did public resort to vigilante action. Onitsha vigilantes killed several suspected criminals in 1979. In July 1989, after a gang of about thirty armed men terrorized and looted a neighborhood in Onitsha without police intervention, residents vented their rage on known and suspected criminals and lynched four before riot police eventually restored order.

Drug-related crime emerged as a major problem in the 1980s. At least 328 cocaine seizures were made between 1986 and 1989, and the number of hard drug convictions surged from 8 in 1986 to 149 in 1989, with women accounting for 27 percent of the 275 total convictions during this period. Drug-induced psychoses accounted for 15 percent of admissions to four psychiatric hospitals in 1988. In a related development, the federal Ministry of Health reported in 1989 that about one-half of the drugs available in Nigeria were imitations, leading to a series of counterfeit and fake drugs decrees imposing increasingly higher penalties for violations.

Nigerians also participated heavily in international drug trafficking. One study found that 65 percent of the heroin seizures of 50 grams or more in British airports came from Nigeria, which was the transit point for 20 percent of all heroin from Southwest Asia. Another study disclosed that 20 percent of the hard drug cases in Britain involved ships of the Nigerian National Shipping Line. By the late 1980s, Nigerians were arrested almost daily in foreign countries, and hundreds languished in foreign jails for drug trafficking.

Security and Anticrime Measures

The Buhari and Babangida military administrations relied heavily on decrees and special tribunals to regulate public life and punish offenders. Soon after his takeover on December 31, 1983, Buhari issued a decree imposing life imprisonment on anyone found guilty of corruption, and he set up four tribunals consisting of three senior officers and a judge to try almost 500 political leaders detained since the coup. State Security (Detention of Persons) Decree Number 2 of 1984 suspended constitutional freedoms, empowered the chief of staff, Supreme Headquarters, to detain indefinitely (subject to review every three months) anyone suspected of "acts prejudicial to state security or . . . [contributing] to the economic adversity of the nation." The decree also authorized any police officer or member of the armed forces to arrest and imprison such persons. Likewise, the Recovery of Public Property (Special Military Tribunals) Decree Number 3 of 1984 set up tribunals to try former officials suspected of embezzlement and of other forms of misappropriation, also without right of appeal. The Exchange Control and Anti-Sabotage Tribunal dealt with certain economic crimes; a new press control law, Decree Number 4 of April 1984 (rescinded August 1985), was enforced by a similar special tribunal, without appeal rights. The Special Tribunal (Miscellaneous Offences) Decree covered a wide range of offenses, including forgery, arson, destruction of public property, unlawful vegetable cultivation, postal matters, and cheating on examinations. By July 1984, Buhari had issued twenty-two decrees, including two retroactive to December 31, 1983, prescribing the death penalty for arson, drug trafficking, oil smuggling, and currency counterfeiting. In a related attempt to combat public indiscipline, Buhari's chief of staff, Brigadier General Tunde Idiagbon, launched a largely symbolic and ineffective nationwide War Against Indiscipline (WAI) campaign in the spring of 1984.

Babangida's AFRC allowed the WAI campaign to lapse and took several other measures to mitigate Buhari's draconian rule, including abolition in July 1986 of the death sentence under Decree Number 20 of 1984 for illegal ship bunkering and drug trafficking, and setting up an appeal tribunal for persons convicted under decrees 2 and 3 of 1984. However, the Babangida regime continued the Armed Robbery and Firearms Tribunals under which most of the death sentences were carried out without appeal. By early 1987, more than 300 people had been executed after conviction by these tribunals, and in 1988 another 85 executions were known to have been carried out under their sentences. The Treason and Other Offences (Special Military Tribunal) Decree of 1986 empowered the AFRC to constitute another special tribunal to try military and civilian personnel for any offenses connected with rebellion. Special tribunals were also set up to hear cases arising out of civil disorders, such as the religious riots in Zaria in March 1987.

The most controversial decree remained Decree Number 2. In 1986 Babangida extended the initial detention period from three to six months but rescinded the extension after a public outcry. However, he extended detention authority to the Ministry of Internal Affairs in addition to the police and military authorities. In mid-1989 seventy to ninety persons were being held under its provisions, and in October the Civil Liberties Organisation appealed to the government to abrogate the decree and to release all those detained under it. In January 1990, the FMG amended the decree to shorten the precharge detention period to six weeks from six months, but in March the minister of justice stated that the decree would continue until the inauguration of the Third Republic.

Babangida's regime took additional legal and enforcement measures to combat illegal drug smuggling, including setting up special drug tribunals that meted out long prison terms and heavy fines; under these tribunals 120 convictions were attained by late 1987. Air transport laws were also toughened to deal with drug trafficking, and in November 1989 the minister of justice announced that a special tribunal would be set up to try air transport crimes. In October 1988, the minister of defense announced the establishment of a special "drug squad" to apprehend drug traffickers at home and abroad. Decree Number 48 of January 1990 established a National Drug Law Enforcement Agency to eliminate the growing, processing, manufacturing, selling, exporting, and trafficking of hard drugs, and the decree prescribed stiffer penalties for convicted offenders. Although Babangida had abolished the death penalty for convicted drug dealers, by the end of the decade there were public calls to restore it. Stricter security measures were introduced at Murtala Muhammad International Airport in 1989 to curb a crime wave there, and a plan was instituted in August 1989 to control black market activities.

The worldwide scope of crime demanded international cooperation to combat it. In 1982 Nigeria and Cameroon decided to conclude extradition agreements. Nigeria also signed a regional security, law enforcement, and extradition treaty with Benin, Ghana, and Togo in December 1984; the treaty covered criminal investigation, dissident activities, currency and drug trafficking, and other criminal and security matters. In 1987 Nigeria and the United States concluded a mutual law enforcement agreement covering narcotics trafficking and expanded cooperation in other key areas. A related antidrug memorandum of understanding with the United States in March 1990 provided for a joint task force on narcotics and assistance to the new National Drug Law Enforcement Agency. A similar legal assistance pact with Britain to combat crime and drug trafficking was signed in September 1989. Nigeria also concluded an antidrug trafficking accord with Saudi Arabia in October 1990.

In the final analysis, domestic conditions will likely determine the fate of the Babangida regime and its successors for the foreseeable future. Although externally secure, Nigeria's internal problems were legion and daunting. The most salient were political fragility and instability; a military determined to be the final arbiter of political life; endemic domestic discord deeply rooted in ethnic and religious cleavages; overtaxed, ineffective, corrupt, and politicized internal security forces and penal institutions; and anticrime measures hopelessly inadequate to the task. Under such conditions, Nigeria faced major challenges in its political transition to the Third Republic.

* * *

There is voluminous literature on Nigerian military history and national security affairs. Much relevant material is published in Nigeria but is not readily accessible abroad.

Nigeria's regional strategic situation and outlook are evaluated by John M. Ostheimer and Gary J. Buckley's chapter, ''Nigeria,'' in *Security Policies of Developing Countries;* and by Pauline H. Baker's ''A Giant Staggers: Nigeria as an Emerging Regional Power'' in *African Security Issues* and ''Nigeria: The Sub-Saharan Pivot'' in *Emerging Power: Defense and Security in the Third World.* Its participation

in the ECOWAS defense pact is examined in Michael J. Sheehan's
"Nigeria and the ECOWAS Defence Pact"; its maritime interests
and strategy are discussed in Sheehan's "Nigeria: A Maritime Pow-
er?" and in Olutunde A. Oladimeji's "Nigeria on Becoming a Sea
Power." Bassey Eyo Ate's "The Presence of France in West-
Central Africa as a Fundamental Problem to Nigeria" and Ekido
J.A. MacAnigboro and Aja Akpuru Aja's "France's Military Policy
in Sub-Saharan Francophone States: A Threat to Nigeria's National
Security" have analyzed the Franco-Nigerian security dilemma.
Julius Emeka Okolo's "Nuclearization of Nigeria" and Oye Ogun-
badejo's "Nuclear Capability and Nigeria's Foreign Policy" dis-
cuss Nigeria's nuclear policy options.

Data on military forces and order of battle are available in such
annual publications as *The Military Balance,* published by the International Institute for Strategic Studies in London, and the various Jane's yearbooks. Supplementary information is available in
John Keegan's *World Armies* and in the annual *Defense and Foreign
Affairs Handbook.* Statistics and other information on arms transfers, military spending, and armed forces are contained in the United States Arms Control and Disarmament Agency's annual *World
Military Expenditures and Arms Transfers* and in the Stockholm International Peace Research Institute's annual *World Armaments and Disarmament.*

Internal security and human rights conditions are evaluated an-
nually in the *Amnesty International Report* and in the United States
Department of State's *Country Reports on Human Rights Practices. The
International Law of Human Rights in Africa,* compiled by M.
Hamalengwa et al., is a useful reference for African states.

Country briefs on police forces are found in John M. Andrade's
World Police and Paramilitary Forces and in Harold K. and Donna
Lee Becker's *Handbook of the World's Police.* Alan Milner's now-dated
The Nigerian Penal System provides essential historical background
that is supplemented by Oluyemi Kayode's chapter, "Nigeria,"
in *International Handbook of Contemporary Developments in Criminology.*

Finally, specialized current news sources and surveys are indispensable for research on contemporary national security affairs.
The most useful and accessible include the annual *Africa Contemporary Record* and such periodicals as *Africa Research Bulletin, Africa
Confidential, Defense and Foreign Affairs Weekly, Jane's Defence Weekly,
International Defense Review,* and the most useful single source, *African Defence/Afrique Défense.* (For further information and complete
citations, see Bibliography.)

Appendix

Table 1. *Metric Conversion Coefficients and Factors*

When you know	Multiply by	To find
Millimeters	0.04	inches
Centimeters	0.39	inches
Meters	3.3	feet
Kilometers	0.62	miles
Hectares (10,000 m²)	2.47	acres
Square kilometers	0.39	square miles
Cubic meters	35.3	cubic feet
Liters	0.26	gallons
Kilograms	2.2	pounds
Metric tons	0.98	long tons
....	1.1	short tons
....	2,204	pounds
Degrees Celsius	9	degrees Fahrenheit
(Centigrade)	divide by 5 and add 32	

Table 2. *Population Estimates by State, 1987*

State	Population	State	Population
Akwa Ibom	5,100,000	Kwara	3,400,000
Anambra	7,200,000	Lagos	4,100,000
Bauchi	4,800,000	Niger	2,200,000
Bendel	4,900,000	Ogun	3,100,000
Benue	4,800,000	Ondo	5,500,000
Borno	6,000,000	Oyo	10,400,000
Cross River	1,900,000	Plateau	4,000,000
Gongola	5,200,000	Rivers	3,400,000
Imo	7,300,000	Sokoto	9,000,000
Kaduna	3,300,000	Federal Capital	
Kano	11,500,000	Territory (Abuja)	300,000
Katsina	4,900,000	TOTAL	112,300,000

Source: Based on information from Economist Intelligence Unit, *Country Report: Nigeria* [London], No. 1, 1990, 10.

325

Table 3. *Enrollment, Number of Schools, and Number of Teachers in Public Primary Schools by State, 1983-84 to 1985-86*

State [1]	1983-84			1984-85			1985-86		
	Total Enrollment	Number of Schools	Number of Teachers	Total Enrollment	Number of Schools	Number of Teachers	Total Enrollment	Number of Schools	Number of Teachers
Anambra	838,470	2,084	34,267	928,738	2,071	27,074	n.a.	2,071	n.a.
Bauchi	326,472	1,830	8,542	284,120	1,830	14,526	308,267	1,798	6,256
Bendel	927,708	1,736	36,860	660,751	1,743	21,446	758,572	1,772	17,903
Benue	953,568	2,700	28,943	441,641	2,018	n.a.	n.a.	n.a.	n.a.
Borno	445,999	2,090	8,137	444,360	1,858	10,009	470,200	1,858	10,0 09
Cross River	872,370	1,660	24,833	845,745	1,524	24,354	616,654	1,489	15,792
Gongola	518,369	1,857	11,899	359,552	1,447	8,645	384,246	1,460	10,244
Imo	793,867	2,011	27,562	849,703	2,012	20,235	887,039	2,010	20,301
Kaduna	1,134,475	2,885	30,099	1,261,918	2,885	14,646	816,696	2,948	n.a.
Kano	752,278	3,063	18,137	762,593	3,108	16,944	765,226	3,108	n.a.
Kwara	865,972	1,305	17,944	882,864 [2]	1,305 [3]	16,362	n.a.	n.a.	n.a.
Lagos	632,528	967	14,944	650,937	962	6,943	662,380	888	16,613
Niger	462,074	1,164	10,034	460,182	1,164	11,320	451,010	1,164	6,802
Ogun	445,168	1,288	12,856	359,515	1,288	14,870	369,261	1,277	11,2 03
Ondo	693,997	1,627	22,294	567,612	1,726	14,870	453,397	1,608	16,824
Oyo	2,070,362	1,907	32,987	1,982,525	2,740	n.a.	n.a.	n.a.	n.a.
Plateau	524,299	1,687	15,656	545,702	1,687	13,719	511,607	1,375	15,103
Rivers	369,363	1,119	14,449	320,935	1,110	12,624	345,059	1,081	11 ,826
Sokoto	705,777	4,038	18,482	717,898	2,509	1,782	724,625	2,452	13,013
Federal Capital Territory (Abuja)	45,155 [2]	198	1,865	45,155 [2]	201		47,244	203	1,683
TOTAL	14,378,271	37,216	390,790	13,372,446	35,188	235,499	8,571,483	28,562	173,572

n.a.—not available.
[1] Akwa Ibom and Katsina did not become states until September 1987 and are therefore not included.
[2] Provisional.
[3] 1983-84 figure.

Source: Based on information from Nigeria, Office of Statistics, *Social Statistics in Nigeria, 1985*, Lagos, 1986, 80.

Table 4. Enrollment in Secondary Schools by State, 1980-81 to 1983-84

State [1]	1980-81 Students	1980-81 Percentage	1981-82 Students	1981-82 Percentage	1982-83 Students	1982-83 Percentage	1983-84 Students	1983-84 Percentage
Anambra	153,378	7.7	250,611	9.7	180,729	6.0	117,506	3.9
Bauchi	18,007	0.9	25,989	1.0	37,330	1.2	19,792	0.7
Bendel	253,075	12.7	351,006	13.6	369,508	12.2	383,571	12.8
Benue	38,314	2.0	75,261	2.9	n.a.	n.a.	n.a.	0.0
Borno	27,164	1.4	36,275	1.4	n.a.	n.a.	n.a.	0.0
Cross River	176,940	8.9	151,182	5.9	168,816	5.6	162,999	5.4
Gongola	29,284	1.5	42,835	1.7	62,356	2.1	77,894	2.6
Imo	277,649	13.9	305,386	11.9	279,414	9.3	270,898	9.0
Kaduna	50,659	2.5	55,153	2.1	98,868	3.3	140,909	4.7
Kano	32,000	1.6	35,167	1.4	62,477	2.1	74,701	2.5
Kwara	34,333	4.2	92,536	3.6	113,129	3.7	133,937	4.5
Lagos	165,563	8.3	191,309	7.4	225,195	7.5	232,657	7.8
Niger	12,882	0.6	14,945	0.6	160,848 [2]	5.3 [2]	66,652	2.2
Ogun	109,525	5.5	136,232	5.3	160,848 [2]	5.3 [2]	181,654	6.1
Ondo	178,309	9.0	258,549	10.0	304,452	10.1	299,144	10.0
Oyo	244,490	12.2	373,266	14.5	557,295	18.5	571,227	19.0
Plateau	35,444	1.8	47,367	1.8	71,947	2.4	90,327	3.0
Rivers	72,916	3.7	86,502	3.4	111,475	3.7	92,627	3.1
Sokoto	32,501	1.6	44,630	1.7	45,630	1.5	74,615	2.5
Federal Capital Territory (Abuja)	0	0.0	1,767	0.1	5,460	0.2	7,978	0.3
TOTAL [3]	1,942,433	100.0	2,575,968	100.0	3,015,777	100.0	2,999,088	100.0

n.a.—not available.

[1] Akwa Ibom and Katsina did not become states until September 1987 and are therefore not included.

[2] As published.

[3] Percentages may not add to totals because of rounding.

Source: Based on information from Nigeria, Office of Statistics, *Social Statistics in Nigeria, 1985*, Lagos, 1986, 67.

Table 5. *Enrollment in Federal Universities by State,*
1980–81 to 1984–85

State [1]	1980–81	1981–82	1982–83	1983–84	1984–85 [2]
Anambra	10,290	11,838	12,139	12,193	12,200
Bauchi	0	263	512	595	700
Bendel	5,694	6,489	7,005	9,528	9,000
Benue	0	193	366	451	600
Borno	2,569	3,244	4,131	5,505	5,600
Cross River	2,798	3,687	4,816	4,816	5,000
Gongola	0	0	128	221	350
Imo	0	224	364	565	600
Kaduna	11,681	12,586	14,029	13,374	13,400
Kano	2,479	2,861	3,376	3,777	4,000
Kwara	2,010	2,784	3,512	4,622	5,000
Lagos	12,365	12,757	9,891	10,800	11,000
Niger	0	0	0	160	300
Ogun	0	0	0	236	350
Ondo	0	0	148	274	400
Oyo	17,855	21,095	22,454	24,007	24,000
Plateau	3,047	3,933	4,798	4,983	5,000
Rivers	1,754	2,428	2,916	3,302	3,500
Sokoto	883	1,366	2,063	2,534	3,000
TOTAL	73,425	85,748	92,648	101,943	104,000

[1] Akwa Ibom and Katsina did not become states until September 1987 and are therefore not included.
[2] As published.

Source: Based on information from Nigeria, Office of Statistics, *Social Statistics in Nigeria,*
1985, Lagos, 1986, 83.

Table 6. *Medical Personnel and Facilities, 1985*

	Number	Per 100,000 Population
Doctors	14,757	15.3
Nurses	45,976	47.6
Midwives	39,137	40.5
Dentists	899	0.9
Hospital beds		
Federal	11,793	n.a.
State	41,371	n.a.
Local	9,272	n.a.
Private	12,751	n.a.
Missions	10,020	n.a.
Community, corporation, and industrial	1,319	n.a.
Joint public/private sector	1,279	n.a.
Total hospital beds	87,805	

n.a.—not available.

Source: Based on information from Nigeria, Office of Statistics, *Social Statistics in Nigeria,*
1985, Lagos, 1986, 45.

Table 7. *Federal Government Budget, 1986-90* (in millions of naira) [1]

	1986	1987	1988 [2]	1989 [3]	1990 [3]
Revenues					
Petroleum profits	8,108	19,027	20,934	22,521	38,627
Other	4,194	6,072	6,377	6,893	9,138
Total revenues	12,302	25,099	27,311	29,414	47,765
Expenditures					
Current	7,697	15,646	19,409	21,235	27,208
Capital	8,527	6,373	8,340	9,797	12,555
Total expenditures	16,224	22,019	27,749	31,032	39,763
Allocations to state and local					
governments	4,333	8,970	11,722	12,197	20,442
Adjustments	0	0	0	0	-1,892
Balance	-8,255	-5,890	-12,160	-13,815	-14,332

[1] For value of the naira—see Glossary.
[2] Provisional.
[3] Projected.

Source: Based on information from Economist Intelligence Unit, *Country Profile: Nigeria, 1990-91,* London, 1990, 37.

Table 8. *Labor Force by Sector, 1983*

Sector	Number (in thousands)	Percentage
Employed		
Agriculture, forestry, and fishing	9,296	33.5
Mining and quarrying	103	0.4
Manufacturing	1,343	4.8
Utilities	318	1.1
Construction	909	3.3
Trade, hotels, and restaurants	6,534	23.5
Transportation, communications, and storage	1,123	4.1
Finance, insurance, real estate, and business services	204	0.7
Community, social, and personal services	7,081	25.5
Other	865	3.1
Total employed	27,776	100.0
Unemployed	1,677	n.a.
TOTAL	29,453	n.a.

n.a.—not applicable.

Source: Based on information from Paul Hackett, "Nigeria—Economy," in *Africa South of the Sahara, 1990,* London, 784.

Table 9. *Gross Domestic Product by Sector, 1986-88* [1]
(in billions of naira) [2]

Sector	1986	1987	1988
Agriculture, forestry, and fishing	31.2	31.9	32.3
Crude petroleum	11.4	10.2	11.3
Mining and quarrying	0.4	0.4	0.5
Manufacturing	7.3	7.7	8.3
Utilities	0.4	0.3	0.3
Construction	1.3	1.1	1.1
Transportation	2.7	2.7	2.9
Communications	0.2	0.2	0.3
Wholesale and retail trade	12.1	13.6	14.1
Hotels and restaurants	0.7	0.7	0.7
Finance and insurance	2.4	2.6	3.0
Real estate and business services	0.3	0.3	0.3
Housing	1.9	1.9	2.0
Government services	5.0	5.0	5.0
Other	0.6	0.6	0.7
TOTAL [3]	77.9	79.3	82.6

[1] At 1984 factor cost.
[2] For value of the naira—see Glossary.
[3] Figures may not add to total because of rounding.

Source: Based on information from Economist Intelligence Unit, *Country Profile: Nigeria, 1990-91,* London, 1990, 15.

Table 10. Balance of Payments, 1984–88
(in millions of United States dollars)

	1984	1985	1986	1987	1988
Exports [1]	11,827	13,369	6,599	7,702	7,419
Imports [1]	8,844	7,634	4,063	4,178	5,000
Trade balance	2,983	5,735	2,536	3,524	2,419
Invisibles (credit)	489	403	344	276	380
Invisibles (debit)	-3,034	-3,254	-2,371	-3,845	-3,800
Net private transfers	-299	-260	-131	-20	-34
Net official transfers	-26	-1	-5	-5	-22
Current account balance	113	2,623	373	-70	-1,057
Investment	200	489	199	67	881
Other long-term capital	-638	-2,307	-1,440	-3,616	-3,492
Short-term capital	-912	-1,920	-91	1,167	1,273
Capital account balance	-1,350	-3,738	-1,332	-2,382	-1,338
Errors and omissions	271	-138	-191	-311	-63
Counterpart items	-9	-445	-40	56	-58
Foreign authorities reserves	0	0	0	1,829	0
Exceptional financing	1,446	1,753	612	4,641	4,503
Change in reserves (- means increase)	-471	-55	578	-104 [2]	514 [2]

[1] f.o.b.—free on board.
[2] As published.

Source: Based on information from Economist Intelligence Unit, *Country Profile: Nigeria, 1990–91*, London, 1990, 46.

Table 11. *Production of Major Agricultural Commodities, 1985-88*
(in thousands of tons unless otherwise indicated)

Commodity	1985	1986	1987	1988
Food crops				
Beans	611	732	688	690
Cassava	1,378	1,546	1,486	1,587
Corn	1,190	1,336	1,202	1,370
Melons	147	153	145	150
Millet	3,684	4,111	3,905	4,170
Plantains	1,113	1,127	1,071	1,549
Rice	196	283	297	307
Sorghum	4,991	5,455	5,182	5,534
Yams	4,738	5,209	4,886	5,042
Total food crops	18,048	19,952	18,862	20,399
Commercial crops				
Cocoa	110	100	105	200
Coconuts	102	104	105	108
Cottonseed	46	30	32	38
Palm kernels	360	350	353	545
Palm wine *	4,882	4,940	4,951	4,986
Peanuts	621	640	657	706
Rubber	58	60	51	81
Sesame	35	35	34	36
Shea nuts	100	103	104	109
Soybeans	114	100	107	121
Sugarcane	862	897	852	888
Total commercial crops	7,290	7,359	7,351	7,818
TOTAL	25,338	27,311	26,213	28,217

* In thousands of liters.

Source: Based on information from Economist Intelligence Unit, *Country Profile: Nigeria,*
1989-90, London, 1989, 18; and Economist Intelligence Unit, *Country Profile: Nigeria,*
1990-91, London, 1990, 18-19.

Table 12. Major Imports, 1985–88
(in millions of naira) *

Commodity	1985	1986	1987	1988
Food and live animals	1,200	802	1,874	1,948
Beverages and tobacco	9	14	31	86
Animal and vegetable fats and oils ..	71	125	66	83
Crude materials (inedible)	350	194	800	667
Mineral fuels	61	42	77	255
Chemicals	1,108	1,039	3,017	4,838
Manufactured goods	1,612	1,237	4,485	5,650
Machinery and transportation equipment	2,414	2,278	6,828	10,282
Other	238	253	684	1,091
TOTAL	7,063	5,984	17,862	24,900

* For value of the naira—see Glossary.

Source: Based on information from Economist Intelligence Unit, *Country Profile: Nigeria, 1990-91,* London, 1990, 43-44.

Table 13. Major Exports, 1984–88
(in millions of naira) [1]

Commodity	1984	1985	1986	1987	1988 [2]
Cocoa beans	183	182	371	1,498	2,627
Cocoa products	32	57	54	62	86
Palm kernels and products	16	6	8	30	103
Petroleum	8,841	11,224	8,368	28,209	29,293
Rubber	17	4	29	61	290
Other [3]	-1	248	91	501	739
TOTAL	9,088	11,721	8,921	30,361	33,138

[1] For value of the naira—see Glossary.
[2] Provisional.
[3] Includes statistical discrepancy, which accounts for negative figure.

Source: Based on information from Economist Intelligence Unit, *Country Profile: Nigeria, 1990-91,* London, 1990, 43.

333

Table 14. Major Trading Partners, 1985–88
(in percentages)

Year	Britain	Canada	France	Italy	Japan	Netherlands	Spain	United States	West Germany	Other	Total
Exports
1985	5.2	n.a.	10.8	n.a.	n.a.	4.2	5.4	19.8	13.7	40.9	100.0
1986	4.9	2.7	8.4	n.a.	n.a.	0.3	2.9	26.9	12.6	41.3	100.0
1987	2.6	2.0	5.7	n.a.	n.a.	3.9	8.3	37.7	7.7	32.1	100.0
1988	2.3	2.8	5.1	n.a.	n.a.	4.8	9.6	36.2	7.1	32.1	100.0
Imports
1985	17.3	n.a.	8.1	4.9	7.4	3.1	n.a.	9.6	9.2	40.4	100.0
1986	17.0	n.a.	10.1	5.2	4.0	5.1	n.a.	8.4	13.7	36.5	100.0
1987	16.4	n.a.	8.4	6.7	7.3	5.1	n.a.	6.2	11.2	38.7	100.0
1988	14.5	n.a.	9.8	6.4	6.4	3.8	n.a.	7.4	10.7	41.0	100.0

n.a.—not available.

Source: Based on information from Economist Intelligence Unit, *Country Profile: Nigeria, 1989–90*, London, 1989, 42, 43; and Economist Intelligence Unit, *Country Profile: Nigeria, 1990–91*, London, 1990, 44–45.

Table 15. Crude Petroleum Production, Selected Years,
1967–89
(in millions of barrels per day)

Year	Quantity	Year	Quantity
1967	333	1979	2,306
1969	564	1981	1,440
1971	1,628	1983	1,235
1973	2,140	1985	1,491
1975	1,861	1987	1,270
1977	2,184	1989	1,662

Source: Based on information from E. Wayne Nafziger, *The Economics of Political Instabili-*
ty: The Nigerian-Biafran War, Boulder, Colorado, 1983, 150; Central Bank of Nigeria,
Economic and Financial Review [Lagos], 23, June 1985, 80; and Economist Intelligence Unit, *Country Profile: Nigeria, 1990–91,* London, 1990, 25.

Table 16. Revised Transition Timetable, 1987–92
(as of December 1990)

Year	Quarter	Event
1987	Third quarter	Establishment of Directorate of Social Mobilization, National Electoral Commission, and Constitution Drafting Committee.
	Fourth quarter	Elections to local governments on non-party basis.
1988	First quarter	Establishment of National Population Commission, Code of Conduct Tribunal, and Constitutional Assembly.
1989	Second quarter	Lift of ban on party politics.
	Third quarter	Announcement of two recognized and registered political parties.
	Fourth quarter	Election of local governments on political party basis.
1990	First and second quarter	Election of state legislatures and state executives.
	Third quarter	Convening of state legislatures.
	Fourth quarter	Swearing in of state executives.
1991	First, second, and third quarters	Census.
	Fourth quarter	Local government elections.
1992	First and second quarters	Elections of federal legislature and convening of National Assembly.
	Third and fourth quarters	Presidential elections. Swearing in of new president and final withdrawal by the armed forces.

Table 17. Major Army Equipment, 1990

Type and Description	Country of Origin	In Inventory
Tanks		
T-55 main battle tanks	Soviet Union	60
Vickers Mk 3 main battle tanks	Britain	97
Scorpion light tanks	-do-	100
Scimitar light tanks	-do-	5
Armored vehicles		
Saladin Mk 2 reconnaissance	Britain	20
AML-60 reconnaissance	France	120
AML-90 reconnaissance	-do-	60
Ferret reconnaissance	Britain	25
Fox reconnaissance	-do-	55
VBL M-11 reconnaissance	France	10
Steyr 4K-7FA armored personnel carriers	Austria	300
Saracen armored personnel carriers	Britain	10
Panhard M3 armored personnel carriers	France	n.a.
ERC-90 Lynx armored cars	-do-	40
ERC-90 Sagaie armored cars	-do-	40
EE-9 Cascavel armored cars	Brazil	100 (on order)
Artillery		
M1942 76mm guns	n.a.	n.a.
M-56 105mm guns	n.a.	200
D-30/-74 122mm guns, howitzers	n.a.	200
M46 130mm howitzers	n.a.	n.a.
Bofors FH-77B 155mm howitzers	Sweden	24
Palmaria 155mm self-propelled howitzers	Italy	25
81mm mortars	n.a.	200
BM-21 122mm rocket launchers	Soviet Union	n.a.
Antitank weapons		
Carl Gustav 84mm	Sweden	n.a.
M-40A1 106mm	n.a.	n.a.
Air defense weapons		
ZPU 14.5mm	Soviet Union	n.a.
20mm	n.a.	60
ZU-23 23mm	Soviet Union	n.a.
ZSU-23-4 23mm self-propelled	-do-	30
L/60 40mm	n.a.	n.a.
Roland missile launchers	France	16
Blowpipe man-portable missiles	Britain	48

n.a.—not available.

Source: Based on information from *The Military Balance, 1990–1991,* London, 1990, 139; and *World Defense Almanac* (Special Issue: *Military Technology*), January 1989, 231.

Table 18. Major Navy Equipment, 1990

Type and Description	Country of Origin	In Inventory
Frigates		
Meko-360H with 1 Westland Lynx Mk 89 MR/SR helicopter and 8 Otomat surface-to-surface missile (SSM) launchers	West Germany	1
Training vessel with helicopter deck .	Netherlands	1
Missile craft		
Lürssen-57 patrol frigates with 4 Otomat SSMs	West Germany	3
Combattante IIIB with 4 Exocet MM-38 SSMs	France	3
Corvettes		
Vosper Mk 9 with Seacat triple surface-to-air missiles (SAMs)	Britain	1
Vosper Mk 3	–do–	1
Large patrol craft		
Brooke Marine	–do–	4
Abeking and Rasmussen	West Germany	4
Coastal patrol craft		
Intermarine	Italy	14
Simoneau	France	6
Danen	Netherlands	6
Van Mill	–do–	5
Watercraft	Britain	2
Swiftships	United States	4
Rotork Sea Truck	n.a.	4
Minesweepers		
Intermarine Lerici-class	Italy	2
Amphibious		
FDR type Ro-Ro-1300 tank landing ships	West Germany	2
Support ships		
Bulldog-class survey ship	Britain	1
Van Lent training ship	Netherlands	1
Tugs (1 firefighter)	Netherlands/ West Germany	8
Launchers	n.a.	56
Naval aviation		
Westland Lynx Mk 89 MR/SR helicopters	Britain/France	3

n.a.—not available.

Source: Based on information from *The Military Balance, 1990-1991,* London, 1990, 139; and *Jane's Fighting Ships, 1989-90,* London, 1989, 399-404.

Table 19. *Major Air Force Equipment, 1990*

Type and Description	Country of Origin	In Inventory
Fighters		
Alpha Jet light attack/trainer	West Germany	21
MiG-21 MF Fishbed	Soviet Union	6
MiG-21 MF (being modernized)	-do-	12
MiG-21 UTI Mongol	-do-	4
Jaguar deck	Britain	15
Trainers		
L-39	Czechoslovakia	12
MB-339AN	Italy	12
MiG-21 UTI	Soviet Union	2
Bulldog	Britain	25
Transports		
C-130H	United States	6
C-130H-30	-do-	3
Do-228 VIP	West Germany	3(?)
F-28	-do-	1
G-222	Italy	5
Do-28D transport/liaison	West Germany	18
Do-128-6 transport/liaison	-do-	18
Gulfstream II VIP	United States	2
Boeing 727-30 VIP	-do-	1
Piper PA-31 Navajo	-do-	3
BAe 125-700	Britain	1
Maritime patrol/search and rescue		
F-27	Netherlands	2
Helicopters		
Bo-105D attack	West Germany	15
Bo-105D maritime reconnaissance/search and rescue	-do-	4
Bo-105C/D transport	-do-	4
SA-316B Alouette III	France	10
SA-3300 Puma transport	-do-	2
AS-332M Super Puma transport	-do-	6 (on order)
CH-47 Chinook	United States	5 (on order)
Hughes 300 training	-do-	14

Table 20. Arms Imports by Supplier, 1978-87
(in millions of United States dollars)

Supplier	1978-82	1983-87
Britain	150	340
Bulgaria	0	20
China	0	5
Czechoslovakia	5	60
France	250	130
Italy	40	350
Soviet Union	90	90
United States	20	140
West Germany	280	70
Other	10	310
TOTAL	845	1,515

Source: Based on information from United States, Arms Control and Disarmament Agency, *World Military Expenditures and Arms Transfers, 1972-1982.* Washington, April 1984, table III, 95; and United States, Arms Control and Disarmament Agency, *World Military Expenditures and Arms Transfers, 1988,* Washington, June 1989, table III, 111.

Bibliography

Chapter 1

Adamu, Mahdi. *The Hausa Factor in West Africa.* Zaria, Nigeria: Ahmadu Bello University Press, 1978.

Afigbo, A. *Ropes of Sand: Studies in Igbo History and Culture.* Ibadan: Oxford University Press, 1981.

Ajayi, J.F. Ade, and Michael Crowder (eds.). *History of West Africa.* (3d ed.) (2 vols.) London: Longman, 1988.

Ayandele, E.A. *The Missionary Impact on Modern Nigeria, 1842–1914.* London: Longman, 1966.

de St. Jorre, John. *The Nigerian Civil War.* London: Hodder and Stoughton, 1972.

Dusgate, Richard H. *The Conquest of Northern Nigeria.* London: Cass, 1985.

Falola, Toyin, and Julius Omozuanvbo Ihonvbere. *The Rise and Fall of Nigeria's Second Republic, 1979–1983.* London: Zed Books, 1985.

Fika, Adamu. *The Kano Civil War and British Over-Rule.* London: Oxford University Press, 1978.

Flint, John. *Sir George Goldie and the Making of Nigeria.* London: Oxford University Press, 1960.

Forrest, Thomas. *Politics, Policy, and Capitalist Development in Nigeria, 1970–1990.* Boulder, Colorado: Westview Press, 1992.

Ikime, Obaro. *The Fall of Nigeria.* London: Heinemann, 1977.

Ikime, Obaro (ed.). *Groundwork of Nigerian History.* Ibadan: Heinemann Educational Books for Historical Society of Nigeria, 1980.

Isichei, Elizabeth. *A History of the Igbo People.* London: Macmillan, 1976.

Lovejoy, Paul E. *Transformations in Slavery: A History of Slavery in Africa.* Cambridge: Cambridge University Press, 1983.

Lovejoy, Paul E., and Jan S. Hogendorn. *Slavery in Muslim Nigeria. The Abolition of Slavery under British Rule.* Cambridge: Cambridge University Press, forthcoming 1992.

Nicolson, I.F. *The Administration of Nigeria, 1900–1960: Men, Methods, and Myths.* Oxford: Clarendon Press, 1969.

Paden, John N. *Ahmadu Bello, Sardauna of Sokoto: Values and Leadership in Nigeria.* London: Hodder and Stoughton, 1986.

Phillips, Anne. *The Enigma of Colonialism: British Policy in West Africa.* Bloomington: Indiana University Press, 1989.

Smith, Robert S. *Kingdoms of the Yoruba.* (3d ed.) Madison: University of Wisconsin Press, 1988.

Stremlau, John J. *The International Politics of the Nigerian Civil War, 1967–1970.* Princeton: Princeton University Press, 1977.

Tumano, Tekena N. *The Evolution of the Nigerian State: The Southern Phase, 1898–1914.* London: Longman, 1972.

———. *Nigeria and Elected Representation, 1923–1947.* London: Heinemann, 1966.

Usman, Yusufu Bala (ed.). *Studies in the History of the Sokoto Caliphate.* Zaria, Nigeria: Ahmadu Bello University Press, 1979.

Watts, Michael. *Silent Violence: Food, Famine, and Peasantry in Northern Nigeria.* Berkeley: University of California Press, 1983.

Chapter 2

Achebe, Chinua. *Anthills of the Savannah.* New York: Doubleday, 1987.

Adenubi, A. (ed.). *Timeless Tai: A Collection of the Writings of T. Solarin.* Lagos: F and A, 1985.

Agboola, S.A. *An Agricultural Atlas of Nigeria.* Oxford: Oxford University Press, 1979.

———. "Some Factors of Population Distribution in the Middle Belt of Nigeria." Pages 291–97 in John Charles Caldwell and Chukuka Okonjo (eds.), *The Population of Tropical Africa.* London: Longman, 1968.

Akintola, J.O. *Rainfall Distribution in Nigeria, 1892–1983.* Ibadan: Impact, 1986.

Alubo, S. Ogoh. "Doctoring as Business: A Study of Entrepreneurial Medicine in Nigeria," *Medical Anthropology,* 12, 1990, 305–24.

———. "The Political Economy of Doctors' Strikes in Nigeria: A Marxist Interpretation," *Social Science and Medicine,* 22, No. 4, 1986, 467–77.

———. "Power and Privilege in Medical Care: An Analysis of Medical Services in Post-Colonial Nigeria," *Social Science and Medicine,* 24, No. 5, 1987, 453–62.

Andreski, I. *Old Wives' Tales: Life-Stories from Ibibioland.* New York: Schocken, 1970.

Aronson, I. *The City Is Our Farm.* Boston: G.K. Hall, 1978.

Baker, Pauline H. *Urbanization and Political Change: The Politics of Lagos, 1917–1967.* Berkeley: University of California Press, 1974.

Barbour, Kenneth Michael, et al. *Nigeria in Maps.* New York: Africana, 1982.

Bascom, William Russell. *The Yoruba of Southwestern Nigeria.* New York: Holt, Rinehart, and Winston, 1969.

Beckett, Paul. *Education and Power in Nigeria.* London: Hodder and Stoughton, 1977.

Berry, Sara. *Fathers Work for Their Sons: Accumulation, Mobility, and Class Formation in an Extended Yoruba Community.* Berkeley: University of California Press, 1985.

Bohannan, Paul J. *Tiv Economy.* Evanston, Illinois: Northwestern University Press, 1968.

———. "The Tiv of Nigeria." Pages 513–46 in James L. Gibbs, Jr. (ed.), *Peoples of Africa.* New York: Holt, Rinehart, and Winston, 1965.

Bohannan, Paul, and Laura Bohannan. *A Source Notebook on Tiv Religion.* New Haven: Human Relations Area Files, 1969.

Bradbury, R.E. "The Kingdom of Benin." Pages 1–35 in Daryll Forde and Phyllis Mary Kaberry (eds.), *West African Kingdoms in the Nineteenth Century.* London: Oxford University Press, 1967.

Caldwell, John Charles, and Pat Caldwell. "The Cultural Context of High Fertility in Sub-Saharan Africa," *Population and Development Review,* 13, 1987, 409–37.

———. "Fertility Control as Innovation: A Report on In-depth Interviews in Ibadan, Nigeria." Pages 233–51 in E. van de Walle (ed.), *The Cultural Roots of African Fertility Regimes: Proceedings of the Ife Conference, February 25–March 1, 1987.* Ile-Ife, Nigeria: Department of Demography and Social Statistics, Awolowo University, and Population Studies Center, University of Pennsylvania, 1987.

———. "The Limitation of Family Size in Ibadan City, Nigeria." Pages 347–63 in E. van de Walle (ed.), *The Cultural Roots of African Fertility Regimes: Proceedings of the Ife Conference, February 25–March 1, 1987.* Ile-Ife, Nigeria: Department of Demography and Social Statistics, Awolowo University, and Population Studies Center, University of Pennsylvania, 1987.

Caldwell, John Charles, and Chukuka Okonjo (eds.). *The Population of Tropical Africa.* London: Longman, 1968.

Callaway, Barbara. *Muslim Hausa Women in Nigeria.* Syracuse: Syracuse University Press, 1981.

Chubb, L.T. *Ibo Land Tenure.* (2d ed.) Ibadan: Ibadan University Press, 1961.

Church, Ronald James Harrison. *West Africa.* (8th ed.) London: Longman, 1980.

Clarke, John I., and Leszek A. Kosinski. *Redistribution of Population in Africa.* London: Heinemann, 1982.

Cline-Cole, J.A. Falola, H.A.C. Main, M.J. Mortimore, J.E. Nichol, and F.D. O'Reilly. *Wood Fuel in Kano.* Tokyo: United Nations University Press, 1990.

Cohen, Abner. *Custom and Politics in Urban Africa.* Berkeley: University of California Press, 1969.

Cohen, Ronald. *Dominance and Defiance: A Study of Marital Instability in an Islamic African Society.* Washington: American Anthropological Association, 1971.

––––––. *The Kanuri of Bornu.* New York: Holt, Rinehart, and Winston, 1967.

Dada, Ayorinde. *National Conference on Mass Failure in Public Examinations.* Ibadan: Heinemann, 1987.

Duru, R.D. "Problems of Data Collection for Population Studies in Nigeria with Particular Reference to the 1952/53 Census and the Western Region." Pages 71–77 in John Charles Caldwell and Chukuka Okonjo (eds.), *The Population of Tropical Africa.* London: Longman, 1968.

Eades, Jeremy Seymour. *The Yoruba Today.* New York: Cambridge University Press, 1980.

Economist Intelligence Unit. *Country Report: Nigeria* [London], No. 1, 1990.

Ejiofor, Lambert U. *The Dynamics of Igbo Democracy.* New York: Oxford University Press, 1981.

Eleazu, Uma O. *Nigeria: The First 25 Years.* Ibadan: Heinemann, 1985.

Ekong, Ekong E. *Sociology of the Ibibio: A Study of Social Organization and Change.* Calabar, Nigeria: Scholars Press, 1983.

Fadipe, N.A. *The Sociology of the Yoruba.* Ibadan: Ibadan University Press, 1970.

Fafunwa, A. Babs. *History of Education in Nigeria.* London: Allen and Unwin, 1974.

Faulkner, O.T., and J.R. Mackie. *West African Agriculture.* London: Cambridge University Press, 1933.

Floyd, Barry. *Eastern Nigeria: A Geographical Review.* London: Macmillan, 1969.

Forde, Daryll, and G.I. Jones. *The Ibo and Ibibio-Speaking Peoples of South-Eastern Nigeria.* (Ethnographic Survey of Africa, Western Africa, Pt. 3.) London: Oxford University Press for the International African Institute, 1950.

Forde, Daryll, and Phyllis Mary Kaberry (eds.). *West African Kingdoms in the Nineteenth Century.* London: Oxford University Press, 1967.

Forde, Daryll, and Richenda Scott. *The Native Economies of Nigeria.* London: Faber and Faber, 1946.

Gibbs, James L., Jr. (ed.). *Peoples of Africa.* New York: Holt, Rinehart, and Winston, 1965.

Gilliland, Dean S. *African Religion Meets Islam: Religious Change in Northern Nigeria.* Lanham, Maryland: University Press of America, 1986.

Green, Margaret Mackeson. *Land Tenure in an Ibo Village in South-Eastern Nigeria.* (Monographs on Social Anthropology, No. 6.) London: Lund, Humphries for London School of Economics and Political Science, 1941.

Grove, Alfred Thomas. *The Changing Geography of Africa.* Oxford: Oxford University Press, 1989.

Hansen, Art, and Della E. McMillan (eds.). *Saharan Africa.* Boulder, Colorado: Lynne Rienner, 1987.

Hill, Polly. *Rural Hausa.* Cambridge: Cambridge University Press, 1972.

Hopkins, Anthony G. *An Economic History of West Africa.* London: Longman, 1973.

Huth, W.P. *Traditional Institutions and Land Tenure as Related to Agricultural Development among the Ibo of Eastern Nigeria.* Madison, Wisconsin: Land Tenure Center, 1969.

Idachaba, Francis Sulemanu, et al. *Rural Infrastructures in Nigeria.* (7 vols.) Ibadan: Ibadan University Press, 1985.

Ityavyar, Dennis. "Background to the Development of Health Services in Nigeria," *Social Science and Medicine,* 24, No. 6, 1987, 487-99.

_____. "Health Services Inequalities in Nigeria," *Social Science and Medicine,* 27, No. 11, 1988, 1223-35.

Kowal, Jan M., and A.H. Kassam. *Agricultural Ecology of Savanna: A Study of West Africa.* Oxford: Clarendon Press, 1978.

Kowal, Jan M., and Donata T. Knabe. *An Agroclimatological Atlas of the Northern States of Nigeria.* Zaria, Nigeria: Ahmadu Bello University Press, 1972.

Lagemann, Johannes. *Traditional African Farming Systems in Eastern Nigeria.* Munich: Weltforum, 1977.

Mabogunje, Akin L. *Urbanization in Nigeria.* New York: Africana, 1962.

Marris, Peter. *Family and Social Change in an African City: A Study of Re-Housing in Lagos.* London: Routledge and Kegan Paul, 1962.

Martin, Susan. *Palm Oil and Protest: An Economic History of the Ngwa Region, South-Eastern Nigeria, 1800-1980.* Cambridge: Cambridge University Press, 1988.

Mason, Michael. "Population Density and 'Slave Raiding': The Case of the Middle Belt in Nigeria," *Journal of African History,* 10, 1969, 551-64.

Melson, Robert, and Howard Wolpe (eds.). *Nigeria: Modernization and the Politics of Communalism.* East Lansing: Michigan State University Press, 1971.

Morgan, William Basil, and John Charles Pugh. *West Africa.* London: Methuen, 1969.

Morgan, William Thomas Wilson. *Nigeria,* London: Longman, 1983.

Mortimore, Michael J. *Adapting to Drought: Farmers, Famines, and Desertification in West Africa.* Cambridge: Cambridge University Press, 1989.

Morton-Williams, Peter. "The Yoruba Kingdom of Oyo." Pages 36–69 in Daryll Forde and Phyllis Mary Kaberry (eds.), *West African Kingdoms of the Nineteenth Century.* London: Oxford University Press, 1967.

Nadel, Siegfried Frederick. *A Black Byzantium: The Kingdom of Nupe in Nigeria.* London: Oxford University Press for International Institute of African Languages and Culture, 1942.

Netting, Robert M. *Hill Farmers of Nigeria: Cultural Ecology of the Kofyar of the Jos Plateau.* Seattle: University of Washington Press, 1968.

Nicholson, Sharon. "Climate, Drought, and Famine in Africa." Pages 107–28 in Art Hansen and Della E. McMillan (eds.), *Saharan Africa.* Boulder, Colorado: Lynne Rienner, 1987.

Nigeria. Office of Statistics. *Social Statistics in Nigeria, 1985.* Lagos: 1986.

_____. Office of Statistics. *Social Statistics in Nigeria, 1986.* Lagos: 1987.

_____. Office of Statistics. *Social Statistics in Nigeria, 1987.* Lagos: 1988.

_____. Office of Statistics. *Social Statistics in Nigeria, 1988.* Lagos: 1989.

_____. Office of Statistics. *Social Statistics in Nigeria, 1989.* Lagos: 1990.

Njaka, Elechukwu Nnadibuagha. *Igbo Political Culture.* Evanston: Northwestern University Press, 1974.

Norman, David W., Emmy B. Simmons, and Henry M. Hays. *Farming Systems in the Nigerian Savanna: Research and Strategies for Development.* Boulder, Colorado: Westview Press, 1982.

Nye, Peter Hague, and David J. Greenland. *The Soil under Shifting Cultivation.* (Technical Communication No. 51.) Harpenden, Hertfordshire, United Kingdom: Commonwealth Bureau of Soils, 1960.

Okonjo, Chukuka. "A Preliminary Medium Estimate of the 1952 Mid-Year Population of Nigeria." Pages 78–95 in John Charles

Caldwell and Chukuka Okonjo (eds.), *The Population of Tropical Africa*. London: Longman, 1968.

Otite, Onigu. *Autonomy and Independence: The Urhobo Kingdom of Okpe in Modern Nigeria*. Evanston: Northwestern University Press, 1973.

Ottenberg, Phoebe. "The Afikpo Ibo of Eastern Nigeria." Pages 1–39 in James L. Gibbs, Jr. (ed.), *Peoples of Africa*. New York: Holt, Rinehart, and Winston, 1965.

Ottenberg, Simon. *Leadership and Authority in an African Society: The Afikpo Village Group*. Seattle: University of Washington Press, 1971.

Ozigi, A.O. *Education in Nigeria*. London: Allen and Unwin, 1981.

Paden, John N. *Religion and Political Culture in Kano*. Berkeley: University of California Press, 1973.

Peel, John David Yeadon. *Aladura: A Religious Movement among the Yoruba*. London: Oxford University Press for International African Institute, 1968.

Peshkin, Alan. *Kanuri School Children*. New York: Holt, Rinehart, and Winston, 1972.

Pullan, Robert Alan. "The Concept of the Middle Belt: A Climatic Definition," *Nigerian Geographic Journal* [Lagos], 5, 1962, 39–52.

Sada, Pius O., and F.O. Odemerho. *Environmental Issues and Management in Nigerian Development*. Ibadan: Evans Brothers, 1988.

Schram, Ralph. *A History of the Nigerian Health Services*. Ibadan: Ibadan University Press, 1971.

Smith, M.G. "The Hausa of Northern Nigeria." Pages 119–55 in James L. Gibbs, Jr. (ed.), *Peoples of Africa*. New York: Holt, Rinehart, and Winston, 1965.

Smith, Mary F. *Baba of Karo: A Woman of the Muslim Hausa*. London: Faber and Faber, 1954.

Smith, Robert S. *Kingdoms of the Yoruba*. (3d ed.) Madison: University of Wisconsin Press, 1988.

Soyinka, Wole. *Ake: The Years of Childhood*. London: Collings, 1981.

_____. *Isara: A Voyage Around 'Essay.'* New York: Random House, 1989.

_____. *The Man Died: Prison Notes of Wole Soyinka*. New York: Harper and Row, 1982.

Stenning, Derrick J. *Savannah Nomads*. London: Oxford University Press, 1959.

Thomas, M.F., and G.W. Whittington. *Environment and Land Use in Africa*. London: Methuen, 1969.

Trimingham, John Spencer. *Islam in West Africa*. London: Oxford University Press, 1959.

Uchendu, Victor Chikezie. *The Igbo of Southeast Nigeria*. New York: Holt, Rinehart, and Winston, 1965.
Udo, Reuben K. *Geographical Regions of Nigeria*. London: Heinemann, 1970.
United Nations. Food and Agriculture Organization. *Atlas of African Agriculture*. Rome: 1986.
Van de Walle, E. (ed.). *The Cultural Roots of African Fertility Regimes: Proceedings of the Ife Conference, February 25–March 1, 1987*. Ile-Ife, Nigeria: Department of Demography and Social Statistics, Awolo University, and Population Studies Center, University of Pennsylvania, 1987.
Watts, Michael. *Silent Violence: Food, Famine, and Peasantry in Northern Nigeria*. Berkeley: University of California Press, 1983.
Wente-Lukas, Renate. *Handbook of Ethnic Units in Nigeria*. Stuttgart: Steiner, 1974.
World Bank. *Population Growth and Policies in Sub-Saharan Africa*. Washington: 1986.
————. *The World Bank Atlas, 1988*. Washington: 1988.

Chapter 3

Acharya, Shankar N. "Perspectives and Problems of Development in Sub-Saharan Africa," *World Development*, 9, February 1981, 109–47.
Africa South of the Sahara, 1990. London: Europa, 1989.
Alhaji, Alhaji Abubakar. "Amplification of the 1990 Budget," *Management in Nigeria* [Lagos], 26, January–February 1990, 13–23.
Arnold, Guy. *Modern Nigeria*. London: Longman, 1977.
Babangida, Ibrahim Badamasi. "The March Towards a New Sustainable Political and Economic Order in Nigeria," *Management in Nigeria* [Lagos], 26, January–February 1990, 7–12.
Bienen, Henry, and V.P. Diejomaoh (eds.). *The Political Economy of Income Distribution in Nigeria*. New York: Holmes and Meier, 1981.
Bulow, Jeremy, and Kenneth Rogoff. "Cleaning up Third World Debt Without Getting Taken to the Cleaners," *Journal of Economic Perspectives*, 4, Winter 1990, 31–42.
Callaghy, Thomas M. "Toward State Capability and Embedded Liberalism in the Third World: Lessons for Adjustment." Pages 115–38 in John Waterbury et al., *Fragile Coalitions: The Politics of Economic Adjustment*. New Brunswick, New Jersey: Transaction Books, 1989.

Central Bank of Nigeria. *Annual Report and Statement of Accounts, 1987.* Lagos: 1988.

_____. *Annual Report and Statement of Accounts, 1988.* Lagos: 1989.

_____. *Annual Report and Statement of Accounts, 1989.* Lagos: 1990.

_____. *Economic and Financial Review* [Lagos], 23, June 1985, 80.

Claessens, Stijn, and Ishac Diwan. "Liquidity, Debt Relief, and Conditionality." Pages 213–25 in Ishrat Husain and Ishac Diwan (eds.), *Dealing with the Debt Crisis.* Washington: World Bank, 1989.

Coleman, James Smoot. *Nigeria: Background to Nationalism.* Berkeley: University of California Press, 1958.

Collier, Paul. "Oil and Inequality in Rural Nigeria." Pages 191–217 in Dharan Ghai and Samir Radwan (eds.), *Agrarian Policies and Rural Poverty in Africa.* Geneva: International Labour Organisation, 1983.

Crowder, Michael. *The Story of Nigeria.* London: Faber and Faber, 1962.

Economic Commission for Africa. *The Abuja Statement.* (Proceedings of Conference, Abuja, June 15–19, 1987.) Abuja, Nigeria: 1987.

_____. *African Alternative Framework to Structural Adjustment Programmes for Socio-Economic Recovery and Transformation (AAF-SAP).* (E/ECA/CM.15/6/Rev. 3.) Addis Ababa: 1989.

_____. *ECA and Africa's Development, 1958–1983.* (E/ECA/CM. 9/20.) Addis Ababa: 1983.

_____. *Survey of Economic and Social Conditions in Africa, 1983–1984.* (E/ECA/CM 11/16.) Addis Ababa: 1985.

Economist Intelligence Unit. *Country Profile: Nigeria, 1989–90.* London: 1989.

_____. *Country Profile: Nigeria, 1990–91.* London: 1990.

Eicher, Carl K. and Carl Liedholm (eds.). *Growth and Development of the Nigerian Economy.* East Lansing: Michigan State University, 1970.

El Samhouri, Mohammed. "Flexible Exchange Rates and Export Instability: The Impact of the Post-1973 International Monetary System on the Developing Countries." (Ph.D dissertation, Kansas State University, 1989.)

Erbe, Susanne. "The Flight of Capital from Developing Countries," *Intereconomics,* 20, November–December 1985, 268–75.

Fage, J.D. *A History of West Africa: An Introductory Survey.* Cambridge: Cambridge University Press, 1969.

Ghai, Dharan, and Samir Radwan (eds.). *Agrarian Policies and Rural Poverty in Africa.* Geneva: International Labour Organisation, 1983.

Hackett, Paul. "Nigeria—Economy." Pages 775–89 in *Africa South of the Sahara, 1990.* London: Europa, 1989.

Husain, Ishrat, and Ishac Diwan (eds.). *Dealing with the Debt Crisis.* Washington: World Bank, 1989.

International Labour Organisation. "Jobs and Skills Programme for Africa." *First Things First: Meeting the Basic Needs of the People of Africa.* Addis Ababa: 1981.

Jane's World Railways, 1989–90. (Ed., Geoffrey Freeman Allen.) Coulsdon, Surrey, United Kingdom: Jane's Information Group, 1989.

Lessard, Donald, and John Williamson (eds.). *Capital Flight and Debt.* Washington: Institute for International Economics, 1987.

Lewis, Flora. "Oil Crisis of '73 Wreaking Economic Havoc," *Kansas City Times,* November 22, 1988, 7.

Lewis, W. Arthur. *Reflections on Nigeria's Economic Growth.* Paris: Organisation for Economic Co-operation and Development, 1967.

Meier, Gerald M. (ed.). *Leading Issues in Economic Development.* New York: Oxford University Press, 1976.

Meier, Gerald M., and William F. Steel (eds.). *Industrial Adjustment in Sub-Saharan Africa.* New York: Oxford University Press, 1989.

Nafziger, E. Wayne. *The Economics of Developing Countries.* Englewood Cliffs, New Jersey: Prentice Hall, 1990.

_____. *The Economics of Political Instability: The Nigerian-Biafran War.* Boulder, Colorado: Westview Press, 1983.

Nelson, Joan M., et al. *Fragile Coalitions: The Politics of Economic Adjustment.* New Brunswick, New Jersey: Transaction Books, 1989.

_____. *Inequality in Africa: Political Elites, Proletariat, Peasants, and the Poor.* New York: Cambridge University Press, 1988.

Nicolson, I.F. *The Administration of Nigeria, 1900–1960: Men, Methods, and Myths.* Oxford: Clarendon Press, 1969.

Nigeria. Ministry of Economic Development. *Third National Development Plan, 1975–1980.* (2 vols.) Lagos: 1975.

_____. Ministry of Information. *Second National Development Plan, 1970–74.* Lagos: 1970.

_____. Ministry of National Planning. *Fifth National Development Plan, 1981–85.* Lagos: 1980.

_____. Office of Statistics. *Social Statistics in Nigeria.* Lagos: 1985.

Nigerian Economic Society. *Poverty in Nigeria: Proceedings of the 1975 Annual Conference of the Nigerian Economic Society.* Ibadan: Ibadan University Press, 1975.

Nwankwo, G.O. *The Nigerian Financial System.* London: Macmillan, 1980.

Okigbo, Pius N.C. "Interpersonal Income Distribution in Nigeria." Pages 313-29 in Nigerian Economic Society, *Poverty in Nigeria: Proceedings of the 1975 Annual Conference of the Nigerian Economic Society*. Ibadan: Ibadan University Press, 1975.

———. *National Development Planning in Nigeria, 1900-92*. London: Currey, 1989.

Okotie-Eboh, Festus Sam. *The Rededication Budget: Budget Speech, 31st March 1965*. Lagos: Ministry of Information, 1965.

Population Reference Bureau. *1990 World Population Data Sheet*. Washington: 1990.

Rake, Alan. "And Now the Struggle for Real Development," *African Development*, Nos. 10-12, December 1976, 1263-64.

Rimmer, Douglas. "Alternatives to Structural Adjustment and the Future of the Nigerian Economy." Paper for Conference on Democratic Transition and Structural Adjustment in Nigeria, Hoover Institution, Stanford, California, August 25-29, 1990.

Rogoff, Kenneth. "Symposium on New Institutions for Developing Country Debt," *Journal of Economic Perspectives*, 4, Winter 1990, 3-6.

Schatz, Sayre P. *Nigerian Capitalism*. Berkeley: University of California Press, 1978.

———. "Pirate Capitalism and Inert Economy of Nigeria," *Journal of Modern African Studies*, 22, March 1984, 45-57.

Schenk, Herbert H., and Leo Waldrick. *1984 World's Submarine Telephone Cable Systems*. Washington: GPO for National Telecommunications and Information Administration, Department of Commerce, 1984.

Sklar, Richard L. *Nigerian Political Parties: Power in an Emergent African Nation*. Princeton: Princeton University Press, 1963.

Stolper, Wolfgang F. *Planning Without Facts: Lessons in Resource Allocation for Nigeria's Development*. Cambridge: Harvard University Press, 1966.

———. "Problems of Development Planning." Pages 819-23 in Gerald M. Meier (ed.), *Leading Issues in Economic Development*. New York: Oxford University Press, 1976.

———. "Social Factors in Economic Planning with Special Reference to Nigeria." Pages 225-30 in Carl K. Eicher and Carl Liedholm (eds.), *Growth and Development of the Nigerian Economy*. East Lansing: Michigan State University, 1970.

United Nations. Centre for Development Planning, Projections, and Policies. "Implementation of Development Plans: The Experience of Developing Countries in the First Half of the 1970s," *Journal of Development Planning*, No. 12, 1977, 1-69.

————. Department of International Economic and Social Affairs. *World Economic Survey, 1990.* New York: 1990.

United Nations Development Programme and the World Bank. *African Economic and Financial Data.* Washington: 1989.

United Nations Fund for Population Activities. "Nigeria: Background Report Needs Assessment for Population Assistance." (Working paper prepared for Population Council, UNFPA Workshop.) New York: October 1979.

Waterbury, John, et al. *Fragile Coalitions: The Politics of Economic Adjustment.* New Brunswick, New Jersey: Transaction Books, 1989.

World Bank. *Accelerated Development in Sub-Saharan Africa: An Agenda for Action.* Washington, 1981.

————. "Impact of Adjustment Policies on Manufacturing in Nigeria." Pages 139–42 in Gerald M. Meier and William F. Steel (eds.), *Industrial Adjustment in Sub-Saharan Africa.* New York: Oxford University Press, 1989.

————. *Nigeria: Medium-Term Development Prospects.* Washington: 1989.

————. *Sub-Saharan Africa. From Crisis to Sustainable Growth: A Long-Term Perspective Study.* Washington: 1989.

————. *World Debt Tables, 1990–1991: External Debt of Developing Countries, Country Tables,* 2. Washington: 1990.

————. *World Development Report, 1982.* New York: Oxford University Press, 1982.

————. *World Development Report, 1985.* New York: Oxford University Press, 1985.

————. *World Development Report, 1986.* New York: Oxford University Press, 1986.

————. *World Development Report, 1989.* New York: Oxford University Press, 1989.

————. *World Development Report, 1990.* New York: Oxford University Press, 1990.

World Bank and International Finance Corporation. *Social Indicators and Development.* Washington: 1987.

World Radio TV Handbook, 1990. (Ed., Andrew G. Sennitt.) Hvidovre, Denmark: Billboard, 1990.

(Various issues of the following periodicals were also used in the preparation of this chapter: *African Business* [London]; *Africa Report; Africa Research Bulletin* [Exeter, United Kingdom]; *Economist* [London]; *Financial Times* [London]; Nigeria, Office of Statistics, *Digest of Statistics* [Lagos] and *West Africa* [London].)

Chapter 4

Adamolekun, Ladipo. *Politics and Administration in Nigeria.* Ibadan: Spectrum Books, 1986.

Adamolekun, Ladipo. (ed.). *Nigerian Public Administration, 1960-1980.* Ibadan: Spectrum Books, 1985.

Adamu, Haroun, and Alaba Ogunsanwo. *Nigeria: The Making of the Presidential System—1979 General Elections.* Kano, Nigeria: Triumph, 1983.

Adejuyigbe, Omolade, Leo Dare, and Adevanti Adepoju (eds.). *Creation of States in Nigeria: A Review of Rationale, Demands, and Problems.* (Papers presented at National Conference on Creation of States in Nigeria, February 24-28, 1982, University of Ife.) Lagos: 1982.

Adekson, J. Bayo. *Nigeria in Search of a Stable Civil-Military System.* Boulder, Colorado: Westview Press, 1981.

Afonja, Simi, and Tola Olu Pearce (eds.). *Social Change in Nigeria.* London: Longman, 1986.

Aguda, T. Akinola. *The Judiciary in the Government of Nigeria.* Ibadan: New Horn Press, 1983.

Ajayi, J.F. Ade, and Bashir Ikara (eds.). *Evolution of Political Culture in Nigeria.* Ibadan: Ibadan University Press for Kaduna State Council for Arts and Culture, 1985.

Ake, Claude (ed.). *The Political Economy of Nigeria.* London: Longman, 1985.

Akindele, R.A. "Nigeria's External Economic Relations, 1960-1985," Pt. 1. *Afrika Spectrum* [Hamburg], 1, 1986, 5-34.

——. "Nigeria's External Economic Relations, 1960-1985," Pt. 2. *Afrika Spectrum* [Hamburg], 2, 1986, 143-61.

Akindele, R.A., and Bassey E. Ate. "Nigeria's Foreign Policy, 1986-2000 A.D.: Background and Reflections on the Views from Kuru," *Afrika Spectrum* [Hamburg], 3, 21, 1986, 363-70.

Akpan, Ntieyang Udo. *The Struggle for Secession, 1966-70.* London: Cass, 1972.

Aluko, Olajide (ed.). *Essays on Nigerian Foreign Policy.* London: Allen and Unwin, 1981.

Anifowose, Rem. *Violence and Politics in Nigeria: The Tiv and Yoruba Experience.* New York: Nok, 1982.

Asobie, H.A. "Bureaucratic Politics and Foreign Policy: The Nigerian Experience, 1960-1975," *Civilisations* [Brussels], 30, Nos. 3-4, 1980, 253-70.

Awa, Eme O. *Federal Government in Nigeria.* Berkeley: University of California Press, 1964.

Awolowo, Obafemi. *Awo: Autobiography of Chief Obafemi Awolowo.* Ibadan: 1960.

_____. *The People's Republic.* Ibadan: Oxford University Press, 1968.

_____. *Thoughts on Nigerian Constitution.* Ibadan: Oxford University Press, 1968.

Ayeni, Victor, and Kayode Soremekun (eds.). *Nigeria's Second Republic.* Lagos: Daily Times, 1988.

Ayoade, John A.A. "Ethnic Management in the 1979 Nigerian Constitution," *Publius,* 16, No. 2, Spring 1986, 73–90.

Azikiwe, Nnamdi. *My Odyssey: An Autobiography.* London: Hurst, 1970.

Bello, Ahmadu. *My Life: An Autobiography.* London: 1962.

Bienen, Henry. *Political Conflict and Economic Change in Nigeria.* London: Cass, 1985.

Bienen, Henry, and V.P. Diejomaoh (eds.). *The Political Economy of Income Distribution in Nigeria.* New York: Holmes and Meier, 1981.

Biersteker, Thomas J. *Multinationals, the State, and Control of the Nigerian Economy.* Princeton: Princeton University Press, 1987.

Coleman, James Smoot. *Nigeria: Background to Nationalism.* Berkeley: University of California Press, 1958.

Collins, Paul. *Administration for Development in Nigeria: Introduction and Readings.* Lagos: African Education Press, 1980.

de St. Jorre, John. *The Nigerian Civil War.* London: Hodder and Stoughton, 1972.

Diamond, Larry. *Class, Ethnicity, and Democracy in Nigeria: The Failure of the First Republic.* Syracuse: Syracuse University Press, 1988.

Diamond, Larry, Juan J. Linz, and Seymour Martin Lipset (eds.). *Democracy in Developing Countries: Comparing Experience with Democracy.* Boulder, Colorado: Lynne Rienner, 1990.

Dudley, Billy J. *Instability and Political Order: Politics and Crisis in Nigeria.* Ibadan: Ibadan University Press, 1973.

_____. *An Introduction to Nigerian Government and Politics.* Bloomington: Indiana University Press, 1982.

_____. *Parties and Politics in Northern Nigeria.* London: Cass, 1968.

Elaigwu, J. Isawa. *Gowon: The Biography of a Soldier-Statesman.* Ibadan: West Books, 1986.

Falola, Toyin (ed.). *Britain and Nigeria: Exploitation or Development?* London: Zed Books, 1987.

Falola, Toyin, and Julius Omozuanvbo Ihonvbere. *The Rise and Fall of Nigeria's Second Republic, 1979–83.* London: Zed Books, 1985.

Gambari, Ibrahim Agboola. *Party Politics and Foreign Policy: Nigeria During the First Republic.* Zaria, Nigeria: Ahmadu Bello University Press, 1980.

Garba, Joseph Nanven. *Diplomatic Soldiering: Nigerian Foreign Policy, 1975-1979.* Ibadan: Spectrum Books, 1987.

Gboyega, Alex. *Political Values and Local Government in Nigeria.* Lagos: Malthouse Press, 1987.

Graf, William. "Issues and Substance in the Prescription of Liberal-Democratic Forms for Nigeria's Third Republic," *African Affairs* [London], 88, No. 350, January 1989, 91-100.

_____. *The Nigerian State.* London: Currey, 1989.

Harbeson, John (ed.). *The Military in African Politics.* New York: Praeger, 1987.

Ibrahim, Jibrin. "The Political Debate and the Struggle for Democracy in Nigeria," *Review of African Political Economy* [Sevenoaks, Kent, United Kingdom], No. 37, December 1986, 38-48.

Ihonvbere, Julius Omozuanvbo. "Economic Contraction and Foreign Policy in the Periphery: A Study of Nigeria's Foreign Policy Towards Africa in the Second Republic," *Afrika Spectrum* [Hamburg], 3, 22, 1987, 267-84.

Ikporukpo, C.O. "Politics and Regional Policies: The Issue of State Creation in Nigeria," *Political Geography Quarterly* [London], 5, No. 2, 1986, 127-39.

Joseph, Richard A. *Democracy and Prebendal Politics in Nigeria: The Rise and Fall of the Second Republic.* New York: Cambridge University Press, 1987.

_____. "Principles and Practices of Nigeria's Military Government." Pages 67-91 in John Harbeson (ed.), *The Military in African Politics.* New York: Praeger, 1987.

Kastfelt, Niels. "Rumours of Maitatsine: A Note on Political Culture in Northern Nigeria," *African Affairs* [London], 88, No. 350, January 1989, 83-90.

Kirk-Greene, Anthony Hamilton Millard (ed.). "A Sense of Belonging: The Nigerian Constitution of 1979 and the Promotion of National Loyalty," *Journal of Commonwealth and Comparative Politics* [London], 26, No. 2, July 1988, 158-72.

_____. *Crisis and Conflict in Nigeria: A Documentary Sourcebook.* (2 vols.) London: Oxford University Press, 1971.

Kirk-Greene, Anthony Hamilton Millard, and D. Rimmer. *Nigeria since 1970: A Political and Economic Outline.* New York: Africana, 1981.

Luckham, Robin. *The Nigerian Military: A Sociological Analysis of Authority and Revolt: 1960-67.* Cambridge: Cambridge University Press, 1971.

Mackintosh, John P. (ed.). *Nigerian Government and Politics.* London: Allen and Unwin, 1966.

Madunagu, Edwin. *Problems of Socialism: The Nigerian Challenge.* London: Zed Books, 1982.

Miles, William F.S. *Elections in Nigeria: A Grassroots Perspective.* Boulder, Colorado: Lynne Rienner, 1988.

Nwabueze, Benjamin Obi. *A Constitutional History of Nigeria.* Essex, New York: Longman, 1982.

_____. *Nigeria's Presidential Constitution: The Second Experiment in Constitutional Democracy.* London: Longman, 1984.

Nwokedi, Emeka. "Sub-Regional Security and Nigerian Foreign Policy," *African Affairs* [London], 84, No. 335, April 1985, 195–209.

Okonjo, I.M. *British Administration in Nigeria, 1900–1950: A Nigerian View.* New York: Nok, 1974.

Olowu, Dele. "Bureaucratic Corruption and Public Accountability in Nigeria: An Assessment of Recent Developments," *International Review of Administrative Sciences* [Brussels], 51, No. 1, 1985, 7–12.

Oluleye, James J. *Military Leadership in Nigeria, 1966–1979.* Ibadan: Ibadan University Press, 1985.

Othman, Shehu. "Classes, Crises, and Coup: The Demise of Shagari's Regime," *African Affairs* [London], 83, No. 333, October 1984, 441–61.

Oyediran, Oye (ed.). *Essays on Local Government and Administration in Nigeria.* Lagos: 1988.

_____. *Nigerian Government and Politics under Military Rule, 1966–79.* New York: St. Martin's Press, 1979.

Oyovbaire, Sam Egite (ed.). *Federalism in Nigeria: A Study in the Development of the Nigerian State.* New York: St. Martin's Press, 1984.

Paden, John N. *Ahmadu Bello, Sardauna of Sokoto: Values and Leadership in Nigeria.* London: Hodder and Stoughton, 1986.

_____. *Religion and Political Culture in Kano.* Berkeley: University of California Press, 1973.

Panter-Brick, S.K. (ed.). *Nigerian Politics and Military Rule: Prelude to the Civil War.* London: Athlone Press, 1970.

_____. *Soldiers and Oil: The Political Transformation of Nigeria.* London: Cass, 1978.

Post, Ken. *The Nigerian Federal Election of 1959.* Ibadan: 1963.

Sanda, A.O., Olusola Ojo, and Victor Aveni (eds.). *The Impact of Military Rule on Nigeria's Administration.* Ile-Ife, Nigeria: Faculty of Administration, University of Ife, ca. 1987.

Schwarz, F. *Nigeria: The Tribes, the Nation, or the Race—The Politics of Independence.* Westport, Connecticut: Westview Press, 1965.

Shaw, Timothy M., and Julius Omozuanvbo Ihonvbere. *Towards a Political Economy of Nigeria: Petroleum and Politics at the (Semi)-Periphery.* Brookfield, Vermont: Avebury, 1988.

Sklar, Richard L. *Nigerian Political Parties: Power in an Emergent African Nation.* Princeton: Princeton University Press, 1963.

Stremlau, John J. *The International Politics of the Nigerian Civil War, 1967-1970.* Princeton: Princeton University Press, 1977.

Suberu, Rotimi Timothy. "Federalism and Nigeria's Political Future: A Comment," *African Affairs* [London], 87, No. 348, July 1988, 431-39.

Teal, Francis. "Domestic Policies, External Constraints, and Economic Development in Nigeria since 1950," *African Affairs* [London], 87, No. 346, January 1988, 69-81.

Tukur, Mahmud, and Tunji Olagunju (eds.). *Nigeria in Search of a Viable Polity.* (Papers presented at Conference on Institutional and Administrative Perspectives for National Development.) Zaria, Nigeria: Baraka Press, 1972.

Ukwu, I. Ukwu (ed.). *Federal Character and National Integration in Nigeria.* Kuru, Nigeria: National Institute for Policy and Strategic Studies, 1987.

Vivekananda, F., and B.E. Aigbokhian. "Militarization and Economic Development in Nigeria," *Scandinavian Journal of Development Alternatives* [Stockholm], 6, Nos. 2-3, 1987, 106-21.

Whitaker, C. Sylvester. *The Politics of Tradition: Continuity and Change in Northern Nigeria, 1946-66.* Princeton: Princeton University Press, 1970.

Williams, Gavin (ed.). *Nigeria: Economy and Society.* London: Collings, 1976.

Zartman, I. William (ed.). *The Political Economy of Nigeria.* New York: Praeger, 1983.

Chapter 5

Achike, Okay. *Groundwork of Military Law and Military Rule in Nigeria.* Enugu, Nigeria: Fourth Dimension, 1978.

Africa Contemporary Record: Annual Survey and Documents, 1987-88. (Eds., Colin Legum and Marion E. Doro.) New York: Africana, 1989.

Agbakoba, Olisa. "In Defence of National Security: An Appraisal of the Nigerian Intelligence System," *Afrika Spectrum* [Hamburg], January-February 1984, 51-58.

Alubo, S.Ogoh. "Human Rights and Militarism in Nigeria." Pages 197-207 in George W. Shepherd, Jr. and Mark O.C.

Aniko (eds.), *Emerging Human Rights.* Westport, Connecticut: Greenwood Press, 1990.

Amnesty International Report, 1989. London: Amnesty International, 1989.

Andrade, John M. "Nigeria." Page 149 in John M. Andrade (ed.), *World Police and Paramilitary Forces.* New York: Stockton Press, 1985.

Arlinghans, Bruce E. (ed.). *Africa Security Issues.* Boulder, Colorado: Westview Press, 1984.

Ate, Bassey Eyo. "The Presence of France in West-Central Africa as a Fundamental Problem to Nigeria," *Millennium* [London], 12, No. 2, Summer 1983, 110–26.

Baker, Pauline H. "A Giant Staggers: Nigeria as an Emerging Regional Power." Pages 76–97 in Bruce E. Arlinghaus (ed.), *African Security Issues.* Boulder, Colorado: Westview Press, 1984.

————. "Nigeria: The Sub-Saharan Pivot." Pages 267–303 in Rodney W. Jones and Steven A. Hildreth (eds.), *Emerging Powers: Defense and Security in the Third World.* New York: Praeger, 1986.

Beaver, Paul. *World Naval Aviation.* Coulsdon, Surrey, United Kingdom: Jane's Information Group, 1989.

Becker, Harold K., and Donna Lee Becker. *Handbook of the World's Police.* Metuchen, New Jersey: Scarecrow Press, 1986.

Boam, T.A. "Nigeria's Staff College," *Army Quarterly and Defence Journal* [Tavistock, Devon, United Kingdom], 108, No. 3, July 1978, 269–77.

Carter, H. Marshall, and Otwin Marenin. "Students and Police in Nigeria: The Power of Stereotypes," *Africa Today,* 27, No. 4, 1980, 21–34.

Clayton, Anthony, and David Killingray. *Khaki and Blue: Military and Police in British Colonial Africa.* Athens: Ohio University Center for International Affairs, 1989.

Defense and Foreign Affairs Handbook, 1989. Alexandria, Virginia: International Media, 1989.

Denholm-Young, C.P.S. "R.W.A.F.F.," *Army Quarterly and Defence Journal* [Tavistock, Devon, United Kingdom], 105, No. 1, January 1975, 60–66.

Diamond, Larry. "Nigeria Update," *Foreign Affairs,* 64, No. 2, Winter 1985-86, 326–36.

Economist Intelligence Unit. *Country Profile: Nigeria, 1989–90.* London, 1989.

————. *Country Report: Nigeria.* Nos. 1–4. London, 1990.

Encyclopedia of the World's Air Forces. New York: Facts on File, 1988.

Gastil, Raymond D. *Freedom in the World: Political Rights and Civil*

Liberties, 1987–88. Westport, Connecticut: Greenwood Press, 1988.

Hamalengwa, M., C. Flinterman, and E.V.O. Dankum (eds.). *The International Law of Human Rights in Africa: Basic Documents and Annotated Bibliography.* Boston: Nijhoff, 1988.

Hanning, Hugh (ed.). *The Peaceful Uses of Military Forces.* New York: Praeger, 1967.

Humana, Charles (ed.). *The Economist World Human Rights Guide.* New York: Facts on File, 1986.

Jane's Fighting Ships, 1989–90. (Ed., Richard Sharpe.) London: Jane's Information Group, 1989.

Jane's Weapon Systems, 1988–89. (Ed., Bernard H.L. Blake.) London: Jane's Information Group, 1988.

Johnson, Elmer H. (ed.). *International Handbook of Contemporary Developments in Criminology,* 2. Westport, Connecticut: Greenwood Press, 1983.

Jones, Rodney W., and Steven A. Hildreth (eds.). *Emerging Powers: Defense and Security in the Third World.* New York: Praeger, 1986.

Kayode, Oluyemi. "Nigeria." Pages 473–93 in Elmer H. Johnson (ed.), *International Handbook of Contemporary Developments in Criminology,* 2. Westport, Connecticut: Greenwood Press, 1983.

Keegan, John (ed.). *World Armies.* (2d ed.) Detroit: Gale Research, 1983.

Kolodziej, Edward A., and Robert E. Harkavy (eds.). *Security Policies of Developing Countries.* Lexington, Massachusetts: Lexington Books, 1982.

Labayle Couhat, Jean, and Bernard Prezelin (eds.). *Combat Fleets of the World, 1988–89.* Annapolis: Naval Institute Press, 1988.

MacAnigboro, Ekido J.A., and Aja Akpuru Aja. "France's Military Policy in Sub-Saharan Francophone States: A Threat to Nigeria's National Security," *Strategic Analysis* [New Delhi], April 1989, 107–19.

Mba, Nina. "Kaba and Khaki: Women and the Militarized State in Nigeria." Pages 69–90 in Jane L. Parpart and Kathleen A. Staudt (eds.), *Women and the State in Africa.* Boulder, Colorado: Lynne Rienner, 1989.

The Military Balance, 1989–1990. London: Brassey's for International Institute for Strategic Studies, 1989.

Milner, Alan. *The Nigerian Penal System.* London: Sweet and Maxwell, 1972.

Nigeria. Executive Office of the President. Department of Information. *Nigeria 1982: Official Handbook.* Lagos: Academy Press, n.d.

359

————. National Assembly. *Government of the Federal Republic of Nigeria: Approved Budget, 1983 Fiscal Year.* Lagos: 1983.

————. Office of Statistics. *Annual Abstract of Statistics, 1986.* Lagos: n.d.

"Nigeria." In *DMS Market Intelligence Report: Middle East and Africa.* Coulsdon, Surrey, United Kingdom: Jane's Information Group, October 1989.

"Nigeria." Pages 147–52 in Hugh Hanning (ed.), *The Peaceful Uses of Military Forces.* New York: Praeger, 1967.

"Nigeria: The Army's Role," *Army Quarterly and Defence Journal* [Tavistock, Devon, United Kingdom], 115, No. 2, April 1985, 135–40.

Nigeria's New Government: A Confidential Report on the Structure, Policies, and Personalities of the Babangida Administration. Washington: Defense and Foreign Affairs, October 1985.

Nigeria Year Book, 1987. Apapa, Nigeria: Times Press, 1987.

Nzimiro, Ikenna. "Militarization in Nigeria: Its Economic and Social Consequences," *International Social Science Journal* [Oxford], 35, 1 (No. 95), 1983, 125–39.

Ogunbadejo, Oye. "Nuclear Capability and Nigeria's Foreign Policy." Pages A136–A151 in Colin Legum (ed.), *Africa Contemporary Record,* 16. New York: Africana, 1985.

————. "Nuclear Nonproliferation in Africa: The Challenges Ahead," *Arms Control,* 10, No. 1, May 1989, 68–86.

Okolo, Julius Emeka. "Nuclearization of Nigeria," *Comparative Strategy,* 5, No. 2, 1985, 135–57.

————. "Securing West Africa: The ECOWAS Defence Pact," *World Today* [London], 39, No. 5, May 1983, 177–84.

Oladimeji, Olutunde A. "Nigeria on Becoming a Sea Power," *Proceedings of the United States Naval Institute,* 115, 3, March 1989, 69–74.

Omu, Paul Ufuoma. "The Nigerian Command and Staff College, Jaji: Ten Years of Development and Success," *Army Quarterly and Defence Journal* [Tavistock, Devon, United Kingdom], 117, No. 2, April 1987, 166–70.

Ostheimer, John M., and Gary J. Buckley. "Nigeria." Pages 285–303 in Edward A. Kolodziej and Robert E. Harkavy (eds.), *Security Policies of Developing Countries.* Lexington, Massachusetts: Lexington Books, 1982.

Oyewole, A. *Historical Dictionary of Nigeria.* (African Historical Dictionaries, No. 40.) Metuchen, New Jersey: Scarecrow Press, 1987.

Parpart, Jane L., and Kathleen A. Staudt (eds.). *Women and the State in Africa.* Boulder, Colorado: Lynne Rienner, 1989.

Sheehan, Michael J. "Nigeria: A Maritime Power?" Pages 395-407 in Jeffrey C. Stone (ed.), *Africa and the Sea*. Aberdeen: Aberdeen University African Studies Group, 1985.

_____. "Nigeria and the ECOWAS Defence Pact?," *Army Quarterly and Defence Journal* [Tavistock, Devon, United Kingdom], 117, No. 1, January 1986, 9-15.

Shepherd, George W., and Mark O.C. Aniko (eds.). *Emerging Human Rights*. Westport, Connecticut: Greenwood Press, 1990.

Stone, Jeffrey C. (ed.). *Africa and the Sea*. Aberdeen: Aberdeen University African Studies Group, 1985.

Taylor, Michael J.H. "Nigeria." Page 112 in *Encyclopedia of the World's Air Forces*. New York: Facts on File, 1988.

United States. Arms Control and Disarmament Agency. *World Military Expenditures and Arms Transfers, 1972-1982*. Washington: GPO, 1984.

_____. Arms Control and Disarmament Agency. *World Military Expenditures and Arms Transfers, 1988*. Washington: GPO, 1989.

_____. Arms Control and Disarmament Agency. *World Military Expenditures and Arms Transfers, 1989*. Washington: GPO, 1990.

_____. Department of State. *Country Reports on Human Rights Practices for 1989*. (Report submitted to United States Congress, 101st, 2d Session, Senate, Committee on Foreign Relations, and House of Representatives, Committee on Foreign Affairs.) Washington: GPO, 1990.

World Armaments and Disarmament: Stockholm International Peace Research Institute Yearbook, 1989. Oxford: Oxford University Press, 1989.

World Defense Almanac (Special Issue: *Military Technology*), January 1989.

(Various issues of the following publications were also used in the preparation of this chapter: *Africa Confidential* [London]; *African Defence/Afrique Défense* [Paris]; *Africa Research Bulletin* [Exeter, United Kingdom]; *Defense and Foreign Affairs Weekly; Jane's Defence Weekly* [Coulsdon, Surrey, United Kingdom]; and *International Defence Review* [Coulsdon, Surrey, United Kingdom].)

Glossary

fiscal year (FY)—An annual period established for accounting purposes. Through FY 1979–80 the Nigerian government's fiscal year ran from April 1 to the following March 31. The latter fiscal year was succeeded by a nine-month FY 1980 that ended December 31, 1980. From January 1, 1981, the fiscal year was made coterminous with the calendar year.

GDP (gross domestic product)— A value measure of the flow of domestic goods and services produced by an economy over a period of time, such as a year. Only output values of goods for final consumption and for intermediate production are assumed to be included in final prices. GDP is sometimes aggregated and shown at market prices, meaning that indirect taxes and subsidies are included; when these have been eliminated, the result is GDP at factor cost. The word *gross* indicates that deductions for depreciation of physical assets have not been made.

GNP (gross national product)—GDP (*q.v.*) plus the net income or loss stemming from transactions with foreign countries. GNP is the broadest measurement of the output of goods and services by an economy. It can be calculated at market prices, which include indirect taxes and subsidies. Because indirect taxes and subsidies are only transfer payments, GNP is often calculated at a factor cost, removing indirect taxes and subsidies.

International Monetary Fund (IMF)—Established along with the World Bank (*q.v.*) in 1945, the IMF is a specialized agency affiliated with the United Nations and is responsible for stabilizing international exchange rates and payments. The main business of the IMF is the provision of loans to its members (including industrialized and developing countries) when they experience balance of payments difficulties. These loans frequently carry conditions that require substantial internal economic adjustments by the recipients, most of which are developing countries.

Lomé Convention—A series of agreements between the European Economic Community (EEC) and a group of African, Caribbean, and Pacific (ACP) states, mainly former Euopean colonies, that provide duty-free or preferential access to the EEC maket for almost all ACP exports. The Stabilization of Export Earnings (Stabex) scheme, a mechanism set up by the Lomé Convention, provides for compensation for ACP exports lost

363

through fluctuations in the world prices of agricultural commodities. The Lomé Convention also provides for limited EEC
development aid and investment funds to be disbursed to ACP
recipients through the European Development Fund and the
European Investment Bank. The Lomé Convention is updated
about every five years. Lomé I took effect on April 1, 1976;
Lomé II, on January 1, 1981; Lomé III, on March 1, 1985;
and Lomé IV, on December 15, 1989.

middle belt—Traditionally an ethnic and political zone stretching from east to west across the central section of Nigeria and
inhabited by many minor ethnic groups who had been unable
to obtain significant political influence because of long-term
dominance by the Hausa-Fulani and Kanuri emirates. As used
by economists and geographers, the term does not always coincide with ethnic and political divisions but usually designates
the area between the characteristic northern and southern economies; in this context the area extends roughly from 7°30'N
to 11°N. Since the civil war of 1967–70 and the replacement
of the former administrative regions by states, use of the term
has diminished among Nigerians who wish to downplay the
regional connotation formerly attached to it.

naira (N)—Nigeria's basic currency unit. It is subdivided into
100 kobo (k). The naira was introduced on January 1, 1973,
replacing the Nigerian pound (*q.v.*) at the rate of two naira for
one pound. At that time N1 equaled US$1.52. The naira sub-
sequently lost value against the dollar; average exchange rate
in 1990: N8.04 per US$1.00.

Nigerian pound (N£)—Basic currency unit until January 1, 1973,
when it was replaced by the naira (*q.v.*). N£1 was valued
at US$2.80 until December 1971; thereafter N£1 equaled
US$3.04.

Paris Club—The informal name for a consortium of Western
creditor countries that have made loans or have guaranteed
export credits to developing nations and that meet in Paris to
discuss borrowers' ability to repay debts. The organization has
no formal or institutional existence and no fixed membership.
Its secretariat is run by the French treasury, and it has a close
relationship with the World Bank (*q.v.*), the International
Monetary Fund (*q.v.*), and the United Nations Conference on
Trade and Development (UNCTAD).

Sahel—A narrow band of land bordering the southern Sahara,
stretching across Africa, and including northern Nigeria. It is
characterized by an average annual rainfall of between 150 and
500 millimeters and is mainly suited to pastoralism.

Special Drawing Right(s) (SDR)—A monetary unit of the International Monetary Fund (IMF) (*q.v.*) based on a basket of international currencies consisting of the United States dollar, the German deutsche mark, the Japanese yen, the British pound sterling, and the French franc.

Sudan—Geographical region (northern reaches now more commonly referred to as the Sahel) stretching across Africa from Cape Verde on the Atlantic Coast to the Red Sea between 8° and 16° north latitude, just south of the Sahara Desert, characterized by savanna and semiarid steppe. Term derived from Arabic *bilad as sudan* (literally "land of the blacks"). Not to be confused with Sudan, the country.

World Bank—Informal name used to designate a group of three affiliated international institutions: the International Bank for Reconstruction and Development (IBRD), the International Development Association (IDA), and the International Finance Corporation (IFC). The IBRD, established in 1945, has the primary purpose of providing loans to developing countries for productive projects. The IDA, a legally separate loan fund but administered by the staff of the IBRD, was set up in 1960 to furnish credits to the poorest developing countries on much easier terms than those of conventional IBRD loans. The IFC, founded in 1956, supplements the activities of the IBRD through loans and assistance specifically designed to encourage the growth of productive private enterprises in the less developed countries. The president and certain senior officers of the IBRD hold the same positions in the IFC. The three institutions are owned by the governments of the countries that subscribe their capital. To participate in the World Bank group, member states must first belong to the International Monetary Fund (IMF—*q.v.*).

Index

"Ali Must Go" Day, 243, 306
Alkali courts, 126
Al Kanemi, 21
Aloma, Idris, 14
Amakiri, Minere, 242
Amin, Idi, 264
Aminu Kano International Airport, 192
Amnesty International, 308
Anambra Basin, 87
Anambra State, 238, 315; health care in, 147; industry in, 286; politics in, 74; yellow fever in, 150
Anang, 107
Anas, Malik ibn, 126
Anglican Church, 105, 128, 129
Anglo-Nigerian Defense Pact, 243
Angola, 16, 69, 258, 264
Angola-Namibia accords, 250, 268
Anyaoku, Emeka, 250
Apapa, 277
Arab-Israeli dispute, xxxi
Aradu, 278, 284
Arafat, Yasir, xxxi
archaeological research, 4-5, 10
area, 87
Argungu, 20
armed forces, 268-301; attitudes toward, 295-98; buildup, 300; capabilities of, 294-95; civic action role of, 301; conditions in, 288-89; under constitution of 1979, 271; constraints on, 294-95; cooperation programs, 262; corruption in, 295, 299, 318; demobilization of, xxv, 65-66, 69, 256, 289, 301; educational qualification for, 287; federal principle applied to, 227; missions of, 273; organization of, 272-73; pay and benefits in, 81, 288; peacekeeping role of, 269; personnel turnover in, 299; political neutrality in, 298; political role of, 298-99; problems in, 289; professionalization of, xxxiii; public disenchantment with, xxxii; quotas in, 288; recruitment for, 287-88, 298; reduced, 272; restructuring of, xxxi, 217, 224, 272, 295; selectivity of, 287-88; size of, xxxii, 256, 272; technical assistance to, 284; training, 262, 290-94; uniforms, ranks, and insignia, 295; women in, 288
Armed Forces Consultative Assembly, 222, 273
Armed Forces Rehabilitation Centre, 289
Armed Forces Ruling Council (AFRC),

xxv, 81, 222, 230, 232, 272, 305, 307; ethnic distribution in, 78; personnel changes in, 255; prisoner amnesties under, 316
Armed Robbery and Firearms Tribunals, 320
arms: diversity in, 283-84; domestic, 256, 286; foreign, 256, 269, 284, 294, 299; procurement, 283-87, 294; standardization of, 285-86; value of, 284, 300
army, 273-75; capabilities of, 294; demobilization of, xxxi, 78; Eighty-second (Airborne) Division, 273-74; enrollments, 288; First Mechanized Infantry Division, 273; geographic areas of responsibility, 273; Guard Brigade, 274; historical origins of, 269; internal security by, 310; light aviation force, 275; number of troops in, 273; organization of, 273; rapid deployment force, 275; reserves, 274-75; restructuring of, 275; role of, in return to civilian rule, 273; Second Mechanized Infantry Division, 273; tensions of, with police, 312; Third Armored Division, 273; uniforms, ranks, and insignia, 295
Army Command and Staff College, 291
Army School of Artillery, 291
Arochukwu, 18
Aro confederacy, 17-18, 19, 33; commercial empire, 18; oracle of, 18; religious influence, 18; slave trade by, 17, 23; trade by, 25
Asante expedition (1873-74), 269
Ashland Oil, 186
Asika, Ukapi, 61
associations (*see also under individual types of associations*), 39, 308
Auchi, 205
austerity: under Babangida, 81, 222; under Buhari, 77, 78; demonstrations against, 305; under Obasanjo, 220; opposition to, 200; under Second Republic, 229
Australia, 64
Austria, 250; matériel acquired from, 286
Awolowo, Obafemi, 39, 47, 49, 58, 66, 70, 209, 211, 228; Action Group under, 40, 42, 73, 161, 212; convicted of treason, 50, 52; released from prison, 57
Azikiwe, Nnamdi, 40, 41, 47, 74, 209; as governor general, 47-48, 211; as president of republic, 50, 54, 55

Published Country Studies

(Area Handbook Series)

550-65	Afghanistan	550-87	Greece
550-98	Albania	550-78	Guatemala
550-44	Algeria	550-174	Guinea
550-59	Angola	550-82	Guyana and Belize
550-73	Argentina	550-151	Honduras
550-169	Australia	550-165	Hungary
550-176	Austria	550-21	India
550-175	Bangladesh	550-154	Indian Ocean
550-170	Belgium	550-39	Indonesia
550-66	Bolivia	550-68	Iran
550-20	Brazil	550-31	Iraq
550-168	Bulgaria	550-25	Israel
550-61	Burma	550-182	Italy
550-50	Cambodia	550-30	Japan
550-166	Cameroon	550-34	Jordan
550-159	Chad	550-56	Kenya
550-77	Chile	550-81	Korea, North
550-60	China	550-41	Korea, South
550-26	Colombia	550-58	Laos
550-33	Commonwealth Caribbean, Islands of the	550-24	Lebanon
550-91	Congo	550-38	Liberia
550-90	Costa Rica	550-85	Libya
550-69	Côte d'Ivoire (Ivory Coast)	550-172	Malawi
550-152	Cuba	550-45	Malaysia
550-22	Cyprus	550-161	Mauritania
550-158	Czechoslovakia	550-79	Mexico
550-36	Dominican Republic and Haiti	550-76	Mongolia
550-52	Ecuador	550-49	Morocco
550-43	Egypt	550-64	Mozambique
550-150	El Salvador	550-35	Nepal and Bhutan
550-28	Ethiopia	550-88	Nicaragua
550-167	Finland	550-157	Nigeria
550-155	Germany, East	550-94	Oceania
550-173	Germany, Fed. Rep. of	550-48	Pakistan
550-153	Ghana	550-46	Panama

550-156	Paraguay	550-53	Thailand
550-185	Persian Gulf States	550-89	Tunisia
550-42	Peru	550-80	Turkey
550-72	Philippines	550-74	Uganda
550-162	Poland	550-97	Uruguay
550-181	Portugal	550-71	Venezuela
550-160	Romania	550-32	Vietnam
550-37	Rwanda and Burundi	550-183	Yemens, The
550-51	Saudi Arabia	550-99	Yugoslavia
550-70	Senegal	550-67	Zaire
550-180	Sierra Leone	550-75	Zambia
550-184	Singapore	550-171	Zimbabwe
550-86	Somalia		
550-93	South Africa		
550-95	Soviet Union		
550-179	Spain		
550-96	Sri Lanka		
550-27	Sudan		
550-47	Syria		
550-62	Tanzania		

☆ U.S. GOVERNMENT PRINTING OFFICE: 1992 311-824/60006